Karen Peterson

CULTURE IN EXILE

Russian Emigrés in Germany,
1881-1941

CULTURE IN EXILE

Russian Emigrés in Germany, 1881-1941

ROBERT C. WILLIAMS

Cornell University Press | Ithaca and London

First published 1972 by Cornell University Press.
Published in the United Kingdom by Cornell University Press Ltd.,
2–4 Brook Street, London W1Y 1AA.

International Standard Book Number 0-8014-0673-0
Library of Congress Catalog Card Number 77-162543

Printed in the United States of America by Vail-Ballou Press, Inc.

Librarians: Library of Congress cataloging information
appears on the last page of the book.

For Ann, who understands,
and for Peter and Margaret,
who will understand.

—◆{ }◆—

Preface

Historians, like other men, must frequently admit a certain discrepancy between their intentions and the consequences of their actions. I first intended this book to be a political and intellectual history of the Russian colony in Berlin in the 1920's; what finally resulted was a more comprehensive study of Russians in Germany from the 1880's through the 1930's. There are two reasons for this change. First, a study such as that by Hans-Erich Volkmann, which discusses the post-1917 Russian emigration within the chronological limits of the 1920's, loses sight of the traditional framework of Russian-German relations and of Russians in Germany, particularly the pre-1914 emigration which was to be so crucial for the later diaspora.[1] Second, a look at the life of Berlin Russians in the 1920's quickly reveals the importance, as intermediaries between Russians and German society, of two non-Russian ethnic groups—Russian Jews and Russian Germans—whose arrival in Germany antedated the war and whose influence in Germany was, tragically, extended into the Third Reich. In the end it seemed more fruitful to consider a series of emigrations to Germany, initiated by pressures of Russification and industrialization under Alexander III, accelerated by the revolutionary storms of 1905 and 1917, and completed during Stalin's First Five-Year Plan.

Such a definition of an era of political migration from Russia

[1] Hans-Erich Volkmann, *Die Russische Emigration in Deutschland, 1919–1929* (Würzburg, 1966).

vii

to Germany coincides with recent interpretations of the Russian Revolution as a crisis induced by the responses of Imperial and Soviet governments alike to the pressures of Russian economic backwardness.[2] If the "traditional" Russian exiles in Weimar Germany were the political flotsam and jetsam of 1917 and the civil war, the more continuous migration of Russians to Germany was the legacy of Russia's forced transformation from an agrarian autocracy into an industrial world power. Russians had traditionally come to Germany to travel, to study, and to write, and Germany for many meant "the West," the modern world with its technological superiority and its apparent soullessness. It was paradoxical that while living in Germany and pursuing their studies at the feet of German philosophers, many Russians found their own identity in relation to the European family of man. Often their disillusionment with what the West had produced was converted into an optimism concerning what Russia might become, an attitude encouraged by Europeans critical of their own society.

Migration played a crucial role in German perception of Russia and Russian attitudes toward Germany. Life in the West and contact with Westerners inside Russia, as well as with European literature, helped Russians form their opinions about the West. European travelers and immigrants in Russia were equally important in conveying information back to their homelands. With the migration of Russians into Germany at the end of the nineteenth century came a stream of those "Westernized" elements of Russian society who were bicultural or "marginal," familiar with Russian life yet still tied by family, language, and memory to their European origins or predilections. Notable among them were the Russian Germans and the Jews of the Western borderlands. Aliens within the Russian Empire, they were destined to play a critical role in Germany as experts on Russia, examples of Russians, and mediators between other Russians and German society. Like the Russian émigrés' story, theirs is also largely untold. Several recent studies have focused on the biographies of significant Russian Jews and

[2] C. E. Black, ed., *The Transformation of Russian Society* (Cambridge, Mass., 1960); Theodore Von Laue, *Why Lenin? Why Stalin?* (New York, 1964).

Germans, notably Lou Andreas-Salomé, Theodor Schiemann, Alexander Parvus (Helphand), Yury Osipovich Martov, Rosa Luxemburg, and Max Erwin von Scheubner-Richter.[3] What has been ignored is the social history of the migration which fostered them and
what one contemporary historian has described as "the role (one
that is completely neglected by conventional national history)
played by non-national or supra-national groups which arose as a
result of political or religious emigrations or from scattered minorities."[4]

Like all histories, this is a selective one. Like all social histories,
it is also holistic, focusing on the political and intellectual behavior
of certain groups of men and not on their individual life stories.
It is the story of cultural conflict, as well as political exile. Russians
in Germany were in "the West"; to the Germans themselves they
appeared as "Easterners." They arrived in Germany during a period when European civilization appeared to have played itself out
in the tumult of World War I; this added to their tragic situation
a symbolic role as both a danger and a "light from the East," capable of either destroying or reviving an old world. As the first uprooted castoffs of the twentieth century's "time of troubles," they
claimed to speak with authority of the consequences of revolution.
Why some were heard and others ignored will be considered in this
study.

It is both an advantage and a disadvantage that the background
and values of the author do not coincide with those of his subjects.
Middle-class America in the 1950's and 1960's is far removed from
the life of Russian exiles in the 1920's, let alone in the years before
1914. To overcome this gap I have talked with a number of émigrés,
corresponded with them, read their memoirs and their newspapers,

---

[3] Rudolph Binion, *Frau Lou: Nietzsche's Wayward Disciple* (Princeton,
1968); K. Meyer, *Theodor Schiemann als politischer Publizist* (Frankfort on
the Main, 1956); Z. A. B. Zeman and W. B. Scharlau, *The Merchant of Revolution: The Life of Alexander Israel Helphand (Parvus), 1867–1924* (London,
1965); Israel Getzler, *Martov* (Cambridge, 1967); J. P. Nettl, *Rosa Luxemburg*
(London and New York, 1966); Walter Laqueur, *Russia and Germany* (London 1965) on Scheubner-Richter.

[4] Herbert Lüthy, "What's the Point of History?" *Journal of Contemporary
History*, III, No. 2 (1968), 7.

and generally tried to empathize with their past hopes and fears. They have given me not only information but a sense of the reality of a topic too often brought alive only by reconstruction of periodicals and archives. They have also convinced me that the Russian émigrés themselves conceive of the history of the Russian emigration in terms of their own circle of friends and colleagues. To talk with a monarchist, a liberal, and a Menshevik about life in Berlin in the 1920's is to discover three totally different worlds, outlooks, and ways of life in exile. Their contacts are limited, the prejudices strong; and the issues are still alive. In this case, then, the "meaning" given this particular social, political, and intellectual upheaval by the historian must necessarily differ from the various and sometimes mutually inconsistent meanings derived firsthand from its participants. This book, therefore, is less about the obvious political and economic sufferings of exiles than about the cultural links forged and broken by Russians in Germany, and especially about those bicultural individuals who, knowing both Russia and Germany and being accepted completely by neither, built a bridge from a Russian island to the German mainland.

I have followed the Library of Congress system of transliteration from Russian to English, with the following exceptions for proper names: (1) An individual's own spelling of his name in English is used (Roman Goul, Boris Nicolaevsky). (2) Soft signs are not transliterated (Talberg, not Tal'berg). (3) *Y* rather than *ii* at the beginning and end of names (Gorky), *Ya* rather than *ia* (Yashchenko), and *Yu* rather than *iu* (Yudin). (4) I have generally used English versions of common first names (Paul, Peter, Alexander).

My research is based in large measure on the unpublished archives and memoirs of the Russian emigration, as well as on the private reminiscences of a number of émigrés still living. I am indebted to the staff of the Hoover Library in Palo Alto, California, for making available to me not only the unpublished collections of S. D. Botkin, P. N. Wrangel, V. A. Maklakov, M. N. Giers, A. A. von Lampe, N. V. Ustrialov, the Okhrana, and the Kadet party but also a number of émigré and German periodicals not available elsewhere. Virginia Downes of the YMCA Historical Archive in New York was particularly helpful in indicating materials related to that organization's work among Russian émigrés in Berlin in the 1920's. The rich collection of émigré memoirs and correspondence of the Columbia University Russian Archive was examined through the generous kindness of Philip E. Mosely and L. F. Magerovsky, curator of the Archive. In addition I am grateful to the Wiener Library in London, the International Institute for Social History in Amsterdam, the Bundesarchiv in Koblenz, the German Foreign Ministry Archives in Bonn, the Bavarian State Archive, and the Institute for Contemporary History in Munich for similar research hospitality.

I would also like to thank the editors of the following publications for permission to reprint portions of articles that originally appeared in these journals: *Slavic Review*, XXVII, No. 4 (December 1968); *Canadian Slavonic Papers*, IX, No. 2 (1967); *Journal of Contemporary History*, I, No. 4 (1966); *The Wiener Library Bulletin*, XXIII, Nos. 2, 3 (1969); *Comparative Studies in Society and History*, XII, No. 2 (1970) (Cambridge University Press); *The Yale Review*, LX, No. 2 (1971) (copyright Yale University).

Above all I am grateful to those émigrés who responded patiently in interviews and correspondence to my many questions concerning Russian life in Germany in this period. Boris Sapir, Boris Nicolaevsky, Grigory Aronson, and Alexander Erlich recalled the early years of the Menshevik emigration. Roman Goul contributed his knowledge of "Scythianism" and Smena Vekh. Information on the Kadet party faction in Berlin was obtained through the kindness of Boris Elkin, Mrs. Vladimir Nabokov, Alexis Goldenweiser, and V. O. Gessen. Mark Vishniak and Alexander Kerensky spoke of the brief period of Social Revolutionary activity in Berlin in 1922.

On the cultural side of the emigration, the late Fedor Stepun contributed his own experiences. Paul Anderson and Donald Lowrie provided useful information on the work of the YMCA with Nikolai Berdiaev and other religious philosophers. Mrs. Helen Pahlen Woolley was kind enough to share her recollections on the Baltic German community. On the more obscure early phases of intellectual life in Berlin in 1920, two former members of the Mir i Trud circle—Vladas Stanka (V. B. Stankevich) and Yury Ofrosimov —were especially helpful.

Preface

The travel and correspondence involved in this study would not have been possible without the generous help extended by the Russian Research Center of Harvard University, the American Philosophical Society, and the American Council of Learned Societies. I am also grateful to Walter Laqueur and Werner Philipp for indicating the location of certain émigré periodicals in Germany; Hans-Erich Volkmann of the Herder Institute in Marburg, Germany, was also most helpful in sharing his knowledge of émigré life in the 1920's.

Intellectually, I owe a debt of gratitude to Theodore Von Laue, who taught me that moral concern and creative interpretation are as important for history as erudition, and Richard Pipes, who by example and counsel has shown me that history must be not only true and new, but literate. My wife, Ann, has managed not only to endure the sowing and reaping of a book in its many stages but to raise two children at the same time. I am indebted to all of them, and would share the responsibility for any shortcomings with none of them.

R. C. W.

St. Louis, Missouri

Contents

Contents

—◦◦{ }◦◦—

Illustrations

Following page 140

Theodor Schiemann
Rosa Luxemburg and Alexander Parvus
Vasily Vasilievich Biskupsky, 1915
Metropolitan Evlogy and Northwest Army families at Altengrabow, 1919
P. M. Avalov and Northwest Army delegation in Potsdam, 1921
Bad Reichenhall, Bavaria
Max Erwin von Scheubner-Richter, 1918
Yu. O. Martov and Theodor Dan, 1922
Alexander Stein
Rafael Abramovich
General P. N. Krasnov, 1922
Alexander Kerensky, 1918
Maxim Gorky in Berlin, 1921
Grand Duke Kirill Vladimirovich
Russian Orthodox Church, Wilmersdorf
General P. N. Wrangel, 1927

—◦◄◄ ►►◦—

Abbreviations for Archives

A	Antikomintern Collection, Hoover Library, Palo Alto, California
AA	Politisches Archiv, Auswärtiges Amt, Bonn
AGFM	Archives of the German Foreign Ministry, National Archives, Washington, D.C.
BA	Botkin Archive, Hoover Library
BA/RD	Archive of the Russian Delegation (part of BA)
BC	Botkin Collection, Russian Archive, Columbia University, New York
BGSA	Bayerische Geheime Staatsarchiv, Bavarian State Archive, Munich
BHSA	Bayerische Hauptstaatsarchiv, Bavarian State Archive
DAI	Deutsche Auslandsinstitut Archiv, Bundesarchiv, Koblenz
FC	Freyenwald Collection, Wiener Library, London
GA	Giers Archive, Hoover Library
HA	Nazi Party NSDAP Hauptarchiv, Hoover Library (film)
KA	Kautsky Archive, International Institute of Social History, Amsterdam
KDA	Kadet Party Archive, Hoover Library
LA	Lampe Archive, Hoover Library
MaA	Maklakov Archive, Hoover Library
MiA	Miller Archive, Hoover Library

Abbreviations for Archives

Records	"Captured German Records filmed at Alexandria, Virginia," National Archives, Washington, D.C.
TA	Archives of Mrs. Tschaikovsky (part of BA), Hoover Library
TC	Tödtli Collection, Wiener Library
UA	Ustrialov Archive, Hoover Library
WA	Wrangel Archive, Hoover Library
YMCA	YMCA Historical Archive, New York
ZC	Zenkovsky Collection, Columbia University

CULTURE IN EXILE

Russian Emigrés in Germany,

1881-1941

The spiritual nausea and haughtiness of every human being who has suffered deeply—how deeply one can suffer almost determines the order of rank—his shuddering certainty, which permeates and colors him through and through, that by virtue of his suffering he *knows more* than the cleverest and wisest could possibly know, and that he knows his way and has once been at home in many distant, terrifying worlds of which *"you know nothing"*—this spiritual and silent haughtiness, this pride of the elect of cognition, of the "initiated," of the almost sacrificed, finds all kinds of disguise necessary to protect itself against contact with officious and pitying hands, and against everything that is not a peer in suffering. Deep suffering makes noble; it separates.

Friedrich Nietzsche

⸺⦅ I ⦆⸺

The Imperial Heritage

Exiles

Historians generally dislike lost causes. They prefer to explain what happened, rather than what might have succeeded, and have consequently neglected the story of political emigrations. The study of émigrés is, of course, full of methodological pitfalls for the unwary: biased accounts of past issues, outright forgeries of documentary evidence, personal recriminations that serve to distort political reality, and a pervasive mood of bitterness, acrimony, nostalgia, and endless hope. Yet the story is important, not only because of its intrinsic merit as a political phenomenon, but also because of the effect that exiles have had both in their place of refuge and in their homeland when they have been able to return. He who would ignore the émigrés might do well to recall that the experience of exile helped fashion the political careers of Marx, Lenin, and Trotsky, as well as of Charles II and Louis XVIII.

In European history the emergence of political exiles is a relatively recent phenomenon, coinciding with the rise of nation-states out of the religious wars of the sixteenth and seventeenth centuries and the era of revolutions that followed. Only with the secular loyalties of citizenship could there be the secular disloyalties of exile, forced or voluntary. The history of political exiles involves the collective habits of those Europeans who fled persecution or upheaval at home to seek not only personal refuge or religious freedom, but also political recovery. But the political behavior of such sojourners has not attracted the attention of historians, who have concerned themselves with many related movements of migration: economic shifts inside Europe and across the sea, the flight of persecuted religious or national minorities, literary exiles, and wartime refugee movements.

The exile experience in general, of course, is as old as man, who has too often had to flee persecution to seek refuge by the waters of Babylon. It has its roots in the Wandering Jew, the early Christians, and their religious successors, the Marian exiles, Puritans, and Huguenots of a later age. But flight from home for political, rather than religious or economic, reasons first emerged as the legacy of the English Civil War, the Glorious Revolution, and the turmoil in France after 1789. For some, emigration was only a strategic retreat; for others, it became a lifelong tragedy. The Royalists who fled Cromwell and the Bourbon exiles who survived Napoleon's reign lived to effect a Restoration; the Jacobites died in foreign lands along with Bonnie Prince Charlie, or made peace with the regime they had fled. Until the nineteenth century most spoke out in defense of the legitimacy of an old order of things, resisting to one degree or another the new sovereignty of peoples expressed by new governments.

In the nineteenth century the typical exile was not the defeated minister or landowner but the expectant revolutionary. Mazzini spent his years of waiting in England preparing for the day of the *Risorgimento*. Others fled abortive revolutions to await new opportunities. For those who attempted without success to overthrow the existing regimes in Poland in 1830, France in 1848, and Russia in 1881, exile often became a way of life and the only means of engaging in clandestine political activity. The Polish leader Adam Czartoryski and his countrymen in Paris, the "forty-eighters" in London, and the Russian revolutionaries intimidated by the regicide of Alexander II were among the many who had to choose exile in order to remain political. Some, like Marx, the Russian socialist Alexander Herzen, and the anarchist Michael Bakunin, wrote powerful tracts that crossed Europe's boundaries more easily than they, but did not live to see the awaited upheaval; others, like

Lenin and Trotsky, survived to return in triumph from exile. In both cases their aim was not restoration but revolution.

In the twentieth century the experience of political exiles has been more variegated. The émigré politics created by totalitarian revolutions in Russia, Italy, and Germany have produced a mingling of representatives of an "old regime" with a more frustrated type of exile, unhappy with old and new orders alike. More numerous than their émigré ancestors, they have also been more divided, representing factions as hostile to each other as to the regimes of Stalin, Mussolini, and Hitler. Yet the experience of political frustration in a foreign land has remained as common to the twentieth century as it had been to the seventeenth.

The traditional pattern of exile politics and political exile may be broadly summarized as follows: Alone in a foreign land, the exile longs for a remembered or imagined Golden Age; his stay seems only temporary at first, until the shock of indigence and downward social mobility makes him realize its permanence; he becomes a "stateless" person, a man without a country, deprived of citizenship at home and denied it abroad; culturally, he is torn between isolation on an island of exiles and immersion in a sea of foreigners; with the passing of time, émigré political unity collapses under the pressure of old issues, abrasive personalities, and new movements; in a life of despair and enforced leisure, many émigrés turn from politics to writing long novels or short polemics which place the blame for the upheaval that drove them abroad on evil men who will soon be ousted by divine intervention, historical forces, or the popular will; only the second generation, raised in exile, finds political reconciliation and cultural assimilation possible.

The Russian emigration of the twentieth century has shared many of these characteristics. Nostalgia for a "shipwrecked world," as the Countess Kleinmichel called it, they saved old currency and passports or formed shadow governments in expectation of an imminent and inevitable Bolshevik collapse. Aristocrats found themselves in new careers as waiters, translators, journalists, or taxi drivers. They lost their status as citizens at the hands of the

Soviet government in the 1920's, found it difficult to obtain visas, passports, and citizenship elsewhere, and often became forlorn bearers of the League of Nations' "Nansen passports," legal evidence of their statelessness. Supported by various foreign governments during the Russian Civil War, the exiles waited in vain for a peasant or workers' uprising at home. Waiting produced further fissures and disputes in old political parties whose memory of past divisions surpassed any desire for exile unity. As if to compensate for its political collapse, the emigration flooded Europe and the United States with its culture: books, translations, journals, newspapers, the memoirs of grand dukes, the art of Kandinsky and Chagall, the music of Stravinsky and Rachmaninoff, and the stories of Ivan Bunin and Vladimir Nabokov.

Unlike the Bourbons, the Russians never effected a Restoration. Unlike the Jacobites, they never had the unity provided by an accepted Pretender. Unlike the English Royalists of the seventeenth century, they were unable to retain their citizenship. Yet in the twentieth century several million citizens of Imperial Russia were forced to live out their lives far from their native soil, hoping against hope for the day they might return. In so doing they shared in the exile experience.

The Russian emigration to Germany before 1917 was, of course, vastly different from the postrevolutionary colony. Smaller in numbers, it tended naturally to be dominated by the political left hostile to the Imperial regime rather than the political right hostile to the Bolsheviks. Seen in this light, many of the prewar émigrés returned to play important roles in Soviet Russia and many of the leaders of the Imperial government found themselves suddenly transformed into exiles. Others, like the Mensheviks, found emigration an all too familiar way of life both before and after 1917. In fact, those Russians who had found refuge in Germany before the war were precisely those best able to adjust to German life after 1917 and to facilitate the adjustment of those for whom the exile experience was new.

Studies of the political refugee in the twentieth century have concentrated on emigration as a tragic and traumatic involuntary state of isolation produced by moving from an old and familiar

homeland to a new and not always receptive place of exile.[1] Hannah
Arendt in her classic study of totalitarianism describes how the upheavals of war and revolution in Central and Eastern Europe in
1914–1918 were followed by "migrations of groups who, unlike
their happier predecessors in the religious wars, were welcomed
nowhere and could be assimilated nowhere," the "stateless" persons
who moved from country to country in Europe in the 1920's and
1930's in search of citizenship.[2] Political refugees have been considered political objects rather than political subjects, part of the
frustrated, alienated, uprooted, lonely, and unwanted elements
which formed the recruiting grounds for subsequent political mass
movements.[3]

The Russian emigration to Germany before and after World War
I was also a social process of severe dislocation, personal unhappi-
ness, and general frustration. As such it proved highly conducive to
utopian or millenarian thinking and political extremism, rather
than to moderation. In the language of the sociologist it may be
said that many Russians experienced severe "deprivation," a "negative discrepancy between legitimate expectation and actuality . . .
where conditions decline by comparison with the past, where it
is expected that they will decline in the future by comparison with
the present"; often this led to a "millenarian ideology" which "justi-
fies withdrawal" and reassures those who have been deprived that

[1] For example, K. Cirtautas, *The Refugee: A Psychological Study* (Boston,
1957).

[2] Hannah Arendt, *The Origins of Totalitarianism* (2d ed.; New York, 1958),
pp. 267 ff.

[3] An example of this approach is this description of the political refugee:
"Hunted revolutionary or banished monarch, dissident intellectual or fugitive
politician, the exile does not seek a new life and a new home in a foreign
land. He considers his residence abroad strictly temporary and will not and
cannot assimilate to a new environment. His thoughts and actions remain
oriented toward the land he continues to call his own as he waits impatiently
for the day when altered conditions will permit him to return home. His emotional and intellectual roots remain firmly imbedded among his own people—
frequently to a greater degree than before his departure. In this sense he
ceases to be an exile as soon as he resolves to break the bonds that tie him to
his native land and endeavors to start life anew beyond its borders" (Lewis
Edinger, *German Exile Politics: The Social Democratic Executive Committee
in the Nazi Era* [Berkeley and Los Angeles, 1956], p. vii).

5

the social order from which they were removed will not survive for long and which "frees them to indulge in phantasy about the ideal society, or to attempt to build it in isolation or through violent attempts against the existing order." [4] For many Russian émigrés such an ideology took the form of two alternative "ways out" of the apparent crisis of the modern world in general and their status as refugees in particular: the East and the West.

Russian émigré literature has often reflected the polarities of two vaguely articulated worlds: "the West," the colonial, imperialist, bourgeois, industrial society of prewar Europe, and "the East," the new, anticolonial, antibourgeois, preindustrial world of the non-European or "backward" nations of the globe traditionally idealized by European thinkers critical of their own countries. To a Russian, the West might mean technical civilization and the East culture; or the West might mean the old Holy Alliance of conservative multinational empires in Central and Eastern Europe and the East a barbaric horde moving on the old Europe; or the West might mean Marxism and the East oriental despotism, as for many Russian socialists. Whatever the specific meaning for each group of émigrés, "West" and "East" were perhaps the most important words in the vocabulary of the times, as they had been for Russians in Europe for generations. For the new language of the émigrés expressed an old problem of identity for Russians living in the West (which often meant in Germany): Were they of the East or of the West? Asiatics or Europeans? And which was superior?

The Russian emigration to Germany before and after 1917 was in fact much unlike the classic pattern of political emigrations. The frustration, utopianism, and political factionalism were all present. But there were also deeper currents at work. The movement of Russians to Germany was traditional. Many Russians were of German ancestry and had friends or relatives in Germany. Many non-Russians had looked to Berlin and Vienna for political support against Great Russian domination. The Russian political right was Germanophile. Russian intellectuals were nurtured on German

---

[4] D. F. Aberle, "A Note on Relative Deprivation Theory as Applied to Millenarian and Other Cult Movements," in S. L. Thrupp, ed., *Millennial Dreams in Action: Essays in Comparative Study* (The Hague, 1962), pp. 210, 214.

thought, often in German universities. Travel and study in Germany had long been a source of cultural conflict for Russians for whom Germany symbolized "the West" with its mixed blessing of technical progress and economic well-being. Conversely, the Russian in Germany was, in the German mind, a symbol of the backward but exotic "East." If the Russian emigration had its specific political roots in the tragic events of political persecution, revolution, and civil war, it also had its more traditional roots in this mechanism of cultural contact, comparison, and conflict.

Thus it was no surprise that many Russians who fled to Germany after 1917 had been there before the war to study, to travel, or to carry on illegal political activity. Similarly there were Russians living in Germany in the 1920's who emigrated before 1914, became partly assimilated into German life, and were thus able to play important roles as intermediaries between the postwar emigration and its German environment. The two most important such groups were the Baltic Germans and the Jews from the Russian Empire, both increasingly persecuted because of their nationality after the 1880's and drawn naturally to Germany because of a need for political refuge and strong cultural ties. In the years before the First World War they became "marginal men":

The individual who through migration, education, marriage, or some other influence leaves one social group or culture without making a satisfactory adjustment to another finds himself on the margin of each but a member of neither. He is a "marginal man" . . . poised in psychological uncertainty between two (or more) social worlds; reflecting in his soul the discords and harmonies, repulsions and attractions of these worlds, one of which is often "dominant" over the other; within which membership is implicitly if not explicitly based upon birth or ancestry (race or nationality); and where exclusion removes the individual from a system of group relations.[5]

Often bilingual, brought up on both Russian and German classical literature, sometimes in German schools in Russia, the Baltic Germans and the Jews felt culturally at home in both Germany and

[5] E. V. Stonequist, *The Marginal Man: A Study in Personality and Culture Conflict* (New York, 1937), pp. 2–3, 8.

7

Russia. To a lesser degree, Russian royalty and intellectuals (and any exiles) also exhibit certain qualities of the "marginal man."

One characteristic of these "marginal men" was that when in Germany they were usually looked upon as "Russians" or "Easterners," whereas in Russia they were often considered to be the "German" or "Westernized" element in society. Consequently, for many of them, this "duality of cultures" produced in them a "duality of personality—a divided self." [6] For them the question whether they were Russians or Europeans, Easterners or Westerners, was a particularly acute one. In Germany they interpreted Russia for the Germans now with disdain, now with admiration, often depending on their anticipation of repulsion or attraction toward Russia on the part of their German audience. "The Russians," one émigré has written, "have always despised the Germans and at the same time admired and even worshipped some of them." [7] Nowhere was the tension between these two extremes greater than in the "marginal man."

"Marginal Men": Russia's Germans and Germany's Russians

Since the first quarter of the eighteenth century, the relationship between Russians and Germans has been far more complex than the normal diplomatic ties between Russia and the German principalities would indicate. [8] The powerful positions held by the Baltic Germans in Russian state service and at the Russian court since the days of Biron, the influx of German colonists to lands along the Volga and in South Russia under Catherine II, the intermarrying of Russian and German royalty, the traditional attraction of German thought for the Russian intelligentsia and of German technology for the Russian entrepreneur and the Russian state, and the conservative alliance of Russia and Prussia throughout most of the

[6] *Ibid.*, p. 217.

[7] Victor Frank, "Russians and Germans: An Ambivalent Heritage," *Survey*, No. 44–45 (October 1962), p. 66.

[8] There is no significant monograph on Russian-German relations as a whole. On twentieth-century ties see the essay by Walter Laqueur, *Russia and Germany* (London, 1965). On Germans in Russia see the bibliography of Karl Stumpp, *Das Schrifttum über das Deutschtum in Russland: Eine Bibliographie* (Stuttgart, 1958).

8

nineteenth century all made up a complicated relationship between the two societies of which diplomatic ties were only one part. To Russians, Germany often meant Europe, the West and the modern world, just as for Germans, Russia, along with China and Japan, was considered part of the East. Some observers have gone as far as to describe Russia as a German colony.[9]

The idea of a colonial relationship between Russia and Germany was based not so much on the economic backwardness of the former as on the fact that many Germans had migrated to Russia and achieved positions of importance within the government, the army, and the agrarian economy. Likewise, Russians came to Germany to learn, rather than to teach. Thus the emigration of Germans to Russia and Russians to Germany became not merely a population exchange but a crucial fact in the political and intellectual life of both countries.

The first Germans to settle on land which was to become part of the Russian Empire came as conquerors, as merchants, and as missionaries. In the twelfth century a substantial number of Crusaders, Hansa traders, and missionaries first moved into the Baltic littoral to establish the beginnings of German dominance over the native (Latvian, Estonian, and Lithuanian populations.) Under the hegemony of the Livonian Order until the mid-sixteenth century, the region later passed into the hands of stronger neighbors: the Poles, the Swedes, and (by the Treaty of Nystadt in 1721) the Russians. The "Baltic German" rulers of the area were more than happy about the final arrangement, by which they agreed to render service to the Russian government in return for managing their own provincial affairs, which they understood to mean unrestricted control over the peasantry. Loyal servants of the Russian crown, they

---

[9] The idea that Russia was a German "colony" was popular during World War I. See the books by I. M. Goldstein, *Voina, germanskie sindikaty, russkii eksport i ekonomicheskoe izolirovanie Germanii* (Moscow, 1915) and *Nemetskoe igo i osvoboditel'naia voina* (Moscow, 1915). A Soviet variation on the theme may be found in B. B. Grave, "Byla li tsarskaia Rossiia polukoloniei?" *Voprosy istorii*, 1956, No. 6, pp. 63–74. A recent Western overstatement of the idea is Werner Keller, *East Minus West Equals Zero* (New York, 1962) which suggests that all Russian accomplishments have been the result of European, especially German, thought and technology.

remained in fact and in outlook a *Herrenvolk* in their own domain, the bearers of Western civilization to an untutored Baltic native population, owners of the land, and comptrollers of trade between the towns of North Germany and Central Russia. Already by the sixteenth century they had emerged as a unique bicultural group, neither German nor Russian but able to act as intermediaries and translators for the diplomatic and economic traffic between Ivan IV's Muscovy and his Lithuanian and Prussian neighbors.[10]

In the sixteenth century a second type of German began to appear in Russia: the diplomat, military expert, scientist, doctor, and technical adviser, making up the group of so-called Moscow (and later St. Petersburg) Germans. Together with the Dutch and English visitors under Ivan IV, they were settled to the southeast of Moscow in the 1560's and 1570's in the area for foreigners known as the German Settlement (*nemetskaia sloboda*). Initially, these "Germans" were limited to the Habsburg diplomats who represented the interests of the Holy Roman Empire, particularly against the Turkish menace to Europe, and reconnoitered what was still an unknown land on the trade routes to Persia and Cathay. In the 1550's Ivan IV initiated the first, unsuccessful, attempt to enroll German doctors, druggists, printers, and artisans in Russian service; but the German presence in Russia remained limited to a few hardy adventurers who took up arms as members of Ivan's private army, the dread Oprichnina.[11] Until the end of the Thirty Years' War foreign dominance in Russia was primarily limited to the English and the Dutch, despite Boris Godunov's recruitment of a few doctors and goldsmiths and his dispatch of six Russian students to Lübeck.

The settling of Germans in Moscow dates from the middle of the seventeenth century. Habsburg, Saxon, and Brandenburg-Prussian diplomats were joined now by a number of refugees from the Thirty Years' War from Holstein, Gotha, Mecklenburg, Hamburg, and Lübeck. Baltic Germans fleeing Swedish troops entered the ranks of Tsar Aleksei's army. The increasing number of German

---

[10] A. Bilmanis, "Grandeur and Decline of the German Balts," *Slavonic and East European Review*, No. 22 (December 1944), pp. 50–80.

[11] Friedrich von Adelung, *Kritisch-literärische Übersicht der Reisenden in Russland bis 1700* (St. Petersburg, 1846) I, 136–175, 205–208.

army officers, shipbuilders, goldsmiths, artisans, doctors, and printers who made their way east at this time is attested to by the influx into the Russian language of the technical terms for their
various trades, as well as by the appearance of the first Lutheran
church in the *sloboda* to serve the growing German community
there.[12] By the time of Peter the Great the foreign German Settlement was well established, and augmented by the addition of more
military men. St. Petersburg, too, developed a substantial German
community. To Peter's German technicians were added the Baltic
German followers of Empress Anne and her co-ruler Biron in the
1730's, the Holstein supporters of the future Peter III, and the
entourage of Sophie of Anhalt-Zerbst, later Catherine II. The intellectual, artistic, and sartorial Gallomania of the courts of Eliza-
beth and Catherine dominated the latter part of the eighteenth
century in Russia, but did not eliminate either the retinues of
Russia's German rulers or the influx of German mathematicians
and scientists whose control over the St. Petersburg Academy of
Sciences gave them reason to find in Russia a true "Paradise of
Scholars."

Another type of German—the peasant colonist from south and
southwest Germany—began to come to Russia during the reigns
of Catherine II and Alexander I. In her manifesto of July 22, 1763,
Catherine offered German settlers land in South Russia, freedom
of religion, freedom from taxes, and the right to self-administration.
The result was a steady migration of veterans, bankrupt nobility,
artisans, students, and poor peasants into Russia, first along the
Volga River, later on the northern shores of the Black Sea and in
the Caucasus when these newly-won regions became available for
settlement after 1800. German immigration to Russia reached a
peak in the wake of the Napoleonic wars which produced military
destruction, poor harvests, high prices, and famine. In 1816–1817
some fifteen thousand residents of Württemberg and Swabia joined
the great *Auswanderung* to Russia.[13] The motives were more than
economic, however. Many saw in Russia the land where God would

[12] S. C. Gardiner, *German Loanwords in Russian, 1550–1690* (Oxford, 1965).
[13] Mack Walker, *Germany and the Emigration, 1816–1885* (Cambridge,
Mass., 1964), p. 31. See also Georg Leibbrandt, *Die Auswanderung aus
Schwaben nach Russland, 1816–1823* (Stuttgart, 1928) and *Ostwanderung
der Württemberger, 1816–1822* (Leipzig, 1941).

assemble the righteous during the last days before instituting a thousand-year Kingdom. This religious *Schwarmerei* left a deep imprint on those sturdy German colonists who were to remain in Russia, and their tidy villages and farms later became the envy of their Russian neighbors and a source of their own sense of superiority.

By the 1820's the Baltic Germans, their St. Petersburg and Moscow co-nationals, and the South Russian colonists were established within the Russian Empire as loyal and privileged citizens. The Russian attitude toward them was one of envy, expressed in the apocryphal story of the Russian general whose ultimate request was to be promoted to the rank of "German," and in Pushkin's sarcastic comments in *Evgeny Onegin* regarding those citizens of Russia who "had the misfortune to be German." Like Goncharov's Stolz in *Oblomov*, the Russian German in Russian literature was a man who was both efficient and necessary, but also stiff and formal: the elderly tutor, the watchmaker, the dentist (such as Finkel in Chekhov's "A Gentlemen Friend") the artisan, and the bandmaster. Germans could be drunken, rude, and greedy, but also meticulous, economical, sentimental, and dreamy. The Russian German was never a positive hero, but he was not yet the jackbooted soldier or the dull-witted "boy with pants" which would emerge in the 1870's with the unification of Germany and the rise of Pan-Slavism.[14]

The Russian Germans themselves varied greatly in their attitudes toward Russia and in their ability to assimilate. Some of the more outspoken Russian patriots among the Decembrists were of Russian-German origin. High status and frequent intermarriage could often facilitate assimilation. "We must be Russians," wrote a young Baltic German army officer in 1818; "we can be Russians, and we will be Russians." [15] Until the attack upon the Russian Germans began in the second half of the nineteenth century, this sense of loyalty toward the Russian government remained.

Culturally, however, many Russian Germans became "marginal,"

---

[14] J. Sazonova, "The German in Russian Literature," *American Slavic and East European Review*, IV, No. 1 (1945), pp. 50–79.

[15] H. Lemberg, *Die nationale Gedankenwelt der Dekabristen* (Cologne, 1963), p. 77.

caught up between their German ancestry and cultural heritage and their Russian environment. "I belong inwardly to two worlds," recalled a Baltic German, "a border-dweller in space as well as in time, a Viking and a child of the steppes carrying within me both the oldest tradition and the remotest future." [16] "Looking back on my formative years," wrote a member of Moscow's German colony, "I am clearly aware that, depending on temporary influences, I was at times torn between Russian and German culture. In the end German influences far predominated; but it would not be wrong to say that I have always had two home countries, Germany as well as Russia. I am attached to both of them with affection and nostalgia." [17]

There was an important difference, however, between the sense of superiority experienced by the Baltic and South Russian Germans who lived among the Russian, Ukrainian, or Latvian peasantry and the more cosmopolitan outlook of the Moscow and St. Petersburg Germans who dealt with the most "westernized" elements of Russian society. The first type, as one Russian observed, "lived in large groups which kept their national identity and their ties to their German *Vaterland*" and "considered that they owed their allegiance to the Throne and not to Russia"; the Moscow and St. Petersburg Germans, on the other hand, "lacked an exaggerated sense of national exclusiveness and remained ever open to influences from their mother country as well as from their newly acquired domicile, Russia." [18]

The choice posed by the Russification campaign of Alexander III after 1881 was, therefore, assimilation or emigration. "Do we want to be Germans," asked one Balt, "or do we want to be Balts? Do we want to give up our nationality or our homeland?" [19] For those

[16] Hermann Keyserling, *Europe* (New York, 1928), p. 315.

[17] Gustav Hilger and A. Meyer, *The Incompatible Allies* (New York, 1953), p. 12.

[18] G. Tschebotarioff, *Russia, My Native Land* (New York, 1964), pp. 32–33; and Otto von Taube, a Baltic German poet, in *Die literarische Welt*, December 8, 1933, cited in A. von Gronicka, *Henry von Heiseler* (New York, 1944), p. 18.

[19] A. von Freytag-Loringhoven, in *Deutsche Monatschrift für das gesamte Leben der Gegenwart*, V (1906), 604–605.

who chose to emigrate to Germany, the traditional identity problem was even more complex. In Germany, too, they were outsiders, despite the adulation of the *Auslandsdeutschen* propaganda. "I have known some of them," recalled a Russian émigré, "who, while in Russia, seemed to feel more like Germans, but later, when they found themselves in Germany after the Revolution, felt more like Russians." [20] Such a life on the margin of two cultures made the Russian Germans ideal interpreters and intermediaries for other Russians and Germans; it also created an inner turmoil and a sense of inadequacy that often led either to a peculiarly ferocious brand of German nationalism and Russophobia, or to a new enthusiasm for Russian culture.

Like the Germans who migrated to Russia, those Russians who lived in Germany experienced a sense of heightened national consciousness through exposure to Western ideas and patterns of life. Paul Tillich once observed that "there is not simply an accidental but an essential relationship between mind and migration, that mind in its very nature is migratory and that human mental creativity and man's migrating power belong together." [21] In this sense emigration, like superior social standing or exposure to European thought, provided another dimension to the process of alienation and estrangement from Russian society at large that became a defining characteristic of the Russian intelligentsia in the nineteenth century. Referring to Alexander Herzen, Dostoevsky remarked that he "did not emigrate; he did not begin Russian emigration;—no, he was already born an emigrant. They all, akin to him, were ready-born emigrants, even though the majority of them never left Russia." [22] Already estranged from the backwardness and oppression they saw around them, young Russians sought knowledge and freedom in the West; paradoxically, many of them ended by idealizing in the abstract, past or future, a Russia whose present reality they had fled.

Russians first began to go abroad in substantial numbers in the eighteenth century, most often to Germany. Russian students and

[20] Tschebotarioff, *Russia*, p. 33.   [21] *Social Research*, IV (1937), 295.
[22] Fedor Dostoevsky, *Diary of a Writer* (New York, 1949), I, 5.

merchants had lived in East Prussia since the 1500's, but it was only in the 1730's that Russian students began to appear at German universities. The major centers were Halle, Marburg, Göttingen, and Jena, where several thousand Russians had already matriculated by 1800, primarily in such technical studies as medicine, law, chemistry, physics, and mathematics. The Russian government frequently sponsored education abroad as a means of bringing technical expertise into their own country. Too often, however, Russian students returned fired by the political and social ideas of the Enlightenment and eager to change their homeland into a better place, as Catherine II discovered in the case of Alexander Radishchev, who returned from five years at Leipzig to become an outspoken critic of serfdom.[23]

For many Russians the result of foreign travel and study was a sense of suspension between Russian reality and European culture. A literary example was Pushkin's Lensky, a "half-Russian, German-bred":

> Vladimir Lensky, handsome, youthful,
> A Kantian, unspoiled and truthful,
> Whose soul was shaped in Göttingen,
> And who could wield the poet's pen.
> From misty Germany, Vladimir
> Had brought the fruit of learning's tree.[24]

By the end of the eighteenth century, imitation of European manners and thought by Russians was slowly transformed into a compensating enthusiasm for Russia herself. The travels of the writer Denis Fonvizin convinced him that "everything with us is better, and we are bigger people than the Germans." [25] European romanticism, with its assertion of the values of feeling and the heart against the rationalism of the Enlightenment, provided further fuel for Russian nationalism, already fired by the victory over Napoleon.

[23] Eduard Winter, *Halle als Ausgangspunkt der deutschen Russlandkunde im 18. Jahrhundert* (Berlin, 1953), p. 288.

[24] *Eugene Onegin*, II, vi, from Avrahm Yarmolinsky, ed., *The Poems, Prose and Plays of Pushkin* (New York: Random House, 1936; copyright 1936 and renewed 1964 by Random House, Inc.).

[25] Hans Rogger, *National Consciousness in Eighteenth-Century Russia* (Cambridge, Mass., 1960), p. 83.

"The German romantic rejection of the West," as one historian has
observed, "was adopted with similar arguments by many Russians,
who however included Germany in the rejected West." [26] In the
nineteenth century this resulted in the paradox that those Russians
who were so attracted to German thought and culture were at the
same time hostile toward Germany. The literary critic Vissarion
Belinsky was an admirer of "the profound, soulful, many-sided
German spirit" but found in his travels in 1847 that the Germans in
reality were "honorable and stupid." [27] "I loved Germans without
knowing them," wrote Gogol, "or perhaps I confused German
erudition, German philosophy and literature with the Germans,"
whom he found to be living in a country "nasty, begrimed, and
smoke-blackened by the huge quantity of tobacco." [28]

The disgust with life in Europe often resulted in a feeling of
sentimental attachment for Russia at a distance. Herzen's remark
in exile in 1851 that "I never felt more clearly than now how Russian I am" was not unique. Gogol, too, found it easier to write
Dead Souls in Germany, France, and Italy than in Russia. Only
after his trips abroad in the 1860's could Dostoevsky speak with
authority of the decadence of the European bourgeoisie. The poet
Fedor Tiutchev too created his idealized "Russia" during two decades of exile in Munich, embodying it with the very qualities he
found lacking in the West.[29] For many more Russians, life abroad
became an education in the real or imagined value of life at home.
That they found men like Schelling, Franz Baader, and Varnhagen
von Ense enthusiastic about the future of Russia only served to re-
enforce this feeling.

With the Great Reforms of Alexander II and the emergence of the
radical intelligentsia, Germany became not merely a center of

[26] Hans Kohn, *The Mind of Modern Russia* (New Brunswick, N.J., 1955),
pp. 9–10.

[27] Vissarion Belinsky, letter of Sept. 29, 1847, from Berlin to Paul Annenkov,
cited in Herbert Bowman, *Vissarion Belinsky* (Cambridge, Mass., 1954),
p. 188.

[28] From Gogol's letters to M. P. Balabina of May 30 and September 5,
1839, in C. R. Proffer, ed., *Letters of Nikolai Gogol* (Ann Arbor, Mich., 1967),
pp. 79, 82.

[29] Richard Gregg, *Fedor Tiutchev: The Evolution of a Poet* (New York and
London, 1965).

16

learning but a place of refuge. Student reading rooms at Heidelberg, Karlsruhe, Berlin, and Leipzig became the foci of political discussions. Illegal books, pamphlets, and journals were printed on Russian presses at Leipzig, and Russian revolutionaries jostled with Russian police agents. But with the unification of Germany and the subsequent government persecution of socialists in the 1870's many Russians moved on to London, Zurich, or Paris. Only in the 1880's did Germany again take its place as a major center of Russian exile politics and student activity.[30]

Life in Germany was often made easier for Russians by the bicultural facility of those Russian Germans and Russian Jews who migrated there. Both these groups shared not only a general familiarity with the German language but a position of political isolation. In addition to their vast differences in social positions (the favored position granted the Baltic aristocracy, the Moscow and St. Petersburg merchants, and the South Russian colonists and the forced isolation imposed upon Jews in the Pale of Settlement), neither Germans nor Jews were completely assimilated into Russian life. Russian nationalists often spoke of both groups in one breath as alien elements in the Russian body politic. Thus Ivan Aksakov observed that "the Jews, like the Germans, do not acknowledge the existence in Russia of a Russian nationality and doubt (for the Germans it is a question that they settled negatively long ago) whether the Russians were really the masters in the Russian land." [31] It was their position on the cultural and political margin of Russia and Germany which made them ideal intermediaries for Russians in Germany.

Until the 1880's Russian Germans and Russian Jews were most important in making Russian literature available in German translation. A Moscow German, J. G. Richter, first translated Karamzin's *Letters of a Russian Traveler* into a Western language. In the

---

[30] On Russians in Germany in the 1860's see B. P. Koz'min, "Russkaia geidel'bergskaia koloniia 1861–1863 gg. i Gertsen," *Iz istorii revoliutsionnoi mysli v Rossii: Izbrannye trudy* (Moscow, 1961), pp. 488–498; also the journal edited by Ivan Golovin, *Blagonamernyi* (Leipzig, 1861).

[31] Stephen Lukashevich, *Ivan Aksakov* (Cambridge, Mass., 1965) p. 111.

1820's other Baltic Germans produced translations of Russian writers in journals in Riga and St. Petersburg, introduced the writings of Pushkin to their German literary friends, and edited the first anthology of Russian poetry in German. Also influential in introducing Russian literature into Germany were Baron Leonhard von Budberg, the translator of Lermontov's *A Hero of Our Times*, Alexander Wulffert, the editor of the *St. Petersburger Zeitung* in the 1820's and 1830's, and Wilhelm Wolfsohn, a Russian Jew from Odessa and prolific translator. It was largely due to the linguistic facility of these men that Russian literature was well received in Germany long before it became known in either France or England.[32]

The Baltic Germans were also important in cultivating an enthusiasm for Russia as an exotic and religious culture. The best known was the mystic Baronness Julie von Krüdener, follower of Swabian pietism and confidante of Alexander I, who cultivated his enthusiasm for a "Holy Alliance" of powers led by Russia against the revival of revolutionary French expansionism. It was she who provided the link between Alexander and the Württemberg pietists and encouraged their anticipation that salvation in a time of disorder would come from the East, that she was the "Woman of the Sun" who would lead all true Christians to the promised land in mankind's last hours, and that Alexander was "the protector of the flock which believes in the new kingdom of Christ on earth." Her apocalyptic portrait of Russia had a profound effect not only upon those Germans who emigrated there but upon Russian nationalist circles in the 1830's and 1840's as well.[33] Boris von Uexküll was another Balt who, as a student of Hegel, developed further for German listeners the theme of Russia's religious possibilities and future potential.[34]

By the 1860's and 1870's, however, Baltic German attitudes to-

[32] H. Raab, *Die Lyrik Pushkins in Deutschland* (Berlin, 1964); V. I. Kuleshov, *Literaturnye sviazi Rossii i zapadnoi Evropy v XIX veke* (*pervaia polovina*) (Moscow, 1965).

[33] E. J. Knapton, *The Lady of the Holy Alliance: The Life of Julie de Krüdener* (New York, 1939); Leibbrandt, *Auswanderung*, pp. 78–98.

[34] George von Rauch, "Boris von Uexküll und Hegels Russlandbild," *Baltische Hefte*, IV, No. 1(October 1957), pp. 26–34.

ward Russia were beginning to shift from attraction to repulsion. The emancipation of the serfs in 1861 and the growth of Pan-Slav sentiment unleashed changes in Russia hostile to the position of a minority which was both upper-class and non-Russian; Bismarck's unification of Germany provided a new center of attraction. Those Balts who began to come to Germany at this time were increasingly Germanophile and Russophobe. Julius Eckardt, the editor of the *Rigaer Zeitung*, was particularly influential in Germany, where his attacks on the Russian government and Russian nationalism gained him entry into journalistic and diplomatic circles and helped to popularize the plight of Russia's Germans. As an adviser of Bismarck and Holstein, a diplomat, a journalist, and a cofounder of the Verein für Sozialpolitik, Eckardt became the prototype of that later variety of Baltic German whose Russian loyalties were so easily replaced by German nationalism.[35]

By 1881, when the murder of Alexander II precipitated the policies of national Russification and social reaction that characterized the reign of Alexander III, a certain pattern of Russian emigration had been established. Neither Russia's Germans nor Germany's Russians had found what they expected in their new homeland. The Russian Germans obtained their land and their exemptions from military service and taxes, but even these were being threatened in a society whose progress in education, industrialization, and administration was making German expertise expendable and whose government was proving increasingly inhospitable. Russians in Germany had expected a kingdom of philosophers, not of beer and parades. In both countries nationalism was making the position of minorities unpleasant. In the 1880's the response of the Russian Germans and the Russian Jews was flight, mainly to the United States and South America but also to Germany. It was in Germany that they contributed by their political hostility and their cultural mediation to German public opinion on Russia in the years before the war. As both interpreters and examples, they formed the point of contact between the Russian emigration

[35] E. Teidoff, "Julius von Eckardt," *Deutsche Post aus dem Osten*, XIII, No. 11 (November 1941), pp. 11–12 and XIV, No. 2 (February 1942), pp. 1–2.

and German society, symbols and salesmen of the barbaric and exotic sides of Russian life.

The First Wave: 1881–1914

Until the 1890's Russia was a country of immigration, not emigration. Since the sixteenth century Europeans had come to Russia as military advisers, merchants, tutors, doctors, bureaucrats, court painters, and architects. Often they were Germans. From 1828 to 1915 some 1,459,000 Germans had settled in Russia, representing 35.1 per cent of Russia's total immigration during that period. But in the 1880's and 1890's the repressive policies of the Russian government managed not only to stem the flow of immigrants into Russia but to increase sharply emigration from Russia. From 1860 to 1889, 2,147,000 foreigners settled in Russia while 1,129,000 Russian citizens left the country; from 1890 to 1915 the process was reversed: while some 1,786,000 persons came to live in Russia, emigration rose steadily so that 3,348,000 people left Russia in these years.[36] Most of the new émigrés, nearly half of them Jews, settled not in Western Europe but in the United States. In Germany, too, there was a marked rise in immigration from Russia after 1881. The German census figures for 1880 recorded 15,097 Russians passing through Germany, 46,971 for 1900, 106,639 for 1905; by 1910 there were 137,697 Russians traveling or living in Germany—over half the total number of Russians in Western Europe.[37]

The Russian government generally discouraged emigration and did what it could to control it. To minister to the religious needs of the Russian colony in Germany and to maintain political loyalties, it encouraged an Orthodox priest, Aleksei Maltsev, to establish the St. Vladmir Brotherhood in Berlin in 1890. The Brotherhood was primarily a welfare organization, devoted to the erecting of Russian churches in places frequented by Russians—Hamburg, Darmstadt, Baden-Baden, and Bad Kissingen—and the publishing of Russian religious literature. Some accused it of

[36] V. V. Obolensky (Osinsky), *Mezhdunarodnye i mezhkontinental'nye migratsii v dovoennoi Rossii i SSSR* (Moscow, 1928), pp. 108, 110.
[37] *Statistik des deutschen Reichs*, Vol. 240 (Berlin, 1915), p. 153.

being an agency of "Slavophile propaganda," an arm of Alexander III's Russification policies abroad; Maltsev himself viewed it as "a wonderful means of familiarizing enlightened European society with our church service, truly the best in the world." [38] Should ideology lose its appeal, there was always the Okhrana, whose main function was the gathering of intelligence concerning the activities of Russian revolutionaries and students in Germany. The Berlin office of the Okhrana was organized in 1901 under the direction of A.M. Harting and was part of the official Russian representation in Berlin, housed in the consulate and using diplomatic channels for correspondence. Beside intercepting mail and watching students, especially those of a "typically Jewish type," it provided security for Russian royalty abroad.[39]

Not only was there a new political emigration of Russians to Germany after 1900, but traditional cultural relations were also being politicized. The old marital ties between Russian and German royalty had once been the foundation of a conservative and anti-Polish alliance. They survived the diplomatic revolution precipitated by the Franco-Russian alliance of the 1890's unimpaired, but after 1900 German politicians were tempted to turn these old ties to political use.

After Alexander II married Princess Marie of Hesse-Darmstadt, members of the Russian royal family came to Germany frequently. Many Romanovs became seasonal or permanent émigrés from Russia by marriage, Germanized or Anglicized considerably in thought, manners, and dress. In the 1870's the usual stamping grounds for Russian royal visitors to Germany were the Schloss Heiligenberg in Hesse-Darmstadt and the nearby royal summer palace of the dukes of Hesse-Kassel. But when Alexander's daughter Marie married Alfred, Duke of Edinburgh, in 1873, and her

---

[38] W. Kahle, "Fragen der russisch-orthodoxen Theologie, dargestellt am Lebenswerk des Berliner Propstes A. P. Malzew (1854–1915)," *Kyrios*, II (1962), 141; *K xv-letiiu Sv. Kniaz-Vladimirskago Bratstva v Berline* (Berlin, 1906).

[39] V. K. Agafonov, *Zagranichnaia okhranka* (Petrograd, 1918), pp. 45–49; Aziat, *Russkie shpiony v Germanii* (Berlin, 1904); L. D. Menshikov, *Russkii politicheskii sysk za granitsei* (Paris, 1914), and the Okhrana Archive at the Hoover Library, Boxes 4, 18, 19, 35.

daughter Viktoria Melita married Grand Duke Ernst August of Hesse-Darmstadt in 1894, the locus of visits was extended to include Coburg, Karlsruhe, and a villa at the Tegernsee south of Munich. Here in the decades before 1914 a great clan of inter-married Russian, German, and English royalty gathered to exchange the latest family news, to arrange future marriages, to gossip, and to enjoy an atmosphere of quiet isolation and *Gemütlichkeit*. When Nicholas II married Alix of Hesse-Darmstadt in 1894 he became an intimate member of this little world.

It was not surprising that many Russian members of this royal family felt quite at home in Germany, despite ominous political developments. Grand Duke Kirill Vladimirovich, pretender to the Russian throne in the 1920's and 1930's, was surrounded by German maids, tutors, and relatives as a young man, and recalled that his aunt, Grand Duchess Alix of Saxe-Altenburg, "always spoke German to us." [40] Kirill himself, because of his marriage to his divorced cousin Viktoria, spent the years from 1905 to 1910 in exile at Coburg, where he indulged his passion for hunting and motor-cars. The Leuchtenbergs, a lesser branch of the Romanov family, spent considerable time before the war at their ancestral castle of Seeon in Bavaria; Duke Georg of Leuchtenberg lived there from 1906 until 1914 convalescing from wounds received during the Russo-Japanese War, and became fast friends with Duke Leopold of Bavaria. For many of these royal exiles Russia remained a land about which they knew all too little. "We were brought up in a Fool's Paradise," one of them later admitted, "carefully guarded from reality," so that even on visits to Russia they felt "on guard, a little hostile, or anyhow watchful, so that we could not blend entirely nor feel quite at home." [41]

After 1900 the family relationship between Russian and German royalty had a diminishing influence on diplomacy. Some Germans continued to look back to the good old days of close Russo-Ger-

[40] Grand Duke Cyril, *My Life in Russia's Service—Then and Now* (London, 1939), p. 17.

[41] Gleb Botkin, *The Woman Who Rose Again* (New York, 1937), p. 64; Grand Duke Alexander, *Once a Grand Duke* (New York, 1932), pp. 151–153; "Leikhtenbergskii gertsogskii dom," *Entsiklopedicheskii slovar'* (Brockhaus-Efron) (St. Petersburg, 189–), XVIIA, 506–507; Queen Marie of Roumania, *The Story of My Life* (London, 1934), I, 205, 217.

man relations on the basis of dynastic intermarriage. Even in 1906 the German ambassador in St. Petersburg felt that "at that time there was still reason to consider the close friendship which had existed for the last century between the reigning houses the strongest bond between Germany and Russia, as in the past."[42] But German policy toward Russia was hardly determined by such sentimental considerations. "The Russians will need us," predicted Friedrich von Holstein, head of the Wilhelmstrasse's Political Section, in 1895, "before we will need them." [43]

Accordingly, in the years before 1914 the bonds between the courts of Berlin and St. Petersburg became a weapon of German policy, not its determinant. German pressure was no longer exerted at the level of official diplomacy but through the institution of personal military attachés of both emperors which dated from the early nineteenth century. Two of these men, Major General Lamsdorff and naval attaché Hintze, were attached to the court of St. Petersburg where they probably had a greater influence than the German ambassador. The German attachés in St. Petersburg and the Russian naval attaché in Berlin, Captain Pauli, were the personal emissaries between William II and Nicholas II and the bearers of that touching exchange of letters known as the "Willy-Nicky correspondence." Lamsdorff, who served in this capacity from 1904 to 1914, was declared by William to be "responsible for reports only to me personally, and is forbidden once for all to report or communicate with anybody else, either General Staff or Foreign Office, or Chancellor." [44] Similarly, William preferred dealing with his cousin through a Russian military attaché rather than the stout, somewhat pompous, but amiable Russian ambassador in Berlin from 1895 to 1912, Count N. D. Osten-Sacken.

At first Holstein was annoyed by a separate correspondence

[42] Freiherr von Schoen, *The Memoirs of an Ambassador* (London, 1922), p. 32.

[43] Holstein to Hugo von Radolin, Berlin, July 2, 1895, in Norman Rich and M. H. Fischer, eds., *The Holstein Papers*, III (Cambridge, 1961), 528.

[44] William II to Nicholas II, Berlin, June 6, 1904, in *Die Grosse Politik der europäischen Kabinette, 1871–1914* (Berlin, 1921-) XIX, No. 1, pp.182–184. See also G. Lambsdorff, *Die Militärbevollmächtigten Kaiser Wilhelms II. am Zarenhofe, 1904–1914* (Berlin, 1937).

between rulers which might interfere with policy as he saw it. But by the late 1890's the composing of the Willy-Nicky letters was in the firm hands of the Wilhelmstrasse.[45] The birthday congratulations, court gossip, and Easter eggs exchanged by the Admiral of the Atlantic and the Admiral of the Pacific became a carefully organized part of German plans to involve Russia in Asia against England and Japan, leaving Germany with a free hand against France. "By cultivating dynastic ties," recalled the German ambassador, "we were still able to keep on good terms with Russia on the whole, so long as her immense strength sought and found a wide field for expansion in the Asiatic East."[46]

But the political use of dynastic ties only revealed their steady erosion. William might ramble on in his letters about the Yellow Peril, the "old tradition which always united our families for the benefit of our countries," "our old friendly relations with Russia," and "the maintenance of peace and of monarchical institutions."[47] But in fact such an appeal to the memory of past ties no longer overrode the more pragmatic considerations of power politics, as indicated by the refusal of the astounded foreign offices in both Berlin and St. Petersburg to endorse the Treaty of Björko agreed between the two emperors personally in 1905. But these ties did promote common action in the face of a threat recognized by both Russia and Germany. The two governments continued to find it profitable to maintain a close watch on the forces of revolution and Polish nationalism. To this end the Russian Okhrana agents and the police presidium in every German city worked hand in hand in the years before the war.

The type of Russian student attending German universities was also changing after 1900. Since the 1730's Russians had come to Germany to sit at the feet of the great German thinkers and had returned with feelings of ambivalence toward "the West."

[45] F. Rosen, *Aus einem diplomatischen Wanderleben* (Berlin, 1931), II, 10; Johannes Haller, *Philip Eulenberg: The Kaiser's Friend* (New York, 1930), I, 307.

[46] Schoen, *Memoirs*, p. 222.

[47] N. F. Grant, ed., *The Kaiser's Letters to the Tsar* (London, 1920), March 28, 1898, and January 8, 1909.

Germany was the land not only of Kant and Schiller, but also of beer and bourgeois uniformity. The traditional attraction of German thought continued to exist for upper-class Russians after 1900; Boris Pasternak, Fedor Stepun, Nikolai Berdiaev, and Boris Vysheslavtsev were among those drawn to Marburg to study the neo-Kantianism of Hermann Cohen and Friedrich Lange. But after 1900 they were not typical of Russian students in Germany. The cultured few were replaced by a wave of lower-middle-class students, many of them Jewish, who came to the technical high schools as well as the universities to study not philosophy but medicine, chemistry, engineering, and law. The number of Russian students enrolled in German universities and high schools nearly tripled between 1900 and 1914. In the universities alone some five thousand Russians registered during the summer and winter semesters of 1912–1913, primarily at Berlin (1,174), Leipzig (758), Munich (552), Königsberg (435), Heidelberg (317), and Halle (283).[48] Russians made up more than half the number of foreign students at most universities and often a majority of them was Jewish.

The attraction of German university towns for young Russians in these years was their cultural life. "Recalling our past and asking ourselves what drew us to Germany, which meant Europe for us," wrote a Russian student, "we inevitably arrived at the same conclusion: its culture." Boris Pasternak's ecstatic "Farewell philosophy, farewell youth, farewell Germany!" expressed a similar emotion. Some returned from their studies to Russia imagining themselves the "bearers of a superior culture"; others became convinced that "the average German was morally and spiritually more stupid and narrow than the average Russian" and returned with a heightened sense of Russia's superiority over bourgeois civilization. Whatever their reaction, they tended to live a somewhat isolated life in Germany in their own student colonies. This was in marked contrast to those Russian Jews and Germans who found assimilation so easy. S. L. Frank knew German well enough to translate the writings of his German teachers into

---

[48] B. Brachmann, *Russische Sozialdemokraten in Berlin, 1895–1914* (Berlin, 1962), p. 196.

Russian; Fedor Stepun, a Balt, not only found life in Heidelberg, Baden-Baden, and Karlsruhe extremely natural and pleasant, but helped to launch a joint Russo-German philosophical journal, *Logos*, which appeared simultaneously in both languages in Moscow and Tübingen in 1910.[49]

Russian intellectuals, writers, and artists who did settle in Germany before 1914, however, found that a veritable cult of things Russian had developed among middle-class intellectuals in Germany, reversing the traditional one-way attraction. The appearance in translation of the classics of nineteenth-century Russian literature was one reason for this revived interest in Russia; another was the mood of despair among the younger generation in Germany which led to a great fascination with Russia and "the East" as a way out of the boredom and sameness of bourgeois European society. The West was organized, civilized, repressed, mechanized, and dehumanized; the East was still untouched, primitive, unrepressed, natural, religious, and wise. Russia was a symbol of this way out to the East, and Dostoevsky was a symbol of Russia. In contrast to England, where he had the reputation of a somewhat morbid and unsavory novelist, Dostoevsky was read in prewar Germany as a visionary prophet who portrayed an underground world beneath the façade of modern society a world which was somehow more real and which, it has been suggested, provided a vicarious experience of forbidden emotions for middle-class readers.[50] The writings of Tolstoi were equally popular in Germany after 1881. Occasionally a reviewer would grumble about a "national danger for German literature" or dismiss *War and Peace* as a "historical-military chauvinist pamphlet of a typical Russian against Western culture." But most German writers, like Timm Kroeger, were attracted by the rich panorama of Russian life which they found in Tolstoi's descriptions of peasants and Cossacks and his use of Biblical imagery in a quest for reli-

[49] L. Zander, "O F. A. Stepune i o nekotorykh ego knigakh," *Mosty*, 1963, No. 10, p. 319; Boris Pasternak, *Safe Conduct* (London, 1959), p. 224; Fedor Stepun, *Byvshee i nebyvsheesia* (New York, 1956).

[50] T. Kampmann, *Dostojewskij in Deutschland* (Münster, 1931); L. Lowenthal, "The Reception of Dostoevsky's Work in Germany: 1880–1920," in R. N. Wilson, ed., *The Arts in Society* (Englewood Cliffs, N.J., 1964).

gious meaning. Like Dostoevsky, Tolstoi was read in Germany not as a social or political thinker but as a Russian prophet with a special vision of the conscious and unconscious life of men.[51]

It is striking to note that German interest in Russia before the war was based upon little more than cursory reading of the works of Russian writers. Russia was largely an unknown quantity, a mysterious country peopled by characters from Gogol, Turgenev, Tolstoi, and Dostoevsky, both backward and dangerous, exotic anl terrible, capable of either revivifying or destroying bourgeois Europe. Because of this lack of information about Russia, many Russians in Germany in these years found themselves pressed into service as interpreters of Russian life.

The best known of these was the writer and literary critic Dmitry Merezhkovsky, considered a "European" in Moscow literary circles, only by virtue of his translated commentaries on Russian literature widely read in Germany. He provided for the German reading public precisely the interpretations it craved about Russia. He wrote knowingly of an imminent "third kingdom" that would mark the final phase of world history, a phase in which the Holy Ghost would appear and reconcile Father and Son, spirit and flesh, into some new and ultimate unity. Through Merezhkovsky and his interpretation of Dostoevsky the young Moeller van den Bruck derived all his knowledge about Russia and much of the framework of his later work, Das Dritte Reich.[52] Thomas Mann borrowed wholesale from him the characterization of Pushkin, Dostoevsky, and Tolstoi respectively as the "Goethe," "Dante," and "Michelangelo" of the East, as well as his enthusiasm for that mysterious "third kingdom" that would replace Western civilization.[53] It was while reading Merezhkovsky, re-

[51] W. Hammer, "The German Tolstoy Translations," Germanic Review, XII (January 1938), 49–61; C. M. Purin, "Tolstoi und Kroeger: Eine Darstellung ihrer literarischen Beziehungen," University of Wisconsin Studies in Language and Literature, XXII (1925), 217–245.

[52] Fritz Stern, The Politics of Cultural Despair (New York, 1965), pp. 239, 380, n. 9; H. Schwierskott, Arthur Moeller van den Bruck und der revolutionäre Nationalismus in der Weimarer Republik (Göttingen, 1962), p. 17.

[53] L. Venohr, Thomas Manns Verhältnis zur russischen Literatur (Meisenheim-an-Glan, 1959), p. 80.

called Stefan Zweig, that he first heard the news from Sarajevo in the summer of 1914.

The contribution of Russian intellectuals to German life after 1900 was in sharp contrast to their previous experience as humble students of German thought. The modish mysticism of Rudolf Steiner's "anthroposophy" movement, originally a branch of English theosophy, had an enormous appeal for Andrei Belyi and other Russians, but also was itself greatly influenced by those Russians who introduced into the movement the writings of the religious philosopher Vladimir Soloviev. The colony of Russian artists in Munich—Kandinsky, Yavlensky, Grabar, Kardovsky, Marianne Verefkin—came to Germany in the late 1890's to study European impressionism and stayed on to contribute Russian themes and their own talents to German expressionism and the postwar Bauhaus movement. In many more cases Russians came to Germany to learn and stayed to teach.

These two types of Russians who had traditionally come to Germany—royalty and intellectuals—continued to participate in German life in the years before the First World War. But they were no longer alone.

The politics of the new emigration to Germany were quite naturally politics of the left. Since the death of Alexander II in 1881 Russian political exiles had lived mainly in England and Switzerland. The first Marxist party in Russia, G. V. Plekhanov's Group for the Emancipation of Labor, had its headquarters in Geneva in these years. But in the late 1890's, as more and more Russians were forced into exile either to obtain an education or for participation in the strikes and student riots that marked the turn of the century in Russia, Germany became an important center of émigré politics. Germany offered printing facilities, a common border with Russia across which illegal literature could be smuggled, relative safety from Russian police agents familiar with Swiss haunts, and separation from the "elders" of the Russian revolutionary movement on which the younger activists looked with increasing disdain. From 1900 until 1905 Germany became a key center of Russian socialist and liberal exiles, looking to the German socialist movement for support and to the Russian student emigration for membership.

For decades Russian socialists had admired German social democracy as the largest and best organized European workers' movement. Since the 1880's Plekhanov and Paul Akselrod had been personal friends of Kautsky and Bernstein, contributed articles on Russia to the socialist daily *Vorwärts* and Kautsky's journal *Die neue Zeit,* and received assistance from the SPD in shipping Marxist literature from Geneva into Russia. But many Russians, particularly the younger generation, were increasingly suspicious of the growing trend toward reformism and trade-unionism within the German labor movement. In Russia coexistence with the dominant political system for economic motives was less popular. In fact in Germany the "orthodox" counterattack against Bernstein's first critique of Marx, which had appeared in *Die neue Zeit* in January 1898, was led not by Kautsky but by three émigré Marxists: Plekhanov, Rosa Luxemburg, and Alexander Parvus (Helphand).

In 1898, however, the tiny Union of Russian Social Democrats Abroad in Berlin was highly sympathetic to Bernstein's ideas. Organized as a link between Plekhanov's circle in Geneva and Russian social democrats in St. Petersburg, the Union soon resented the domination of the "elders" and came increasingly under the control of the new émigrés. Between 1898 and 1900 the four leaders of the Union—Wilhelm Bucholtz, S. N. Prokopovich, E. D. Kuskova, and V. V. Grishin (Kopelzon), the Bund representative abroad—succeeded in breaking away from Plekhanov and in turning the Union and its new journal, *Rabochee delo,* into an independent organization not unsympathetic to German reformism. In April 1900 Plekhanov's group in Geneva withdrew from the Union and decided to establish a new organ of Russian Marxism abroad.

In the spring of 1900, members of the Russian Social-Democratic Workers' Party (RSDRP) began to leave Russia for Germany for this purpose. Potresov arrived in March and Lenin followed four months later. In August they met with Plekhanov, Vera Zasulich, and Akselrod in Geneva to discuss plans for setting up the new journal, *Iskra*. The "elders" favored Switzerland as a location for *Iskra*, the "youngsters" Germany. In the end Lenin and Potresov won out. In late August 1900 Lenin arrived in Nuremberg, where a German socialist, Adolf Braun, helped to arrange for the publication of *Iskra* at Leipzig through a Polish typographer. On September 6 Lenin arrived in Munich, where he was shortly joined by Potresov and Zasulich, and later, in March 1901, by Martov. Plekhanov remained in Geneva, Akselrod in Zurich. From the end of 1900 to the spring of 1902, then, Munich became the home of Lenin and Krupskaia, his wife, the center of operations for *Iskra*, and a new colony of Russians abroad.[54]

As an illegal journal *Iskra* was forced to keep one step ahead of the German and Russian police, who were aware of its existence from the start. After four issues had appeared in Leipzig it proved necessary to move printing operations to Munich, then to Stuttgart, and finally in April 1902 to London. In Stuttgart *Iskra* and its theoretical companion *Zaria* were printed by the SPD publisher Dietz, who also printed the first edition of Lenin's *What Is To Be Done?* and helped the *Iskra* circle arrange the channels necessary for moving RSDRP literature into Russia. The Munich circle, which began to call itself the League of Russian Revolutionary Social-Democrats Abroad in October 1901, worked with the Group for Assisting Russian Revolutionary Social Democracy in Berlin in this matter. RSDRP literature was brought into Berlin, stored in the basement of the *Vorwärts* building, and sent off to Russia via East Prussia, Upper Silesia, and Austrian Galicia in the metal waistcoats and false-bottom suitcases of sympathetic Sunday "travelers." Even after *Iskra* had moved out of Germany in 1902, its lines of communication were to remain important for the Bolsheviks down to 1914.[55]

---

[54] Leo Stern, ed., *Die Auswirkungen der ersten russischen Revolution auf Deutschland von 1905–1907* (Berlin, 1956), II, xvii; X. Streb, *Lenin in Deutschland* (Berlin, 1957); F. Donath, *Lenin in Leipzig* (Berlin, 1958).

[55] D. Geyer, *Lenin in der russischen Sozialdemokratie* (Cologne, 1962), p. 206; Boris Nicolaevsky, ed., *A. N. Potresov: Posmertnyi sbornik proizvedenii* (Paris, 1937), pp. 40–43; *Pis'ma P. B. Aksel'roda i Iu. O. Martova* (Berlin, 1925), p. 21, n. 9, p. 60, n. 2; Osip Piatnitsky, *Memoirs of a Bolshevik* (New York, 1933), pp. 51–75.

Political infighting and splitting were characteristic of Russian political exiles before 1905, and the Bolshevik-Menshevik schism after 1903 was but one example of this. In Germany in these years the presence of Bernstein's supporters, Lenin's circle, the Mensheviks, Polish socialists, Bundists, and liberals made it particularly difficult for the SPD to decide which of these groups to support. Dietz helped Peter Struve publish the liberal journal *Osvobozhdenie* in Stuttgart from 1902 to 1904 at the same time as he was assisting Lenin and Plekhanov. Struve had Plekhanov's permission to edit a supplement to *Zaria* with Dietz, but his publication of an article by Sergei Witte, the Russian Finance Minister, quickly ended his relationship with exile Russian Marxists. Instead he formed his own liberal journal abroad with the help of the historian P. N. Miliukov and a number of other Russians in Germany uneasy about the direction in which Russian socialism was moving: Bernstein's admirers Prokopovich and Kuskova, the economist Tugan-Baranovsky, and a young student of philosophy later associated with the Vekhy circle, S. L. Frank. Another Russian liberal active in Germany was G. B. Iollos, the Berlin correspondent of *Russkie vedomosti,* whose own journal *Russische Korrespondenz* provided a running account in German of the Russian government's persecution of Jews and socialists from 1904 until World War I. The liberals never struck deep roots in Germany, however. They had few personal contacts there (except for Georg Simmel and Max Weber) and after 1905 most liberals returned to Russia to pursue careers in parliamentary politics that revealed a new middle-class nationalism hostile to Germany.[56]

Thus the Russian emigration to Germany after 1900 found fertile ground for political activity. But what struck most Germans about the emigration when it was "discovered" during the stormy events of 1904–1905 in Russia was not that it was simply in radical opposition to the Russian government. Rather they were impressed

[56] D. Shakhovskoi, "Soiuz osvobozhdenie," *Zarnitsy: Literaturno-politicheskii sbornik,* II, No. 2 (1909), pp. 82–171; Geyer, *Lenin,* pp. 275–285; Max Weber, "Zur Lage der bürgerlichen Demokratie in Russland," *Archiv für Sozialwissenschaft und Sozialpolitik,* XXII, (1906), 234–353. On Iollos see A. K., "Inostrannaia pressa v Berline," *Golos Rossii,* May 5, 1920, pp. 2–3; *Byloe,* 1912, No. 14, pp. 5–14.

by the association between radicalism and the Jewish student emigration, and between Pan-German sentiment and the Baltic German emigration. The last two decades of the nineteenth century were years of great hardship for Russian Jewry. The assassination of the tsar in 1881 was followed by the first pogroms and by new restrictive legislation: with only a few exceptions, Jews were limited to the towns of the Pale of Settlement; by the July 1887 circular of the Ministry of Education, Jews could not exceed 10 per cent of the student body at schools within the Pale, 5 per cent outside it, and only 3 per cent in Moscow and St. Petersburg; no business could be conducted on Sundays or on Orthodox holidays; in 1891, 20,000 Jews were expelled from Moscow. As a result hundreds of thousands of Russian Jews, denied even those civil liberties available to other Russian citizens, began to leave Russia for Europe, the United States, and Palestine. Many of those who stayed behind, as well as many who left Russia, moved easily into the ranks of the radical opposition movement.[57]

Germany was an important place of refuge for Russian Jews. In the 1880's there began a virtual stampede to German universities and technical high schools, where a curriculum of medicine, engineering, science, and law provided both career opportunities and the possibility of work in the public service. Driven out of Russia for political reasons they found German culture familiar and accessible. "They knew Germany," recalled Chaim Weizmann, "they spoke German, and they were vastly impressed by German achievement, German discipline and German power." [58] The majority setttled in the cities of Prussia and Saxony where they found jobs as factory workers, artisans, and craftsmen. Jewish students also were most in evidence in these two provinces. They soon formed their own clubs, circles, and reading rooms, Zionist and socialist alike.

The great wave of Jewish emigration from Russia began in connection with the political reaction that followed the death of

[57] Leonard Schapiro, "The Role of the Jews in the Russian Revolutionary Movement," *Slavonic and East European Review*, 40 (1961), 148–168; Lev Deich, *Rol' evreev v russkoi revoliutsionnoi dvizhenii* (Berlin, 1923).
[58] Chaim Weizmann, *Trial and Error* (Philadelphia, 1949), p. 165.

Alexander II. In the spring of 1882 thousands massed along the western border seeking passage to Hamburg for transit to the United States, Australia, or South America. With the aid of the Alliance Israélite Universelle in Paris and the German Central Committee for Russian Jewish Refugees, hundreds of thousands of Jews passed through Germany in the 1880's. The Hamburg-American Line, which carried about 5,000 Russians annually in the 1870's, carried 30,000 in 1886 and 77,000 in 1891. The Russian Jews visible to Germans in these years were a pathetic mass of hungry and tired refugees, plodding wearily with their few belongings from one soup kitchen or compulsory delousing bath to another. The identification of the Jews with various diseases, so popular in the wake of World War I, originated in these years. The citizens of Hamburg were certain that they were responsible for the cholera epidemic that hit the city in the summer of 1892.[59]

By the 1890's there was a sizable Russian Jewish colony in Berlin made up mainly of students. When Weizmann arrived there in 1895, he found not only an organized Russian Student Union but also an active Zionist movement around Achad Ha-am and the Russian Jewish Scientific Union. Small groups of Russian Jewish students were also beginning to appear in other German university towns, particularly at the Bergakademie in Freiburg and the Technical High Schools of Darmstadt and Karlsruhe. Most were pleased to find that anti-Semitism was much less apparent in Germany in the 1890's than in Russia. Their sense of isolation was derived more often from German Jews, who looked upon them as a less civilized, if somewhat exotic, branch of their people. Only after 1900 did the immigration of the Jews begin to play a role in German public opinion and politics.[60]

The number of Russian Jews in Germany after 1900 was often overestimated. The total from Russia, Poland, Galicia, the Buko-

---

[59] Z. Szajkowski, "The European Attitude to East European Jewish Immigration (1881–1893)," *Publications of the American-Jewish Historical Society*, XLI, No. 2 (December 1951), pp. 127–160; H. Weichmann, *Die Auswanderung aus Österreich und Russland über die Deutschen Hafen* (Berlin, 1913); H. Frederic, *The New Exodus: A Study of Israel in Russia* (London, 1892).

[60] Weizmann, *Trial and Error*, pp. 38–40.

vina, Hungary, and Rumania—the so-called *Ostjuden*—did increase from 41,000 in 1900 to more than 70,000 by 1910, and those coming from the Russian Empire from 13,000 to 21,000 in the same period. But the number of Russian Jews actually decreased relative to the number of non-Jewish Russians in Germany during this time span. Moreover, some 70,000 German Jews left their homeland between 1900 and 1910, balancing the influx of *Ostjuden*; by 1910 only 79,000 out of 615,000 Jews in Germany (13 per cent) were foreigners.[61] The claim by some Germans that a tide of Eastern Jews was sweeping into Germany before the war was considerably exaggerated.

What produced such exaggeration was the involvement of the Jewish student emigration in both German and Russian social democracy. Although nearly half the number of Russians studying at some German universities and high schools in these years were Jews, the total number of Jewish students from Russia who lived in Germany at any given time before 1914 was never much more than one thousand. Their ability to move easily into both SPD and RSDRP circles made them not only useful go-betweens for Russian and German socialists but gave them prominence in the German mind despite their relatively small number.

Wilhelm Adolfovich Bucholtz was probably the most important example of a Russian émigré involved in both socialist movements before the war. Rosa Luxemburg and Parvus were better known, but Bucholtz was a more significant link between the SPD and Russian émigré circles. It was not clear whether Bucholtz, born in 1867 in Orenburg of German parentage, was a "Russian" or a "German." Formally a Prussian citizen, he was educated in Russian schools, and for his part in the Kazan student riots of 1887 was exiled to Samara, where he first met Lenin. In 1891 the Russian government extradited Bucholtz; he came to Berlin for the first time. When Lenin arrived there in the summer of 1895 he was surprised to find that Bucholtz was already a figure of some importance in German socialist circles, a correspondent for *Vorwärts* on Russian affairs, and a friend of Kautsky and Wilhelm

[61] S. Adler-Rudel, *Ostjuden in Deutschland, 1880–1940* (Tübingen, 1959), pp. 2, 18, 22, 29, 163.

Liebknecht. In 1900 he was important in the organization of *Iskra* and *Zaria* because of his connections with the SPD and his Prussian citizenship. In arranging with Dietz and the SPD for the printing of Russian literature and the subsidizing of the financially desperate RSDRP he could avoid the police surveillance which would have followed any Russian engaged in the same activity. After the 1903 split within the RSDRP Bucholtz remained an important liaison between the SPD and the Berlin Mensheviks, with whom he met from time to time and whose literature he helped to smuggle into Russia. After 1910 he joined another émigré from Riga, Alexander Stein, in editing the Menshevik *Russisches Bulletin*, a journal carrying news of the Russian labor movement to the Berlin colony and its German friends.

Parvus was a more familiar figure in German socialist affairs before the war. An émigré from Odessa who came to Germany in 1891, he began his career as a radical critic of Bernstein in the 1890's and ended it as a chauvinist and war profiteer after 1914.[62] As a *Vorwärts* contributor in the 1890's, he was among the first to bring the existence of a labor movement in Russia to the attention of German socialists. In the pages of the two SPD dailies which he edited in Saxony before 1905, the *Leipziger Volkszeitung* and the *Sächsische Arbeiterzeitung* in Dresden, he and his two Polish exile friends, Rosa Luxemburg and Julian Marchlewski, provided a running commentary on events in Russia and a critique of reformist tendencies within the German labor movement. Bernstein's followers were not unaware of a certain "Eastern" element among his detractors, and after 1898 Parvus for a time found Russian exile circles more receptive to him than his former German friends. For Lenin and Krupskaia he was almost the only tie to the world beyond the Russian colony. Parvus received all incoming mail for *Iskra*. It was in Parvus' Schwabing apartment that Lenin first met Rosa Luxemburg, that Trotsky stayed when in Munich, and that eight numbers of *Iskra* were printed on a hectograph machine borrowed from SPD friends in Berlin. Parvus and March-

---

[62] Z. A. B. Zeman and W. B. Scharlau, *The Merchant of Revolution: The Life of Alexander Israel Helphand(Parvus), 1867–1924* (London, 1965); K. Haenisch, *Parvus* (Berlin, 1925).

lewski also ran a publishing house in Munich for a time, designed
to make the works of Russian authors, among them Gorky, available to German readers. Like other Russian Jews in Germany,
Parvus became an "intermediary between two worlds," a man
who could "write for the Russian press on the German socialist
movement and took pleasure in introducing the young generation
of the Russian socialists to his German comrades." Among his
German socialist friends in Dresden, Parvus was known as "the
Russian," whereas Krupskaia remembered him as an "extreme
left-winger . . . interested in Russian affairs." [63] To some Parvus
was a Russian, to others a German. The fact that he was not quite
either enabled him to appear to be both.

The best known of the Russian émigrés involved in German
socialism, of course, was Rosa Luxemburg. Like many educated
Jews, she found Germany familiar (her father had traveled there
frequently on business) and arrived there in 1898 as a fervent
admirer of German civilization. In Switzerland and then Germany
she immersed herself easily in German socialist life, writing essays
for *Die neue Zeit* and succeeding Parvus as editor of the *Sächsische Arbeiterzeitung* after the latter's expulsion from Dresden.
By 1901, however, there were complaints within the SPD about
the "unpleasant tone in the party press produced by the male
and female immigration from the East," as one critic put it. Rosa's
radicalism, her enthusiasm for the revolution of 1905, and her
doctrine of the mass strike were all part of her gradual shift
away from German socialism to what she considered the "real
hope of cultural as well as political salvation" in the more extreme
Russian and Polish movements. Like Parvus, she remained a victim of what her recent biographer has called "the acute Russian-
German dichotomy" in her life. Considered an "Easterner" within
the SPD, she remained for Lenin neither a Pole nor a Russian
socialist but one of "the German comrades." Thus her initial
ability to mediate between two cultures ultimately became a
liability resulting in her rejection by both.[64]

[63] N. Krupskaia, *Memories of Lenin* (New York, 1930), I, 67.
[64] J. P. Nettl, *Rosa Luxemburg* (London and New York, 1966), I, 31, 52,
163, 187; II, 512.

The Russian Germans, like the Jews, were also victims of Russification at the end of the century. Many South Russian colonists, Moscow and St. Petersburg Germans, and Balts emigrated to Germany before the war. The poorer colonists fled for various reasons, among them land hunger, the pressures of Russification in the schools and churches, and a June 4, 1871, law requiring military service. Encouraged in Germany by the Evangelical church and the Royal Colonization Commission for Posen and West Prussia, some 50,000 Volhynian Germans migrated into Germany between 1900 and 1914, mainly to Prussia, Posen, Silesia, Brandenburg, Schleswig-Holstein, and Hanover. Many more passed through on their way to Canada and the United States. In Germany they received a warm reception. The government established a Welfare Society for German Returnees in Berlin in 1909 to look after their economic and legal needs, and a number of publicists worked enthusiastically to draw the attention of German public opinion to the plight of *Deutschtum* abroad.[65]

Although fewer of them emigrated, the Moscow and St. Petersburg Germans also caught the attention of Germany at this time. German diplomats in Russia enjoyed friendly relations with these groups, and the embassy in St. Petersburg followed developments in the pages of the major Russian-German newspaper there, the *St. Petersburger Zeitung*. One St. Petersburg German, the writer Henry von Heiseler, still found it easy to move back and forth between the two cultures. A resident of Munich from 1898 to 1914, he continued to visit Russia, to inform his literary friends around Stefan George of Russian literary developments, and to translate the works of Russian authors into German. Heiseler typified the cosmopolitanism of the Moscow and St. Petersburg Germans in his ability to become what his biographer terms "a

[65] K. Stumpp, "Die Auswanderung der deutschen Kolonisten aus Russland (1873–1914)," in *Der Wanderweg der Russlanddeutschen* (Stuttgart and Berlin, 1939), pp. 162–171; F. Rink, "Deutsche Rückwanderung aus Wolhynien in früheren Jahren," *Deutsche Post aus dem Osten*, XI, No. 12 (December 1939), p. 5; A. Mergenthaler, "Russlanddeutsche Rückwanderer in den Jahren 1900 bis 1918," *ibid.*, pp. 7–8; T. Bassler, *Das Deutschtum in Russland* (Munich, 1911); A. Faure, *Das Deutschtum in Süd-Russland und an der Wolga* (Munich, 1907).

mediator between Germany and Russia, between East and West." [66]

Unfortunately, many Baltic Germans who emigrated to Germany did not share his ecumenical attitude. Like the Russian Jews, the Baltic Germans who emigrated to Germany in the years before 1914 were politically disaffected because of persecution by the Russian government and capable of assimilation because of cultural and linguistic ties to Germany. But within the social fabric of the Russian Empire they were quite distinct, a conservative landholding aristocracy in the northwest which proudly traced their ancestry to the Teutonic Knights and the Livonian Order, and their loyalty to the Russian crown to the early eighteenth century. Since Peter the Great they had been an important servitor class within the government. The list of Benckendorffs, Lievens, Korffs, Stackelbergs, Kleinmichels, and Lamsdorffs who had served the Russian Empire as civil servants, diplomats, army officers, and professors was a long one. Most remained loyal to the crown until 1917. But toward the end of the nineteenth century there were growing signs of discontent among the Baltic nobility, and some of the more discontented found their way to Germany.[67]

The Great Reforms of Alexander II, the Russification policies of Alexander III, and the beginnings of industrialization, all wrought great changes in the Baltic. A new Russian professional class of educated men and women reduced the dependence of the state on the services of the Baltic Germans. Russification affected not only the native Latvian and Estonian population of the region but the German upper class as well. Industrial change brought a restless non-German labor force into the towns and encouraged both nationalist and socialist sentiments among the local peasantry and intelligentsia. The Russian government not only did not support the Baltic Germans in coping with these changes, but provoked them by its policies. Baltic Germans had traditionally looked upon the Russia they inhabited with the mixed

[66] Gronicka, *Henry von Heiseler*, p. 190.

[67] On the Baltic Germans see especially H. Rothfels, "The Baltic Provinces: Some Historic Aspects and Perspectives," *Journal of Central European Affairs*, IV (1944), 117–146; C. Lundin, "The Road from Tsar to Kaiser: Changing Loyalties of the Baltic Germans, 1905–1914," *ibid.*, X (1950). 223–255.

disdain and fascination characteristic of the colonial and paternalistic master. But after 1900, and particularly after the revolution of 1905, the mood among the German upper class in the Baltic provinces was one of "better dead than Slav." [68]

Baltic Germans had traditionally come to Germany for study or travel. Here they found that while they were considered "Germans" in Russia, they passed for "Russians" in Germany. Their familiarity with both cultures gave them peculiar expertise in Germany concerning Russia. By the 1880's their message was becoming more hostile than friendly. Victor Hehn, in his widely read *De Moribus Ruthenorum: Zur Charakteristik der russischen Volkseele* (Stuttgart, 1892), portrayed Russia as an oriental despotism in which the cleanliness, prosperity, and organization of the German population in the Baltic and South Russia contrasted with the surrounding dirty, unorganized, and repulsive Slavic natives. Julius Eckardt, now the editor of the liberal *Die Grenzboten* and informant on Russian affairs for the Foreign Office, pointed out the dangers facing the Baltic Germans in Russia and warned of the perils of "Pan-Slavism." In Bismarck's Germany there was little interest in *Auslandsdeutschtum,* but after 1900 Baltic Germans found increasing sympathy in Germany, and their role in German society became an impressive one, especially where Russia was concerned. Both the Russian ambassador in Berlin and the German military attaché in St. Petersburg were Balts. Paul Rohrbach, the Imperial Commissar for Settlement in German Southwest Africa, who urged German expansion in the Near East in his *Die Bagdadbahn* (1902), flavored his many articles in *Preussische Jahrbücher* and other journals with an anti-Russian condiment. The theologian Adolf von Harnack became the confidant of William II on religious matters and an active supporter of nationalist campaigns to help the Balts. The "Russian expert" of the German General Staff was Hugo von Freytag-Loringhoven, later Chief of Staff. Among the active supporters of the Pan-German League were Alfred Geiser, its business manager, and Friedrich Lezius, a professor of theology. Balts in the aca-

[68] E. Stackelberg-Sutlem, *Ein Leben in baltischen Kampf* (Munich, 1927), p. 105.

demic world included Reinhold Seeberg, professor of theology at the University of Berlin; Johannes Haller, who taught medieval history at Marburg and Tübingen; and the cultural historian George Dehio, also at Tübingen. After 1914 many of these men became advisers to the German High Command in the East on the administration of the occupied Baltic provinces. But even before the war their influence on German policy and opinion concerning Russia was such that the historian Friedrich Meinecke later uttered a warning against ever again accepting "Balto-centric" views of Russia which considered her inferior and underestimated her "vitality." [69]

The most influential Baltic German of the Russophobic variety in prewar Germany was Professor Theodor Schiemann. Schiemann was primarily a historian specializing in Russia, and his seminar on East Europe at the University of Berlin was the first of its kind in Germany. But in the 1890's he also interpreted Russian events for the conservative reading public through his weekly foreign affairs column in the *Kreuzzeitung,* became an adviser on Russia to Holstein at the Wilhelmstrasse, and was a member of the court camarilla of William II. His personal influence on William was considerable. During the 1914–1918 war he saw many of his ideas become reality for a time: the restoration of German power in the Baltic provinces; the colonizing of Poland, Galicia, and the Ukraine with Germans; the reduction of Russia to her pre-Petrine boundaries. The so-called Schiemann school within the German General Staff and the Foreign Ministry became synonymous with German aggrandizement in the East; in 1917 it was probably Schiemann who persuaded William to annex formally Latvia and Estonia. Until his death in January 1921 Schiemann remained an outspoken proponent of a German policy and a Russian system of government which would guarantee the rights of the German upper classes in the Baltic "one of those

[69] F. Epstein, "Friedrich Meinecke in seinem Verhältnis zum Europäischen Osten," *Jahrbuch für die Geschichte Mittel- und Ostdeutschlands* (Tübingen, 1954), pp. 134–135; A. Zahn-Harnack, *Adolf von Harnack* (Berlin, 1936), pp. 339–355, 383; H. C. Meyer, *Mitteleuropa in German Thought and Action, 1815–1945* (The Hague, 1955), pp. 95–102; F. Fischer, *Griff nach der Weltmacht* (Düsseldorf, 1961), pp. 346–352.

Balts," as Chancellor Bülow put it, "who see the world and every event from the narrow angle of local patriotism." [70]

Schiemann's views on Russia and the Russians were not unlike those of his close friend Victor Hehn. The Russians, like the Slavs in general, were a primitive and backward people: nomadic, uneducated, uncivilized, barbaric, but also innately religious. Until Peter the Great, Russia resembled an Oriental kingdom, but Peter and the procession of German rulers, bureaucrats, and colonists who succeeded him managed to introduce some order into the country. This "Westernization" of Russia, however, was a superficial process. It created only a *Scheinkultur*, a layer of European influence beneath which lay traditional weakness and disorder. In particular, Russian military power was vastly overrated in Europe. Since the Polish uprising of 1863 deep anti-Western and anti-German forces had emerged in Russia, and it was this threat rather than that of Russia's armies which was most dangerous for Germany. The old order was collapsing in Russia under the pressure of anti-state elements: writers, intellectuals, socialists, nihilists, Jews. The delicate balance between tsar and empire, Russians and non-Russians, was tipping toward disaster for the Baltic Germans. The only solution was the creation in Russia of a government of law (*Rechtstaat*) which could guarantee the rights of the cultured, German element in Russian society.[71]

Schiemann's hostility toward the Russian government and his underestimation of Russian military power were a welcome message for some German policy makers. Most Balts of any prominence in Germany agreed with his views to some extent; those who did were more apt to achieve prominence than those who did not. But not all Balts shared his colonial mentality. For many, it was Russia's very primitiveness that attracted them: her untouched vastness, her religiosity, her soul—all those elements, in short, which European civilization could neither understand nor over-

---

[70] Bernhard von Bülow, *The Memoirs of Prince Bülow* (Boston, 1931), II, 594; on Schiemann see K. Meyer, *Theodor Schiemann als politischer Publizist* (Frankfort on the Main, 1956).

[71] For Schiemann's views on Russia see Meyer, *Schiemann*, pp. 88–115, and the collection of Schiemann's *Kreuzzeitung* articles entitled *Deutschland und die grosse Politik* (Berlin, 1910–1912).

whelm. But all too often, cultural attraction was mixed with political hostility.

Those Russian Germans who did feel a deep attraction toward Russia were no less successful in disseminating their views abroad before 1914, not among policy makers but among European intellectuals. The remarkable friend of Nietzsche and Freud, Lou Andreas-Salomé, a St. Petersburg German, introduced the poet Rainer Maria Rilke to the magic of Russia on two long trips in 1899 and 1900. With her help Rilke was able to see Russia for himself, to visit Tolstoi, to see the churches of Kiev and the peasants along the Volga and to immerse himself in the exotic, sacred, dark, and untouched land which seemed to recall his own childhood.[72] Moeller van den Bruck had been introduced to Merezhkovsky in Paris in 1902 by two Baltic German sisters, Lucie and Less Kaerrick. Lucie later became Moeller's second wife, while Less translated the famous Piper Verlag edition of Dostoevsky's works. Rudolf Steiner also married a Balt, Marie Sievers, who introduced the writings of Vladimir Soloviev into Steiner's circle and later translated a number of his works into German.[73]

The best known of the Russophile Balts, although his popularity came in the wake of the war, was the philosopher and mystic Hermann Keyserling. After two years at the University of Dorpat, Keyserling came to Heidelberg in 1900 to study natural science. But like many of his generation he found that science raised more questions than it could answer. He turned to more philosophic writings then in vogue: Houston Stewart Chamberlain's *Foundations of the Nineteenth Century*, the works of the Austrian mystic Rudolf Kassner, the writings of Kant and Schopenhauer. From science he passed to mysticism. After a period of "frenzied reading in the British Museum," Keyserling learned that the revolution of 1905 in Russia had destroyed his family estate at Rayküll.

[72] "Letters of Rainer Maria Rilke to Helene * * *," *Oxford Slavonic Papers,* IX (1960), 129–164; I. S. Mackey, *Lou Salomé: Inspiratrice et Interprète de Nietzsche, Rilke et Freud* (Paris, 1956); R. Binion, *Frau Lou: Nietzsche's Wayward Disciple* (Princeton, 1968).

[73] H. Weisberger, *Aus dem Leben von Marie Steiner-von Sievers* (Dornach, 1956).

From 1906 to 1908 he lived in Berlin, claiming to have visions and studying yoga. In 1908 he returned again to the Baltic, where he lived as a gentleman farmer for the next three years.

In 1911 Keyserling decided to escape the confines of Europe by taking a long trip to the Far East. Upon his return he produced an enormous travel diary (*Reisetagbuch*) which has been compared with Oswald Spengler's *Decline of the West* and which ran through seven German editions between 1918 and 1923. "Europe has nothing more to give me," Keyserling announced in his book, in which he portrayed the "partially developed peoples" of the world as superior to Europe precisely because of their lack of "civilization." "Yes, Russia," he wrote, "the Russia of the simple peasant, is today probably the only province of Christendom which is near to God." He rhapsodized about the "delicate soul of the Slav" and "the Russian peasant, that primitive man, who seems absolutely incapable of any organization, in whom no form of objectivity, not even that of the concept of duty, meets with understanding, who obeys exclusively his uncontrolled subjectivity." Russia, in short, was a part of the non-European world, a world superior to Europe because it had not yet been Europeanized.[74]

The careers of Schiemann and Keyserling reflected two extremes in the Baltic German mind: hostility toward and fascination with Russia. Sometimes they coexisted. Those most critical of Russia also found it somewhat exotic, and those familiar with Russian culture often harbored fears of the forces of Russian political life. It was indicative of Baltic Germans now leaving Russia and of the mood of prewar Germany that Schiemann's colonial attitude found a strong resonance, and Keyserling's musings on the Russian soul went largely unheard. Most Balts in Germany before 1914 would have agreed with Schiemann's ominous warning in 1916: "Russia is a danger that will remain and with which future generations will have to deal, unless we release them from this danger"[75] In 1905 they spelled out this danger in Germany.

[74] H. Keyserling, *The Travel Diary of a Philosopher* (New York, 1925), I, 16, 227; II, 70, 337.
[75] Meyer, *Schiemann*, p. 204.

The revolution of 1905 made most Germans aware for the first time of the size and composition of the Russian emigration to Germany. German attitudes toward the emigration, however, were determined not only by its "radical" nature and its association with events inside Russia, but by considerations of foreign policy as well.

From the outbreak of the Russo-Japanese War early in 1904 until the Algeciras conference at the beginning of 1906, Germany made a last attempt to revive Bismarck's policy of alignment with Russia. Russian involvement in the Far East and the outbreak of revolution in the winter of 1904–1905 made it clear that Russia could pose no serious threat to Germany in Europe in the event of war there. How Germany should take advantage of this situation was less clear. The danger was that the Anglo-French entente might be broadened to include Russia, leading to the "encirclement" of Germany by hostile powers. Two lines of policy suggested themselves to German leaders: William II favored the creation of a "continental alliance" of France, Germany, and Russia directed against England; Bülow and Holstein favored a more aggressive policy directed against France over the issue of rights in Morocco, perhaps with the idea of provoking a "preventive war" against France in the absence of effective Russian support. Both policies assumed that the Russian government was crumbling, an assumption that Russians in Germany were eager to promote.

In the end both policies were pursued in haphazard fashion and neither produced the desired results. By 1907 the encirclement of Germany was complete. The Russo-German Treaty of Björko, signed on board the kaiser's yacht in the summer of 1905, proved abortive. But important conclusions were drawn concerning Russia by German policy makers in 1905. Both the Wilhelmstrasse and the General Staff assumed that Russia, in the wake of a Japanese victory and revolution at home, could not be considered a serious threat in a future war and that the bulk of the German army could be directed against France. After 1905 Germany feared not Russian power but Russian weakness, the danger that the flames of revolution might not only consume the government of Nicholas

II but spread to Germany itself. Some Russians in Germany gave warning of this danger; others exemplified it.

Until 1905 the German government was more aware of the existence of Russians in Germany than was German public opinion. Since the 1880's suspicious Russians had been kept under surveillance and a treaty between Russia, Prussia, and Bavaria signed in 1885 provided for the extradition of "undesirable aliens." After 1900 the Okhrana agents in Germany and the Berlin police kept a close watch on the growing number of émigré student clubs and socialist circles. But few Russians were extradited, since there were advantages for the Russian government in having its political opponents out of the country. "We have to put up with an officially recognized colony of anarchists in Berlin for the sake of the Russians," William complained in 1903, "in order to lighten for the 'Little Father's' police agents the task of watching them"; he whimsically suggested to Bülow a "mass execution of these rascals."[76] On occasion Russian or Polish students were arrested, as in December 1901 when a group of them had broken up a lecture by Schiemann at the University of Berlin because of its anti-Slav tone. But it was only in the winter of 1903–1904, when more arrests occurred, that the issue of Russians in Germany became a matter of public concern.

"Is the Imperial Chancellor aware," an SPD Reichstag delegate asked Bülow in January 1904, "that the Russian government maintains police agents on German territory to keep Russian and German citizens under surveillance?" Bülow admitted as much, but added that since 1900 there had been only three cases of extradition of known "anarchists" from Prussia to Russia.[77] Expulsion, not extradition, was the more common penalty. Between 1902 and 1909 only seven Russians were actually turned over to the Russian police, although many were expelled. Such was the case with fourteen "undesirable aliens" in the spring of 1904, after the police had arrested and interrogated over one hundred

[76] William II to Bülow, December 27, 1903 (*Letters of Prince Bülow*, trans. Frederic Whyte [London, 1930], p. 24).

[77] *Stenographische Berichte über die Verhandlungen des Reichstags*, February 4, 1904, pp. 1363–1407; hereafter *Verhandlungen*.

Russian students. Others were expelled that summer after the trial of nine German socialists in Königsberg revealed the extent of SPD cooperation in the smuggling of illegal Russian literature out of Germany. By the time news of the 1905 revolution reached Berlin the activity of Russian radicals was already a hotly debated issue.

On January 23, 1905, the first reports of Bloody Sunday and the outbreak of revolution in Russia reached Berlin. In the following months the SPD and the German labor unions responded to the fresh wind from the East that revitalized the forces of radicalism against those of reformism within the movement. Over 500,000 German workers were involved in work stoppages, strikes, and lockouts in 1905—more than the total for the previous five years. For all of 1905 and into 1906 German socialists followed the news from Russia with great interest through a daily column in *Vorwärts*. The SPD collected some 350,000 marks to aid Russian revolutionaries inside Russia and abroad.[78] The fact that the ideological justification of the new radicalism, Rosa Luxemburg's *Mass Strike, Party and Trade Unions*, had been written by an "Easterner" was not lost on German opinion. The very enthusiasm of German socialists for the revolution and the discovery of Russian revolutionaries within the SPD heightened the fears of similar violence in Germany. None were more eager to promote this fear of revolution and to draw attention to its evil effects than the Baltic Germans.

At first the Balts found little support in Germany for their cause. In early 1904 the editors of the Pan-German League's journal, *Alldeutsche Blätter,* refused to believe warnings that the Baltic Germans were in any danger, but by the spring of 1905 conservative circles showed a growing awareness of their plight. When one writer argued that German culture was disappearing in the Baltic and that the area was "no province of Germanism," he was sharply attacked by Alfred Geiser. By the autumn of 1905 the League was busy raising funds to help the Baltic Germans recover their land and property and to emigrate to Germany if they so desired.

[78] C. Schorske, *German Social Democracy, 1905–1917* (Cambridge, Mass., 1955), p. 31; L. Stern, *Auswirkungen*, II, lix.

Throughout 1905 Schiemann and other Balts pointed out the dangers which revolution held for their countrymen in an area of the world where, as Georg Cleinow, a St. Petersburg German, put it, "the more powerful West European culture has won out over the semi-Asiatic." [79]

The winter of 1905–1906 brought a wave of looting, murder, and general destruction in the Baltic provinces. Baltic Germans in Germany lost no time in lobbying to help their homeland in its hour of need. In December 1905 members of the Pan-German League traveled to various cities making speeches on behalf of the Balts. At the annual meeting of the League in Leipzig on December 16–17 a resolution demanded that the German government send ships to Riga, Reval, and Libau to protect Germans in those cities and to bring back to Germany those who wished to emigrate. The League also recommended that a note be sent to the Russian government asking that law and order be preserved in the region. Two weeks later, there went out a formal call for monetary donations to help the Balts.[80]

The Balts cultivated sympathies far beyond the confines of the League, primarily in conservative circles, in the press, and within the government establishment. Schiemann urged that Baltic German refugees in the eastern provinces be moved into Prussian Poland as a bulwark of Germanism. The *Preussische Jahrbücher* wrote that the "oldest and greatest colony of Germanism" was in danger of being overwhelmed by the forces of revolution. In the Reichstag, the conservative deputy Libermann von Sonnenberg urged the government to help "the most valuable element in the whole Russian Empire," Baltic Germans both in Russia and in Germany, and feared that a "less desirable immigration from Russia" of Jews might be expected. In socialist circles, of course, the Balts were the undesirable elements in Russia. For the SPD leader August Bebel they were simply eastern Junkers, an oppressive landowning

---

[79] *Die Grenzboten*, 1905, No. 3, p. 451; *Alldeutsche Blätter*, January 23, 1904, March 11, June 17, September 30, 1905.

[80] *Alldeutsche Blätter*, December 30, 1905. Schiemann, Geiser, and Harnack were among the Balts most active in the League campaign.

class in the Baltic which for centuries had kept the native Latvian population under its thumb.[81]

The Baltic Germans had some effect on German policy, as well as on public opinion. In late December 1905 German transport ships arrived in Riga to evacuate Balts who desired to come to Germany and the cruiser *Lübeck* and some torpedo boats were held at Memel in case of further violence in the provinces. There was no direct intervention, but there was strong support for the Balts not only in their homeland but also in Germany. The Prussian *Staatsministerium* observed that the revolution had increased the number of Russian refugees coming to Germany and that most were either Jews or "Russian citizens of German origin." Bülow cared little about the Jews ("the revolution in Russia is their work") but encouraged the admission of Balts. Schiemann urged raising the fees at German universities and high schools to keep out the "less gifted Slavic and Jewish students," admitting only Orthodox Russian and Baltic German students.[82] He also used his friendship with William II to put pressure on the Russian government to protect the Balts. In a letter of January 29, 1906, to Nicholas, William wrote that Berlin was "full of noble families who have fled from the Baltic provinces," people who "find themselves in a particularly sorry state, for they have lost everything: their castles have been burned, their property destroyed and their forests plundered."[83] In 1906 the German government could do little more to help the Balts. But an irredentist cause had been established, and it would become an important propaganda point in 1914. "I will never consent to leave the Baltic provinces in the lurch," William is said to have told Schiemann in July 1906; "I shall go to their assistance, and they must be incorporated in the German Empire. I shall not raise a finger to do this as long as the present

[81] *Preussische Jahrbücher*, January 1906, pp. 172–178; *Deutsche Monatschrift für das gesamte Leben der Gegenwart*, January 1906, pp. 544–545; *Verhandlungen*, December 12, 1903, p. 12, and February 14, 1906, pp. 1213, 1272, 1291.

[82] R. Wittram, *Drei Generationen: Deutschland-Livland-Russland, 1830–1914* (Göttingen, 1939), pp. 314–336; Stern, *Auswirkungen*, I, 139, 152.

[83] W. Goetz, *Briefe Wilhelms II an den Zaren, 1894–1914* (Berlin, 1920), p. 222.

Russian government maintains itself, but I could never leave the Balts to their fate." [84]

Despite William's blustering in defense of the Balts, the Wilhelmstrasse remained cautious. The consulate in Riga was well aware of the sufferings of the Germans at the hands of the radicals in 1905, and the Foreign Office itself helped arrange emigration to Germany and loans to landowners whose estates faced bankruptcy as a result of the turmoil of these years. But most diplomats were wary of Baltic German lobbying for more extensive German intervention in Baltic affairs. In the autumn of 1906 the Riga consulate warned Berlin against the "loud and noisy agitation" of Balts in Germany, particularly within the Pan-German League and its *Alldeutsche Blätter*, "which has a number of Balts on its editorial staff." The German government, it noted, should be extremely careful of falling victim to "the hundreds of Baltic émigrés and other officious emissaries of *Baltentum*" who were capable of "destroying friendly, neighborly relations between Germany and Russia." For the moment, the fears of the diplomats were unfounded. Only with the outbreak of all-out war would the dreams of a German annexation of the Baltic be temporarily fulfilled.[85]

German attitudes toward Russian Jews in Germany during 1905–1906 were quite different. William pointed out to Nicholas, as if he did not already know, that Jews like Trotsky, Parvus, and Luxemburg were the "leaders of the revolt" in Russia. This was a strong impression in Germany too. Of the 360 Russian students at the University of Berlin in 1905, 261 were Jewish. Were not many of them being trained for revolution? Early in 1904 the Pan-German League had already suggested limiting the number of Jews entering Germany from Russia. "Why doesn't Rosa Luxemburg go back to Russia?" wrote Friedrich Naumann in *Die Hilfe* in October 1905. Was this "Jewish foreigner" not already a dominant influence within German social democracy? echoed the *Kon-*

---

[84] Bülow, *Memoirs*, II, p. 266.

[85] Riga to Reichskanzler, September 3, 1906 (AGFM, Auswärtiges Amt Akten UC I/237, 218–227); Riga to Reichskanzler, March 21, 1907 (*ibid.*, 262). German reports on the Baltic situation in general from 1881 to 1914 are contained in AGFM, UC I/236, frames 491–821, and UC I/237, frames 1–268.

servative Korrespondenz. For many Germans "Russian," "radical," and "eastern Jew" became linked together after 1905 as a single type of undesirable.[86]

The fear of an influx of revolutionary Jewish students from the East never quite disappeared from the German mind after 1905. It did not become pathological until after the war, but until 1914 it remained a powerful part of general Russophobia. On August 31, 1906, Bülow wrote to William that the expulsion of all "Russian immigrants, especially Jews," was desirable. The aim of Russian socialists, wrote the *Kreuzzeitung,* was nothing less than an "organized Jewish proletariat" in Russia and Germany. "The political police," Sonnenberg said in the autumn of 1907, "must pay close attention to the machinations of the Russian-Jewish students who study revolutionary propaganda at our universities and dynamite at our technical high schools, who set up seminars for the science of revolution and laboratories for dynamite bombs in our midst." One Reichstag delegate even recommended "blocking the border against any Russians who do not come here with evidence of certain positive attitudes toward us." In the spring of 1908 one conservative deputy still felt there was a "rising danger of an immigration from the East" of Russian Jews. When an SPD deputy protested against the expulsion of a Russian Jew from Germany in the spring of 1911, his reference to him as a "Russian" provoked only anti-Semitic remarks on the right.

But after 1907 the issue of Russians in Germany never assumed the proportions it had reached during the revolutionary events of 1905. Although the number of Russians in Germany increased until it reached a peak in 1912–1913, their political activity was less noticeable. There were two reasons for this. First, with the institution of the Duma and the legalization of political parties greater activity became possible within Russia itself. Many Russians had returned from exile at the beginning of 1905 and were able to remain. Second, the German police and Russian agents in Germany tightened their watch on all suspicious activity. In the spring of 1907 they

[86] L. Stern, ed., *Die russische Revolution von 1905–1907 im Spiegel der deutschen Presse* (Berlin, 1961).

raided a "reading room" in the Berlin suburb of Charlottenburg, discovered stores of Bundist and Bolshevik literature, and expelled one student. Several months later Maxim Litvinov and two other Bolsheviks were expelled from Prussia for running an illegal printing press. In Dresden the police expelled five Russians from Saxony because they participated in the Reichstag election campaign for the SPD. In June 1909 twelve Russian socialists went on trial in Dresden and arrests followed in Mannheim, Darmstadt, Heidelberg, and Braunschweig.

Thus émigré political activity died down after 1907. From 1909 to 1912 the Bolshevik journal *Proletarii* was brought to Leipzig from Geneva and Paris, stored in the basement of the SPD daily *Leipziger Volkszeitung* building, and sent to Russia. But the police were now well aware of such activities. It became more difficult for Jewish students to enter a German high school or university and easier for them to be expelled. By 1908 the number of Russian students at the University of Berlin had declined almost to its 1901 level of 250, a drop of 200 since the summer of 1906. In April 1911 the Bavarian government reduced the number of Russian students at the University of Munich from 393 to under 200. Heidelberg, too, limited the number of foreign students to 15 per cent of the total student body and the number from any single country to 7 per cent.[87]

Despite these limits, a sizable colony of Russian students remained in Germany until the outbreak of war in 1914. The German reaction against them, exemplified by the student demonstrations against Russian Jews at Mannheim and Weinheim in the spring of 1913, led to a desire among the students for even closer organization. A Russian student congress was held at Karlsruhe in February 1913, followed by a meeting of a Zionist group at Darmstadt and the appearance of a new Union of Jewish Students from Russia. This in turn only served to heighten the Russophobia already present within the German student community. In May 1914 students at the universities of Bonn and Jena voted to impose their own

[87] Brachmann, *Sozialdemokraten*, pp. 102, 185.

numerus clausus upon Russian-Jewish students. Thus until the war the issue of the *Ostjuden* continued to agitate German opinion and to contribute to its Russophobia.[88]

By 1914 there were also signs of a mellowing of opinion toward Russia in Germany, for example, the formation in Berlin, in October 1913, of the German Society for the Study of Russia by one of Schiemann's students, Otto Hoetzsch. Its purpose was "to further the completely non-political character of Russian studies in Germany." [89] A younger generation of Russian experts was now emerging, knowledgeable and willing to break with the anti-Russian and anti-Slav rhetoric of its Baltic German teachers. Hoetzsch himself, who succeeded Schiemann as the *Kreuzzeitung*'s Russian expert, warned throughout the war against the Baltic notion that Russia was a weak and disorganized society which would collapse under German pressure in a matter of weeks or months. But the polemics of wartime were to reveal that Hoetzsch's view was still that of a minority in Germany, and that German opinion was more responsive to the warnings of the "Russian danger" and the promises of Russian weakness disseminated by the Balts.

In 1914 Germany went to war against a Russia which it feared but did not quite comprehend. The emigration was not the only factor in generating this fear. The old images of the Russian steamroller, of Cossack cavalry and peasant hordes riding out of the East, of a revolution which would unleash Polish discontent, still remained. But the Russian emigration made a major contribution to prewar political Russophobia. Most Germans knew Russia largely from the pages of Russian literature. What Russians in Germany before the war said and what they did made a great impression. They not only filled an information gap concerning Russia; they were themselves examples of Russians.

But both the Russians and the Russia which they portrayed

---

[88] On Russian students in Germany on the eve of the war see the journal *Studencheskii listok: Periodicheskii organ posviashchennyi interesam studenchestva iz Rossii v Germanii*, Nos. 1 (May 20, 1913), 2 (June 28, 1913), and 5–6 (February 14, 1914).

[89] W. Markert, "Die deutsch-russischen Beziehungen am Vorabend der ersten Weltkrieg," in Markert's *Deutsch-russische Beziehungen von Bismarck bis zur Gegenwart,* (Stuttgart, 1964), p. 58.

were more diverse after 1900 than previously. Royalty still recalled the good old ties between Russia and Prussia, intellectuals the joys of German philosophy. But for the new political emigration of socialists and non-Russians, the Russian government was a hostile and despotic force. The Baltic Germans and the Jews were culturally most suited to convey this attitude, and for political reasons eager to do so. For German conservatives and the middle classes the Balts portrayed a Russia dangerous because it was weakened by revolution; for the German left, the Jews described a powerful and brutal autocracy. Each reflected broader sentiments of nationalist and socialist dissent; each was critical of the other: the Jews of the Balts because of their association with the Russian state, the Balts of the Jews because of their involvement in the revolutionary movement. Neither created anti-Russian sentiment in Germany; both reinforced it. The fascination of some German intellectuals for Russian culture notwithstanding, Germany went to war in 1914 in part to defend itself from dangers in the East. Political hostility overcame cultural receptivity.

II

The Time of Troubles:
1914-1921

War and the Emigration

Until 1914 the migration of Russians to Germany had been a relatively peaceful and tranquil process. The summer visits of royalty, the student university semesters, and the revolutionaries' drab years of waiting were nothing like the great social and political upheaval that followed Sarajevo. Even the relatively large emigration of Jews and Germans from Russia in the prewar years gave no warning of the storm to come. Most Russians in Germany before 1914 had been voluntary exiles; unhappy as they might be, they had been able to choose emigration. Now the ranks of Russians in Germany were swollen by masses of involuntary exiles, men and their families whose fate was determined not by choice but by the vagaries of war, revolution, and civil war. The new breed of exile was not a student or a revolutionary but a war prisoner, an army officer, or a landowner. The prewar exiles either left Germany or were put under surveillance; the German government even used some of them for wartime services against Russia. The war and postwar refugees, in contrast, soon became a major political and social problem in Germany.

Most Russians in Germany in the summer of 1914 were as surprised at the outbreak of war as most Europeans. Those who could do so fled immediately to Russia or Switzerland to escape the rash of anti-Russian outbreaks that paralleled attacks on Germans unfortunate enough to be caught in Moscow or St. Petersburg. The Russian embassy and the property of the Russian church owned by the St. Vladimir Brotherhood were looked after by the Spanish embassy in Berlin, which also undertook to represent the interests of Russian war prisoners as they began to arrive. The prisoners, in fact, soon constituted the bulk of the Russians in Germany. Even as late as the time of the Armistice in November 1918 there were still over a million Russian POW's in Germany, despite six months of attempts at repatriation.[1]

As the first prisoners poured into Germany in the spring of 1915 they were indiscriminately placed in a series of camps throughout the country. The German military, however, soon hit upon the idea of separating out the non-Russian nationalities as a potential reservoir of anti-Russian forces who might serve with the German army. To this end the Germans established special barracks for Moslem prisoners at Zossen, for Ukrainians at Rastatt, and for Belorussians and Russian Germans as well. Here they were subjected to German propaganda.[2] A camp newspaper, *Russkii vestnik,* published in Berlin beginning in December 1915 and soon claiming a circulation of over one hundred thousand, carried news of Russia and the war and developed endlessly the theme that Germans were friends, not enemies, of Russia and that life in the prison camps was really not unbearable.[3] Like the Jewish refugees before the war, the Russian prisoners often were introduced to German life with a bath and prolonged delousing. The presence of infection and sickness among the Russian prisoners—a common enough problem for both sides on the Eastern front—kept alive the image of Russia as a land of dirt, insects, and disease. The Russians' habit of keeping the doors and windows of their barracks closed helped to spread

[1] C. Hoffmann, *In the Prison Camps of Germany* (New York, 1920); E. Willis, *Herbert Hoover and the Russian Prisoners of World War I: A Study in Diplomacy and Relief, 1918–1919* (Stanford, 1951). For an account of camp life by a Russian prisoner see V. Korsak, *Zabytye* (Paris, 1928).

[2] Hoffman, *Camps,* pp. 81–83.

[3] *Russkii vestnik* appeared twice weekly from 1915 to 1918. A collection of pro-German impressions by Russian prisoners was published as *Russische Kriegsgefangene über ihre Eindrücke in Deutschland* (Berlin, 1917).

the typhus and tuberculosis that flourished owing to food shortages brought about by the British blockade in 1916–1917.

The fact that the German advance occurred in the areas running from the Baltic through Poland and Volhynia into the western Ukraine and Belorussia meant that substantial numbers of Russian prisoners were in fact not Russians but Russian Jews and Germans. It was hardly surprising that Russian Jewry was hard hit by the effects of the war. To the destruction of the fighting was added the persecution suffered at the hands of the Russian army. The Jews were not unfriendly to the Germans, yet now they found themselves treated in Germany as enemy aliens. This was true for civilians and war prisoners alike. Those Russian Jews caught in Germany at the time of the war, numbering about 23,000, found their movements restricted by the police; many were put into internment camps. To these were added some 35,000 Jewish laborers brought into Germany from West Russia and Poland during the course of the war as farm hands and factory workers and 35,000 more war prisoners.[4] German wartime pamphlets pointed to this new source of Jewish immigration as a continuation of the prewar flood of non-Aryan "mongolized Slavs," related the Jews to the Yellow Peril in general, and called for a "border defense" against future immigration.[5] German Jewish committees, headed by such luminaries as the theologian Martin Buber, the philosopher Hermann Cohen, and the Russian-Jewish translator Alexander Eliasberg, attempted to find funds to aid the needy and formed a Jewish Society to Aid Russian Citizens in Berlin in 1916 as a subsection of the American YMCA working among the Russian prisoners. But in general the position of Russian Jews in Germany remained extremely difficult throughout the war.

Russian Germans from the western and southwestern provinces found Germany more attractive than did Russian Jews. The outbreak of the war brought a rash of anti-German attacks not only in Moscow and Petrograd, where the embassy and the offices of the

[4] S. Adler-Rudel, *Ostjuden in Deutschland, 1880–1940* (Tübingen, 1959), p. 61.
[5] G. Fritz, *Die Ostjudenfrage: Zionismus und Grenzschluss* (Munich, 1915).

St. Petersburger Zeitung were sacked, but in the provinces as well. A campaign in the nationalist press and the Duma in the winter of 1914–1915 led to the passing of legislation forcing German colonists living in a 250-mile wide belt between the Baltic and the Black Sea to sell their lands or face expropriation. In December 1915 the law was extended to Finland, Poland, the Caucasus, and twenty-nine provinces of southwest Russia, and in early 1917 to virtually all of the Russian Empire.[6] Many Germans were deported to the East during the war, returning to their homes and then to Germany after the Bolshevik revolution. To the Russian-German prisoners interned at special camps at Berger, Damm, Holthausen, and Insterburg—3,500 in early 1916, 15,400 at the time of the March revolution, and 20,300 by the time of the signing of the Treaty of Brest-Litovsk—were added a number of refugees admitted to Germany under the auspices of the Welfare Society for German Returnees. By the end of the war a total of 33,429 Russian Germans had migrated to Germany, according to the Society, most of them from Volhynia province.[7]

The positive reception accorded the Russian Germans in Germany contrasted markedly to the treatment of the Jews. Prisoners were given privileged treatment in special camps. The Welfare Society was active in settling the colonists and their families on new land, finding them jobs, and caring for the needy, aided by Catholic and Protestant church groups. In the press, too, the Russian Germans were lauded as productive farmers betrayed by the Russian government, whose *Heimatliebe* had drawn them back to the *Reich*.[8]

[6] D. Rempel, "The Expropriation of the German Colonists in South Russia during the Great War," *Journal of Modern History*, IV (1932), 49–67.

[7] A. Mergenthaler, "Russlanddeutsche Ruckwanderer in den Jahren 1900 bis 1918," *Deutsche Post aus dem Osten*, XI, No. 12 (December 1939), pp. 8–10.

[8] A number of German pamphlets sympathetic to the Russian Germans appeared during the war, among them: R. Löw, "Deutsche Bauernstaaten auf Russischer Steppe" (Berlin, 1916), C. Eiffe, "Zwei Millionen Deutsche in Russland" (Munich, 1915), F. Duckmeyer, "Die Deutschen in Russland" (Berlin, 1916), Edmund Schmid, "Die deutschen Bauern in Südrussland" (Berlin, 1917). The countervailing Russian view was that the German colonists were the advanced guard of the German army; see I. I. Sergeev, *Mirnoe zavoevanie Rossii nemtsami* (Petrograd, 1915) and S. P. Shelukhin, *Nemetskaia kolonizatsiia na iuge Rossii* (Odessa, 1915).

For years German policy makers and publicists, encouraged by the writings of Balts such as Schiemann and Rohrbach, had dreamed of a German *Mitteleuropa,* an empire of German-speaking peoples which would include the border states of the Russian Empire: Finland, the Baltic provinces, Poland, Belorussia, Bessarabia, the Ukraine, and the Caucasus.[9] With the steady German advance to the East in 1915, this dream for the first time showed signs of becoming a reality; by the Treaty of Brest-Litovsk in the spring of 1918 it was actually consummated in German military occupation of all of Russia's western borderlands. Germany's far-reaching goals in the East were shared by many elements within German society, from the antitsarist sentiment of the socialists through the dreams of the academic geopoliticians to the more hard-headed plans of Chancellor Bethmann-Hollweg and General Ludendorff; but no group was more enthusiastic about these goals than the Baltic Germans.[10]

From the start of hostilities in 1914 German military activity was accompanied by a political assault on Russia designed to take her out of the war. There were two elements to this assault. The first was a series of attempts to initiate separate peace negotiations with the Imperial, Provisional, and Bolshevik governments, beginning in the winter of 1914–1915, which culminated ultimately in the punitive solution at Brest-Litovsk. The second element involved the various attempts, after the failure of peace negotiations, to overthrow the Russian governments by supporting opposition groups both in Europe and in areas of Russia under German occupation: the revolutionary political parties, the non-Russians, and later the monarchists. This bore fruition in the Bolshevik coup. In every aspect of this campaign the Germans made use of, and were used by, the émigrés and found in their dealings with various opposition groups the utility of the émigrés as intermediaries.

The first attempt at a separate peace in the East was made in the winter of 1914–1915 by Albert Ballin, the head of the Hamburg-American Line. Ballin's intermediary was Josef Melnik, a Russian

[9] H. C. Meyer, *Mitteleuropa in German Thought and Action, 1815–1945* (The Hague, 1955).

[10] F. Fischer, *Griff nach der Weltmacht* (Düsseldorf, 1961), *passim.*

Jew who had been an adviser and secretary to the Russian Finance Minister and Premier Sergei Witte and then the political agent for the Hamburg-America Line inside Russia before the war. During the war Melnik lived in Copenhagen, where he filed reports on Russia with both the German ambassador and Ballin. With the approval of Berlin, Ballin tried for several months in early 1915 to establish contact with Witte and thus engage in peace feelers with the Russian government, but by June these attempts were given up. Undismayed, Ballin turned next to the Baltic Baroness Seydlitz, the widow of a Russian officer living in Norway. Through Seydlitz Ballin hoped to make contact with Madam Vyrubova, the intimate of the Tsarina. But when the Baroness asked for 120 million marks to bribe the Grand Duke Nikolai Nikolaevich, both Ballin and Berlin lost interest.[11]

In the spring of 1917 the collapse of the Imperial government produced a new flurry of hopes for a separate peace which manifested themselves in the dispatch of German representatives to Scandinavia. Among them were Paul Litvin, a wealthy industrialist and friend of Gustav Stresemann, and Georg Cleinow, a journalist and editor since 1909 of the liberal *Die Grenzboten*. Litvin was a Russian Jew who had emigrated to Germany before the war and prospered sufficiently to establish his own heating company. Through Stresemann he was introduced to State Secretary Zimmermann, who used him as a translator and go-between in the Stockholm talks, and later in the negotiations of the supplementary treaties of Brest-Litovsk.[12] Cleinow was a St. Petersburg German whose father had served as an economic adviser to the German embassy there; his studies in East European history and economics at Königsberg, Berlin, and Paris and his frequent trips to Russia before the war brought him to the attention of the German government, which used him as press chief for occupied Poland during the war. In April 1917 the Wilhelmstrasse sent him to Copenhagen to offer peace feelers to the Provisional government.[13] Neither Lit-

[11] L. Cecil, *Albert Ballin* (Princeton, 1967), pp. 278–283.

[12] Hans Gatzke, "Stresemann und Litwin," *Vierteljahreshefte für Zeitgeschichte*, V (1957), 76–90.

[13] On Cleinow see *Neue deutsche Biographie*, III (1957), 279–280; M. Kelchner, "Georg Cleinow und die Grenzboten," *Die Grenzboten*, 1920, No. 1, pp. 2–16.

vin nor Cleinow succeeded in his assignment, but both were admirably suited for the task in their German loyalties and their knowledge of Russia and the Russian language.

The German government also established contact with Russian revolutionary circles abroad through Parvus, who was living in Constantinople at the outbreak of the war. Like many German socialists, Parvus greeted the war as an opportunity to destroy the "reactionary" Russian autocracy; unlike many other Russian socialists abroad he was willing to work closely with the German government to achieve his goals and suggested to the German ambassador in Constantinople that they were essentially the same as those of Russian revolutionaries. In March 1915 Parvus submitted a memorandum to the Wilhelmstrasse urging German financial support of the Russian revolutionary movement at home and abroad; by July he had five million marks at his disposal. From Parvus these funds were passed on to Russian revolutionaries living in Switzerland, including Lenin. In the spring of 1917 Parvus succeeded in persuading the Wilhelmstrasse and the High Command to dispatch several trains with some four hundred Russian exiles, among them Lenin, from Switzerland to Russia via Germany and Sweden. Lenin was hardly a German agent, and may have even been unaware of the source of money received, but Parvus was such an agent. Moreover he was uniquely gifted as the intermediary between two parties unable and unwilling to deal with each other directly, the German government and the Bolsheviks.[14]

German support was also extended throughout the war to representatives of the non-Russian nationalities. The German government spoke constantly of the "emancipation" of Finland, Poland, the Baltic provinces, the Ukraine, and Georgia from Russian control and cast a hopeful eye on the economic resources of the area. To this end they subsidized non-Russian émigré organizations, among them a Georgian committee in Berlin, a Union for the Emancipation of the Ukraine in Vienna, a Jewish committee in Galicia, a Zionist organization in Germany, Finnish émigrés in Stockholm,

[14] On Parvus' wartime activity see Z. A. B. Zeman and W. B. Scharlau, *The Merchant of Revolution: The Life of Alexander Israel Helphand (Parvus), 1867–1924* (London, 1965), *passim.*, and Fischer, *Griff*, pp. 168–173, 471–506.

an Estonian National Committee, and various Baltic German groups. Much of the German effort was merely fishing in troubled waters; but with the occupation of these areas by the German army in 1918 contacts with the émigrés took on an added dimension.[15]

By the winter of 1914–1915 these contacts were already well established. In Constantinople, Parvus had succeeded in putting the German embassy in touch with the Ukrainian émigrés living there, although he shortly turned his efforts to more substantial plans involving the Swiss exiles. In the autumn of 1914 the hitherto obscure Prince Matchabelli had set up a Georgian committee in Berlin and announced plans for a future Caucasian federation aligned with Germany and Turkey. Ukrainian politicians living in Vienna established their own organization in Lvov, approached the Austrian government for support, and were soon brought to the attention of the German government by an influential Polish delegate in the Reichstag.[16] Faced with this outburst of émigré activity, the German government decided to make use of it. At best it would facilitate centrifugal nationalism within the Russian Empire; at worst it would give an air of legitimacy to the advance of the German army into the non-Russian areas.

Coordination of this activity remained firmly in German hands. In late 1914 the Wilhelmstrasse sponsored two Baltic Germans in the establishment of a League of Russia's Foreign Peoples designed to coordinate financial support to various exile groups. Matchabelli's Georgian committee was superseded in 1916 by the more practical German-Georgian Society, which published a series of pamphlets urging a "free Caucasus" and surveying the value of Georgian manganese deposits.[17] The activities of the representatives of the Vienna Ukrainians, Roman Smal-Stocki and Dmitro Doncov, were soon taken over by a group of Baltic German journalists and academicians. Paul Rohrbach and Axel Schmidt, influential journalists and long-time supporters of the idea of a German-dominated *Mitteleuropa*, in 1918 organized the German-Ukrainian Society

[15] Fischer, *Griff, passim.*

[16] Hans Beyer, "Die Mittelmächte und die Ukraine, 1918," *Jahrbücher für Geschichte Osteuropas; Beiheft 2* (Munich, 1956), 18–23.

[17] See David Trietsch, *Georgien und der Kaukasus* (Berlin, 1918) and the pamphlet by "Kaukasielli," "Der Kaukasus im Weltkrieg" (Weimar, 1916).

designed to pressure the German army into a policy of land reform and national autonomy under the Hetmanate, a German-created government.[18]

Much of this exile activity brought no results during the war apart from extensive correspondence with the Wilhelmstrasse, a continuous search for funds, and the publication of pamphlets designed to rally German opinion behind the non-Russians. In the end, the interests of the German war effort and those of the émigrés remained distinct, as evidenced by the incapacity of the Germans to influence Bolshevik policy or control Bolshevik propaganda in Germany in 1918 and the failure of the Ukrainian exiles to alter Germany's punitive policies in Kiev during the occupation. The exception to the rule was the case of the Baltic Germans, whose influence was strong enough to maintain German power in a military effort in their homeland not merely during the war but for a year after the Armistice.

Throughout the war the Balts were the most active group of Russian exiles involved in the German war effort. Following the prewar example of Schiemann, Rohrbach, Haller, and others, the wartime publicists again lauded the Baltic Germans as a superior and oppressed segment of Russian society and urged separation of the area from Russia under German supervision. That the German army achieved this goal was, of course, independent of the lobbying of Balts in Germany. But in 1917–1918 it was the Balts who engineered the political separation of their homeland and were most active in administering the region for Oberost. The ultimate failure of German Free Corps intervention in 1919 and the establishment of an independent Latvia and Estonia only heightened their acute sense of frustration. When they were forced to return once again to Germany it was as even more embittered German nationalists and supporters of the *Auslandsdeutschen*.

Beginning in 1915 Theodor Schiemann and other Balts urged

[18] On Smal-Stocki's activities during the war see Georg Prokoptschuk, *Ukrainer in München* (Munich, 1958), pp. 61–65. Doncov lived in Berlin during the war and engaged in pamphleteering for Ukrainian interests in his "Die Ukrainische Staatsidee und der Krieg gegen Russland" (Berlin, 1915) and "Gross-Polen und die Zentralmächte" (Berlin, 1916). On Rohrbach and his German-Ukrainian Society see Georg Prokoptschuk, *Deutsch-ukrainische Gesellschaft* (Munich, 1963) and its journal *Die Ukraine*, 1918–1926.

the immediate annexation by Germany of the Baltic area as a major war aim. Despite the opposition of Bethmann-Hollweg and the school of Otto Hoetzsch, which urged a separate peace with Russia to free German forces for the war in the West, the Balts found considerable sympathy for their aims within the army High Command and the Foreign Office. By May 1915 the province of Kurland was under German occupation and on July 28 the German nobility of all three Baltic provinces, united in their own Landesrat, requested German protection for an independent state system. This request was reinforced by the assurances of Baron von Uexküll to the German embassy in Stockholm and of the journalist Sylvio Broederich to Bethmann that summer that the Baltic Germans were virtually unanimous in desiring German protection.[19]

Throughout 1915 there was mounting pressure by the Baltic exiles in Germany as well. Broederich urged that the Baltic "homeland" be rescued from the "Muscovite-Mongol" yoke and brought back into the orbit of Western civilization as the Reich province of "Ostland." Max Boehm likewise argued that only the incorporation of the Baltic's "ancient German soil" could save the area from "Russian brutality." Another journalist described the anti-Russian strivings of all the peoples of the western borderlands of the Empire, especially the Baltic Germans and the Jews, and Karl Nötzel noted that the task of Europe must now be to emancipate the Poles, the Ukrainians, and the Armenians from Russian despotism and barbarism. In the best tradition of Rohrbach's *Mitteleuropa* schemes, the Balts emerged once again to portray for Germans the forces of centrifugal nationalism at work in Russia and to dangle the promise of a belt of German-dominated *Randstaaten* before the audience of German public opinion.[20]

[19] Fischer, *Griff*, pp. 233, 246, 346–352; on Uexküll see Lucius to Bethmann-Hollweg, Stockholm, September 10, 1915 (AGFM, T-136, roll SA-139); Broederich had arrived in Berlin in early July, talked with Bethmann, and given lectures on the Baltic Germans to the Berlin Police Club and other civic organizations (Okhrana Archive, Hoover Library, Box 63, VIIc, folder 1A).

[20] Sylvio Broederich-Kurmahlen, *Das neue Ostland* (Berlin, 1915); Max Boehm, *Die Krisis deutschbaltischer Menschen* (Berlin, 1915); Ekkehard Ostmann, *Russlands Fremdvölker: Seine Stärke und Schwäche* (Munich, 1915); Karl Nötzel, *Die Unabhängigkeit der Ukraine als einzige Rettung vor der russischen Gefahr* (Munich and Leipzig, 1915).

In the face of this pressure William II on September 22, 1915, recognized the formal independence of all three of the Baltic provinces under the administration in theory of a German Landesrat. In fact the area now passed into the firm hands of the High Command's Oberost, the government for the occupied provinces in the East. To strengthen German control in the area the High Command also began in 1916 to carry out a plan conceived by Berlin as early as December 1914, namely, to move German colonists from East Prussia and the occupied areas of Galicia, Volhynia, and the Ukraine into the Baltic provinces and Poland. This plan, like the separation of the provinces from the Russian Empire, marked another triumph of Schiemann and the Balts over the counterpressures of Hoetzsch. Throughout 1916 and 1917 the Balts kept up their journalistic campaign in a series of pamphlets enlightening German opinion and the German government concerning the "Russian danger" and the need for a German *Mitteleuropa* which would destroy forever the aggressive threat of "Pan Slavism" and reduce Russia to her seventeenth-century borders.[21] If the Balts did not create or radically alter German policy in the East, they loudly supported it and soon became not merely its proponents but its executors.

From the Revolution to the Armistice

The Germans were no less surprised than anyone else at the sudden collapse of the Romanov dynasty in Russia in the spring of 1917. As the dispatch of the famous "sealed train" of revolutionaries to Petrograd indicated, however, they were well prepared to take advantage of the situation. This was partly owing to the aid of those émigré opponents of the Imperial government who shared with the German High Command a general desire to facilitate the collapse of the old regime in Russia. In the end the Bolshevik *coup*

[21] Notably the seven-volume series edited by Rohrbach and entitled *Die russische Gefahr* (Stuttgart, 1916–1917), which included Axel Schmidt's "Das Endziel Russlands" (1916), Rohrbach's "Russische selbstzeugnisse der Feindschaft" (1916), their joint "Die russische Revolution" (1917), and Johannes Haller's "Die russische Gefahr im Deutschenhause" (1917), an attack on Otto Hoetzsch. Hoetzsch responded with his *Russische Probleme* (Berlin, 1917), where he criticized the Russophobia of the Balts.

d'état seemed to mark a singular achievement of German wartime policy by bringing to power a group of individuals dedicated to taking Russia out of the war.

From the March 1917 revolution until the Armistice in November 1918 the German government, like the Allies, was concerned with events in Russia primarily insofar as they affected the prosecution of the war on the western front. Germany needed in Russia a government willing to sign a peace treaty which would guarantee food supplies needed to alleviate the desperate shortages of the Central Powers; to this end the German government had arranged the transportation of Bolshevik leaders into Russia in April 1917 in hopes of breaking the Provisional government's war effort at home, if not in the trenches. But in the weeks and months that followed the Bolshevik revolution in November it became apparent that the Bolsheviks in power were not nearly as desirable as the German government had initially assumed. First they dragged their feet over the signing of a separate peace at Brest-Litovsk. Then their own inability to control Russia forced the German High Command to extend its own lines of supply and communications deep into Russian territory and to waste valuable manpower in occupation.

German disillusionment with the Bolsheviks extended from the Moscow embassy of Count Mirbach to Berlin. In early December 1917 State Secretary Kühlmann wrote that the Bolshevik government would remain in power for only a short time.[22] Chancellor Hertling in a January 9, 1918, speech to the Reichstag gave them only a few months of grace.[23] But if the Bolsheviks were doomed, then what should be German policy in the east? A separate peace was desirable at all costs, but should it be the moderate peace of Kühlmann and the Wilhelmstrasse or the punitive one of the army? The months which followed the signing of the Treaty of Brest-Litovsk brought the answer. Kühlmann was forced to retire in early July 1918 and German policy in the east followed the lines marked

---

[22] Telegram of December 3, 1917, cited in Z. A. B. Zeman, ed., *Germany and the Revolution in Russia, 1915–1918* (Oxford, 1958), p. 94.

[23] G. Rosenfeld, *Sowjetrussland und Deutschland, 1917–1922* (Berlin, 1960), p. 29.

out by General Ludendorff: military occupation of a vast belt of land from Riga to the Kuban and the forced removal of stores of grain to feed the German army in the west.

The Germans also faced the problem of which political faction to support in Russia when the expected Bolshevik collapse occurred. There was general agreement among German policy makers that the most desirable government would be one which could maintain order in Russia and at the same time would be willing to accept German domination of the western lands of the Empire: Finland, the Baltic area, Poland, Belorussia, and the Ukraine. Realizing that the liberal parties in Russia (Octobrists and Kadets) were generally both Ententophile and expansionistic in their aims, Kühlmann favored supporting parties on the extreme left, the Social Revolutionaries if not the Bolsheviks.[24] Whereas Kühlmann assumed that monarchist supporters of the old regime would not accept German domination of the *Randstaaten*, Ludendorff felt they would do so and were the only faction worth supporting:

Though we now negotiate officially only with the Soviet government we should at the same time entertain relations with other movements in Russia, in order not to find ourselves suddenly high and dry. We cannot rely on Kerensky's partisans, because they are dominated by the Entente. We have to acquire contacts with the right-wing monarchist groups and influence them so that the monarchist movement would be governed by our wishes as soon as it gained influence.[25]

And once again Ludendorff's authority proved too much for Kühlmann. Throughout 1918 the Germans flirted with various monarchist groups in Russia, first in Moscow and Petrograd and later in Kiev. But they continued to maintain official relations with the Bolshevik government, even after the assassination of Ambassador Mirbach in July, and to support a "double-tracked" policy toward Russia, as one member of the Wilhelmstrasse defined it.[26]

[24] Kühlmann to Mirbach, Berlin, May 18, 1918 (Zeman, *Germany*, pp. 128–129).

[25] From Ludendorff's memorandum on Germany's policy in the East dated June 9, 1918 (Zeman, *Germany*, p. 136).

[26] Wipert von Blücher, *Deutschlands Weg nach Rapallo: Erinnerungen eines Mannes aus dem zweiten Gliede* (Wiesbaden, 1951), p. 19.

The opposition to the Bolsheviks, like the Russian emigration, defined itself in terms of how much of the Russian Revolution it could accept. For those on the far right, the entire process of modernization beginning with the industrialization program of Witte in the 1890's was anathema; they associated with it the appearance of Jews in positions of prominence, the rise of political parties and a press not entirely subservient to the autocracy, and the general process of limited constitutional government which emerged out of the fires of 1905. Needless to say, they could countenance neither the March nor November upheavals of 1917. The liberal parties, notably the Octobrists and the Constitutional Democrats, generally accepted the economic and political modernization of the country, the wartime alliance with France and England, and even the collapse of the autocracy in the spring of 1917. They tolerated and participated in the Provisional government, although many of them would have preferred some form of limited mon- ⚹ archy. For the socialist parties modernization and industrialization were useful because, according to Marxist theory, they contained the seeds of their own destruction through class struggle and revolution. The Provisional government represented the "bourgeois" phase of the revolutionary process, and the question of when to cooperate with it and when to oppose it was a thorny one; a few Mensheviks and Social Revolutionaries joined with it in hopes of effecting land reform or new labor legislation. The Bolshevik revolution split the socialists into those willing for a time to cooperate with it (the left SR's) and those who soon went into opposition (the majority SR's and most Mensheviks).

The strength of the anti-Bolshevik movement lay in the army. Many officers had long been disgruntled over the collapse of the alliance with Germany in the 1890's and some felt that Russia had fought World War I on the wrong side. Few officers could accept the Provisional government with its toleration of insubordination within the ranks, and many who had not been able to join the march of General Kornilov on Petrograd in the late summer of 1917 would later go over to the armies of Denikin, Kolchak, or Wrangel. It was the old officer corps, together with the Cossacks and a number of right-wing and liberal political leaders, which formed the base of the White movement, starting in the winter of 1917–1918. Together with large numbers of the aristocracy, the landed gentry, and the middle and professional classes, they would constitute the leadership of the Russian emigration as well.

The Russian intelligentsia was more divided. Very few opposed the Bolsheviks from the beginning and many viewed the period of revolution and civil war as a kind of purifying cataclysm ushering in some vaguely defined better world. Typical, perhaps, were those who remained in Russia and found cultural work under the new regime, particularly through Lunacharsky's Commissariat of Education, but were later expelled by the Bolsheviks or simply underwent a gradual change of heart. Thus, while few were to be found in the ranks of the White movement, equally few could retain any great enthusiasm for the Soviet government when in exile.

Finally, the non-Russian borderlands were also an important source of resistance to the Bolsheviks. Hostile in varying degrees to the nationalities policy of the Imperial regime, they found temporary freedom in the impotence of the Provisional government. Finland, Poland, and the Baltic states ultimately emerged as independent nations; the Georgians, the Ukrainians, and the Russian-German colonists of South Russia enjoyed no such success, although all were temporarily separated from Soviet Russia in 1918 by the German occupation army. Indeed, like the prewar Russian, Jewish, and Baltic German émigrés to Germany, those who established contact with the Germans in the occupied borderlands in 1918–1919 were to play a most significant role in the story of the Russian emigration to Germany.

Russian conservative circles seemed an ideal group to support in 1918 not because they held political promise but because they were thoroughly Germanophile. The moderate right, principally the Kadet and Octobrist parties, had supported an aggressive foreign policy before 1914, particularly in the Balkans, directed against both Germany and Austria in alliance with England and France. But strong sympathies for Germany based on the traditional dynastic-conservative alliance which had been broken off in the 1890's continued to exist at court, in the army, among the aristocracy, and within the extreme right-wing groups which sprang up after 1905. Russia, it was said, was being unwillingly pushed into a war with Germany by England. But the tide of prewar Russian opinion continued to flow with England and France, and the long memorandum of February 1914 by P. N. Durnovo, Minister of the Interior, urging a comity of Russian and German interests, went largely unheard.

General sympathy for an alignment with conservative Germany carried over also into the new extreme right-wing political parties which began to appear in Russia after 1900 and particularly after the upheaval of 1905.[27] Representing mainly the upper classes, the army, and the bureaucracy, groups like the Union of the Russian People and the Black Hundreds attempted to gain mass support for the regime through an attack on the entire fabric of Russian society: industrialization, parliamentarism, and the supposed forces behind them, the Jews. Literature such as the notorious *Protocols of the Elders of Zion* purported to reveal Jewish plans to take over the world through such apparently innocent means as financial operations, liberalism, and Freemasonry.[28] The Jews within were also identified with the dark forces of destruction moving on Russia from the East, the Japanese in particular; together they represented "two armies directed simultaneously against the Russian state and the Russian people, the first from the front, the second from the rear."[29]

As Russian nationalists who opposed not only the Jews but all non-Russian nationalities within the Empire, many on the right

[27] On the Russian right see: H. Jablonowski, "Die russischen Rechtsparteien, 1905–1917," in *Russland Studien: Gedenkschrift für Otto Hoetzsch* (Stuttgart, 1957), pp. 43–55; Hans Rogger, "Was There a Russian Fascism? The Union of Russian People," *Journal of Modern History*, XXXVI (1964), 389–415, and "The Formation of the Russian Right, 1900–1906," *California Slavic Studies*, III (1964), 66–94; V. P. Viktorov, ed., *Soiuz russkogo naroda: Po materialam chrezvychainoi sledstvennoi komissii vremennogo pravitel'stva 1917 g.* (Moscow and Leningrad, 1929).

[28] On the *Protocols* see the recent study of Norman Cohn, *Warrant for Genocide* (London, 1967).

[29] G. V. Butmi, *Konstitutsiia i politicheskaia svoboda* (St. Petersburg, 1906), p. 15. Butmi reiterated his tirades against the Jews, British, Japanese, and Masons in a number of other pamphlets.

could tolerate German influence in the western borderlands. But with the outbreak of the war the already dissolving parties of the right split into outspoken patriots who could no longer countenance a friendly attitude toward Germany and those on the extreme right who remained Germanophile. Among the latter was a former Kursk landowner, N. E. Markov, known as Markov II or Markov the Second, who became, along with Dr. A. I. Dubrovin and V. M. Purishkevich, a major figure in right-wing politics after 1905 and the man responsible for obtaining government subsidies for right-wing organizations.[30] A vigorous anti-Semite and advocate of close ties between Russia and Germany, Markov II became the leader of the pro-German faction during the war and subsequently, after the death of Purishkevich in 1920 and Dubrovin two years later, the dominant figure in the right-wing politics of the emigration. In his remarkable polemic *The Wars of the Dark Powers* (Paris, 1928) he predicted a Jewish-Bolshevik takeover of the world through the Comintern and found that the Jews were behind every social upheaval since 1789; Jewish-Masonic control of Russia had begun with the October Manifesto and only a regime like that of Benito Mussolini might have saved her.[31] It was a vicious and absurd message, but one which would find currency in the wake of the Bolshevik revolution not only within the emigration but throughout Europe.

In early 1918 several groups of monarchists and right-wing politicians appealed for German support through the Moscow embassy. When Mirbach's mission had first arrived there in April, Kühlmann's instructions had been simply to maintain good relations with the Bolshevik government in order that the terms of Brest-Litovsk might be fulfilled with a minimum of friction. But

---

[30] Viktorov, *Soiuz*, p. 32. Markov II was born in Kursk province in 1866 and in 1905 had organized the local gentry into a self-defense organization known as the Party of Civil Order. He soon joined the growing right-wing movement in the capitals, became a member of the Main Council of the Union of the Russian People, and was elected to the Third and Fourth Dumas. When Dubrovin broke away from the Union in 1909 to form his own group, Markov II became editor of the journal of the Purishkevich faction, *Vestnik soiuza russkogo naroda*.

[31] N. E. Markov, *Voiny temnykh sil* (Paris, 1928), pp. 120, 138.

Mirbach quickly discovered that Bolshevik control of Russia outside the capitals was questionable, that a number of anti-Bolshevik movements existed, and that Allied representatives were already in touch with them. Mirbach and his embassy staff, therefore, were not unwilling to listen to the schemes of two loosely organized anti-Bolshevik groups in Moscow: first, the so-called "right center" faction, a circle of Octobrists and conservative Kadets around General V. I. Gurko which included Prince G. N. Trubetskoi, the liberal politician Peter Struve, and the former Minister of Agriculture, A. V. Krivoshein;[32] second, a group of right-wing politicians, church officials, and army officers around Markov II which included Patriarch Tikhon, former Prime Minister A. F. Trepov, and Senator A. A. Rimsky-Korsakov, an elderly State Councillor, former governor of Yaroslav province, and long-time supporter of various right-wing groups.[33]

German contact with these shadowy circles in the ensuing months came to little. Markov II and his friends submitted memoranda to the embassy in which they argued that they were the most reliable political leaders for the Germans to support. They also attempted to involve the Germans in a plot to save the Russian Imperial family.[34] The Germans for their part retained informal ties with these groups and encouraged them, but were suspicious of their motives and unimpressed by their political promise. Mirbach admitted in late June that the Bolsheviks were "lost in the long run" but felt that the monarchists he had talked with were "not to be recommended" as an alternative, since they were "too confused and too lazy" and "fundamentally only interested in winning back their former secure and comfortable living-conditions with our help."[35] Mirbach favored instead supporting the moderate parties in Russia, Kadets and

[32] General Fürst Awaloff, *Im Kampf gegen den Bolschewismus* (Glückstadt and Hamburg, 1925), p. 153; Rosenfeld, *Sowjetrussland*, p. 93.

[33] This group is mentioned in AGFM, T-136, roll SA-139 and in N. D. Zhevakov, *Kniaz' Aleksei Aleksandrovich Shirinskii-Shikhmatov: Kratkii ocherk zhizni i deiatel'nosti* (Novyi Sad, 1934), p. 17.

[34] See, for example, the 12-page memorandum submitted to the German embassy in July 1918 and enclosed in the report of Riezler to Bethmann-Hollweg, Moscow, July 20, 1918 (AGFM, T-136, roll SA-140).

[35] Mirbach to State Secretary, June 25, 1918 (Zeman, *Germany*, pp. 137–139).

Octobrists, since "such a combination would ensure that we had a large percentage of the influential men of the industrial and banking worlds serving our essential economic interest." [36] But Mirbach's view was not popular in most German official circles, where it was recognized that alignment with the center and moderate right parties in Russia, even if practical in terms of replacing the Bolsheviks, would entail the abandonment of long-awaited German hegemony in the western borderlands.

The distaste for the Bolsheviks felt by most of the Moscow embassy staff increased when, on July 6, 1918, Ambassador Mirbach was murdered by a member of the left-wing faction of the Social Revolutionary party, possibly with Bolshevik connivance.[37] There was now more embassy sympathy for the monarchist circles with which the staff had been in touch during the previous two months. Rumors flew that a German infantry battalion would be sent to Moscow to provide protection for embassy personnel. But in fact the incident, by turning German opinion against the Bolshevik government, hastened the withdrawal of the embassy and the commitment of Germany, even on the eve of its own collapse in the West, to the anti-Bolshevik cause. Although a new German ambassador, Karl Hellferich, arrived in Moscow to replace Mirbach, he left on August 6 and was soon followed by the entire staff, which moved first to Pskov and then to Reval.

The withdrawal of the German embassy, however, did not free the Germans from the constant pressures of the Russian monarchists. After Brest-Litovsk some 250,000 refugees had flooded into the area occupied by Oberost, particularly the provinces of Smolensk, Vitebsk, and Mogilev. Foreign Commissar Chicherin's complaints that "an incessant stream of refugees is attempting to return to the areas which have been occupied by German troops" and his demand that the German High Command "take all measures necessary to contain mass emigration within the territory of the Russian Soviet Republic" did nothing to stem the tide.[38] At the end of

[36] *Ibid.*, p. 138.

[37] See George Katkov, "The Assassination of Count Mirbach," *St. Antony's Papers, No. 12, Soviet Affairs* (London, 1962), pp. 53–93.

[38] Chicherin's dispatches were reported in the correspondence of April 1918 between the Moscow embassy and Berlin; see AGFM, roll SA-83 (vols. 38–39) and SA-101 (vol. 49).

April a representative of Trepov and Markov II's circle arrived in Pskov and asked the High Command for permission to form three divisions of anti-Bolshevik troops out of Russian war prisoners in Germany. He was followed by a representative of the Grand Duke Paul, seeking financial and military aid for a Romanov restoration, and by G. M. Deriugin, a right-wing Duma representative looking for similar support.[39] Other requests were reported by the German embassy in Kiev. But by the autumn of 1918 the German collapse was imminent, and German reluctance to support the anti-Bolshevik movement was now fortified by German impotence to do so. The Whites turned to the Allies, the Germans to their last area of influence in the East, the Baltic.

While the Germans occupied West Russia and the Ukraine in 1918 they found themselves inadvertently involved in the fate of numerous members of the Russian royal family who had been scattered throughout Russia after the revolution. On the one hand, there was pressure from Berlin on both the Moscow embassy and Oberost to protect Russian royalty living in the German-occupied areas and to intercede with the Bolsheviks on behalf of others, particularly those with German relatives. On the other hand, there was an unwillingness to intervene in such matters lest the Bolshevik leadership be persuaded to take up arms against Germany. In the end the Germans discovered to their surprise that while they could be of little help to Nicholas II and his family, the lesser members of the family living in the German occupation zone could be of use to them.

Immediately following his abdication in March 1917, Nicholas II and his family were arrested at Tsarskoe Selo by a detachment of troops sent by the Provisional government. After an unsuccessful attempt to arrange for their asylum in England, it was decided to move the royal family into the interior of the country. On August 14, 1917, they were taken from Tsarskoe Selo in two railroad trains under military guard and moved to Tobolsk. In the spring of 1918

---

[39] Pskov to Berlin, May 2, 1918 (AGFM, roll SA-83, vol. 38) and May 19, 1918 (SA-83, vol. 39). Also Awaloff, *Kampf*, pp. 131–132, and J. Bischoff, *Die letzte Front: Geschichte der Eisernen Division im Baltikum* (Berlin, 1935), p. 25.

they were moved further east to Ekaterinburg where, on July 17, 1918, the entire family was brutally murdered by their guards.

The whereabouts and fate of the Imperial family was of constant interest to monarchist circles in Moscow in 1918. Krivoshein in January sent an emissary to Tobolsk who returned to report that the family was badly in need of funds, and 250,000 rubles were promptly dispatched to them. Markov II had also talked about his own scheme to save the family since mid-1917 and claimed to have thirty men at his *dacha* in Finland ready to give their lives in such an attempt. One of his emissaries, a cavalry officer named Sergei Markov, soon realized, however, that Markov II's plans were largely imaginary. He decided in June 1918 to turn to the German consulate in Petrograd for help. After a month's delay, he was allowed to send off two telegrams from the consulate to Empress Alexandra's brother, Grand Duke Ernst Ludwig of Hesse, asking for his personal intercession on behalf of the family.[40]

By this time the German embassy in Moscow had already made some attempts, however half-hearted, to intervene for the family. Prince Henry of Prussia had written several letters to the Wilhelmstrasse urging that some action be taken. But the Foreign Office decided that it would only involve itself on behalf of Russian royalty of German descent; it was on this basis that Ambassador Mirbach told Krivoshein and other monarchists in 1918 that they could not attempt to save Nicholas II but only German princesses who had married into Russian royalty. Finally, in mid-July 1918, the embassy received permission from Berlin to press the Bolshevik government concerning the fate of the Imperial family—more specifically, the security of Alexandra—but it was too late. Chicherin did not even bother to answer the query.[41]

The German government was more successful in protecting the lesser Romanovs who had fled to South Russia after the March revolution. Most belonged to the family of Grand Duke Alexander Mikhailovich, who had moved south to the Crimea that spring:

---

[40] Sergei Markov, *Pokinutaia tsarskaia sem'ia, 1917–1918* (Vienna, 1928), pp. 159 ff.; Bernard Pares, *The Fall of the Russian Monarchy* (New York, 1939), pp. 472–502; Awaloff, *Kampf*, pp. 40–44.

[41] Blücher, *Deutschlands Weg*, pp. 27–28.

his mother-in-law the Dowager Empress Maria Fedorovna, his wife Grand Duchess Xenia, and his sister-in-law Olga, with her husband and six sons. Also living there were Grand Duke Nikolai Nikolaevich, his wife Stana of Montenegro, and his brother Grand Duke Peter. Shortly after the Bolshevik revolution the entire group was placed under house arrest by the Bolsheviks. After several months of living in fear of their lives, they were only too happy to be rescued in the spring of 1918 by detachments of German troops which had just occupied the city of Yalta.[42]

It was the policy of the new German ambassador in Kiev, Baron Adolf Mumm von Schwarzenstein, and the two German military officers in charge of the occupation, Field Marshall Eichhorn and General Wilhelm Groener, to make certain that their royal charges in the South received adequate protection in these months. But several members of the family were opposed to accepting aid and protection from the Germans and made their feelings known to Mumm.[43] General Ludendorff finally managed to obtain a pledge from Maria Fedorovna and the grand dukes that they would not attempt to leave the Crimea without first informing the German government. The Germans felt that in the event of a possible restoration it would be wise to have as many friends as possible within the Romanov family; at the same time they had to moderate the demands of Prince Henry of Prussia, Grand Duke Kirill, and others for strong pressure on the Bolsheviks on behalf of other members of the family.

By October 1918 plans were under way to move the Romanovs out of the Crimea before Bolshevik or Ukrainian nationalist troops could move into the area. The Ukrainian hetman, Paul Skoropadsky, arranged with German help for the passage of some aristocrats and royalty to Copenhagen via Germany. But State Secretary Admiral Hintze and the High Command had other plans of moving the entire family into a huge castle near Windau in the Baltic, an area which the Germans hoped to defend at all costs. Before these plans could be put into effect, however, the Armistice had been

[42] Grand Duke Alexander, *Once a Grand Duke* (New York, 1932), pp. 293 ff.

[43] Mumm to Foreign Office, June 4, 1918 (AGFM, T-136, roll SA-139).

declared and British and French forces had landed in the Crimea. For a few months Russian royalty enjoyed the protection of their new guardians before being evacuated on a British battleship in March 1919 to safety.[44]

Outside the area of occupation the Germans retained an interest in any royalty who might combine political promise with pro-German sentiments. The German Foreign Office had kept extensive files on the movements and activity of Russian royalty throughout the war.[45] It had been observed in Berlin that the Grand Duke Kirill was by far the most *deutschfreundlich* of the lot. But German interest in Kirill was short-lived. In June 1918 General Rüdiger von der Goltz, commander in chief of the German troops supporting the Whites in the Finnish civil war, contacted in person the circle of aristocrats and army officers around Kirill and discussed plans for possible military operations against the Bolsheviks.[46] Von der Goltz quickly discovered the impracticability of dealing with this group and did not recommend to Berlin that Kirill be allowed to pass through Germany to Switzerland that summer, since such a decision could only irritate the Bolsheviks while bringing the Germans nothing in return. "This part of the Russian Imperial house," he complained to Ludendorff in September 1918, "has forgotten nothing and learned nothing." [47]

Much more useful to the Germans in 1918 were two lesser members of the Romanov family then living in Kiev, Duke Georg and Duke Nikolai of Leuchtenberg. When war broke out in the summer of 1914, Georg had been caught in Bavaria where he had been convalescing from wounds suffered during the Russo-Japanese War. For some time after his return to Russia he was suspected of pro-German sympathies and even desertion. Nevertheless he served

[44] The plans to evacuate Russian royalty to the Baltic are mentioned in Blücher, *Deutschlands Weg*, pp. 28–29; the Foreign Ministry correspondence is in AGFM, T-136, roll SA-140. See also Grand Duke Alexander, *Once a Grand Duke*, pp. 313–314.

[45] The file on Russian royalty before 1914 is in AGFM, T-136, rolls SA-139 and SA-140.

[46] Rüdiger von der Goltz, *Meine Sendung in Finnland und im Baltikum* (Leipzig, 1920), pp. 92–93.

[47] Von der Goltz's conversation with Ludendorff as reported by Lersner to the Foreign Ministry, October 7, 1918 (AGFM, T-136, roll SA-140).

in various capacities during the war and at the time of the March revolution was assigned to General Brusilov's staff in Kiev. Here he remained, together with his two oldest sons and his brother Nikolai, until the Germans occupied the Ukraine in the spring of 1918. Almost immediately Duke Georg wrote his old friend Duke Leopold of Bavaria, now a commanding officer in Oberost, urging him to carry out a program of land reform in the Ukraine, to forget about the German (and Ukrainian nationalist) dream of a separate Ukraine, and to work toward restoration of a constitutional monarchy in Russia.[48]

Georg also voiced similar hopes to the German representatives in Kiev, Ambassador Mumm and Field Marshal Eichhorn. The Germans, he hoped, would not betray the Russian upper classes as the Entente powers were now doing. Would the Germans not be willing, he asked, to help organize and supply a new anti-Bolshevik army in Kiev made up of officers unwilling to serve with Denikin? The Germans proved receptive, and in the next months Duke Georg worked closely with Eichhorn and Groener on the formation of a "Southern Army" of Russian officers under General P. N. Krasnov. With them, he recalled, he was able to develop a "relationship of trust, since, having lived in Germany the last ten years, I was known there, I knew the German character, achievements and inadequacies, the language and how to deal with them." [49]

Before anything could come of the "Southern Army" Germany agreed to the Armistice, German subsidies came to an end, and the entire project collapsed. But for a time the value of the Leuchtenbergs had been considerable to the Germans. Duke Georg had not only been the intermediary with Russian officers in Kiev but had also kept the Germans informed about the situation among Russian royalty in the Crimea. His brother Nikolai had the job of coordinating the military plans of General Krasnov with those of Ludendorff, to which end he had been sent to Berlin in late August.[50]

[48] Duke Georg's recollections of this period were later published as G. Leikhtenbergskii, *Vospominaniia ob "Ukraine," 1917–1918* (Berlin, 1921).

[49] G. Leikhtenbergskii, "Kak nachalas' 'Iuzhnaia armiia'," *Arkhiv russkoi revoliutsii*, No. 8 (1923), 170.

[50] Mumm to Foreign Ministry, Kiev, July 26, 1918 (AGFM, T-136, roll SA-140).

Politically neither of the Dukes associated with any particular Russian faction in Kiev, although they did endorse the attempt by Krivoshein and others to procure German sponsorship of Grand Duke Mikhail as tsar.[51] With the German withdrawal from Kiev in late 1918, the Leuchtenbergs fled to Bavaria where once more they settled down in the familiar seclusion of Seeon.

With the German occupation of the Ukraine in 1918 the German government found itself faced with yet another political lobby in Russia interested in German support: German colonists living in South Russia. Since before the war both the Foreign Office and Pan-German circles had followed with interest the fate of the Russian German communities and the Treaty of Brest-Litovsk provided accordingly that Russian citizens of German descent would have the right to emigrate to Germany. Now in 1918 the High Command and the Foreign Office received a stream of requests for permission to emigrate from German colonists in the Crimea and the Ukraine. But Ludendorff, not the Pan-Germans, made policy in the East, and Ludendorff agreed only under the condition that émigré Russian Germans would serve in the German army. Faced with the existence of something that the Germans themselves claimed had existed for years—a desire to return home on the part of Germans outside Germany—the German government found itself without a policy.

The wartime policies of the Imperial Russian government had been particularly painful to the Russian German community, linked by language and ancestry with the enemy. By the law of November 3, 1914, there could be no use of the German language in the Russian press and no public assembly of Russian Germans in groups of more than three. Even worse were the notorious property liquidation laws of February 2 and December 3, 1915, whereby German nationals in Russia had to sell all immovable property within eight months or lose it to Russian banks at ten per cent of its assessed value. Large numbers of German colonists living in Volhynia were deported to Siberia during the war. Among them

51 Mumm to Reichskanzler, Kiev, August 23, 1918 (AGFM, T-136, roll SA-140).

were Mennonites who suffered less at first, emphasized their Dutch origins, and were allowed to enter the medical corps in the army to meet their military obligations, rather than carrying arms in the infantry. But they too suffered hardships as the war dragged on and often found themselves interned with Russian Germans for the duration.[52]

In the days which followed the March revolution, however, the Russian Germans, like other national minorities within the Empire, suddenly found themselves with a new freedom. Already on March 18, 1917, a group of thirty leaders from various colonies in South Russia met in Odessa to discuss plans to form an all-Russian union of German colonists (*Kolonistenverband*). German student organizations revived again after a period of wartime somnolence. In mid-May an even larger All-Russian Congress of Russian Germans was held in Odessa and a similar one followed in August in Moscow. But it was only in early November 1917 that a committee with authority to represent the German community in Russia was finally organized under the leadership of a South Russian colonist and minister, Pastor Winckler. But under neither the Provisional government nor the Bolsheviks did the Russian Germans succeed in their attempts to recover land and property lost during the war. Most of their activity amounted to organizing themselves, propagandizing among the scattered colonies, and printing their own pamphlets and newspapers.[53]

Not surprisingly many colonists welcomed the arrival of German troops in South Russia in 1918. Some Mennonities greeted them as saviors and even lent money to the occupation troops.[54] Plans were initiated for the long-awaited emigration to Germany, in accordance with the terms of Brest-Litovsk, but hopes were dashed when a Mennonite committee returned from Berlin in September 1918 to report that by then the economic and political situation in

---

[52] On the fate of the Russian Germans during World War I see Rempel, "Expropriation"; F. Epp, *Mennonite Exodus* (Altona, Manitoba, 1962); A. Krüger, *Die Flüchtlinge vom Volhynien* (Plauen-am-Vogtland, 1937); Edmund Schmidt, *Die deutschen Kolonien im Schwarzmeergebiet Südrusslands* (Berlin, 1919), and *Die Mennoniten-Gemeinden in Russland während der Kriegs- und Revolutionsjahre 1914 bis 1920* (Heilbron-am-Neckar, 1921).

[53] Schmidt, *Kolonien*, pp. 34–35.   [54] Epp, *Exodus*, p. 33.

Germany was growing as bad as in Russia. Nevertheless nearly one hundred Mennonite and German families did leave their homes in the Ukraine in the winter of 1918–1919 with the German occupation forces. Many Volhynian Germans had little choice; on returning from their Siberian wartime exile they found to their dismay that villages had disappeared under the ravages of war and they continued on to Germany. Most of them settled in Saxony where they were surprised to find themselves looked upon by the local population not as Germans, but as Russians.[55]

Pastor Winckler and his committee had even more grandiose plans. In the wake of a series of meetings held in Odessa and other South Russian towns in the spring of 1918 a group of colonists decided to petition the German government not only for permission to emigrate to Germany but also for support in establishing in South Russia and the Crimea a new German province which would be formally incorporated into the Reich. Already in April 1918 Winckler had held conversations with Ambassador Mumm in Kiev concerning the possibility of admitting the German colonies of Bessarabia and the Caucasus to German statehood. Faced with such unanticipated enthusiasm and with the fact that many colonists were contributing funds for the desperately needed Eighth German War Loan, Mumm agreed to arrange for Winckler and two other colonists to travel to Berlin in May to explain their case in person. Throughout the spring and early summer of 1918 Winckler described his plans to a number of government representatives in Berlin, including General Groener, State Secretary Kühlmann, General Ludendorff, and even William himself. But Berlin was no more prepared than Mumm had been to deal with such problems in the face of the worsening military situation. The emigration of German families from Russia was approved in principle, although no concrete steps were taken, and the idea of a German state in South Russia was considered absurd.[56]

During the six months of German occupation of Russia which

[55] Krüger, *Flüchtlinge,* p. 206.
[56] Schmidt, *Kolonien,* pp. 35–37; Wilhelm Groener, *Lebenserinnerungen* (Göttingen, 1957), pp. 401–402; scattered material on the Russian-German colonists during and after World War I is also contained in AGFM, T-136, roll SA-138.

preceded the Armistice it had become clear that strong sympathies for Germany existed among several elements of Russian society. These included the conservative circles made up of right-wing politicians, monarchists, aristocrats, and army officers of the old regime, certain members of the Russian Imperial family, and the Russian Germans. In contrast, talks conducted in Kiev in the summer of 1918 between General Groener, Field Marshal Eichhorn and the Kadet party leaders P. N. Miliukov, V. D. Nabokov, and A. I. Kaminka revealed with equal clarity that Germany could expect little from Russian liberals, vigorous supporters of the Russian war effort, friends of English parliamentary democracy and opponents of German influence in the western borderlands.[57] But how was Germany on the eve of her own defeat in the West to take advantage of such sympathy? Certain individuals with a good knowledge of both Russia and Germany were of help during the occupation in specific situations. Yet as groups the monarchists or the Russian Germans could offer little in return for any support the Germans might have given them. Should direction of the anti-Bolshevik armies mushrooming around the periphery of Russia be left to the Allies? What should be done with the thousands of political refugees and army officers now leaving Russia in the train of the retreating German armies? These and many other questions were soon intertwined with the problem of Russian war prisoners and refugees inside Germany.

Exodus: Politics of the Russian Civil War

The proper beginnings of a Russian emigration to Germany after the upheaval of 1917 date from the winter of 1918–1919, when thousands of refugees began to filter across the border with the retreating German army of occupation. For two years they lived in a state of suspension, observers and participants in the bloody civil war that raged inside their homeland. During this time émigré

[57] These talks are described from the Russian side by Miliukov in "Dnevnik P. N. Miliukova," *Novyi zhurnal*, No. 66 (1961), 173–203, and by Ambassador Mumm in his July 2, 1918, report to the Reichskanzler in AGFM, T-136, roll SA-139. The main reason for the failure of these talks was that while the Kadets urged a return to pre-1914 Russian boundaries the Germans talked enthusiastically about making the Ukraine a "second Bavaria."

politics revolved around questions related not so much to exile survival abroad as to the problems of aiding the White cause. The focus of their efforts was on the large reservoir of Russian war prisoners still left in Germany at the end of the war, and on persuading German officials and public opinion that the evils of the Russian Revolution would reach into Germany if the émigré cause did not receive the whole-hearted support of the Germans. The problems were new ones, but there was continuity too in the dominant role of the Baltic Germans in the politics of the emigration and the appearance of anti-Semitism as a new form of Russophobia.

By the spring of 1918 left-wing agitators, Russian and German, were reaching the POW camps. Repatriation of sick and wounded prisoners to Russia had begun in the winter of 1917–1918, with Red Cross trains running twice a week. Several thousand Russian and German prisoners were being exchanged every day, the Germans now being desperate for manpower on the western front.[58] An unexpected consequence of this exchange was Bolshevik agitation in the camps begun by the first Soviet representative in Berlin, Adolf Joffe, with the assistance of German propagandists drawn ✓from the ranks of the Independent Socialists and the Spartacists. Joffe himself was ingloriously ejected from Berlin in November 1918, but considerable headway had been made. A number of Russians released at the time of the Armistice fraternized openly with the Spartacists. Many were released from the camps and found themselves free to wander about the country or return home at will.[59]

The Armistice brought complete confusion regarding the fate of more than a million Russians still in Germany. Many, like the hero of Arnold Zweig's *Sergeant Grishka*, simply fled on foot to the East, passing an equally pathetic mass migration of German and Austrian prisoners on their way home from Russia. Poland and Lithuania tried without success to seal their borders. For several months the Allies did nothing about repatriation, leaving to the Germans the

[58] Willis, *Hoover*, pp. 11–12.
[59] *Ibid.*, pp. 16–17; H. Helbig, *Die Träger der Rapallo-Politik* (Göttingen, 1958), pp. 29–38.

problem of transporting Russian prisoners out of Germany. But German trains ran only as far as the East Prussian border, where the men were left to fend for themselves. Nevertheless, by January 1919 the number of Russian prisoners still remaining in Germany had probably been reduced to less than 700,000 men.

Then in early 1919 the Allied Armistice Commission proclaimed its interest in the fate of these Russians. On January 19 it forbade the further transportation of Russian prisoners out of Germany. Instead Marshal Foch proclaimed the existence of an Inter-Allied Commission for the Repatriation of Russian Prisoners of War in Berlin under the direction of an English officer, Major-General Sir Richard Ewart, who was later succeeded by Major-General Neill Malcolm. The Allies thus now claimed the right to decide what should be done with more than half a million Russians. The motive was quite clear. Further repatriation could only add manpower to the Red Army and facilitate the spread of Bolshevism inside, and possibly outside, Russia. To prevent this, the Allies were willing to accept the responsibility for feeding and housing these hundreds of thousands of prisoners; the burden fell on Herbert Hoover.

By April 1919 the Allied leaders revealed their true purposes. After stopping the flow of Russian prisoners out of Germany, they suddenly changed their mind and decided to reinstate repatriation proceedings. The Allied plan for "repatriation," however, was not to place Russian prisoners in Soviet hands but rather to send detachments of them off to the Baltic and South Russia to areas occupied by anti-Bolshevik armies. In this way the Allies transformed the issue of the fate of Russian prisoners in Germany into a part of the larger question of anti-Bolshevik military intervention.

The fledgling Weimar government opposed such a policy initially. Not only was Germany supposed to house, feed, and transport these prisoners (a task the Allies themselves were making impossible by confiscating German rolling stock), but German leaders feared reprisals against German prisoners still in Russia for any moves hostile to the Bolsheviks. A German agency for organizing the repatriation of Russian war prisoners had existed since January 1919, even though the Allies claimed jurisdiction over them. This

Reichszentralstelle für Kriegs- und Zivilgefangene was nominally under the direction of an SPD Reichstag deputy, but in fact was dominated by the vigorous personality of Moritz Schlesinger. Schlesinger, a socialist and a businessman, did what he could in 1919 to ship as many Russian prisoners out of Germany as possible and was not averse to dealing directly with the Bolsheviks. But he was in a difficult position, distrusted by the Allies for urging a prisoner exchange with the Bolsheviks and villified by the Bolsheviks for being unable to bring it about.[60]

Few of the Russians who began arriving in Berlin in the winter of 1918–1919, in the wake of the retreating German armies, considered themselves permanent émigrés. Flight from their homeland was a tactical retreat, and their mood was not one of despair but of defiance. Soon the Bolsheviks would fall before the White armies, supported by the Allies, and a return home would be inevitable. Until the collapse of the last of the White armies in the autumn of 1920, Berlin, like other European capitals, was not so much a refugee center as an outpost of the Russian Civil War, especially in the Baltic.

The political headquarters of the Whites abroad was not Berlin, however, but Paris, where the representatives of the Imperial and Provisional governments, as well as the non-Russian minorities, sought representation at the Peace Conference. In 1918 Paris became the center of activity for former Russian ambassadors caught abroad by the revolution, notably Mikhail Nikolaevich Giers, former ambassador to Italy; V. D. Nabokov, ambassador to London; and V. A. Maklakov, the Russian representative in Paris. They were joined by the representatives of the White armies—Prince G. E. Lvov of the government at Omsk and S. D. Sazonov, Kolchak's foreign minister. In the winter of 1918–1919 these men (except for Nabokov and Miliukov, who left for London) constituted themselves as the Russian Council of Ambassadors (Soveshchanie Poslov) in order to represent "Russian" interests before the powers and the negotiators at Versailles. Lvov was elected chairman and

---

[60] Gustav Hilger and A. Meyer, *The Incompatible Allies* (New York, 1953), pp. 23–25; L. Zimmermann, *Deutsche Aussenpolitik in der Aera der Weimarer Republik* (Göttingen, 1958), p. 118.

Generals Shcherbachev and Hermonius were named heads of the Military and Supply Commissions in charge of organizing aid to the armies inside Russia.[61]

In Berlin there was no comparable émigré organization for the simple reason that few refugees had yet arrived. When General Monkevich appeared in Berlin in early March 1919 as the representative of the Council of Ambassadors he observed that the Russian colony there still had no organization to defend its interests. The Russians he met were in a "Germanophile" mood, having returned from Russia with the German army, and there was a need to establish links with the Allies. To satisfy this need Monkevich established the Russian Military Mission in Berlin, unofficially recognized by the Allies as the legitimate émigré body with respect to Russian war prisoners. The prime function of Monkevich and his two assistants, Colonel A. F. Brant and A. F. Gamm (the former Russian consul-general in Berlin), was to ensure that Russian officers were not enrolled by the Germans for the campaign in the Baltic, but held in readiness for Allied dispatch to the army of General Yudenich. In this they failed. When Monkevich left in August, émigré politics was firmly under the control of the Baltic Germans.[62]

The Balts and their Russian allies began to organize themselves in the spring of 1919 under the direction of the Russian Civic Assembly (Russkoe obshchestvennoe sobranie) and its subsidiary Russian Committee. The Committee had been organized on April 3 as a welfare agency, supported by contributions from German business firms. The Assembly first met in May, claiming leadership of the entire Berlin colony. Both groups were dominated by Russian conservative politicians and Baltic Germans. Many were former army officers, and all had high hopes of winning German support for a monarchist army of Russian officers and prisoners of war which would be directed to the Baltic.[63]

Like these early organizations of the colony, the émigré press

[61] John Thompson, *Russia, Bolshevism, and the Versailles Peace* (Princeton, 1966), pp. 62–81.

[62] See the reports of Monkevich to Maklakov of March 10 and March 14, 1919, MaA, Series B, Paquet III, No. 6, folder III.

[63] BA/RD, folder 7 ("The Russian Committee in Berlin, 1919–1920"), folder 9 ("The Russian Civic Assembly in Berlin"), and folder 12 ("The Charity Section of the Russian Committee").

was also dominated by monarchists and Balts. *Luch sveta* (Ray of Light), which appeared in April in Berlin, edited by Colonel F. V. Vinberg, Peter Shabelsky-Bork, and Sergei Taboritsky, channeled the bitterness of the young army officers into a virulent anti-Semitism. It was *Luch sveta* which published the text of the notorious *Protocols of the Elders of Zion* and announced that "the common connection between our revolution and the German one is that both states were overthrown in a completely artificial way by means of a far-flung world network of intrigue and secret dealings of Jewish-Masonic organizations." [64] The daily newspaper *Prizyv* (The Call), organized in the summer of 1919, likewise railed against revolutionaries, the Allies, and the Jews, anticipated an uprising of "the Russian people" against the Bolsheviks, who represented "the powers and forces of the Jewish tribe," and rhapsodized about a "secret connection which unites the Russian and German soul, the fate of Russia and Germany." [65]

The German government was lukewarm toward the émigrés at this time. The Wilhelmstrasse had nothing to do with the French-oriented Russian Military Mission of Monkevich, and received the advances of the Russian Committee coolly. The Ministry of the Interior, too, refused the requests by the Committee that it be given authority to issue visas and passports to the émigrés. The émigrés consequently found it more profitable to deal directly with representatives of the German army in Berlin, officers who shared with the Russians a desire to maintain an anti-Bolshevik presence in the Baltic. Therefore the shadowy relations between General

[64] *Luch sveta*, I (April 1919), 50. Vinberg, born in Kiev in 1869, was a guards officer and a member of two right-wing political groups, the Russian Assembly and the Chamber of the Archangel Michael. Commander of a cavalry regiment during World War I, he became involved in Kornilov's intrigue against the Provisional government in 1917 and was later arrested and imprisoned by the Bolsheviks. In the Peter and Paul Fortress in Petrograd he met Peter Shabelsky-Bork, a young (b. 1893) right-wing army officer whose parents were close to Dubrovin and the Union of the Russian People, and through him his friend Sergei Taboritsky, another young officer. All three later fled to Kiev, where they fought under General Keller, and then to Germany in January 1919. Here they lived together, first in Berlin and after the Kapp Putsch in Munich. The Munich police reports on them are particularly useful: BHSA, MInn 71624.

[65] *Prizyv*, March 3, 1920, p. 4; February 8, 1920, p. 1.

Max Hoffman and other army officers and the circle of the Countess Kleinmichel at the Hotel Adlon or contacts being established between Russian and German army officers in the Baltic itself, proved in the end more significant than official ties with the Weimar government.[66]

The story of German military intervention during the Russian Civil War in the Baltic provinces in 1918–1919 has been told many times, although more often by Germans than by Russians.[67] Here was a remarkable coincidence of interests: the Allies were growing more and more deeply committed against the Bolsheviks; Russian émigré politicians and army officers were seeking a successful war of intervention; German Free Corps troops loosely controlled by the army command in the East (Grenzschutz Ost) were fighting out of habit, if not for excitement or land; and Baltic Germans were eager to turn German policy to their own advantage to regain lost lands and property from Bolsheviks or Latvians. Their meeting place in 1919 was Berlin, where the Weimar government could offer little resistance to a series of projects that often involved the use of Russian war prisoners for anti-Bolshevik purposes. Decisions were left largely in the hands of German commanding officers in

[66] On passports see the note from the German to the Prussian Ministry of the Interior, April 12, 1919 (AGFM, roll SA-102, vol. 60). On Kleinmichel's salon see Blücher, *Deutschlands Weg*, pp. 54, 61, 81.

[67] The monographic literature on the Baltic intervention and the German Free Corps is considerable. Especially good are R. G. L. Waite, *Vanguard of Nazism: The Free Corps Movement in Postwar Germany, 1918–1923* (Cambridge, Mass., 1952); F. W. von Oertzen, *Die deutschen Freikorps, 1918–1923* (5th ed.; Munich, 1939); Claus Grimm, *Jahre deutscher Entscheidung im Baltikum, 1918/1919* (Essen, 1939). Also useful are E. Anderson, "The British Policy toward the Baltic States, 1918–1920," *Journal of Central European Affairs*, XIX (1959), 276–289 and N. Berezhansky, "P. Bermondt v pribaltike v 1919 g.," *Istorik i sovremennik*, 1922, No. 1, pp. 5–87.

The memoir literature includes Awaloff, *Kampf;* Von der Goltz, *Meine Sendung* and *Als politischer General im Osten* (Leipzig, 1936); August Winnig, *Am Ausgang der deutschen Ostpolitik: Persönliche Erlebnisse und Erinnerungen* (Berlin, 1921); K. von Braatz, *Fürst Anatol Pawlowitsch Liewen* (Stuttgart, 1926); Bischoff, *Die letzte Front.* An indispensable collection of documents is E. L. Woodward and R. Butler, eds., *Documents on British Foreign Policy, 1919–1939* (London, 1936), III, part 1. Hereafter *DBFP.*

the Baltic or in East Prussia, men whom neither the Weimar government, the Allied Commission, nor the émigré Russians could control. It was precisely this lack of central direction which gave the politics of the Baltic intervention its air of intensity, intrigue, and unreality.

The formation of a Russian anti-Bolshevik army under German auspices began even before the Armistice. After the murder of Ambassador Mirbach an agreement was signed between German army officers and Russian monarchist politicians in Pskov on October 10 which provided for the creation of a new anti-Bolshevik force of Russian volunteers supported by German money and weapons.[68] That summer Russian officers and men were smuggled out of Bolshevik-held territory behind the German lines and were formed into a Northwest Army designed to secure the ordered withdrawal of German troops from the occupied areas of Russia after the Armistice and then to hold the Baltic against Allied or Bolshevik attack. The officers directing the Northwest Army were Rittmeister Paul von Rosenberg, a Russian guards officer, and Major Willisen, a German general staff officer and friend of General Groener assigned to Grenzschutz Ost. Willisen was an outspoken opponent of any cooperation with the Bolsheviks and, like General Hoffmann, had already become interested in the idea of organizing Russian army officers and monarchists against them.[69]

The Armistice and the German collapse which followed cut short the formation of the Northwest Army. For several weeks German officers insisted on keeping its organization in their own hands, but in late November they reluctantly agreed to turn authority over to a former Duma member, Baron A. A. Krüdener-Struve, a Baltic German. But in December events took a turn for the worse. Most German troops were on their way home. The Bolsheviks had moved

---

[68] Bischoff, *Letzte Front*, p. 25; Awaloff, *Kampf*, pp. 131–132; Anatoly Markov, "Entsiklopediia belago dvizheniia s 1917 po 1958 g.," (n.d.; four vols. typescript at the Hoover Library), I, 8.

[69] Bischoff, *Letzte Front*, p. 25; Awaloff, *Kampf*, pp. 66 ff., 131–132; Otto Schüddekopf, *Linke Leute von Rechts* (Stuttgart, 1960), pp. 63–64; Rittmeister Paul von Rosenberg, "Formirovanie russkikh natsional'nykh chastei na pribaltiiskom fronte," (Berlin, 1919; typescript in the folder "Baltiiskii vopros" of BC).

nearly ten thousand of their own forces into the region around Pskov. Rosenberg, after negotiating unsuccessfully with British officers at Libau for aid, left for Berlin in early January 1919 to seek support. Here he found precisely the manpower needed to organize and staff an anti-Bolshevik army: thousands of German junior officers now filtering back to Berlin from the front and several hundred thousand former Russian war prisoners.[70] He also discovered that he was not alone.

In December 1918 another Russian officer, Major-General Pototsky, arrived in Berlin from Kiev to recruit Russian war prisoners to serve in the anti-Bolshevik Volunteer Army of Anton Denikin. The Allied authorities in Berlin were receptive, and allowed Pototsky's Russian Delegation to begin recruitment under cover of the Red Cross emblem.[71] Rosenberg, disliking both Pototsky and the Allies, decided to turn to the German government instead. In March 1919 he submitted to the Socialist War Minister, Gustav Noske, a "Brief Report on the Northern Army" in which he argued that unless the German government supported an army of Russian volunteers against the Bolsheviks in the Baltic, communism would triumph in Germany.[72] According to Rosenberg, Noske "was very receptive to this project, and after explaining the present political position of Germany advised us to work through the main military headquarters in the East, having promised in turn to send the corresponding instructions there." [73] Noske's plan was in fact vetoed by the Weimar cabinet, fearful of Allied reprisals. Nevertheless it was soon put into effect through less official channels of the Reichswehr and the volunteer Free Corps.

In April and May 1919 Rosenberg was able, with German help, to begin organizing the first detachments of Russian troops for the Baltic. Grenzschutz Ost provided the over-all direction, and German army supply officers supervised the transporting of Russians from German POW camps to Berlin and then to Tilsit and the Baltic through the organization Werbebüro Baltenland. German indus-

[70] Grenzschutz Ost estimated the number of Russian war prisoners in Germany in March 1919 at about 300,000 men, which was probably conservative (Rosenfeld, *Sowjetrussland*, p. 207).

[71] Awaloff, *Kampf*, pp. 53–54, 120–121.   [72] *Ibid.*, pp. 541–543.

[73] Rosenberg, "Formirovanie," p. 7.

trialists and businessmen provided money for the entire project through the Lützow Free Corps. On May 30, 1919, the first train-load of Russian troops left Berlin for the Baltic as a German military band at the rail-siding struck up "God Save the Tsar." It was an un-likely beginning to an unlikely adventure.[74]

The Allied representatives in Berlin were less successful in their negotiations with officers of the Volunteer Army. In Berlin they dealt with Colonel Brant, who claimed jurisdiction over all Russian prisoners in Germany in the name of General Denikin. Having helped establish the Russian Military Mission there, Brant received encouragement from General Malcolm for his project but, like the Allies, was unable to assert any influence over the Reichswehr-con-trolled flow of officers and men to the Baltic that spring and sum-mer. Most of Brant's time was taken up by squabbles with other émigré representatives. In November he was replaced by Sergei Dmitrievich Botkin, representative of the émigré Council of Am-bassadors in Paris whose own Russian Delegation was soon to be-come the most important émigré organization in Berlin. By January 1920 a British observer could report that "Colonel Brant has no access to prisoners of war. He is believed to indulge in propaganda and intrigue when opportunity offers." [75]

Thus the use of former Russian prisoners in the Baltic remained in German hands, at first with Allied consent and later to their dismay. By the end of January 1919 Latvia had been overrun by Bolshevik troops. On February 1 General von der Goltz, commander of German forces in Finland, arrived in Libau to direct the opera-tions of a mixed force of German Free Corps and anti-Bolshevik Russian officers still in the area, designed to hold the Baltic against both the Red Army and the troops of Latvian and Estonian na-tionals. At first the Allies supported the offensive launched in early spring which resulted in the capture of Riga on May 23. But as the deliberations in Paris on the final terms of the Treaty of Versailles drew to a close, the Allies became ever more suspicious that the

---

[74] The organization and financing of the dispatch of Russian and German troops to the Baltic in 1919 is briefly described in *ibid.*, pp. 12–13.

[75] *DBFP*, III, 806–807; on Brant's machinations see the material in LA, folder 49.

main enemy in the Baltic might be not the Bolsheviks but the Germans. On June 12, 1919, the Council of Principal Allied and Associated Powers, sitting in Paris, ordered all German troops to leave the area. Von der Goltz ignored the order. Then on June 24 came the news of the Treaty, with its demand that all German forces be evacuated from the Baltic as soon as possible.

At this point Von der Goltz decided to put his operation under a Russian flag rather than disband it. A shadow anti-Bolshevik Russian army would be created, nominally under the White Russian officers of the Northwest Army but actually organized, financed, and staffed by Germans. Three small Russian detachments were already fighting in the area, under Prince Anatoly Pavlovich Lieven, Colonel P. M. Bermondt-Avalov, and a Colonel Vyrgolich. These forces could be expanded with Russian war prisoners now being shipped out of Berlin. Von der Goltz thus hoped to create an army Russian in form but still German in content. To this end he tried to recruit General V. I. Gurko, former Imperial chief of staff and commander-in-chief of the army under the Provisional government, now living in Copenhagen.[76] But Gurko declined the offer and Von der Goltz's second choice, Prince Lieven, had gone over to the British-sponsored army of General Yudenich, then operating out of Narva. In the end Von der Goltz chose as his Russian "commander" the adventurous Bermondt-Avalov.

Colonel Avalov belonged to the ranks of the young, pro-German Russian army officers who had become increasingly embittered over Russia's military defeat and the ensuing revolution, which they blamed on the British and the Jews. Born in Tiflis in 1884, Avalov claimed to be the son of a Prince Mikhail Antonovich Avalov and his wife, a woman who had later remarried a Russian guards officer named Bermondt.[77] There were less savory rumors, sponsored primarily by the British and by rival émigrés in Berlin, that Avalov was variously a low-born Caucasian of German extraction, part Jewish, a heavy drinker, and even a former band leader in the Russian army.[78] An excellent rider and a popular leader

[76] Bischoff, *Letzte Front*, p. 169; Von der Goltz, *Meine Sendung*, p. 224.
[77] Awaloff, *Kampf*, p. 460.
[78] Blücher, *Deutschlands Weg*, p. 77; DBFP, III, pp. 18, 86–87.

with his men, Avalov had seen service in both the Russo-Japanese War and World War I. In the summer of 1918 he fled to Kiev, where he ran a recruiting office for the German-sponsored Southern Army of Russian volunteers fighting the Bolsheviks. After the Armistice he appeared in Germany with a number of other Russian officers and was interned in a POW camp at Salzwedel. In early 1919 he made an attempt to organize Russian prisoners for use against the Bolsheviks and quickly discovered that Rosenberg and Pototsky were involved in similar activity. When the Reichswehr had completed arrangements for sending Russian troops to the Baltic with Free Corps divisions, Avalov was named one of three Russian commanding officers.[79]

During the summer and early autumn of 1919, Von der Goltz continued to fight in the Baltic, despite Allied pressure to remove him. By the end of the summer he commanded a substantial mixed force of some fifty thousand men, of whom about ten thousand were Russians.[80] But funds were running low. Von der Goltz had warned the Ministry of Finance in a letter of August 1, 1919, that "the Free Corps, which at the moment has no funds to speak of, will fall apart if it is not supported financially by us."[81] Until late September and early October about fifty million marks continued to arrive each month from the Verband für Handel und Industrie through the facilities of the Bleichröder Bank, along with war-surplus weapons and ammunition through the kindness of Krupp industries. But by October 1919 German intervention in the Baltic was coming to an end. The Allies were persistently demanding withdrawal, and German supporters were losing interest; industrialists were having second thoughts about the success of investing in anti-Bolshevik operations in the Baltic, and many were now switching their support to Denikin's forces in the south. In the end Von der Goltz and Avalov failed when their support ran out, but their

[79] Awaloff, *Kampf*, pp. 142–145.
[80] Avalov estimated a total force of 51–52,000 men in the Baltic, of which about 12,000 were Russians (*Kampf*, p. 219). In October 1919 the British estimated there were still 30–50,000 German troops in Latvia and 12,000 Russians (*DBFP*, III, 140–143).
[81] Rosenfeld, *Sowjetrussland*, p. 224.

support only ran out when it appeared that they could not succeed.[82]

Not only were the Allies and the Germans at odds over the use of Russian prisoners in the Baltic intervention, but the Russian émigrés in Berlin were also deeply divided. A. V. Belgard, a right-wing landowner from Kurland, was the leader of a Baltic German faction in Berlin that wished to keep operations in their homeland out of the hands of Avalov, whom they detested as an upstart junior officer. In May when Von der Goltz was searching about for a "Russian" commander, Belgard proposed Lieven, another Balt. In July, when it was clear that Von der Goltz intended to use Avalov as his commander, Belgard left Berlin for Mitau in hopes of convincing Von der Goltz of his mistake.[83] He was accompanied by yet another émigré candidate for control over Russian troops in the Baltic, General Vasily Biskupsky, undoubtedly one of the most universally disliked men of the Russian emigration. Biskupsky was another cavalry officer who arrived in Berlin in early 1919 where he quickly became embroiled with Colonel Vyrgolich against Avalov, with the British against the Germans, and with the Germans for money. Biskupsky told his German friends at the Wilhelmstrasse that he hoped to lead an army of Russian and German troops to the gates of Moscow and then to march on Paris. Unlike General Gurko, Biskupsky had absolutely no qualms about coming forward.[84]

On August 10, 1919, while Belgard and Biskupsky were in Mitau attempting to oust Avalov as commander of the Russian forces, a group of Baltic Germans in Berlin announced the formation of the Supreme Council of the Government of West Russia which would assume the political duties of the Northwest Army. Avalov was "temporarily" named commander-in-chief and A. K. Römmer, a Balt and a former member of the Petrograd Supply Board, was

---

[82] DBFP, III, 135–137, 207–208, 225–229, 294–298; Rosenfeld, Sowjetrussland, p. 229; Bischoff, Letzte Front, p. 185.

[83] Awaloff, Kampf, pp. 245–246; Von der Goltz, Meine Sendung, pp. 221–229; Pamiatka Liventsa, 1919–1929 g. (Riga, 1929), p. 27.

[84] Awaloff, Kampf, p. 245; Blücher, Deutschlands Weg, p. 57; Von der Goltz, Meine Sendung, p. 224.

named "civil governor." [85] The main function of the Council was to convince Allied representatives in Berlin that the anti-Bolshevik effort in the Baltic was in Russian hands; Von der Goltz correctly assumed that it had no real authority.[86] Nor did the Council's claim in early October to be a genuine West Russian government (timed to coincide with the last unsuccessful offensive against Riga) alleviate Allied fears of German control of the Baltic.

By mid-October the Baltic adventure was rapidly coming to an end. Under pressure from both the Allies and the German government, Von der Goltz at last returned to Germany, German economic and military aid came to an end, and the Free Corps were ordered to return home. Avalov's own Russian detachments, distrusted by both the Latvians and the British, followed suit in early November. Many went over to Yudenich and the British. In Berlin, under pressure from the Allies and the German left-wing parties, the recruitment of Russian prisoners and German Free Corps was no longer permitted.[87] German industrialists and Russian émigrés alike had realized the futility of continuing to support Avalov in the Baltic and were turning now to the White armies of General Denikin and Admiral Kolchak.[88] By the end of November the Russian forces of Avalov and Vyrgolich had crossed into East Prussia, where they were disarmed and interned in camps in Silesia: Neisse, Oppeln, and Altengrabow. The Allied Baltic Evacuation Commission an-

[85] The Council chairman was Baron Ludvig Karlovich Knorring and its members included H. V. von Berg; V. M. Poppe; Baron A. P. von Pilchau, chairman of the Latvian Baltic nobility; P. P. Durnovo, son of the former Minister of the Interior; and G. M. Deriugin (DBFP, III, 279).

[86] Von der Goltz, Meine Sendung, pp. 299–303.

[87] The Communists and the Independent Socialists in Germany had opposed the Baltic operation from the beginning. Hugo Haase consistently attacked Noske in the National Assembly for not evacuating all German troops from the area and putting a stop to further recruitment of Germans and Russians in Germany. But it was only in November—and then largely because of Allied pressure—that recruitment was forbidden, arrests made, and the flow of troops from East Prussia brought to a halt (DBFP, III, 118, 180, 224, 299; Waite, Vanguard, pp. 134–136).

[88] Krupp reportedly began shipping small arms and tanks to Denikin at this time and Gurko, Römmer, Von der Goltz, and Biskupsky were all dealing with Admiral Kolchak's representative in Berlin, Baron Korff (DBFP, III, 211–212, 225–229, 261–284).

94

nounced that it would not be responsible for the five thousand Russian officers and men who thus arrived in Germany, accepted dismissal pay, and settled down in the camps to await their fate.[89]

With the collapse of German intervention in the Baltic the affairs of the Berlin Russian colony had also fallen into disarray. Monkevich had returned to Paris in August, leaving the Russian Military Mission in the hands of the wily Brant, who maintained links with both the Inter-Allied Commission and Baltic German circles which he publicly criticized as too Germanophile. The Mission, he reported to General Shcherbachev on September 13, was in a "critical" position because the German government would not recognize it and the affairs of Russian prisoners had passed into the hands of the German government and the Balt-dominated West Russian government.[90] Neither the Allies nor the Russian Council of Ambassadors in Paris would allow Brant to procure available war surplus supplies being offered to him by German firms. Only on December 8, 1919, did the Allied Supreme Council in Paris suggest that the Russians could purchase German weapons and munitions "at their own risk and without the intervention of the Allied powers."[91] Brant's conversations with Ago von Maltzan at the Wilhelmstrasse and with War Minister Noske regarding German support for the dispatch of Russian prisoners and arms to the White armies were no more fruitful. Throughout the winter of 1919–1920 the Mission tried in vain to obtain authority over the remnants of Avalov's forces.

The intrigues of Brant, Biskupsky, Avalov, and the Baltic Germans in Berlin were well known to Russian émigré circles in Paris. Throughout the summer of 1919 plans were laid for the establishment there of a legitimate émigré organization capable of reconciling the warring political factions, attending to the needs of the

---

[89] By mid-December 1919 most Russian officers and men under Avalov and Vyrgolich were in Germany, except for a small number which remained to fight under Yudenich (*DBFP*, III, 244–245, 257–258; Awaloff, *Kampf*, pp. 232–235).

[90] Brant to Shcherbachev, September 13, 1919 (WA, folder 192).

[91] British Military Mission in Berlin to Brant, December 11, 1919 (WA, folder 33).

refugees, and representing the interests of the Russian community to both the Allies and the German government. Brant himself estimated in the autumn that there were already nearly 100,000 Russian refugees in Berlin alone, with no single administrative body capable of speaking for them.[92] It was to provide such organization that Brant was informed in early November that the Council of Ambassadors was sending to Berlin Sergei Dmitrievich Botkin, a former Russian ambassador in Rome, to take over émigré affairs. Neither Botkin nor anyone else realized at the time that he would become the dominant figure in Russian affairs in Germany until the 1930's. Indeed, it is Botkin's stream of intelligent and moderate reports which provide the historian with the most valuable and microscopic glimpse into the life of the Berlin Russian colony.[93]

The Council of Ambassadors conceived of the idea of sending Botkin to Berlin as early as June 1919, when Pototsky, Monkevich, and Brant were active only as an adjunct to the Inter-Allied Commission and concerned mainly with Russian prisoners of war. To give Botkin's mission an air of legitimacy it was thought that he should go as either a representative of the Kolchak government, or an assistant to the Dutch or Spanish missions in Berlin. In the end he arrived in November as a representative of the Red Cross. Here he found expected resistance from Brant but with the assistance of his "prewar connections" with Baron Ago von Maltzan, head of the newly constituted Eastern Section of the Wilhelmstrasse, was able to consolidate the functions of the existing Russian Committee and the Russian Military Mission into a new organization, the Russian Delegation on War Prisoners and Refugees. Never officially recognized by the German government, Botkin's Russian Delegation became within a short time the *de facto* representation of the

[92] Brant to Shcherbachev, November 28, 1919 (WA, folder 192).

[93] Botkin's reports may be found in any (and sometimes all) of five archives: BA/RD, which contains the official file of reports of his Russian Delegation; GA, which contains the reports by Botkin received in Paris by Giers; the Botkin Collection of personal materials at the Columbia University Russian Archive; AA and AGFM, which contain copies of reports received by the German Foreign Ministry. BA/RD is by far the most complete collection, with 67 folders of material, much of which is unavailable in any of the other archives.

Russian colony in Berlin, a position which it maintained against pressures from the left and right into the Nazi era.[94]

Botkin, like other Russian political leaders in Berlin in the winter of 1919–1920, soon found himself embroiled in efforts to organize the dispatch of men and weapons to the last of the White armies forming inside Russia under the direction of General Wrangel. In so doing he continued to work as compatibly as possible with Brant, whose Russian Military Mission had gradually become the "military section" of the Russian Delegation. He also helped organize an émigré Russian Red Cross in Berlin in December 1919 under the direction of Baron A. A. Wrangel, which promptly involved itself with Russian war prisoners. Like other émigré organizations, the Red Cross not only helped to alleviate the daily needs and suffering of the indigent but also lobbied for the White cause. In January 1920 Botkin and Brant had been authorized by General Hermonius to purchase some 70,000,000 cartridges at a cost of 20,000,000 marks through the German Schilde Consortium, and by late February a ship was loading them at Hamburg for dispatch to the Crimea.[95]

In early 1920 the émigrés continued to seek out military support in Berlin. Biskupsky, Brant, A. I. Guchkov, and two former recipients of German aid, General P. N. Krasnov and Hetman Skoropadsky, all wanted control over the remnants of the Northwest Army and war prisoners for future use against the Bolsheviks. Biskupsky's claim to the title of Inspector-General of Volunteer Forces on German Territory was disputed by General Shcherbachev, however, who refused his requests for aid "in view of the political character of your activity in Germany at the present time."[96] To remove the control of Russian troops in Germany from the hands of Biskupsky and Brant, Shcherbachev in April sent on to Berlin

---

[94] The origins of the Russian Delegation are described by Botkin in his retrospective report entitled "Istoricheskaia spravka ob organizatsii In den Zelten S. Botkina," written in 1929 (BA/RD, folder 58). On Maltzan and the émigrés see also Blücher, *Deutschlands Weg*, pp. 52–53, and Zimmermann, *Deutsche Aussenpolitik*, pp. 36–38, 118–119.

[95] On the organization of the Russian Red Cross in Berlin see BA/RD, folder 59, and A. A. von Lampe, *Puti vernykh* (Paris, 1960), pp. 89–108; on ammunition procurement see WA, folders 26 and 33.

[96] Shcherbachev to Biskupsky, February 20, 1920 (LA, folder 26).

Lieutenant General I. A. Holmsen (Khol'msen) a former Russian officer and military attaché who had been active in London shipping former Russian war prisoners to the White armies.[97] He soon discovered that German enthusiasm for selling or shipping war surplus material to Russia had waned because of fear for the safety of German war prisoners still under Soviet control, and he had to report to General Hermonius that the munitions at Hamburg would have to be transferred to France for shipment.[98] To add to the confusion, there arrived in Berlin in July 1920 a representative of General Wrangel, General A. A. von Lampe, who joined in the recruiting efforts through his own Mutual Aid Society for Officers of the Russian Army and Fleet and the Central Union of Russian War Invalids. Like Botkin, Lampe established contacts with Maltzan and his *Ministerialdirektor* Behrendt at the Wilhelmstrasse as an unofficial representative of the Russian colony but found little real support.[99] Along with Holmsen, he headed the military section of Botkin's Russian Delegation. Thus the last effort to support the White armies was subsumed under a single authority coordinated with the efforts of the men in Paris.

In the meantime, Biskupsky, deprived of his official position in Berlin, had embarked on his own scheme to involve a group of Russian, German, and Hungarian army officers in the formation of a "monarchist army" to restore the old regimes of central and eastern Europe. Holmsen was aware of the meetings of Biskupsky, General Hoffmann and others at Hoffmann's house out of which the plan emerged.[100] But the focus of activity was not in Berlin but in Munich, where such right-wing Russians as Vinberg and Markov II had fled in the wake of the Kapp Putsch.

On March 12, 1920, a detachment of German troops from Camp Doberitz outside Berlin, the Erhardt Brigade, marched into the capital and installed as head of a new government an East Prussian

[97] See Holmsen's unpublished memoirs in the Columbia University Russian Archive, "Na voennoi sluzhbe v Rossii: Vospominaniia ofitsera general'nago shtaba," (mimeo; New York, 1953), pp. 70–71.

[98] Holmsen to Hermonius, April 25, 1920 (WA, folder 26).

[99] Botkin to Giers, August 14, 1920 (GA, folder 32); Lampe to Paris, November 22, 1921 (LA, folder 53).

[100] Holmsen, "Sluzhbe," p. 73.

civil servant, Wolfgang Kapp. The Kapp Putsch, as it became known, proved short-lived, primarily because of a successful general strike launched a few days later by German socialists. Kapp and his followers, mainly army officers fresh from the campaigns of 1919 in Silesia and the Baltic and some conservative politicians, resigned within five days of taking office and fled to Munich.

The Berlin press was full of charges of the complicity of Russian army officers in the Kapp affair. The possibility that Russian prisoners might now be used against the Republic from the right could no longer be discounted. Avalov denied any part in the Kapp Putsch, and the camp newspaper at Altengrabow where his troops were interned enjoined Russian officers there to behave correctly and not to become involved in German politics—although only after the failure of the putsch had become evident.[101] But Biskupsky was very much involved. As Kapp's main contact with Russian officers in Berlin, he had apparently signed some agreements with Kapp providing for the "restoration of the monarch in Russia" and future cooperation with Germany. In return Biskupsky received subsidies from Kapp for some of his projects involving the use of Russian prisoners against the Bolsheviks.[102] While there was a distinct comic-opera tone to Biskupsky's machinations in early 1920, they were sufficient to alarm the German press.

The Kapp Putsch succeeded in bringing together a number of right-wing Russian and German officers, many of whom now drifted south to Munich in the aftermath of the affair to escape the Berlin police. In the spring and early summer of 1920 a group of them devised an astounding scheme to organize a counterrevolutionary army of Germans, Russians, Hungarians, and Italians to restore the empires of eastern and central Europe and stamp out Bolshevism. On the German side the two major figures involved were General Ludendorff and his aide, Max Bauer; the émigré Russians were represented by Biskupsky. The plan was to recruit Free Corps troops, Russian war prisoners and émigrés, and members of the Bavarian Einwohnerwehr into a force capable of sweeping through Austria,

[101] *Moment* (Altengrabow), March 20, 1920, p. 1; Awaloff, *Kampf*, p. 438.
[102] J. Trebitsch-Lincoln, *The Autobiography of an Adventurer* (New York, 1932), pp. 158–159.

Bavaria, Czechoslovakia, and then Russia to restore the old monarchies: a "Greater Germany" made up of Germany, Austria, and parts of Poland and Czechoslovakia; a "Greater Hungary" composed of Hungary, Slovakia, Rumania, and Yugoslavia; and a monarchist Russia again ruling Poland, Galicia, and Bessarabia.[103]

The dream of a restoration of the old empires of Central and Eastern Europe toppled by the chaos of war and revolution probably originated at a meeting of disgruntled German army officers at Regensburg in Bavaria in early May 1920. Many had participated in or supported the Kapp Putsch and now sought to regroup their forces for another assault on the Weimar Republic. Among those present were Bauer, Biskupsky, and J. Trebitsch-Lincoln, a Hungarian adventurer who had been Kapp's "press director." Within a few weeks of this meeting Bauer and Trebitsch-Lincoln appeared in Budapest, where they succeeded in interesting a group of Hungarian army officers in the plan. Bauer brought a personal letter to them from Ludendorff, and it was decided that more concrete plans would be made at a meeting in Budapest in June.[104]

In early June, Colonel Bauer telegraphed Major Stephani in Munich to arrange transportation for Ludendorff to Budapest as soon as possible. Stephani himself had been one of the leaders of the anti-Republican National Alliance (Nationale Vereinigung) in Germany, commander of the Potsdam Free Corps and, along with Bauer, a leading officer in the military group around Kapp.[105] But General Ludendorff was now in Berlin attempting to influence preparations for the general elections on June 6 to replace the Weimar National Assembly by a regular Reichstag and so was unable to come to Budapest. When the Budapest meeting finally was held, in the second week in July, Biskupsky and Bauer were the main plotters.

Biskupsky's scheme was little more than a dream, the organization "simultaneously of the whites, reds, greens, separatists, except

---

[103] Information on this affair comes primarily from Trebitsch-Lincoln and the documents published by the Russian émigré daily *Volia Rossii* in Prague: December 5, 7, 8, 9, and 24, 1920.

[104] *Ibid.*, December 5, 1920, p. 1; December 8, 1920, p. 2.

[105] Waite, *Vanguard*, pp. 198, 200, 202.

for those working with Poland, etc." into a huge "general plan" which would restore the monarchies by military means as follows:

(1) The Red Army liquidates Poland and re-establishes the boundaries of 1914;

(2) Wrangel's army fights a holding action until the moment when the 1914 borders are re-established by the Red Army;

(3) Ukrainian partisans attack the Poles;

(4) Belorussians conclude an agreement with Moscow and attack the Poles when the borders are re-established;

(5) Commanding officers of the Red Army (MAINLY Officers of the Old Regime) prepare for an uprising (putsch) and the organization of a military dictatorship;

(6) Wrangel begins an offensive in coordination with the "military center;"

(7) Armies of the Central European states mobilize to face the threat of Bolshevism and attack the Communist armies, with White Russian troops in the vanguard. The people will be prepared through propaganda and the distribution of an unlimited quantity of Russian money to organize an anti-Communist movement in the rear of the Communist army;

(8) Ukrainian partisans commanded by officers of the old regime attack the Communist army from the rear;

(9) Belorussia invites Russian and German volunteers to clear their country of the Communists;

(10) White sympathizers in the Red Army organize an uprising in the capitals and invite Russian, German, and Hungarian volunteers to restore public order;

(11) A union of Russia, Germany, and Hungary is announced on the basis agreeable to all three states, promising eternal peace and mutual economic well-being;

(12) THE THRONES WILL BE RESTORED and the republican states returned to the position which they deserve.[106]

Bauer contributed the idea of a series of acts of political terror to be carried out in Germany and elsewhere by Orgesch, the combination of German nationalist and military organizations which had grown out of the Regensburg meeting. Using Bavaria as a base of operations, the Free Corps would join Austrian paramilitary

[106] *Volia Rossii*, December 5, 1920, p. 2.

forces in occupying south central Europe to the Adriatic. There was also talk of involving Wrangel's military representatives in Paris, the Italian General Caviglia, and the editor of the Milan daily *Popolo d'Italia*, Benito Mussolini, in the operation.[107]

The Budapest conversations, played up by the left-wing press throughout Europe as an international monarchist plot, naturally came to nothing. But like the continual plans for an anti-Bolshevik army discussed by Russian émigrés with General Hoffmann until 1922, the whole affair served at least to establish contact between Russian and German army circles and monarchists. As such it was only an initial episode.

By the end of the summer of 1920 the German government was more receptive to the activities of the Berlin émigrés. The Red Army had failed in its efforts to defeat the Poles on their own territory, and the army of General Wrangel was receiving substantial military aid from France and England. The news in August that the French government would lend its full political and military support to Wrangel produced a sensation among the Russians in Berlin, where Botkin, Lampe, and Holmsen were continuing their efforts to organize the flow of men and munitions to South Russia. The Wilhelmstrasse was at least benevolent about this. Maltzan promised Botkin that the shipment of Russian officers to Wrangel would be allowed if transit visas could be obtained from the Czech government. This proved difficult, however, and by the end of August only 155 Russian officers had succeeded in leaving Germany for the Crimea, traveling individually as civilians. By the time the French government agreed to provide visas in late September, Wrangel's demise was inevitable.[108]

Thus most of the activity in support of Wrangel did not proceed beyond the planning stage in Germany. Avalov talked of raising money in Sweden for a new army under his command and French direction. Krasnov, too, had a scheme for sending a cavalry regi-

[107] *Ibid.*, December 8, 1920, pp. 1–2; Trebitsch-Lincoln, *Autobiography*, pp. 210, 218.
[108] Botkin to Giers, August 23, 1920 (GA, folder 32); Holmsen to Monkevich, August 11, 1920 and to Miller, August 25, 1920 (MiA, folder 17).

ment to the Crimea. By October, German industrialists were preparing to make war surplus materials and weapons available to the émigrés and the Wilhelmstrasse was helping dispatch a German Red Cross mission and a shipment of medical supplies for Wrangel. A Swedish syndicate in Berlin was also planning to supply Wrangel with several thousand hand grenades. But before any of these preparations could be turned into concrete support, Wrangel's army had been defeated and was in the process of evacuation. Most of the Russian officers who succeeded in leaving Germany arrived too late to be of assistance.[109]

The various attempts by émigré army officers to use Russian prisoners of war for their anti-Bolshevik enterprises had not gone unnoticed in Germany. After the return of Avalov's troops from the Baltic in late 1919 the left-wing press had conducted a steady attack on this activity, especially the Communist daily newspaper *Die rote Fahne*, which charged that Russian troops in Germany were actually "soldiers of the Russian Red Army" who were being illegally used in the civil war by "the Bermondt clique in the Foreign Office." In the Reichstag the Independent Socialists in December 1920 charged that "they want to make White Guardists out of the Red Guardists, ready to fight against the Soviet government in Russia or with the reaction against the republic in Germany." The German government, "hand in hand with the Russian counter-revolutionaries," was "carrying on propaganda and planting informers among Russian war prisoners and interned Red Army soldiers"; Avalov's troops at Altengrabow "are not treated as prisoners or even as internees but as Allies." Botkin's Russian Delegation, claimed a USPD delegate "has been recognized by the German government to the extent that the German government accepts the passports which it revises or produces"; Wrangel's representative in Berlin, A. A. von Lampe, was organizing the dispatch of Russian prisoners to South Russia "right under the very eyes of the government." [110]

The Kapp Putsch, the incredible schemes of Biskupsky and

---

[109] Holmsen to Shcherbachev, September 5, October 5, 8, 18, 1920 (LA, folder 52).

[110] *Die rote Fahne*, 1920: January 9, p. 1; May 27, p. 1; October 9, p. 2; *Verhandlungen des Reichstags, I: Wahlperiod 1920*, 346, pp. 1792–1793, 1807.

Bauer, and the attempts to send Russian prisoners of war to Wrangel in 1920 all indicated to the German government the dangers of maintaining Russian prisoners in Germany. If Avalov's Baltic adventure proved to the Soviets the utility of former prisoners in an anti-Bolshevik army of intervention, the Kapp Putsch and the warm relations between Russian officers and their German counterparts indicated to Weimar policy makers the connection between Russian war prisoners and the right-wing enemies of the Republic. By the spring of 1920 direct negotiations between the German and Soviet governments on the completion of repatriation were not merely convenient; they were mutually desirable. It was the reconciliation of the two governments which, in turn, defined the permanent legal statelessness of the Russian émigrés.

Two broad types of relationships between Russia and Germany had seemed possible after the Armistice. The first involved an overturn of the Bolshevik regime in Russia, the restoration of a non-Bolshevik government, and a subsequent alliance with a conservative Germany. Certain German army officers such as Hoffmann, Ludendorff, and Groener supported such a plan, in company with Russian émigrés of various political leanings in Berlin. The second was that foreseen by the Soviet leaders and the German left: a revolution in Germany followed by an alliance between two Soviet neighbors. Both of these relationships depended on the demise of either the Soviet government or the Weimar Republic, that is, not only on mutual interests in foreign policy but on changes in domestic politics as well.

The accommodation between Soviet Russia and Weimar Germany which ultimately emerged in the 1920's was neither of these. Rather it was an alliance between a nonrevolutionary and a revolutionary government predicated on common attitudes which overrode the differences in domestic politics: notably, hostility toward the Allies for the Versailles treaty and the support of White movements in the Russian Civil War; distaste for the new Polish state created from the former territories of Prussia and Russia; and a common interest in military collaboration. In the late summer and early autumn of 1919, when the punitive terms of the Treaty of Versailles became known and the failure of German anti-Bolshevik intervention in the Baltic was recognized, this new relationship began to emerge out of the conversations of Karl Radek, the Soviet leader held in Moabit prison in Berlin, with such realistic and sympathetic Germans as the industrialists Walther Rathenau and Felix Deutsch, the journalist Maximilian Harden, the former German representative in Petrograd, Admiral Hintze, and army officers such as General von Reibnitz and Bauer. In the winter of 1919–1920 these conversations developed into more formal negotiations over the issue of the prisoner-of-war exchange.

Developments in the war prisoner issue paralleled these more general changes in Weimar-Soviet relations. From the Armistice until the spring of 1919 Russian prisoners were involved in various attempts at revolution in Germany aimed at bringing about an alliance between a Soviet Germany and Russia (Joffe's propaganda, the March Days in Berlin, the Bavarian Soviet Republic). In the spring and summer of 1919 other former POW's were directed to the Baltic in an attempt to effect a Russo-German alliance based on the overthrow of Bolshevism in Russia. Thus by the end of 1919 Russian prisoners in Germany had been involved in the failures of two attempts to alter domestic politics in Russia and Germany. But if they could not be used by either government against the other, perhaps their removal could serve to establish a third, more realistic relationship between them.

Therefore, in the end, three factors contributed to the opening up of negotiations between the Weimar and Soviet governments on this issue in the winter of 1919–1920: (1) the Allies by the autumn had abdicated their control over Russian prisoners in Germany; (2) the attempts by Germans to use these prisoners against the Bolsheviks in the Baltic had failed; (3) the existence of substantial numbers of Russian prisoners in German camps was no longer desirable to the German and Soviet governments because of the cost of housing and feeding them and because of their potential or actual involvement in left- and right-wing plots against the Republic.

The Allies, as we have seen, had taken over control of Russian prisoners in Germany in the winter of 1918–1919 because they feared that repatriated prisoners would aid the Bolsheviks and

105

hoped that, if directed to the anti-Bolshevik armies, the prisoners might topple the Bolshevik regime. Lloyd George frankly suggested to the Supreme War Council in Paris on January 12,1919, that "if we decided to fight Bolshevism, this would be one of the methods available." At the same time Marshal Foch announced that the Allies would now send Russian prisoners still in Germany not to Soviet Russia but to "provinces which are free from the Soviets' regime." [111] Within a few months it was clear that to keep hundreds of thousands of Russian prisoners in Germany would be expensive; moreover they might now be profitably employed by German forces in the Baltic. With this in mind the Allied Control Commission in Berlin decided on April 3, 1919, that "the retention of prisoners of war was impossible, and that the Germans should be allowed to organize their repatriation in their own way, provided none were forced to return home who might not wish to." [112] Thus until the early summer of 1919 the Allies supported the shipment of Russian prisoners to the Baltic as an integral part of German intervention in the area.

When the Allies demanded that Von der Goltz withdraw from the Baltic that summer they also forbade the further shipment of Russian prisoners there. Apparently they felt that the Baltic adventure was strengthening German power in the area more than it was hurting the Bolsheviks. Moreover the cost of feeding and housing the prisoners, now being borne by the French government and the British and American Red Cross, was proving larger than expected. Their solution was to let the Germans take over full responsibility for Russian prisoners, including both the cost of retaining them in Germany and their repatriation. While the original decision to wash their hands of the problem was expressed in a Supreme War Council resolution of August 2, 1919, the Allies continued to argue over whether or not to reimburse the German government for expenses in this connection. Finally, in November 1919, the Allies informed the German government that "the Allied and associated powers

[111] *Papers Relating to the Foreign Relations of the United States, 1919: The Paris Peace Conference* (13 vols.; Washington, D.C., 1942–1947), III, 472, 479.

[112] *Ibid.*, IV, p. 706.

have decided to incur no more expenses for the Russian prisoners of war in Germany, except those necessary for the upkeep of their representative to the International Commission in Berlin." [113] It was to prove a fateful decision.

Thus in November 1919 the repatriation of Russian war prisoners represented for Weimar not only an opportunity to open up conversations with the Soviet government, but a political necessity. Attempts to use these prisoners against the Bolsheviks in the Baltic had now proved a failure; those men returning with Avalov to Germany represented a possible threat from the right to the Republic; the Allies had formally declared that the German government was to deal with the problem. All that was needed was a gesture of interest from Moscow. It appeared in the person of Victor Kopp, who arrived in Berlin in November to replace Karl Radek as the informal Soviet representative in Germany.

During the winter of 1919–1920 Kopp sounded out the German government not only on direct negotiations concerning repatriation but also on the conversion of POW missions into consulates. From the start the POW exchange was considered a prelude to normal diplomatic relations. At first the German reaction was tentative. Kopp found considerable enthusiasm only from Schlesinger and Gustav Hilger at the Reichszentralstelle and from Maltzan at the Wilhelmstrasse. Hilger was particularly useful at this time, since he not only was in charge of Russians in German camps but was himself a Moscow German who had emigrated after the Armistice.[114] But otherwise German officials moved slowly, wary of antagonizing the Allies. Probably the Allied publication of a long list of Germans accused of being "war criminals" was the catalyst that

[113] *Ibid.*, IX, p. 383.

[114] Hilger was an invaluable intermediary on the POW exchange. Educated in both Russian and German schools, he returned to Russia in 1910 at the age of twenty-four as a machine-construction engineer. During the war he worked for the Swedish consulate representing the interests of German war prisoners interned in Russia. He stayed on in this capacity for the German government after Brest-Litovsk, but decided to emigrate to Germany after the Armistice. There he became Schlesinger's assistant in charge of Russian prisoners in Germany. In the 1920's and 1930's he played an important role in Soviet-German relations, ultimately as an attaché and adviser at the German embassy in Moscow. See Hilger and Meyer, *Incompatible Allies.*

precipitated the decision of the German government at a secret cabinet session of February 13, 1920, to open formal negotiations with the Soviet government on repatriation.[115] Two weeks later Maltzan informed Botkin that talks with Kopp were about to begin.[116]

On April 19, 1920, the first Soviet-German agreement since the Armistice was signed on "the mutual repatriation of prisoners of war and interned civilians." The agreement provided for the repatriation "without delay" of all Russian prisoners in Germany and German prisoners in Russia who desired to return to their homelands through "welfare centers" in Moscow and Berlin, representing the two governments. More significant for the future, Article III defined as Russian prisoners of war, "all Russians or former Russian subjects who have come into German hands, whether fighting for the former Russian Empire or for the Russian Soviet Republic, or against the Russian Soviet Republic." The treaty thus challenged the legitimacy of any non-Soviet émigré organization in Berlin, such as Botkin's Russian Delegation, and claimed jurisdiction over all Russians in Germany. By such an agreement the Weimar government came close to extending *de jure* recognition to the Soviet government.[117]

The treaty of April 19 was ratified by the Reichstag and the Soviet government in May, as war broke out between Russia and Poland. The successes enjoyed by the Red Army in its advance on Warsaw that summer accelerated Berlin's interest in expanding relations with the Soviet government. Alarmists warned of "Asiatic hordes" pouring into defenseless Germany from the east; Ludendorff told Maltzan that the Russians could easily advance to the Rhine. A second agreement of July 7 between the two governments defined the "scope and duties of welfare centers" to include "in the widest sense the interests of military and civilian prisoners"; it also provided for postal and courier service between Moscow and Berlin.[118] Hilger left for Moscow in early June to handle the

---

[115] Blücher, *Deutschlands Weg*, p. 97.

[116] Botkin to Giers, February 29, 1920 (GA, folder 32).

[117] The text of the treaty is contained in L. Shapiro, ed., *Soviet Treaty Series* (Washington, D.C., 1950), I, 40–41.

[118] *Ibid.*, p. 50.

affairs of German prisoners in Russia, while Kopp remained in Berlin. Finally, toward the end of July, Foreign Minister Walther Simons sent Kopp to Moscow with a letter to his Soviet counterpart, Chicherin, urging the "resumption of normal relations" between Moscow and Berlin." [119]

During late 1920 and early 1921 the final phase of the repatriation story was played out in Berlin and Moscow. The Russian Civil War had ended with a Bolshevik victory; the vindictiveness of the Allies toward Germany was apparent. By March 1921 the final exchange of prisoners between the two countries was completed; the welfare centers in both capitals had lost their *raison d'être*. The way to more permanent relations now seemed open. Thus Hilger and Schlesinger negotiated with Kopp in Moscow the Russo-German treaty of May 6, 1921, which formally supplemented the April 19, 1920, POW agreement but in fact foreshadowed Rapallo. The treaty of May 6 provided for permanent courier service between Germany and Soviet Russia and expanded the jurisdiction of the POW missions in both countries to include now "the protection of the interests of their own nationals." The missions were to have commercial representatives attached to them and would be known as "German Representatives in Russia" and "Representatives of the RSFSR in Germany" respectively. The legitimacy of the émigré Russian organizations was also now denied, since the Soviet delegation would be "the only body representing the Russian state in Germany." [120]

The Russo-German treaty of May 6, 1921, thus marked the shift from the limited ties of the POW exchange to *de facto* recognition of the Soviet government by Weimar Germany. As such it was a triumph for the "Easterners" in Germany, notably Maltzan, Schlesinger, and Hilger, who had long sought such a normalization of relations with Soviet Russia. Not all Germans shared these views. Schlesinger had gone to Moscow in 1921 despite the objections of Behrendt, who opposed any negotiations beyond those related to the prisoner exchange. His views were apparently overridden by

---

[119] Blücher, *Deutschlands Weg*, pp. 97–99; Hilger and Meyer, *Incompatible Allies*, pp. 25–26, 50.
[120] Shapiro, *Treaty Series*, pp. 117–120.

Simons, who had given Schlesinger *carte blanche* in his talks with Kopp. Even at the last moment the agreement seemed in jeopardy when communist-led outbreaks of violence in the Ruhr made many Germans wary of Moscow's intentions and the Kronstadt rebellion made them equally tentative about the stability of the Bolshevik regime. In the end only Simon's tenacity, the signs of stability contained in Lenin's proclamation of the New Economic Policy, and the concurrent Soviet negotiations for a trade agreement with the British government turned the tide.[121]

By the winter of 1920–1921 the Russian Civil War had been brought to a close by the final defeat of Wrangel's army and Soviet-German relations were opening up through the prisoner exchange. The Russian refugees now flooding into Germany were thus no longer simply an adjunct to the White armies and governments inside Russia but political émigrés, defeated at home and facing the prospect of new isolation abroad. It is at this point that one can begin to speak of the existence of the Russian emigration as a political and juridical entity with its own institutions, its own problems. The Russian Germans who had played a significant role in the politics of the civil war—Brant, Holmsen, Lampe, A. A. Wrangel, Vinberg, Countess Kleinmichel, Belgard, and others—would continue to dominate the institutional life of the Russian colony and the monarchist movement. They soon found themselves to be a critical bridge between the Russian emigration and German society, easing the complex process of social and political assimilation for the Russians and acting as influential interpreters of Russian events for the Germans.

121 Hilger and Meyer, *Incompatible Allies*, pp. 65–67.

III

Community of Despair:
Émigré Institutions

A Shipwrecked World

In the period 1919–1923, Germany, in particular Berlin, was the main population center of the Russian emigration. By the end of 1919 approximately 70,000 Russians were living in Berlin alone and were arriving at a rate of more than 1,000 a month. By the autumn of 1920 the total number of Russian refugees in Germany may have been as many as 560,000, including individuals in transit to the United States or other European countries and war prisoners awaiting repatriation. In the spring of 1921 estimates of the total number of Russians living in Germany dropped to below 300,000 and at the beginning of 1922 to less than 250,000. After a rise to nearly half a million again in 1922–1923, when émigrés moved to Germany from France because of Germany's lower cost of living, there was a general exodus from Germany in 1923 to France, Czechoslovakia, the Balkans, Soviet Russia, and elsewhere, caused mainly by the collapse of the mark and the worsening political situation.[1] In 1925, the German census recorded over 250,000 individ-

[1] *Berliner Tageblatt*, December 23, 1919, p. 1; *Rul'*, January 29, 1921, p. 5, and February 4, 1921, p. 4. J. H. Simpson, *The Refugee Problem* (London, 1939), pp. 82, 559, 561. The figure of 300,000 for early 1921 is given by a Soviet study of the emigration (Vladimir Belov, *Beloe pokhmel'e: Russkaia emigratsiia,* [Moscow, 1923], p. 44) and by the Central Information Office of Countess Bobrinsky in Constantinople, which kept statistical data on the emigration from May 1920 until August 1921. The estimate of 230–250,000 Russians in Germany for January 1, 1922, is that of Dr. A. Iziumov and is based on materials in the émigré Prague Archive.

uals in Germany who had lived within the boundaries of the Russian Empire in 1914.[2] But only about 80,000 were Russians; the majority were Poles. After 1923 the number of Russians in Germany steadily declined until by 1930 there were less than 100,000, as compared with close to 200,000 in France at that time. Paris replaced Berlin as the capital of the diaspora.

There were many reasons why Germany became the center of the emigration up until 1923. Geographically, Germany was the closest Western European country which could provide refuge. Entry visas were easy to obtain from the German government. Most important, life in Germany was relatively cheap in these years. Jobs were difficult to find, but the low value of the mark meant that accumulated savings and payments from international and émigré welfare organizations, in U.S. dollars or Swiss and French francs, went a long way. German book publishing was another attraction for émigré writers and politicians. But in 1923 these propitious economic conditions disappeared with the inflation and temporary stabilization produced through conversion to the Rentenmark, a new currency based on German land and industrial facilities. Like the German middle classes, many Russians lost their savings and their jobs. Prices rose drastically and German publishing houses, which had provided employment for many Russians, closed their doors. In short, Germany's advantages relative to Soviet Russia and other Western European countries came to an end and many émigrés moved on.

In its social composition the Russian emigration to Germany in the early 1920's was dominated by two groups from Imperial Russia: the upper classes and the intelligentsia. "The Russian emigration in Berlin," one German observer recalled, "was a pyramid whose point was the only part which remained. The lower and middle classes were missing, along with the workers and peasants, craftsmen and shopkeepers. Instead there were army officers, bureaucrats, artists, financiers, politicians and members of the old court society."[3] To an extent this was true of the Russian emigra-

[2] *Statistik des deutschen Reichs,* Vol. 401 (Berlin, 1930), pp. 456–459.
[3] Wipert von Blücher, *Deutschlands Weg nach Rapallo: Erinnerungen eines Mannes aus dem zweiten Gliede* (Wiesbaden, 1951), p. 53.

tion everywhere, by virtue of the nature of the Bolshevik revolution. But in Paris after 1920 appeared the mass of soldiers and civilians forced to leave Russia with Wrangel's army and in Prague there were large numbers of Ukrainians and Jews of lower- and middle-class origin. The Balkan emigration in turn had a predominance of peasant soldiers from the White armies.[4]

In 1921 and 1922 a gradual shift occurred in the composition of the Russian emigration in Germany. Many monarchists found Germany inhospitable to their political activity and moved on to Paris or the Balkans, and a second wave of intellectuals arrived in Berlin from Soviet Russia and Paris. After 1923, when a large number of political refugees had left Germany, the two dominant non-Russian nationalities remained within the emigration: Russian Germans and Jews, who made up together nearly half of the 250,000 "Russians" in Germany in the 1925 census.[5] Closely linked to Germany by culture and language, they remained there long after Germany had ceased to be the center of the political emigration.

Most Russians in Germany lived in Berlin in these years, particularly in the southwestern suburbs of Schöneberg, Friedenau, Wilmersdorf, and Charlottenburg. This was the high-income residential area of Berlin before the war, with few stores, office buildings, or factories and a large number of attractive homes and parks. Along with its predominantly upper- and middle-class population lived a number of students from the Charlottenburg Technical High School. To the north lay the picturesque Tiergarten, to the east, south, and west the sweep of the outer subway system, the *Ringbahn*, at whose efficiency a generation of Russians had so marveled. It was an area frequented by thousands of Russians before the war and therefore familiar to many, but also an area fitting the social standing of the Russian upper classes.[6]

---

[4] Brief descriptions of the composition of the Russian colonies in Germany, France, Czechoslovakia, and the Balkans are given in Simpson, *Refugee Problem*, pp. 302–318, 377–390, 400–404.

[5] Of 253,069 former citizens of the Russian Empire living in Germany in 1925, 63,500 were Jews and some 59,000 gave German as their first language.

[6] *Erster Verwaltungsbericht der neuen Staatgemeinde Berlin* (Berlin, 1926),

Southwest Berlin became almost a Russian suburb in the early 1920's. Some official Russian organizations were downtown: the Russian church which had been attached to the embassy before the war at Unter den Linden 7; the Ukrainian embassy on the Kronprinzenufer along the Spree River. But the center of the colony was the southwest corner of the city. On the Wielandstrasse to the west of the Tiergarten were the offices of the Society to Aid Russian Citizens in Berlin, established in 1916, and on the Uhlandstrasse the headquarters of the Russian Red Cross and Botkin's Russian Delegation. At either end of the Motzstrasse were the locations of literary cafés frequented by Russian writers and artists: the Pragerplatz and the Nollendorfplatz. At the Stuttgarterplatz on the western fringe of the area was a Russian social club which had been a center for Russian students since 1908. With well over 100,000 Russians living in the area at the peak of the emigration, the Germans often referred to Berlin as "Russia's second capital" and the Kurfürstendamm as the "NEP-skii Prospekt."

For the Russians housing was an especially acute problem, about which they complained endlessly. The red tape of the Berlin housing authorities was formidable and German landlords were often harsh. They demanded advance payments before renting an apartment, and some landlords would only accept their rent in foreign currency, a practice which severely depleted émigré savings and income. Thus the common Russian reaction to German landlords was a bitter one. The Jewish scholar Simon Dubnov complained that his landlady was particularly fond of playing dirty tricks on him, and the writer Vladimir Nabokov described the janitors in Berlin apartment houses as "for the most part opulent bullies who had corpulent wives and belonged, out of petty bourgeois considerations, to the Communist party."[7]

German landlords were often equally suspicious of their Russian tenants. The religious philosopher Nikolai Berdiaev discovered that to reach his two-room apartment through his landlady's living

---

Vols. 15, 17; Karl Baedeker, *Berlin and Its Environs: Handbook for Travellers* (Leipzig, 1910), pp. 175–185.

[7] Simon Dubnow, *Kniga zhizni: Vospominaniia i razmyshleniia*, III (New York, 1957), 18–19; Vladimir Nabokov, *The Gift* (New York, 1963), p. 66.

room he was required to pass along a strip of old carpeting laid down like a path across the rug.[8] When Boris Zaitsev's family became ill their landlord and his wife assumed that they had brought into their household typhoid fever, cholera, or some other equally menacing disease associated in the German popular mind with "Russians." When the Russian doctor arrived they noted duly that he was "a Jew." "Thank goodness," exclaimed Zaitsev's landlord after his tenants had proved to be civilized people; "these Easterners have not spent their time sitting on the divan, didn't mark up the wallpaper, haven't broken any dishes and even tidy up their rooms after a fashion." [9] In the end the day-to-day intimate contact between landlord and émigré helped reinforce hostile attitudes of Russians toward the West and Germans toward Russia which had long existed but rarely derived from such immediate personal experience.

But Berlin was not the only center of Russians in Germany in the 1920's. Munich, too, had its Russian colony, composed primarily of right-wing politicians, aristocrats, and army officers who found Bavaria more receptive to their activity than Berlin, where they were under constant harassment from the police and the left-wing press. Hamburg reported a community of more than a thousand Russians by early 1921. In Düsseldorf and other towns in the Rhineland and Westphalia there were also large numbers of refugees, including many Jews, who found work in the mines while awaiting an opportunity to move on to France or the United States. In Baden-Baden were over five hundred well-to-do Russians, mainly aristocrats from St. Petersburg and Moscow, whose savings were dwindling and who had no prospects for employment. Wiesbaden was another popular location, since one could travel there from France without a visa during the French occupation and then into Germany without the usual formalities. Königsberg, Breslau, Frankfort, Dresden, Leipzig, Stuttgart, Halle, Heidelberg, Götingen—almost every German town had its Russians in these years.[10]

[8] Donald Lowrie, *Rebellious Prophet: A Life of Nicolai Berdyaev* (New York, 1960), p. 160.

[9] Boris Zaitsev, *Drevo zhizni* (New York, 1953), pp. 54–55.

[10] *Rul'*, February 15, 1921, p. 5; S. Adler-Rudel, *Ostjuden in Deutschland, 1880–1940* (Tübingen, 1959), pp. 90–93.

The Russian colony in Berlin soon became a community of its own. One could find Russian theaters, bookstores, doctors, lawyers, hairdressers, stenographers, shops, restaurants, employment agencies, newspapers, journals, and hundreds of other signs of a flourishing and independent existence. Dozens of private societies and political factions competed for the attention of the colony. But there were also émigré organizations which were formed not to promote the political interests of a particular group within the emigration but rather to represent the émigré community as a whole in such common concerns as visas, passports, legal problems, fund-raising, social welfare, and so on. This is not to say that such organizations were not often battlegrounds between political factions or that their personnel did not have strong political views, but their function differed from the political lobbies of specific groups. First and foremost they defended the rights of the émigrés to determine their own affairs in the face of increasing pressure after 1921 from both the German and Soviet governments. For as time passed the Russian emigration appeared to both as a thorn in the side of increasingly friendly relations between the two countries. Then, too, there was competition within the emigration among an increasing number of such organizations which weakened the authority of any one with respect to the German government. The story of the émigré community and its organizations is the story of the erosion and divisions of a politically lost cause. It is also the story of the valuable role of the "marginal men," primarily Russian Germans, in easing the adjustment of the Russian emigration to conditions in Germany.

Organization

The central institution of the Russian colony in Germany was Botkin's Russian Delegation, which served to coordinate refugee work among dozens of lesser organizations and to represent the interests of the community before the German government. As early as March 1920 the Wilhelmstrasse had informed Botkin that he would be granted "special consular functions" which would enable him to stamp and issue passports for Russians seeking to enter or leave Germany.[11] Although the Russian Delegation was never formally recognized by the Germans, Botkin himself was given an identity card normally reserved for foreign diplomats and enjoyed open access to the Foreign Office and the friendship of Maltzan. In April 1921 the Wilhelmstrasse informed the League of Nations that "non-Bolshevik Russians residing in Germany are represented in Berlin by a Delegation which looks after their interests and which, in particular, deals with the question of passports." [12] The warming of Soviet-German relations which culminated in the Treaty of Rapallo in 1922, however, led to pressure by the German government to reduce Botkin's status to that of a private individual rather than an official representative. In May 1922 the name of his organization was changed to the Office of Russian Refugees in Germany and the Wilhelmstrasse became increasingly cool. Despite Botkin's recollection that "the institution remained the same and only the name was changed," he found by 1923 that he could issue "identity cards" but not passports and that his contacts at the Wilhelmstrasse were often "busy" when he called on them. By 1924 his dealings with the Foreign Office were reduced almost to nothing.[13]

Botkin's Russian Delegation and most other organizations in Berlin in the early 1920's were dominated by what came to be known as the "monarchist" camp—former aristocrats, army officers, politicians, and bureaucrats. In all of these groups the Baltic Germans were highly visible. The Russian Civic Assembly, founded in the spring of 1919, was the initial center of the right-wing politicians and the Balts. Some of its seventy-five members in 1920—including chairman A. A. Rimsky-Korsakov, Biskupsky, and the former Procurator of the Holy Synod, A. A. Shirinsky-Shikhmatov—were to become leaders in Russian monarchist politics; an impressive number were Balts. Together with the old Russian Committee it continued to occupy part of a building on the Kaiserallee, re-

[11] Foreign Office note number A4-27/2356 dated March 30, 1920 (BA/RD, folder 58).

[12] *Russian Refugees*, League of Nations Report (Geneva, 1921), C. 126, M. 72, 1921, VII, Annex 2, p. 4.

[13] Botkin to Giers, June 25, September 24, and December 20, 1922 (GA, folder 33); Botkin to Giers, July 5, 1924, and February 13, 1925 (folder 35).

ceived some money from Botkin for its refugee work, but failed to obtain any recognition or support from Maltzan. In the end many of its members left for Munich, where they found financial support from South German industrialists and the papal nuncio in Bavaria, Eugen Pacelli.[14] In the summer of 1921, however, both organizations were included in the Supreme Monarchist Council, a unified monarchist organization established in Berlin. By 1922 what remained of the more aristocratic elements in Berlin were gathered in fraternal organizations such as the Old Club (open only to former members of the Imperial Russian Yacht Club and the English Clubs of Moscow and St. Petersburg) and the Society of Employees of the Ministry of Foreign Affairs. The membership of all these organizations overlapped (Botkin and Gamm belonged to the latter two) and was also sprinkled with a disproportionate number of Balts.[15]

Another important émigré organization in Berlin in the early 1920's was Zemgor or the Zemstvo and Town Committee (Zemsko-Gorodskii Komitet), the continuation in emigration of a wartime Russian organization now centered in Paris. Founded in July 1915 as a committee of business and industrial leaders to coordinate the logistics behind the Russian war effort, by the summer of 1919 Zemgor had ceased to function inside Russia.[16] Most of its leaders had either fled to South Russia or were imprisoned. Some of its members had emigrated, however, and in 1921 the organization was revived in Paris to deal with welfare and education among the émigrés. As such it was concerned primarily with the more needy émigrés, especially in the ranks of Wrangel's army in the Balkans, and accordingly played a relatively minor role in Berlin.[17]

[14] The files of the Russian Committee and the Russian Civic Assembly are located in BA/RD, folders 7, 10.

[15] The files of the Old Club and the Society of Employees of the Ministry of Foreign Affairs are contained in BA/RD, folder 57.

[16] The wartime Zemgor united two previously separate Russian organizations, the Union of Zemstvos and the Union of Towns, which were important elements in civilian support for the Russian war effort. Zemgor's main function was allocating government supply orders to cities and towns, obtaining manufactured articles for the army and passing them on to the War Ministry. See T. Polner, *Russian Local Government during the War and the Union of Zemstvos* (New Haven, 1930).

[17] *Ocherk deiatel'nosti vserossiiskago zemskago soiuza za granitsei (aprel' 1920 g.-1 Ianvaria 1922 g.)* (Sofia, 1922), pp. 134–135.

The chairman of the Berlin Zemgor was Fedor Vladimirovich Shlippe, a member of the Moscow German colony. Born in 1873, Shlippe had been tutored by Germans as a child, had attended German private schools in Moscow, traveled to Chemnitz and Dresden as a young man, and was equally fluent in both German and Russian. After attending a *Gymnasium* in Ekaterinoslav, where his father served on various committees of the local gentry, Shlippe came to Moscow in 1892 to enter the Agricultural Institute. After completing his studies there and at Moscow University, Shlippe in 1899 made his first trip to Germany, visiting Berlin, Dresden, and Munich. Until 1911 he made no more trips abroad, but served as an agricultural expert and administrator in various zemstvos. By 1914 he had become one of the leading figures in zemstvo work, serving under D. M. Shipov in Moscow *guberniia,* and later working closely with Prince Lvov on the organization of Zemgor during the war. Because of his German background, he was finally forced to retire from public life. In Kiev and then in Riga he found other Russian German friends who were equally aware that life in Russia would be even more painful for them as time went on. By the summer of 1920 Shlippe had left Russia for London, where he became the assistant to Count P. N. Ignatiev, then organizing a committee to aid Russian refugees in Germany.[18]

In early 1921 Shlippe arrived in Berlin to head the German office of Zemgor, now operating in Paris under Prince Lvov. His assistant was A. V. Belgard, and his committee was sprinkled with other Russian Germans. In Berlin as elsewhere the functions of Zemgor included finding jobs and housing for refugees, helping establish schools, and running homes for the elderly and the infirm. It also distributed food and clothing to the needy, helped Russian artisans and craftsmen find a market for their products, provided some scholarships for needy students, and gave legal aid and advice. It worked closely with Botkin's Russian Delegation, student organizations, and other émigré agencies, as well as the German govern-

18 The unpublished memoirs of F. V. Shlippe are in the Russian Archive of Columbia University and were written some time during World War II. See pp. 14, 43. Also on Zemgor see "Poriadok voznikoveniia Zemsko-Gorodskogo Komiteta v Germanii i vzaimootnosheniia ego s Rossiiskym Zemsko-Gorodskym Komitetom v Parizhe" (GA, folder 39).

ment. Funds for all these operations came from the American YMCA in Berlin, the German government, and private émigré individuals and organizations.[19]

One problem which plagued Shlippe and Zemgor in these years was the relationship with the Paris organization. Until the spring of 1922 Shlippe's committee was almost an independent organization with only one-third of its funds coming from Paris. But in 1922 the German Ministry of the Interior closed a number of refugee camps and both the German government and the YMCA ceased to support Zemgor, which was forced to maintain them on its own. In the spring of 1923 the Paris office sought to assert its authority over Shlippe's organization in Berlin. By then Zemgor was dependent on the Russian Red Cross for funds, a large part of which came from Paris. Moreover, Prince Lvov now sent his own representative to Berlin in an effort to remove Shlippe. The result was a wasteful duplication of effort and mutual bad feeling which, coupled with the economic and political crisis in Germany that year, led within a few months to the collapse of Berlin's Zemgor. By 1924 it had ceased to exist.[20]

The Russian army in exile also had its own organizations, linked to those in Paris. Beside Lampe's Mutual Aid Society and Central Union of Russian War Invalids there was the elite Society for Officers of the General Staff, a Sailors' Mutual Aid Society, a Society for Former War Prisoners and Internees in Germany, and even a Mutual Aid Society for former officers of the Preobrazhensky guards regiment. In 1921 there were some three thousand Russian officers in Berlin, including those from the Imperial army, the White armies of Avalov, Yudenich, Kolchak, and Wrangel, and the

[19] There is a list of Zemgor members appended to "Poriadok" and in Botkin's report on Zemgor in BA/RD, folder 58. Another source of refugee funds was the American Aid Committee of Count Musin-Pushkin in Berlin, which received money from Princess Cantacuza-Grant in the United States.

[20] "Obzor deiatel'nosti Zemsko-Gorodskogo Komiteta za 1922 god" (GA, folder 39); reports of Botkin to Giers, May 22, 1923, and May 27, 1924 (GA, folder 34); see also the long letter of Shlippe denying this representative's (Izhboldin) right to represent Zemgor in Berlin printed in Rul', May 16, 1923, p. 6.

Red Army as well.[21] Most of their organizations soon turned from politics to welfare work under the supervision of the military section of Botkin's Russian Delegation, headed at first by Holmsen and then in the spring of 1922 by Lampe. Like Botkin, they reported on events of interests in both Germany and Soviet Russia to their superiors in Paris, Generals Miller and Wrangel; through Vladimir Orlov, a former Okhrana agent, Holmsen even kept in touch with the Soviet press and was occasionally given access to German information concerning Soviet border fortifications. The army in general found itself under constant pressure from the monarchists to support various pretenders and factions in emigration and from the German left and the Soviet government to abandon politics altogether. In the wake of Rapallo Lampe wrote that "it is obvious that the Russian army must live through a very difficult period." [22]

Another active center of émigré life in Berlin was the Russian Orthodox church, unusual in that the existence of Maltsev's St. Vladimir Brotherhood before the war provided it with buildings— a Russian library, the old embassy church, a museum, a graveyard, and a large building known as the Alexanderheim, which now became a home for the indigent—money, and land. The Brotherhood also owned church property at Kissingen in Bavaria, Herbersdorf in Silesia, and Hamburg, all of which were frequented by travelers and diplomats before the war.

Two rival centers of church life soon appeared in emigration. The first, in Paris, was the circle of churchmen around Metropolitan Evlogy, who was formally named West European Eparch by Tikhon in 1922. The second group centered in the Balkans around former Metropolitan Antony of Kiev, and originated at the church Sobor (Assembly) held at Sremtsy Karlovtsy in Yugoslavia in the

[21] Lampe's office estimated that there were about 3,000 Russian refugees still living in German POW camps as of January 1, 1922 ("Spravka o kolichestve russkikh bezhentsev, prozhivziushchikh v lageriakh, po sostoianiiu k nachalu ianvaria 1922 goda," LA, folder 28). Holmsen gave the same estimate in his report to General Miller dated October 19, 1921, MiA, Group I, folder 17.

[22] Lampe to Wrangel, May 22, 1922 (WA, folder 213); see also the reports of Holmsen to Miller in MiA, Group I, folder 45.

autumn of 1921. Both groups were actively involved in right-wing politics in emigration and shared common political views, despite their jurisdictional dispute. Antony's epistle of December 3, 1921, expressed his "deep sorrow at the loss of our fatherland and especially that our country has fallen under the power of godless men— Jews and Chinese" and urged a restoration of a monarchist, Orthodox Russia. Both Antony and Evlogy were present at the congress of Russian monarchists held at Reichenhall in Bavaria in the spring of 1921, where Antony made it clear that all "true Russian patriots" should recognize the enemies of Christ and Russia to be "Jewish patriot-revolutionaries." [23]

In Berlin the Alexanderheim became, under the administration of A. V. Belgard, a center for monarchist intrigue in 1919 and 1920. Here Belgard and his friends found a temporary focus for their attempts to organize the dispatch of men and materials to Avalov and Wrangel. Their activity, however ineffective, was not missed by the Independent Socialists in the Reichstag, who attacked the Alexanderheim as a "counterrevolutionary center" with a "net of agents" throughout Germany whose aim was "to enlist Russian citizens, Russian prisoners, and internees for counterrevolutionary aims." [24] The embassy church on Unter den Linden was also revived

[23] B. Szczesniak, ed., *The Russian Revolution and Religion* (Notre Dame, Ind., 1959), pp. 12, 60–62, 244–246. Metropolitan Evlogy (Vasily Georgievsky, 1868–1946) was a former Bishop of Lublin and right-wing representative in the first and second Dumas before 1914. Imprisoned by the Bolsheviks in 1919, he escaped abroad where he was recognized by Tikhon as *de facto* head of the Orthodox church in Western Europe. When his position was revoked in 1930 by Archbishop Sergei, Tikhon's successor, Evlogy recognized the Patriarchate of Constantinople, although he returned to the Moscow fold shortly before his death.

Metropolitan Antony (Aleksei Khrapovitsky, 1863–1936) was a former Metropolitan of Kharkov and Kiev and later head of the Supreme Church Administration for the territory occupied by the White armies during the civil war. In Sremtsy Karlovtsy he attempted to maintain his authority by organizing his own Supreme Administration of Russian Eparchies and Communities Abroad, supposedly encompassing all émigrés of the Orthodox faith. Antony's anti-Semitism is well displayed in his *Khristos spasitel' i evreiskaia revoliutsiia* (Berlin, 1922), pp. 37, 41.

[24] *Verhandlungen des Reichstags, I: Wahlperiod 1920*, 346, pp. 1793, 1805–1806, 1987. The USPD delegates charged that the Berlin police knew of the Vladimir Brotherhood's activity, including the arming of branch organizations in Bavaria with machine guns, but had done nothing to stop it.

after a period of disuse, at first under the priest Znosko and, after the spring of 1921, under Metropolitan Evlogy. Evlogy, who had fled to the Balkans with the remnants of Wrangel's army in late 1920, announced on April 13, 1921, the formation of a Church Parish (Tserkovnyi Prikhod) in Berlin which would minister to the needs of émigré Russians throughout Western Europe. Two months later it was announced in Berlin that Evlogy had been named by Patriarch Tikhon to direct the affairs of the Orthodox church abroad. Evlogy also became actively involved in monarchist politics in Berlin in the spring of 1921, helping prepare for the Reichenhall Congress (at which he gave the opening benediction) and renewing acquaintances with right-wing friends such as Markov II whom he had known before the revolution.[25]

By 1922 the Russian church in Berlin began to decline. Not only were many of its monarchist parishioners leaving for Paris, but both the German and Soviet governments were working against it. Maltzan warned Botkin in early March that the well-known involvement of Evlogy and his priests in right-wing politics would have to cease.[26] Then in June came the news that the grounds and property of the old Russian embassy in Berlin, including its church, had been sold to the Soviet government.[27] Within the emigration, too, the church was losing its appeal. Both inside Soviet Russia and in emigration many were turning to the pro-Soviet Living Church (Zhivaia Tserkov); in early 1923 the Soviet government even organized in Berlin its own Russian Church Administration Abroad and sent five priests there to proselytize.[28] By the autumn of 1923, faced with a number of pressures, Evlogy had transferred the Church Parish from Berlin to Paris.

With the departure of Metropolitan Evlogy and the general exodus of Russians from Germany in 1923 the Orthodox church

[25] Rul', April 6, 1921, p. 3, and June 12, 1921, p. 6; Evlogy, Put' moei zhizni (Paris, 1947), p. 394.

[26] Botkin to Giers, March 4, 1922 (GA, folder 33).

[27] Botkin to Giers, June 25, 1922 (GA, folder 33). The formal transfer of the property took place on June 20.

[28] Report from the American legation in Riga to the U.S. Secretary of State (Szczesniak, Religion, p. 111). In May 1923 Rul' reported that the Soviet government was also shipping antireligious literature into Berlin for distribution among the émigrés (May 20, 1923, p. 3).

throughout Germany suffered a decline. Many émigrés continued faithfully in the religion in which they had been brought up, but in general the Russian churches in Berlin, Wiesbaden, Dresden, Baden, and Leipzig were only poorly attended. The St. Vladimir Brotherhood had ceased to be a church service organization and had become a haven for twenty or thirty right-wing politicians who ran a veterans' home and fought off suits brought by the Soviet government in German courts to confiscate their property.[29]

Beside the semiofficial organizations of the Russian colony there existed in Berlin a number of private groups representing the most diverse professional, social, and national elements. Professional groups included the Society of Russian Doctors, founded in May 1919; the Union of Russian Engineers in Germany; the Union of Russian Lawyers in Germany; the Union of Russian Writers and Journalists; the Union of Russian Merchants, Industrialists, and Financiers; and student organizations like the Student Brotherhood, the right-wing Wünsdorf Union of National Youth, the more liberal Union of Russian Students, and the Russian National Student Union. The children of the emigration attended the St. George *Gymnasium*, the YMCA school at Wünsdorf, and others sponsored by Zemgor. The Ukrainian, Georgian, and Armenian émigrés in Berlin had their own organizations, schools, churches, and offices in Berlin for issuing passports and identity papers. By the winter of 1922–1923 there were some forty organizations in Germany considered significant enough to be represented on the Council of United Russian Institutions and Civic Organizations in Germany.[30] Frus-

[29] Evlogy and Markov II retained their connection with the Vladimir Brotherhood even after they moved to Paris. In 1923 the United Council of Emigré Organizations refused to accept the Brotherhood on the grounds that its claim to be a continuation of the pre-1914 organization was false (*Rul'*, January 28, 1923, p. 5). From 1926 to 1929 the Soviet government tried without success to obtain the Alexanderheim grounds and property through the German courts. Botkin, who defended the Brotherhood's interests, later became the head of the organization, although he disagreed with the politics of many of its members (see the folder entitled "Vladimirskoe bratstvo" of the Botkin Collection in the Columbia University Russian Archive).

[30] *Protokoly s"ezda russkikh iuristov zagranitsei 1–4 oktiabria 1922 goda v Berline* (Berlin, 1922); *Zarubezhnaia russkaia shkola 1920–1924* (Paris, 1924), pp. 149–156; "Informationsblatt des Verband des russischer Gross-Kaufleute, Industriellen u. Financiers in Deutschland 1923–1924" (BA/RD, folder 17).

trated by their failure in the civil war, the émigrés seemed to have found solace in organizing themselves.

Intellectual Life

The central organization in Berlin devoted to the welfare of the poorer émigrés was the Society to Aid Russian Citizens in Berlin, founded in 1916 as a subsection of the YMCA to work with the Russian war prisoners and the predominantly Jewish community caught there by the war. Located in Charlottenburg, it was theoretically devoted to the interests of all Russian citizens in Germany but was later characterized by Botkin as being concerned mainly with "German subjects from Russia" and later with the "Jews and representatives of the left-wing parties." [31] In the 1920's it operated on a shoestring budget and ran two rooming houses for indigents. For a time in 1919–1920 it proved a valuable rallying point for those refugees unwilling or unable to work with the more conservative and aristocratic elements of the emigration. Its members included I. V. Gessen; R. Ya. Glants, who wrote for *Vorwärts* under the name of A. Grigorianz; S. Ya. Shkliaver, a lawyer who later headed the Russian-language branch of the Rudolf Mosse publishing house; I. M. Rabinovich, a lawyer; and the writers V. I. Golubtsov, Yu. V. Ofrosimov, and V. B. Stankevich (Vladas Stanka).[32] It was primarily this group of men who initiated the first phase of Russian intellectual life in Berlin.

In early 1920 the only publishing outlet available to Russian writers not of the monarchist camp was the newspaper *Golos Rossii*

On the Armenians and Georgians see Botkin to Giers, April 14, 1923 (GA, folder 33) and Blücher, *Deutschlands Weg*, pp. 123–124.

[31] Botkin to Giers, March 3, 1928 (BA/RD, folder 65).

[32] *Golos Rossii*, July 15, 1920, p. 3. Stankevich, the leader of the group, was a former secretary to the Trudovik faction in the Duma and a Lithuanian of no particular political affiliation in emigration. Born in 1884, he had been a professor of criminal law before the war, a member of the Petrograd Soviet in 1917, and a military commissar on the northern front that summer. He lived in Berlin from 1919 to 1923 on a Lithuanian passport, and thus legally was not then an émigré. See his *Vospominaniia 1914–1919 g.* (Berlin, 1920) and other publications: *Sud'by narodov Rossii* (Berlin, 1921), *Rossiia i Germaniia* (Berlin, 1922), *Frit'of Nansen* (Berlin, 1923), *Na velikom severe: Iz istorii russkikh poliarnykh puteshestvii* (Berlin, 1923).

Community of Despair

(The Voice of Russia). Stankevich, Alexander Drozdov, A. S. Yashchenko, and Michael Smilg-Benario, a Russian German, were among its steady contributors.[33] If the circle of writers around *Golos Rossii* shared any common platform, it was war-weariness. War in all forms must now be brought to an end in order that the reconstruction of Europe might begin. This included the Russian Civil War, assumed to have been won by the Bolsheviks already by early 1920.[34] If *Golos Rossii* showed any sympathies for the Soviet regime, however, it was more out of tiredness than enthusiasm.

Aside from *Golos Rossii* there was little literary or intellectual activity until 1922. There was a small literary periodical *Rus'*, but it was directed more toward Russian war prisoners than any émigré reading public. Another periodical, *Russkii emigrant*, the organ of the cooperative society Russkaia Koloniia, had high hopes of becoming a major journal for the entire Berlin emigration, but collapsed in late 1920. At that time, however, there was an American Fund organization in Berlin which numbered among its members Stankevich, Gessen, and Golubtsov and provided some money from the United States to support needy Russian émigré writers. A Russian Academic Group was also established in the spring of 1920 to organize educational activity for the emigration, both independently and as an adjunct to the University of Berlin, headed by A. I. Kaminka and including among its members V. D. Nabokov, Stankevich, and Yashchenko.[35]

It was Stankevich who initiated the first significant circle of in-

[33] Smilg-Benario was a minor official in the Ministry of Justice in 1917–1918 who became the main *Golos Rossii* correspondent on the Russian Civil War in 1919–1920. Like so many Russian Germans he found Germany, as his publisher later put it, "just as much his homeland as Russia itself" (*Der Zusammenbruch der Zarenmonarchie* [Vienna, 1928], p. 8). See also his "Na sovetskoi sluzhbe," *Arkhiv russkoi revoliutsii*, No. 3 (1921), 147–189.

[34] *Golos Rossii*, April 21, 1920, p. 3.

[35] *Rus'* was mainly a POW camp journal, of which only two issues appeared in January and February 1920. Russkaia Koloniia was a society of members of the prewar Russian cooperative society Tsentrosoiuz who ran a restaurant, a wholesale outlet, a children's library, and a lecture series in Berlin. *Russkii emigrant* published poems, stories, and émigré news in 1920–1921. Both the colony and its journal disbanded with the appearance of Botkin's Russian Delegation and *Rul'*. See *Golos Rossii*, October 27, 1920, p. 4; *Rul'*, January 13, 1921, p. 3.

126

tellectuals in Berlin in the spring of 1920 and introduced a note of political friction into an otherwise solidly monarchist community. The quiet and scholarly Stankevich called his new society Mir i trud (Peace and Labor); it published two short-lived journals, *Mir i trud* and *Zhizn'* (Life).[36] In the Berlin colony theirs was a still, small voice for "coexistence" between the new Bolshevik regime and the West on the assumption that the choice now was between "peace and culture or a continuous and totally destructive war."[37] From the first meeting of March 9, 1920, until the group's demise in the autumn of that year it provided the beginnings of intellectual acceptance in Berlin of the Soviet regime.

Stankevich's circle was a loosely-linked group of émigré intellectuals of no party affiliation. Included among its members were the writer Roman Goul, Smilg-Benario, Yashchenko, Golubtsov (a distant relative of Nabokov), and Ofrosimov, a poet and later the theater critic for the newspaper *Rul'*. *Zhizn'* was formally edited by Stankevich and Golubtsov. But the technical side of the publication was handled by two prewar Jewish émigrés to Germany: a former Russian businessman named Goldberg, who worked for *Golos Rossii*, spoke Russian with a heavy German accent, and was an uncultured but necessary addition to the circle, and R. Ya. Glants, a member of the SPD and the staff of *Vorwärts*, an intelligent and sympathetic member of Mir i trud. *Zhizn'* was financed largely by émigré contributions, usually made at the well-attended evening meetings of the society. With monarchist sheets such as *Prizyv* for rivals, *Zhizn'* was a temporary rallying point for forces of moderation and reconciliation within the emigration. But in the autumn of 1920 the emigration had outgrown it, and several of its writers now began working for *Rul'*. New literary outlets and new nonmonarchist organizations and political circles were appearing. *Zhizn'* could no longer compete either financially or politically with them.

Another of the many organizations extending aid to the Russian refugees in Berlin in the early 1920's was the Young Men's Christian Association, an American Protestant organization engaged in social

[36] *Zhizn'* appeared as a biweekly in Berlin from April 1 to October 1, 1920.
[37] *Mir i trud: Neperiodicheskii sbornik,* I (1920).

and missionary work throughout the world. Since 1900 the YMCA had been active in Russia, where it had established a Society for Aiding Young Men in Attaining Moral and Physical Development, later known as Maiak (The Lighthouse), which conducted physical education programs, engaged in social work, and offered occasional bible readings. By 1917 Maiak claimed over 1,600 members, mainly among the upper classes, and had become a full member of the World Student Christian Federation.[38] With the Bolshevik revolution, however, most of the non-Russian YMCA secretaries were forced to leave the country, and by 1919 the YMCA office in Petrograd had been closed by the government. Cut off from further work inside Russia, the YMCA began an even more significant phase of work among Russian refugees abroad.

Since the end of 1918 the YMCA had been active among Russian war prisoners still interned in Austria and Germany. By the autumn of 1920 YMCA workers in Berlin had discovered that hundreds of young Russian émigrés were enrolling in German schools or facing problems of education within the Russian colony, offering a "regular and open field for Association activities." They therefore began an extensive program of relief work, Sunday schools, student cooperatives, academic courses, and social affairs among Russians in Berlin. A dormitory for fifty students was established in barracks at Tempelhof field, a "Polytechnicum for Russians" set up for civilian and military internees at the Wünsdorf POW camp, and a large student hall opened in Berlin. YMCA student circles and libraries quickly followed, not only in Berlin but also in Halle, Dresden, Kiel, and other German towns, directed by a former Russian YMCA staff secretary, F. T. Pianov.[39]

The year 1921 brought a sharp expansion in this activity. At a time when most Russian students could not afford to attend Ger-

[38] A general summary of YMCA work in Russia before 1917 and among Russian émigrés after World War I is contained in K. S. Latourette, *World Service* (New York, 1957), pp. 368–383. Much of the following section is written on the basis of unpublished materials in the YMCA Historical Archive in New York: On Maiak see YMCA, World Service Box 7, folders B and C, and the "Memoirs of Ethan T. Colton, Sr.—1872–1952" (MS, YMCA), p. 217.

[39] "Report of the Russian Department for the Month of December 1921" (YMCA, World Service Box 146-A) and "Work for Russian Students in Berlin" (1924) (World Service Box 8, folder D).

man educational institutions, YMCA work in education played an important part in émigré life. In January 1921 the YMCA announced that it would provide funds for fifty Russian students to continue their education in Berlin. Backed by American money, the YMCA soon enlarged its programs. A Russian House was opened in Berlin, providing free meals and pocket money for particularly needy refugees, a Union of Russian Students in Germany was established, and a social club was organized in Charlottenburg. In addition, a Russian correspondence school, which opened in Berlin in the spring of 1921 under the direction of Dr. Paul Anderson, provided thousands of Russians with an education by mail over the next three years and led to the creation of the YMCA Press.[40]

Politically the YMCA tried to maintain a middle ground between the monarchists on the one hand and the Soviet government and its sympathizers on the other. Insofar as was possible, it remained above politics, rendering aid and assistance not only to émigré students and intellectuals but also to scholars inside Soviet Russia until the mid-1920's.[41] Financially independent, the YMCA could deal with the Russian colony in Berlin on its own terms, without interference from German, Soviet, or émigré organizations. But because it worked mainly with the younger generation of émigrés and with intellectuals, the YMCA was not unsympathetic to Soviet Russia in these years. Pro-Soviet intellectuals thus had no small influence within the émigré student movement at this time, playing upon the idealism of youth and the common goal of "working together" to

[40] The Union of Russian Students in Germany, organized in 1920, claimed over 300 members by early 1921; its most important function was to provide financial aid to needy students, derived from émigré donations, the YMCA, and German businessmen. The YMCA correspondence school was originally founded to prepare Russian POW's in Austria, Poland, and Germany for useful work when they returned to Russia and only later became an émigré organization. This school's need for texts led to the creation of the YMCA Press with its Russian-language publishing operation, first in Switzerland, then in Berlin, and after 1924 in Paris. See *Rul'*, January 15, January 18, and February 1, 1921, and "Russian Correspondence School" (YMCA, World Service Box 9, folder E), and N. Klepinin, "Survey of North American YMCA Service to Russians in Europe" (YMCA), pp. 36–38, 90–91.

[41] On YMCA assistance to scholars and writers inside Soviet Russia in the 1920's, see S. M. Keeny, "Relief to Professors" (1924; YMCA, World Service Box 8, folder B).

rebuild Russia. Until 1923 two leading members of the pro-Soviet Smena Vekh (Change of Directions) movement in Berlin, Yashchenko and B. Diushen, were particularly active in the correspondence school, which Yashchenko helped direct until 1923.[42]

Another important educational and intellectual center was the Russian Scientific Institute, organized in the winter of 1922–1923 in Berlin. The idea of the Institute was to provide both an educational institution for émigré students and a clearing house where émigré scholars could follow and discuss developments inside Soviet Russia. The leading émigrés behind the project were three Kadets (Gessen, Kaminka, and A. A. Kizevetter), and a number of intellectuals, among them Nikolai Berdiaev, L. P. Karsavin, I. A. Ilin, Boris Vysheslavtsev, S. N. Prokopovich, and V. I. Yasinsky, the "rector" of the Institute. Some Germans also participated, principally Otto Hoetzsch, Moritz Schlesinger, and representatives of the Ullstein firm, and the Institute was financed largely by private German sources through Hoetzsch.[43]

The success of the Russian Scientific Institute, which opened in the old Architecture Academy in Berlin on February 17, 1923, was short-lived. During the spring and summer of 1923 it offered an exciting series of lectures on a variety of subjects. Kizevetter lectured on eighteenth- and nineteenth-century Russian history, S. L. Frank gave a course on philosophy, Berdiaev turned to Russian intellectual history, and Peter Struve came from Paris to talk on Russian economic history. In the field of law Kaminka lectured on commercial agreements and I. A. Stratonov on the history of Russian law and legal theory. For bright young émigré students it was a paradise, a remarkable assemblage of some of the best minds in emigration.

But the Institute, like other émigré organizations, did not long survive the crisis of 1923 in Germany and the exodus of many of its leading personnel to Paris and Prague. For a time it had re-

[42] "Report" (YMCA, World Service Box 146-A).
[43] I. V. Gessen, "Gody skitanii" (MS, Hoover Library), pp. 86, 165; *Dni*, January 31, 1923, p. 2; *Rul'*, June 6, 1923, p. 5; M. Novikov, "Pervye shagi v emigratsii," *Grani*, No. 38 (1958), p. 129.

placed Zemgor as the main agency for émigré education and benefited from the wave of intellectual expellees in Berlin. But it had also become another battleground between anti-Bolshevik émigrés and the forces of reconciliation, German, émigré, and Soviet. Yasinsky and Schlesinger, who between them controlled funds from the League of Nations and the YMCA, tried to keep the Institute alive as a Russian university, which existed down to 1933. But by the autumn of 1923 the Institute and its faculty had been moved to Prague, where the liberal financial contributions of the Czech government provided a fruitful new base of operations.

Within a few months Berdiaev and the YMCA had also left Germany, although their collaboration continued until World War II. The center of the "religious intellectuals" shifted to Paris, where the search for a spiritual revival continued, now in the St. Sergius Theological Academy. If Berlin had initiated the meeting between the YMCA and Berdiaev's circle, Paris became their new home.

The two most important bases of Russian intellectual life in Berlin in the early 1920's were not organizations but the literary cafés, which provided meeting places for émigré writers and artists, and publishing houses, which provided a market for their work. The cafés were particularly important as social centers where men of the most diverse views could meet and debate, theorize, drink, and listen to the latest stories and poems read by their authors. In Dresden, Leipzig, and other German towns there were similar gathering places and Russian literary organizations, but the focus of intellectual life remained southwest Berlin.

The most important café was the Leon on the Nollendorfplatz, whose second floor rooms became for the Berlin Russians in the early 1920's "almost our club." [44] Not only was it the central gathering place for Russian writers and artists, but it was also the scene of the periodic meetings of the émigré Union of Russian Writers and Journalists in Germany. Primarily the center of the confirmed

[44] A. F. Damanskaia, "6 otryvkov iz vospominanii Avgusty Filippovny Damanskoi" (typescript in the Columbia University Russian Archive, folder 7 ["Berlin 1920–1923 gg."], p. 6. For a brief sketch of this café and its writers, see Z. Arbatov, " 'Nollendorfplatskafe' (Literaturnaia mozaika)," *Grani*, No. 41 (1959), pp. 106–122.

émigré writers, the Leon café also tolerated the "half-way" émigrés who later returned to Soviet Russia: Andrei Belyi, Viktor Shklovsky, Aleksei Tolstoi, Alexander Drozdov, and Gleb Alekseev, among others. But there were other cafés on the Nollendorfplatz too, and it was not unusual in 1922 to find four or five separate literary gatherings or poetry readings going on simultaneously on a given evening.

Émigrés who were more strongly pro-Soviet gathered at the Landgraf café on the Kurfürstendamm not far from the Nollendorfplatz. The Landgraf was also the central meeting place for another writers' organization, the House of Arts, a Soviet literary organization now re-established in Berlin under the symbolist poet Nikolai Maksimovich Minsky. A former editor of a legal Bolshevik newspaper, *Novaia zhizn'*, Minsky had left Russia in 1905, had not experienced the upheaval of 1917 and after, and was able in many cases to reconcile the deep antagonisms between émigré and Soviet writers in Berlin. Founded in November 1921, the House of Arts was frequented mainly by the writers around *Nakanune,* the pro-Soviet Berlin daily, and other "left" intellectuals: Belyi, Tolstoi, Remizov, Ehrenburg, Stankevich, and Yashchenko. But here, as at the Leon café, the lines were still blurred and intellectual exchanges took precedence over political recriminations.[45]

Even more vital than the cafés to émigré intellectual life, however, was the proliferation of books and periodicals. In part this was true of the emigration in general. With the end of the Russian Civil War and the apparent triumph of the Bolsheviks, the written word became a substitute for political activity and at the same time a means of putting the case for or against the Soviet regime before the emigration. The diaspora was a vast reading public, Soviet publishing was almost nonexistent at first, and there was even the possibility of exporting books into Russia. This was true throughout the emigration. But in Germany conditions were particularly favorable for émigré publishing.

By 1900 Germany had become the world's leading book publisher. Her printing, typesetting, and distribution facilities were

[45] *Novaia russkaia kniga,* 1922, No. 1, p. 34; Ilia Ehrenburg, *Men, Years, Life,* Vol. III: *Truce: 1921–1923* (London, 1963), pp. 20–21.

second to none. The German reading public, moreover, had long been interested in Russian literature and a number of translations of classic and contemporary writers had appeared even before the First World War. Germany had also served as a center for émigré Russian publishing activity, literary and political, and Cyrillic type was readily available in a number of publishing firms. Finally, post-war conditions in Germany were ideal: the cost of paper and type-setting was relatively low; thousands of Russian writers and readers were close at hand; and there was a general enthusiasm for things Russian in Germany as a result of the revolution. Berlin soon became the most important single center of Russian book publishing, including Petrograd and Moscow.[46]

Book publishing had reached a peak in Germany on the eve of the war with some 35,000 titles recorded for 1913. Despite the disruptions of four years of war, by 1920 the annual output of books in Germany had returned to the 1911 level of 30,000 titles. It was a remarkable publishing revival, unparalleled in Europe. During 1920, 895 new German publishers had appeared in Germany and abroad, while only 386 had ceased their operations. The Russian emigration to Germany, as one historian of German publishing recalled, played a major role in this revival.[47]

The sheer volume of Russian books published outside Soviet Russia in the early 1920's was remarkable. By June 1924 nearly 4,000 separate titles had been recorded from throughout the diaspora, and no less than 142 Russian publishing firms had appeared abroad, émigré and Soviet, of which 86 were located in Berlin.[48] Here book publishing, like intellectual life in general, reflected the fluidity or even the nonexistence of boundaries between "Soviet" and "émigré" enterprises. Until late 1921 the émigré houses pre-

---

[46] *Katalog knig vyshedshikh vne Rossii* (Berlin, 1924); F. Schulze, *Der deutsche Buchhandel und die geistigen Strömungen der letzten hundert Jahre* (Leipzig, 1925); E. Znosko-Borovsky, "Russkaia kniga vo Frantsii," *Novaia russkaia kniga*, 1922, No. 3, pp. 22–26 and "Pechat' i revoliutsiia," *ibid.*, 1923, No. 3, pp. 119–122.

[47] Schulze, *Buchhandel,* p. 254.

[48] *Katalog,* pp. vii, ix–xvi. Berlin's closest rivals in terms of the number of Russian publishing houses were Paris (12), Prague (9), Reval (6), New York (4), Vienna (3), and Sofia (3).

dominated. But from the end of 1921 until the spring of 1923 Berlin was flooded with various Soviet publishing operations which found conditions there far better than inside Russia and sold to émigré and Soviet readers alike; Petropolis and the firms of Z. I. Grzhebin and I. P. Ladyzhnikov were the best known. Yet many of these firms published the works of both émigré and Soviet writers, as did many of the "literary almanacs" which came out at this time.[49]

Berlin also attracted a number of émigré firms and journals from outside Germany, beginning in the winter of 1921–1922. Along with the influx of émigrés from Paris came journals like *Sovremennye zapiski* and *Russkaia mysl'*, trying to escape the sudden rise in the cost of paper and publishing which plagued France at the time. For the next year and a half Berlin was the scene of an outpouring of Russian books and periodicals. But in 1923 the inflation and its consequences brought an end to the honeymoon: thousands of Russians were leaving Germany; German publishers were being forced to close; conditions for publishing inside Soviet Russia and in other European countries were improving; the Union of Russian Editors and Booksellers in Germany could not change its prices fast enough to keep up with the fall of the mark; when currency finally stabilized, the advantages of the émigrés to German publishers as a source of foreign currency disappeared. Emigré firms moved west to Paris and Soviet ones returned east to Moscow or Petrograd.

The leading émigré publishing house, Slovo, directed by I. V. Gessen, reflected the fate of many similar projects in these years.[50]

[49] Some literary collections were clearly demarcated. The *Al'manakh mednyi vsadnik: Kniga pervaia* (Berlin, 1923), edited by Sergei Krechetov (Sergei Sokolov), was obviously an "émigré" publication, with stories and poems by Bunin, Balmont, Boris Zaitsev, Gleb Struve, Krasnov, and Vladimir Sirin (Nabokov). *Molodaia Rossiia* (Berlin, 1922), edited by Aleksei Tolstoi, was definitely more "Soviet," a collection of short stories by Boris Pilniak, Alexander Drozdov, Konstantin Fedin, and others, as was *Al'manakh "Skify"* (Berlin, 1923). But other collections, such as *Vereteno:Literaturno-khudozhestvennyi al'manakh* (Berlin, 1922), published the stories and poems of émigré and Soviet writers alike, among them Nabokov and Drozdov, Bunin and Pilniak.

[50] This account of the operations of the Slovo house is based on Gessen, "Gody skitanii," pp. 95–122.

Before Gessen arrived in Berlin from Finland in 1919, he was approached by the big Ullstein firm about opening a Russian-language publishing operation in Berlin. The newspaper *Rul'*, in fact, was a side effect of this project. After considerable negotiating, an arrangement was reached whereby Ullstein would provide for the Russians the necessary technical facilities and printing staff and would handle all business arrangements, while Gessen, Kaminka, and other Russians would be in charge of selecting and editing the works to be published. It was initially a satisfactory arrangement on both sides.

The materials published by Slovo were diverse. Originally the plan was to publish primarily Russian classics, which would be generally popular among the émigrés. But soon the works of young émigré writers like Mark Aldanov and V. V. Nabokov were being printed through Slovo. Under Kaminka's direction Slovo also published a periodical devoted to "works of Russian scholars abroad." [51] In 1921 Gessen launched the *Arkhiv russkoi revoliutsii*, another Slovo periodical which published émigré accounts of the civil war until 1937. As Slovo sales expanded in 1921–1922 the Ullstein house established a branch organization, Logos, concerned only with book sales and headed by Gessen.

Slovo always had hopes of sending its books into Russia. Gessen once even persuaded Maltzan to provide a visa for an Ullstein representative who succeeded in obtaining the copyright for the works of several Soviet authors, including Blok, Belyi, and Zamiatin. Such an arrangement, Gessen recalled, "created the illusion of a certain closing of the gap with our homeland." [52] But Slovo was never able to exploit the Soviet book market; not only did the émigrés stoutly refuse to adopt the new orthography required of Soviet books, but their idea of exporting books to Russia came at a time when Soviet publishers themselves were establishing offices in Berlin. Slovo remained an émigré house, and as such declined when the emigration dispersed. Its prosperity came to an end with the inflation and ensuing currency stabilization. Faced with falling

---

[51] Four volumes of *Trudy russkikh uchennykh zagranitsei* appeared in 1922–1923.
[52] Gessen, "Gody skitanii," p. 118.

sales and increasing debts to their German publisher, Gessen and
his associates by 1924 had little choice but to liquidate both Slovo
and Logos by sale.

The rise and fall of the Russian book trade in Berlin coincided
with the period of greatest intellectual ferment within the colony.
Most Russian writers, artists, and scholars who came to Berlin in
these years were there between the autumn of 1921 and the summer
of 1923. Like the emigration in general, they were drawn to
Germany by its nearness to Soviet Russia, its relatively low cost
of living and its publishing opportunities. As a consequence, they
remained relatively isolated from German life. Some had been
expelled from Russia by the Soviet government, others came on
Soviet visas, uncertain about their future. But most had lived for
four or five years under the Soviet regime, unlike the first wave of
émigrés, and had no strong feelings of antipathy toward the Bolsheviks. Concerned with the fate of Russian culture more than politics,
some assumed that Soviet Russia represented a continuation of that
culture, and ultimately they moved back to the East.

A number of émigrés were returning to a Germany they knew
well from years of study abroad before 1914. Several, including
Berdiaev, Stepun, Frank, Ilin and Vysheslavtsev, had all come under the influence of the German neo-Kantian revival during their
terms at Marburg, Heidelberg, and Berlin and continued to show
a strong interest in German intellectual life before and after the
revolution. Nikolai Bubnov, who had studied under Windelband at
Heidelberg, stayed on as a professor there, helping to make Russian
religious thought intelligible to Germans. But others were more disillusioned by a return to their prewar intellectual haunts. Boris
Pasternak, revisiting his beloved Marburg in 1923, found that "Germany was hungry and cold, under no illusions, creating no illusions, her hand held out to the age as if for charity (a gesture not
at all like her), the whole country on crutches." [53]

[53] Nikolai Berdiaev, *Dream and Reality: An Essay in Autobiography* (New
York, 1951), p. 97; Fedor Stepun, *Byvshee i nebyvsheesia* (New York, 1956),
I, pp. 100–118; N. N. Alekseev, "V burnye gody," *Novyi zhurnal*, No. 54
(1958), 161–163; V. V. Zenkovsky, "B. P. Vysheslavtsev kak filosof," *ibid.*,

136

Most intellectuals, however, were simply attracted by the temporarily good postwar situation in Berlin: easy entrance visas, a large Russian colony, a cordial reception from the Germans, and publishing opportunities. The sociologist Pitrim Sorokin found his arrival in Berlin surprisingly pleasant:

I was spared many hardships of the exile's *via dolorosa,* with its pains of violent uprooting, homelessness, nostalgia, its bewilderment, frustrations, and disillusionments. During the first few days of our stay in Berlin, my wife and I were exhilarated by our regained freedom and security. In the friendly circle of the Russian émigrés in Berlin, with their intense intellectual, artistic, and political activities, we felt revitalized and happy. We were not worried about the meagerness of our financial resources and the uncertainty of our future. After the "hell" in which we had existed in Communist Russia, everything appeared quite comfortable and certainly better than that Communist inferno. Lady-Fortune seemed to be smiling at us again.[54]

For those without money there were a number of sources of financial aid, among them the YMCA, the German government, and the Red Cross. There were, of course, the inevitable problems of housing and rents. Even so, Berlin remained a relatively good place to live until the end of 1923. "In Paris," wrote Aleksei Tolstoi to Ivan Bunin, "we would be starving." [55]

But it was the opportunity to publish which made Berlin almost a dream-world for the intellectuals. They published with any one of dozens of houses: Slovo, Gelikon, Efron, Argonauts, Ogon'ki, Petropolis and the firms of Grzhebin and Ladyzhnikov. Literary periodicals sprang up overnight—*Novaia russkaia kniga,* Andrei Belyi's *Epopeia, Beseda,* Drozdov's *Spolokhi*—and were supplemented by the literary "almanacs": *Grani, Molodaia Rossiia, Strugi, Vereteno.* For every abortive literary project there were several successful ventures. Other intellectuals found opportunities for

No. 40 (1955), 249–261; Boris Pasternak, *Safe Conduct* (London, 1959), p. 226. On Bubnov see his *Ostliches Christentum: Dokumente* (Munich, 1923–1925), *Russische Frömmigkeit: Briefe eines Starzen* (Wiesbaden, 1947), *Russische Religionsphilosophen: Dokumente* (Heidelberg, 1956).

[54] Pitrim Sorokin, *A Long Journey* (New Haven, 1963), p. 198.

[55] Ivan Bunin, *Memories and Portraits* (Garden City, N.Y., 1951), pp. 185–186.

steady writing with the big émigré dailies: the poetess A. F. Damanskaia worked for *Dni;* V. F. Khodasevich found employment on Kerensky's *Golos Rossii;* I. I. Aikhenvald and Ofrosimov wrote the literary columns for *Rul'.* Other émigrés, like Mark Aldanov and Marina Tsvetaeva, came from Paris or Prague to participate in the literary renaissance.

Under such conditions many writers outdid themselves. When Aleksei Remizov was not working furiously on new articles or stories he was arranging for the publication of old ones; from Ilia Ehrenburg came nine novels; Andrei Belyi, tortured by his love affair with Asia Turgenev, drinking and dancing his way through every Berlin café, wrote endlessly—articles for *Beseda, Novaia russkaia kniga, Rul',* and his own *Epopeia,* along with no less than nine books in 1922 and 1923 alone.[56]

The cultural radius of Russian Berlin extended even beyond the boundaries of Germany. Marina Tsvetaeva in Prague was one of many who watched with interest the life of the Berlin colony: reading *Rul',* corresponding with friends there, and contributing to Berlin journals—in her case, translations of Maiakovsky's poetry into French for Ehrenburg's journal *Veshch.*[57] In Wiesbaden, Merezhkovsky and Bunin watched Berlin and read its literature. Many others came to Berlin only briefly and returned to Paris or Prague with news of the colony. Still others conveyed news of Berlin activities to journals outside Germany, as Fedor Stepun did in the pages of *Sovremennye zapiski.* Berlin for a time was the cultural hub of the diaspora.

But Berlin was also a political crossroads in these years. It was here that émigrés made the agonizing decision whether to proceed west into emigration or to return to Soviet Russia. Many had al-

---

[56] Beside his *Lalazar: Kavkazskii skaz* (Berlin, 1922), Remizov wrote a number of articles and published his earlier *Povest' o Ivane Semenoviche Stratilatove* (1909) and *Rossiia v pis'menakh,* a collection of stories written in 1917–1918. Ehrenburg wrote *Julio Jurenito, Trust D. E.,* and *The Love of Jeanne Ney,* among others. Belyi's nine volumes are *Putevye zametki* (Berlin, 1922), *Zvezda* (Moscow, 1922), *Stikhi o Rossii* (Berlin, 1922), *Posle razluki* (Berlin, 1922), *Vozvrashchenie na rodinu* (Moscow, 1922), *Sirin uchenogo varvarstva* (Berlin, 1922), *Zapiski chudaka* (Berlin, 1922), *Glossaloliia* (Berlin, 1922), *Vospominaniia o Bloke* (Berlin, 1923).

[57] "Pis'ma Mariny Tsvetaevy k Romanu Guliu," *Novyi zhurnal,* No. 58 (1959), 169–189; Ehrenburg, *Truce,* pp. 26–27.

ready made up their minds: they stayed a few months, a year, and then moved on to Paris. For some, the decision was slow and painful, made more difficult by the pleas of Soviet intellectuals that they return to Russia. A few decided on emigration. Others chose to return to Russia. For some it was hardly a difficult choice, but others had come to Berlin with the full intention of leaving their homeland permanently, and only after considerable soul-searching did they decide to return.

The coexistence in Berlin of those who had decided to emigrate and those who planned to return to Soviet Russia made the choice that much more difficult for the undecided. Many of the most active members of the intellectual community in Berlin were living on Soviet visas and intended from the beginning to return, among them Gorky, Ehrenburg, Boris Pasternak (who was in Berlin only to visit his parents and publish his poetry with Grzhebin), and Mikhail Gershenzon (who lived in Badenweiler and came to Berlin for periodic medical treatment).[58] Then there were the Soviet writers like Maiakovsky and Sergei Esenin, who were traveling abroad in these years and stopped off in Berlin. But often an individual could not easily be labeled "Soviet" or "émigré." Only a few of them, like Merezhkovsky and B. P. Vysheslavtsev, could be recognized as outwardly hostile to the Bolshevik regime.[59] For the romanticism of a new Russia and a new culture was widespread, and the political lines were not yet drawn.

In the end, most émigré intellectuals were caught up in the enthusiasm for Russia and "the East" characteristic of the postwar era in Europe. Driven to the West for political reasons, they continued to believe in the cultural mission of the East to revive

[58] "Pis'ma M. O. Gershenzona k V. F. Khodasevichu," *Novyi zhurnal*, No. 60 (1960), 222–235.

[59] Merezhkovsky remained an advocate of military intervention, to the extent of backing Hitler, until his death. Ilin, a friend of Lampe and Duke Georg of Leuchtenberg, belonged to a circle of White army officers who advocated "Christian terror" against the Bolsheviks. He was also active in the Russian Scientific Institute, edited *Russkii kolokol* (Berlin, 1927–1930), and produced a collection of essays on Russia entitled *Welt vor dem Abgrund—Politik, Wirtschaft und Kultur im kommunistischen Staate* (Berlin, 1931). Vysheslavtsev was later employed writing anti-Bolshevik literature for the Nazis' Anti-Comintern organization. See A. A. Lampe, *Puti vernykh: Sbornik statei* (Paris, 1960), pp. 193–195 and Alekseev, "Burnye gody," pp. 161–163.

Europe. "Europe cannot always go on playing the fool," wrote Roman Goul, "she must realize that Russia's salvation will be her own salvation." "Our Russian apocalypsis began in Russia," warned Merezhkovsky, "but will end in Europe; our collapse is Europe's collapse, our salvation is Europe's salvation." [60] It was an assertion which could only weaken the case of the emigration against the Bolsheviks.

Unification and Statelessness

The multiplication of émigré organizations, often overlapping in function or working consciously at cross-purposes, quickly became intolerable. Not only did it complicate the lives of the émigrés, but it meant that the German government was often vaguely informed or completely ignorant of the status and authority of any given group or individual from the colony with which it was dealing. Both the leaders of the émigré community and German officials desired an end to this confusion and hoped for some single organization which would represent the emigration on matters of common concern.

Already in early 1921 F. V. Shlippe and the Russian Red Cross had made futile attempts to register Russians in Berlin in order to obtain data on the size and composition of the colony and to enable lost friends and relatives to find each other. But such a task soon proved too much for them. In April 1921 a group of leaders of various civic and professional organizations met in Berlin and decided to create a single émigré council to work with the Russian Red Cross on problems facing the community at large. The need for some form of unity was accentuated by the claim of the Soviet government one month later that it legally represented the interests of all Russians in Germany. Finally on June 21 some fifty delegates representing over thirty different émigré organizations met under the chairmanship of Shlippe once again to consider the question of a single émigré council. [61]

The plans discussed at this meeting had been worked out in

[60] Roman Goul, *V razseian'i i sushchie* (Berlin, 1923), p. 27; *Rul'*, November 11, 1921, pp. 4–5.
[61] *Rul'*, 1921: January 22, p. 5; February 4, p. 3; April 16, p. 5; May 18, pp. 1–2; June 23, p. 3.

Theodor Schiemann (From
K. Meyer, *Theodor Schie-
mann als politischer Pub-
lizist*, Frankfort, 1956)

Rosa Luxemburg and Alexander Parvus (*center*) (Courtesy of Ullstein, Berlin)

Vasily Vasilievich Biskupsky, 1915, (Courtesy of J. J. Augustin Verlag, Glückstadt)

Metropolitan Evlogy and Northwest Army families at Altengrabow, 1919 (Courtesy of J. J. Augustin Verlag, Glückstadt)

P. M. Avalov and Northwest Army delegation in Potsdam, 1921 (Courtesy
of J. J. Augustin Verlag, Glückstadt)

Bad Reichenhall, Bavaria (Photographed by the author)

Max Erwin von Scheubner-Richter, 1918, in Riga (From Paul Leverkuehn, *Posten auf ewiger Wache: Aus dem abenteuerreichen Leben des Max von Scheubner-Richter*, Essen, 1938)

Yu. O. Martov (*left*) and Theodor Dan, 1922, in Berlin (Courtesy of Boris Sapir and the International Institute for Social History, Amsterdam)

Alexander Stein (Courtesy of Boris Sapir and the International Institute for Social History, Amsterdam)

Rafael Abramovich (Courtesy of Boris Sapir and the International Institute for Social History, Amsterdam)

General P. N. Krasnov, 1922 (Courtesy of the Hoover Library, Palo Alto)

Alexander Kerensky, 1918 (Courtesy of the Hoover Library, Palo Alto)

Maxim Gorky in Berlin, 1921 (Courtesy of Ullstein, Berlin)

Grand Duke Kirill Vladimirovich (Courtesy of J. J. Augustin Verlag, Glückstadt)

Russian Orthodox Church, Wilmersdorf (Photographed by the author)

General P. N. Wrangel, 1927 (Courtesy of the Hoover Library, Palo Alto)

recent months by a committee of émigré leaders which included Shlippe, A. V. Belgard, and L. B. Lütz. But the émigrés had difficulty agreeing on specifics. How would a single authority be financed? How would common policy be agreed upon? How much power should be delegated to it? How would decisions be made on issues that divided the colony, such as whether or not to organize famine aid for Russia in 1921? As a result, little was accomplished until the autumn of 1921. Even then the initiative came not from the émigrés themselves but from Schlesinger, now the League of Nations representative in Germany for Russian refugee affairs, and from the German government, which created a Commissar for Russian Refugees under the Ministry of the Interior. The first commissar promptly asked émigré leaders to submit to him a memorandum on the organization of a single agency with which he might deal on refugee affairs.[62]

On December 6, 1921, the Council of United Russian Institutions and Civic Organizations in Germany met under the leadership of Shlippe, Botkin, the Kadet leader V. D. Nabokov, and Senator A. A. Rimsky-Korsakov.[63] Also attending were A. A. Wrangel from the Russian Red Cross and Senator Belgard from Zemgor. During the next year the Council met periodically at the Ministry of the Interior, with German Red Cross representatives, and with Fridtjof Nansen, League of Nations High Commissioner for Refugees, when he came to Berlin in September 1922. Each member of the Council was given responsibility for specific problems—Botkin for legal matters, Shlippe for health and education, S. A. Smirnov for housing and employment, and so on. Practical work in such areas, however, was left to the appropriate member organizations. After some attempts to raise money through lotteries, social events, and even movies, the Council in the end decided to leave fund-raising up to the individual organizations as well. In the end the Council remained a coordinating body of émigré leaders whose primary function was to represent the community to outsiders.

From its inception the Council was plagued by political prob-

---

[62] *Rul'*, December 30, 1921, p. 5.

[63] The activity of the Council is described in "Ocherk deiatel'nosti soveta i soveshchaniia ob"edinennykh russkikh organizatsii i uchrezhdenii v Germanii za 1922 g." (GA, folder 33). See also BA/RD, folder 67.

lems. When Smirnov began dealing with Schlesinger in the spring of 1922 on money matters, the monarchists vigorously objected. Within the Council it became clear that the split between the forces of anti-Bolshevism and the forces of reconciliation would widen before it narrowed. The meeting of July 24, 1922, was particularly agitated over the question of future relations with the German Red Cross "Russian Section" and the department of the Ministry of the Interior, now both in the hands of Schlesinger. Within the Council the organizations represented were classified as "right," "left," and "center" politically in order to maintain some kind of numerical balance among them. But this served only to exacerbate the causes of conflict.

Thus by the end of 1922 the Council had established itself as the representative organization for the émigré community but was torn by internal disputes. The addition of five "center" organizations in the winter of 1922–1923 was of no help in solidifying the Council politically.[64] New émigrés were arriving every day now, many of them much more sympathetic to the Bolsheviks than the earlier refugees. Then, too, Schlesinger was encouraging them against the "old" émigré leaders, intriguing with the new Zemgor representative from Paris against Shlippe, and organizing the Russian Scientific Institute with Professor V. I. Yasinsky. The Institute now began to replace Zemgor as the primary agency for émigré education. Moreover Schlesinger now controlled the flow of funds from two major sources to the émigrés: the YMCA and the League of Nations. With Zemgor and the Russian Red Cross almost bankrupt, the control of such funds was a powerful political lever.[65]

By 1923 the Council, like other émigré organizations, had become largely dependent financially and politically on more powerful outside agencies: the German government, the League of Nations, and the YMCA. Relations between the old émigrés, with their strong antipathy to the Soviet regime, and these agencies, which for one reason or another had come to accept the Bolsheviks *de facto* or *de*

---

[64] "Pamiatnaia zapiska ob ob"edinenii russkikh uchrezhdenii i obshchestvennykh organizatsii v Germanii. 5 sentiabria 1922 g.–15 aprelia 1923 g." (LA, folder 22).

[65] Botkin to Giers, September 8, 1924 (GA, folder 35).

jure as the government of Russia, became increasingly cool. In the following years relations between the "old" and the "new" émigrés and their organizations were marked by suspicion, intrigue, jurisdictional disputes, and mutual accusations. The mass exodus of Russians from Germany in 1923 also helped to undercut the authority of the émigré Council. By the summer of 1924 it had ceased to exist and its functions had been taken over by the German government. The evolution of the emigration from a political community to a community of political refugees was complete.[66]

The erosion of the political authority of the émigré community was also expressed in the erosion of their juridical status. Former citizens of Imperial Russia, they were faced after 1922 with the choice of becoming Soviet citizens or stateless (staatenlos) persons, men without a country. There was a third alternative—to become a German citizen—but this was a complicated process which generally required ten to twenty years of residence in Germany and was undertaken mainly by the Russian Germans.[67] Thus the early 1920's saw the émigrés lose their power to control their own affairs on such important matters as visas, passports, marriage and divorce. They became refugees whose status was largely determined by the German government and in German courts by an attitude that remained until 1933 "always cool, but at the same time correct." [68]

Until 1914 the status of Russians in Germany had been determined by treaties, principles of international law, and German law. In general the rights to hold property, to engage in business transactions, and to receive legal counsel enjoyed by Russians in Germany were greater than equivalent rights of German citizens in Russia. No visas were required to enter Germany, and passports were demanded of Russians only because of the more stringent passport formalities imposed by the Russian government. During the war, of course, the rights of Russians in Germany were abrogated and the number of Russians entering the country was reduced

[66] Botkin to Giers, June 16, 1925, and August 26, 1924 (*ibid.*).

[67] Simpson, *Refugee Problem*, p. 601; A. Goldenweiser, "Die Rechtslage der russischen Flüchtlinge," II ("Deutschland"), 49 (typescript, private collection).

[68] Goldenweiser, "Rechtslage," p. 2.

143

almost to zero. These rights were again returned, however, with the signing of the Treaty of Brest-Litovsk.[69]

Beginning in 1919 all foreigners entering or leaving German territory had to carry a passport and receive a visa stamp on crossing the border. Foreigners were also required to report to the local police within forty-eight hours of their arrival to receive another personal identity card (*Personalausweis*) to move about within Germany and to obtain permission to reside there (*Aufenthaltsbewilligung*). The term of residence was specified on the entrance visa and could only be altered by permission, first from the Foreign Office in Berlin and then from the local police. A Prussian law of November 17, 1920, standardized the duration of the *Personalausweis* at six weeks to three months, after which it had to be renewed. (It was later extended to six months because of the enormous paperwork involved.) [70]

Until the treaty of May 6, 1921, there was no formal Soviet representation in Berlin and hence no way for Russian émigrés to receive a Russian passport except through Botkin's Russian Delegation. Most Russians at this time were living on an incredible variety of passports which had been issued not only by the Imperial Russian and Provisional governments but also by the various regional authorities of the White armies. Botkin, through negotiations with Maltzan at the Foreign Office, had received for his Delegation the right to issue the *Personalausweis* needed by every émigré at regular intervals not only for residence in Germany but also in order to receive an exit visa from the German government. This small yellow identity card (*gelber Ausweis*) could be obtained either at the Delegation in person or by mail from other parts of Germany, and then required the sanction of the local police. Until 1923 it was possible for representatives of the Russian Delegation and the Russian Red Cross to obtain from the Wilhelmstrasse not only the German *Ausweise* but also foreign passports to leave Germany for another country.[71]

[69] I. M. Rabinovich, *Russkie v Germanii: Iuridicheskii spravochnik* (Berlin, 1921) and "Spravka ob uzakoneniiakh i pravilakh deistvuiushchikh dlia inostrantsev v Germanii dlia v"ezda v stranu, prozhivaniia v nei i vyezda iz neia" (GA, folder 32).

[70] *Rul'*, August 11, 1921.

[71] Botkin to Giers, February 22, 1924 (GA, folder 34).

But the treaty of May 1921 marked the beginning of a steady undermining of these rights. Henceforth the Soviet representative in Berlin could also issue *Ausweise* and passports. Moreover, Soviet decrees of October 28 and December 15, 1921, deprived of their Russian nationality and citizenship all those refugees who had (1) left Russia without a Soviet visa after November 7, 1917, or (2) lived abroad for a period of five years or more and not obtained a Soviet passport or nationality certificate by June 1, 1922.[72] With the conclusion of the Treaty of Rapallo on April 16, 1922, and after German recognition of the Soviet government, those Russians who refused to recognize the authority of Russia's rulers were now legally stateless. In practice it was still possible to obtain *Ausweise* and passports from the Russian Delegation until 1924, although the German government was under constant pressure from the Bolsheviks not to issue them.[73]

Because of the availability of both Soviet and non-Soviet Russian passports in Germany, the system of Nansen certificates never became widely employed. Fridtjof Nansen, the sixty-year old polar explorer, League of Nations High Commissioner for Refugees since September 1921, had developed in 1922 an identity certificate (known as the "Nansen passport") valid for one year which would provide for stateless persons a measure of freedom and legal protection and would be issued by the country of refuge. A Nansen office was opened in Berlin in 1922 by Moritz Schlesinger, its head until 1931, but the German government found little reason to convert to this system and preferred to deal with both the Soviet representatives and Botkin. Whereas in some countries the Nansen passport was mandatory, in Germany only a few were actually issued. Until 1924 it was still easy for an émigré to get his transit or exit visa from Botkin.[74]

The Treaty of Rapallo affected the entire legal status of Russians in Germany, as well as the passport system. According to German law foreigners whose cases were being tried in German courts would usually be dealt with according to the laws of their own

[72] Simpson, *Refugee Problem*, p. 233.

[73] Botkin to Giers, February 22, 1924 (GA, folder 34).

[74] Simpson, *Refugee Problem*, pp. 197–207, 239–242; Goldenweiser, "Rechtslage," pp. 8 ff.; Hans-Erich Volkmann, *Die russische Emigration in Deutschland, 1919–1929* (Würzburg, 1966), pp. 32–45.

country. Until the treaty of May 6, 1921, this meant for Russians in Germany that they would be tried according to Imperial Russian law. But in the second half of 1921 there was a steady shift in this position, marked by oscillation and indecision in cases before the German courts. With Rapallo the émigrés became legally stateless, and hence would be judged by German law in accordance with the law of the country of which they were most recently a citizen—interpreted to mean Soviet Russia. Except in a few isolated cases, German courts in practice now began to follow this guideline, to the dismay of most émigrés.[75]

The most frequent legal problems arose from cases concerning émigré marriage and divorce. After Rapallo neither was recognized as valid in Germany unless concluded in either German or Soviet civil courts. In several cases émigrés who had married or divorced in areas occupied by the White armies during the Russian Civil War suddenly found themselves considered in German courts to be unmarried or bigamists. Marriage and divorce in emigration raised similar problems. In the autumn of 1921 a German court refused to recognize the divorce of a Russian woman, which had been granted by an Orthodox ecclesiastical court headed by Metropolitan Evlogy, until it had also been sanctioned by a German civil court.[76] Henceforth divorce demanded not only the permission of the Orthodox church abroad but also of a German court.

Thus by 1923 the transformation of Russian émigrés into men without a country was largely completed. To the constant pressure to become Soviet citizens was added the difficulty of becoming German ones. Expulsion from Germany or a German province was another constant threat, should an émigré for any reason be designated an "undesirable alien." But in practice this threat was usually used only in cases of those who, like Avalov or other right-wing political figures, chose activity frowned upon by the Weimar government. In general, German policy toward the Russian community in the 1920's was one of toleration. "The German government," wrote Botkin in early 1924, "looks upon all of us as political émigrés whose extradition is impermissible."[77]

[75] Botkin to Giers, March 5, 1924 (GA, folder 34).
[76] Rul', October 8, 1921, p. 5.
[77] Botkin to Giers, February 22, 1924 (GA, folder 34), p. 12.

The Non-Russians

Not all former citizens of the Russian Empire now in emigration in Germany were Russians. There were large numbers of Ukrainians, Poles, Jews, Balts, Georgians, Armenians, and Russian Germans in Germany in these years, and often they had their own organizations. The most active communities were those of the Russian Germans and the Jews, some of whose organizations antedated the war. Organizations of the other non-Russian nationalities, however, were more ephemeral. Often they were an unanticipated legacy of Germany's wartime policy of lending political, economic, and military support to non-Russians against the central government in hopes of facilitating the disintegration of Russia's war effort. It was a policy which now haunted the Wilhelmstrasse.

The center of the Ukrainian nationalist emigration before and after the war was not Berlin but Vienna. During the war a group of Ukrainian exiles headed by Dmitro Doncov and calling themselves the Union for the Emancipation of the Ukraine had engaged in nationalist propaganda there under the watchful eyes of the Austrian government. Doncov had lived in Berlin for a time during the war, where he wrote articles and pamphlets against the Poles and the Russians. But with the March 1917 revolution Doncov and a number of other Ukrainian exiles had returned to Kiev to participate in the Rada government. When the German army of occupation decided in late April 1918 to install their own "Ukrainian" ruler, they chose not a Ukrainian nationalist politician but a Russian Guards officer, Paul Petrovich Skoropadsky.[78]

As a result the rule of "Hetman" Skoropadsky, from April 29,

[78] For the story of events in the Ukraine in these years see John Reshetar, *The Ukrainian Revolution, 1917–1920* (Princeton, 1952). Skoropadsky was a Russian cavalry officer who had served in the same regiment with P. N. Wrangel in 1905 and in World War I as commander of the 34th Army Corps and ADC to Nicholas II. Stationed near Kiev at the time of the March 1917 revolution, Skoropadsky as a conservative landowner and army officer was hardly enthusiastic about either the Rada government or the Bolsheviks. In April 1918 he convinced General Groener that he was the man to replace the Rada with a dictatorship capable of meeting German grain delivery quotas while quelling peasant unrest. He was accordingly made "hetman" on April 29, 1918, with the blessings of leading landowners and the Bishop of Kiev.

1918, until his formal abdication on December 14, was sustained only by the presence of German troops and was suspect to all who considered themselves either liberal socialist or nationalist on the Ukrainian political scene. Although his government did have its own Foreign Ministry and was allowed to negotiate with the Bolsheviks during the summer of 1918, its autonomy was always questionable. Skoropadsky's government was primarily a facade and any serious policy had to be approved in Berlin. When the Republican army of Simon Petliura moved on Kiev in December, Skoropadsky had little choice but to flee to Germany. It was an inglorious form of emigration for the hetman. Disguised as a German army doctor, he made his way to Berlin in a trainload of wounded German troops and was hidden by the Wilhelmstrasse in a house in Friedenau to protect him from assassination at the hands of Ukrainian nationalists. Here he lived for several weeks under the name of Blochau (which he soon changed to one which sounded less Semitic, Reichoranta) to await the arrival of his wife, appropriately disguised as a German army nurse.[79]

Until the end of 1920 Skoropadsky and his entourage lived in Berlin, competing with supporters of Petliura for the political backing of the German Foreign Office and the possession of some four hundred million marks still credited to "the Ukrainian government" at the Reichsbank for grain deliveries made in 1918. The Wilhelmstrasse for a time retained an interest in Skoropadsky as a possible future Ukrainian political leader and also as a source of information on events in the Ukraine during 1919. But Skoropadsky in German eyes was not a serious contender for leadership in any future Ukraine; he was more interested in obtaining the funds at the Reichsbank. Rejected by the Ukrainian "national center" in Vienna, headed by his former Foreign Minister, Dmitro Doroshenko, Skoropadsky now drifted into political isolation, to emerge only with the rise of the "monarchist" movement in emigration in early 1921.

With the collapse of the hetmanate in late 1918 a new staff of Ukrainians had appeared in Berlin to occupy the old quarters of the Ukrainian embassy on the Kronprinzenufer. These were the representatives of Petliura's new government in Kiev, headed by

[79] Blücher, *Deutschlands Weg*, p. 41.

148

the Galician scholar Roman Smal-Stocki. Smal-Stocki quickly established his own relationship with the Wilhelmstrasse, the traditional point of contact for the more politically minded émigrés. Once every week he would visit Wipert von Blücher, the Eastern Section Legationsrat assigned to the Russian émigrés, to report on Ukrainian developments and to protect Ukrainian interests against the "Great Russian generals" Denikin and Kolchak and their sympathizers in Berlin. Like Skoropadsky, he also attempted to unearth the funds now sealed in the Reichsbank and claimed by every "Ukrainian" faction in emigration. But the Germans trusted the stability of Petliura's government no more than any previous one in Kiev. Smal-Stocki's attempts to portray his government as the last line of defense against Bolshevism (which he admittedly was also telling British diplomats in Berlin) only met with an understanding but unproductive cordiality.[80]

Petliura's position in Berlin was further compromised in the spring of 1920 when he allied himself with the Polish army of General Pilsudski, then marching on Kiev. Germany had counted on an independent Ukraine as a counterweight not only to Russia but also to an independent Poland. Now Petliura, for whom the Germans had little sympathy in 1918, had gone over to the Poles himself. Attempts by Smal-Stocki to describe this as a purely tactical maneuver met a stony response in Berlin. Nor was it surprising that the German government turned down Petliura's request for military advisers from the Reichswehr that summer. By the end of November 1920 the Bolsheviks had occupied Kiev, Petliura and his government had fled to Poland, and the doors of the Ukrainian embassy in Berlin were formally closed. Smal-Stocki himself, however, continued to occupy the building as a political lobbyist until November 1922, when he was removed only with the aid of the Berlin police. Like Botkin's Russian Delegation, his Vertrauenstelle für Ukrainische Flüchtlinge continued to handle the daily passport, visa, and legal problems of Ukrainian émigrés in Germany.[81]

[80] *Ibid.*, pp. 41, 84, 86–89; Botkin to S. D. Sazonov, May 7, 1920 (GA, folder 32).

[81] Blücher, *Deutschlands Weg*, pp. 50, 88, 90; G. Frants, "Evakuatsiia germanskimi voiskami Ukrainy (zima 1918–1919 g.)," *Istorik i sovremennik*, 1922, No. 2, p. 269; Botkin to Giers, February 21, 1923 (GA folder 33).

Neither Smal-Stocki nor Skoropadsky and their Ukrainian friends had limited themselves to dealings with the Germans in 1920. Arnold Margolin, a Jewish lawyer from Kiev who had been a leading figure in the Rada government in 1917 and later a lobbyist for Ukrainian interests at the Paris Peace Conference in 1919, already in March 1920 was attempting to get the British government to pressure the Germans into releasing to him the well-publicized Ukrainian account at the Reichsbank. But Skoropadsky, too, had his representative in London, explaining to the British Foreign Office that Skoropadsky was not really "pro-German," while asking the Wilhelmstrasse for money to keep a "Ukrainian" representative in London on a permanent basis. In letters to both Berlin and London he dangled Ukrainian trade opportunities and urged a program of Anglo-German economic cooperation in resurrecting the Ukraine under the political leadership of Skoropadsky. Smal-Stocki also approached both German and British officials in Berlin with proposals of joint backing for a future Ukraine under Petliura. In the end, the obvious Bolshevik victory in the Russian Civil War reduced all these proposals to unreality in the eyes of their intended supporters.[82]

By 1921 Ukrainian politicians in Berlin could claim to represent no effective political authority other than themselves. The Wilhelmstrasse lost interest in supporting them and Maltzan now referred their requests for money to German businessmen.[83] But although the centers of the Ukrainian emigration were now Vienna, Warsaw, and Paris, a substantial Ukrainian community remained in Berlin in these years. Like the Russians, they had their clubs, welfare societies, their Union of Ukrainian Students, and even a Ukrainian choir. But like the Russian organizations, these too suffered from the passage of time and the pressures of the Soviet government, which took over the Ukrainian embassy in the autumn of 1922. For them, too, the Treaty of Rapallo marked their transformation from

[82] AGFM, T-120, roll 3073, 6612/E498303-363.

[83] *Ibid.*, particularly the letters of his representative, Stepanovsky, dated November 9 and December 11, 1920, to Dr. Karl von Schubert, which were sent on to Maltzan. Stepanovsky proposed the investment of German capital in a joint "English-German Company for the Reconstruction of the Ukraine," in which he hoped some Italians would also be involved.

claimants to Ukrainian nationality and political authority into *Staatenlosen.*

Like the Ukrainians in Berlin, the Georgians were a legacy of German wartime policy. German military and industrial circles had long been interested in Georgia for its valuable deposits of oil and manganese, and during the war Count Schulenberg, the German consul at Tiflis, has established a Georgian Committee in Berlin under Prince Matchabelli as a kind of government in exile. A Georgian legion had also been formed by Schulenberg, which saw service with the Turkish army in Anatolia for a time. In 1918 the German government had entered into friendly and profitable relations with the Georgian Menshevik government and established ties between Georgian leaders and German socialists which were maintained after the Armistice. The small Georgian colony in Berlin, however, was essentially a Menshevik colony, its existence temporary, and its connections more with German social democracy and the Russian Mensheviks than with the émigré community at large. The Georgians, however, like the Armenians in Berlin, were allowed certain rights as individuals to issue passports and visas and to be represented at the Wilhelmstrasse on an unofficial basis.[84]

But the most active and flourishing non-Russian communities in emigration proved to be those of the Russian Germans and the Jews. Some of their organizations had grown up in Berlin before the war and were now revived in a new form. Others developed, like their Russian counterparts, out of the needs of the immediate post-war situation. Often individuals from these groups, particularly Balts and Jews, could move easily into émigré Russian or German life and were not attached to any particular organization. Yet for large numbers of Russian-German and Jewish émigrés, especially the former peasant colonist or the Jewish craftsman or artisan, such

[84] Blücher, *Deutschlands Weg,* pp. 123–124. For an account of Georgian émigré politics in Berlin see Chapter V below. Two Armenians in Berlin—one Grinfel'd, born in England, and Nazariants, prewar Berlin correspondent of the Kadet daily *Rech'*—actually enjoyed semidiplomatic status and extraterritorial rights until the spring of 1922, when they were reduced to the status of private individuals. They continued to run their own *Vertrauenstelle* for Armenians in Berlin. See Botkin to Giers, April 14, 1923 (GA, folder 33).

individuals played an important part in the economic and cultural adjustment to German life.

The Baltic Germans, as we have seen, were often active within the Russian community where they were able to employ their familiarity with Germany in the first years of the emigration. But they also had their own organizations. *Ausweise* and passports could be obtained from a special office for Baltic German émigrés. Then there were Baltic German churches and choirs, welfare organizations and clubs. There was a Baltic Red Cross, independent of the Russian organization. Even in Hamburg there was a Russian-German Club of thirty or forty members. Then there were the inevitable political circles of Balts, such as the Guide to Economic Interests in the East, which under various guises tried to encourage German interest in rescuing the Baltic area from the threat of Soviet Russia.[85]

The Russian Germans from other areas of Russia also had their organizations in Germany. Beside the Society for Russian Citizens of German Origin, there were two other similar organizations represented on the Council of émigré organizations: the Union of German Colonists and the Union of Former Students of Moscow's German Schools. There were a number of other smaller groups of Russia's *Auslandsdeutschtum* which also attracted the attention of German nationalists: the Union for Germans Abroad, the Union of Volga Germans, and the Union of Colonized Areas of Russia. There was even a private school for Russian Germans in Berlin, established in December 1920 and modeled after the German *Kirchenschulen* of prewar Moscow and St. Petersburg. Like the Balts, these groups also engaged in both political and welfare activity, drawing constant attention to the plight of their countrymen still in Russia and providing some kind of community life for those in Germany.[86]

[85] *Rul'*, January 29 and February 15, 1921, p. 5.
[86] Johannes Schleuning, *Aus tiefster Not: Schicksale der deutschen Kolonisten in Russland* (Berlin, 1922); "Die Deutsch-Russische Schule—Berlin, 1920–1945," *Heimatbuch der deutschen aus Russland*, 1962, pp. 77–81.

But the Russian-German colonists differed enormously from the Balts in their economic and social status. Mainly peasant families, they found themselves in a much more tragic position in postwar Germany, often homeless, with little food, clothing, or money and utterly bewildered by the catastrophic events which had brought them there. Few were as able as the more cosmopolitan and upper-class Balts to adjust to their new position. But in Germany they were helped by organizations such as the Society to Aid German Returnees in Berlin, which had helped Germans emigrate from Russia since before the war, or by such international organizations as the Red Cross or the American Relief Administration. More aid came from Russian Germans who had emigrated to Canada and the United States before 1914 and were now engaged in sending food and clothing to their countrymen inside and outside of Russia.[87]

For the Mennonites, as for many other Russian-German families, Germany was a transit point on the way to join friends and relatives in North America. In the spring of 1920 a German government "study commission" had met with a number of German Mennonites at Heilbronn-am-Neckar to organize a German Mennonite Aid society to help the Mennonite families who had fled South Russia with the German army in the winter of 1918–1919. About seventy-five needy families were finally settled in barracks at a Bavarian army parade ground at Lechfeld, near Augsburg. Additional colonists who arrived in Germany during the famine years of 1922 and 1923, often afflicted with cholera or trachoma, were housed there until their health could meet Canadian immigration requirements. Despite attempts to turn Lechfeld into an agricultural colony, it remained essentially a temporary home for most of its members. But the attraction to German culture and feeling of disdain for *die dumme Russen* was increased by their experience here. "Germany's care for her adopted children in these rescue operations," recalled one Mennonite, "reinforced the impact of German culture upon the Russian Mennonites and explains in part

[87] *Heimatbuch*, 1957, pp. 175–180; H. H. Fischer, *The Famine in Soviet Russia, 1919–1923* (Stanford, 1927), pp. 462–467.

why Germany and German culture had held a continuing attraction for them, both in Canada and South America." [88]

In their economic and social status the Jews coming to Germany from Russia after the war were not unlike the German colonists. For the most part they were craftsmen, artisans, and laborers from the towns of the Pale of Settlement. Unlike the colonists, however, they were not well received in Germany, although conditions had improved somewhat since before the war. During the war Russian Jews in Germany were often treated as enemy aliens, despite their own antipathy to the Russian government. Along with the talk of a Jewish danger in the East came demands for immigration restrictions. On April 23, 1918, the Prussian government forbade the further admission of Jewish seasonal laborers from Poland, although their traditional migration revived gradually within a year. Despite restrictions and hardships, Germany remained after 1917 a haven for Jewish refugees seeking sanctuary from pogroms and civil war.

By the end of 1918 there were approximately 160,000 foreign Jews living in Germany. More than half of these had lived there since before 1914 and the remainder were mainly war prisoners or workers imported forcibly from Russia and Poland during the war. Of the 90,000 Jews who had lived in Germany even before the war, about 23,000 were from the Russian Empire. In the wake of the revolution and war there was a new influx of some 75,000 more Ostjuden into Germany, although 47,000 of these had left Germany again within a few years, returning to Poland or moving on to Western Europe and the United States.[89]

A number of Jewish cultural, social, and educational groups had existed in Germany since before 1914. By 1916 the Verein Perez, one of the more important Jewish societies, claimed a membership of

[88] F. Epp, *Mennonite Exodus* (Altona, Manitoba, 1962), pp. 63, 143, 168–170; *Die Mennoniten-Gemeinden in Russland während der Kriegs- und Revolutionsjahre 1914 bis 1920* (Heilbronn-am-Neckar, 1921), pp. 106–109. The Mennonites were not Germans but ancestors of Swiss and Dutch Anabaptists who had moved into Germany in the sixteenth century and on to Russia in the late 1700's.

[89] Adler-Rudel, *Ostjuden*, pp. 60–61; Simpson, *Refugee Problem*, pp. 526–527.

almost seven hundred.[90] But the main organization for Jewish immigrants from Russia was the so-called Labor Aid Office or Arbeiterfürsorgeamt, set up by the Prussian Ministry of Internal Affairs in 1919. The Office soon became a kind of consulate for *Ostjuden* arriving in Germany in 1919 and 1920. With a network of local welfare and labor organizations attached to it, its main function was to protect the legal rights of Jewish immigrants and to help them find jobs and housing.

There were a number of other Jewish organizations. The general Union of Eastern Jews, organized in the spring of 1920, worked closely with the Labor Aid Office on matters concerning Jewish émigrés from Russia. There was also a Union of Russian Jews, headed by a former judge and State Councillor Jacob Teitel, which was very active in helping to obtain and distribute funds for poor families. The older ORT (Organization for Rehabilitation and Training) society, a Jewish labor organization founded in Russia in 1880, had also moved its headquarters to Berlin, where a World ORT Union was organized in 1921. It now became the central labor agency coordinating the affairs of Jewish workers in Germany, Poland, Rumania, and the Baltic states. Even the Jewish Red Cross, founded in Russia in 1912, was active in Berlin in these years.

Berlin also became the main cultural center for East European Jewry in the 1920's. The Jewish theater flourished, Jewish reading rooms and libraries were well attended, and numerous books and periodicals in Hebrew and Yiddish appeared with a Berlin imprint. By 1923 Germany was second only to the United States as a producer of Jewish books.[91] The home of Poale Zion on the Linienstrasse became a great meeting place for old friends from Warsaw, Cracow, Kiev, or Vienna; the Zionist socialist organization issued two journals: *Jüdische Arbeiterstimme* in German and the literary-political periodical *Unsere Bewegung* in Yiddish. The operations of the YIVO Institute for Jewish Research also moved to Berlin from Geneva. In 1921 the Eastern Jewish Historical Archive was established in Berlin to investigate the pogroms of 1919–1921 in the Ukraine and Belorussia.

The Russian Jewish socialist organization known as the Bund

[90] Adler-Rudel, *Ostjuden*, p. 64.   [91] *Ibid.*, p. 108.

was another element in the Berlin Jewish colony. Like the Zionists, many Bundists were soon involved in activities outside their own circle, the international labor movement, and were on their way to the United States to join friends or relatives. Within the emigration in Berlin their organization was only of minor significance, although as individuals some Bundists became involved in the work of the Russian Menshevik colony and thus with the German labor movement. For a short time the Bund newspaper, *Der Morgenstern*, was published in Berlin, and the Bund historical archive was moved from Geneva to the basement of the *Vorwärts* offices in Berlin with the help of German socialists.

The size of the Jewish emigration to Germany at this time and the involvement of a number of Jews in the socialist movement helped exacerbate an already strong German feeling against Eastern Jews. A number of laws were passed to restrict or eliminate their immigration. A German law of February 24, 1920, specified that all alien workers needed a German visa to come to Germany, which in turn required having a job promised in advance through the state employment office (Deutsche Arbeiterzentrale) and living quarters arranged through the housing authorities. Permission to hire aliens was granted by the Arbeiterzentrale only to employers whose wages were fixed according to those paid to German workers; conversely, a foreign laborer could remain in Germany only as long as he could find an employer who had such permission.[92] In theory such legislation was aimed at preventing immigration in general and protecting the rights of German workers; in fact Jewish immigrants from the East suffered the most from its restrictions.

Other German legislation and policy was aimed directly at the Jews. In a memorandum of March 16, 1920, submitted to the Prussian government during the wave of unrest that followed the Kapp Putsch, General Hans von Seeckt proposed that all *Ostjuden* in Berlin be interned in camps. Many Jews were in fact arrested and interned in the following months. Thousands were expelled from Bavaria and Silesia. In early 1921 the situation became even worse

[92] *International Labor Review*, I (1922), 204; J. Brown, *World Migration and Labour* (Amsterdam, 1926), pp. 226–227.

when Dominicus of the Democratic party replaced the socialist Severing as Prussian Minister of Internal Affairs. On February 26, 1921, a decree was promulgated providing for the interning of undesirable aliens (*lästige Ausländer*) on sometimes flimsy pretexts, including inability to produce one's personal identity card upon request. In both Prussia and Saxony hundreds of Jews found themselves confined to barracks in the camps at Stargard and Cottbus. With Severing's return to office, however, the worst excesses ceased. By 1923 most of the camps had been closed and an August 23, 1923, edict limited internment to those previously convicted of antistate activity. By the end of that year, as the political situation in Germany at last appeared to be stabilizing, the interning of undesirable aliens was halted completely.[93]

A sketch of the internal political and cultural life of the Baltic-German and Jewish colonies in Berlin, however, does not explain their importance in German and Russian émigré life in the 1920's. Nor was the relative size of these two groups within the emigration important in itself. More significant was their ability to play an active part within either Russian or German political and cultural life and to serve as interpreters, organizers, and intermediaries between Russians and Germans. Within the émigré community and its organizations the Baltic Germans appeared as key figures, mainly because these organizations were dominated by upper-class Russians. For this reason the Baltic Germans generally gravitated to the right on the émigré political spectrum and the Jews to the left. Thus in the German mind the Baltic Germans were linked with the conservative defense of the old Europe and the Jews with the forces of change and revolution. For the political left in Germany the Balts appeared as the purveyors of reaction, imperialism, and monarchism—qualities associated with the old order in Europe. For the political right the *Ostjuden* were revolutionaries, Bolsheviks, the architects of the Bavarian Soviet Republic, and the Asiatic bearers of the disease of revolution in Germany. Moreover, both the Baltic Germans and the Jews among the émigrés helped rein-

[93] Adler-Rudel, *Ostjuden*, pp. 115–121.

force these attitudes in Germany toward the other group, the Balts as frequent anti-Semites and the Jews as critics of the reactionary Baltic barons. Just as before the war, their role in interpreting Russia to Germans revealed the relative ease with which they were able to adjust to the political and cultural life of the two countries.

⸺❦ IV ❧⸺

Politics of Adjustment

The Russian political circles that began to emerge in Germany during and after the Russian Civil War were generally regroupings of traditional Russian parties. Indeed, the monarchists, the liberals, and the socialists in exile differed as much among themselves as they did from the Bolsheviks, as the subsequent failure of anti-Bolshevism to cement émigré disputes indicated. Their support thus came more often from their German hosts than from their fellow émigrés, and it was to like-minded German political circles that the monarchists, Constitutional Democrats, and Mensheviks turned in Berlin in the early 1920's. In seeking out German ideological comradeship, financial backing, and publishing facilities, the Russians soon found that the indispensable intermediaries were often prewar émigrés or people familiar with Germany, particularly Russian Germans and Jews. In fact, all three of these factions moved quickly into German political life through the mediation of four such "marginal" or "Westernized" individuals: Max Erwin von Scheubner-Richter and Alfred Rosenberg for the monarchists, Iosif Vladimirovich Gessen for the Kadets, and Alexander Stein for the Mensheviks. All four spoke German, had been to Germany before the war, and were able to play a key role both in organizing the first Russian political groupings in Berlin and in finding outlets for the various shades of anti-Bolshevik sentiment that developed in the German press.

Politics of Adjustment

The Monarchists

Since the Bolshevik revolution was a revolution from the left, it was not surprising that the politics of the Russian emigration in Germany in the early 1920's were primarily politics of the right. Conservative politicians and army officers of the old regime had played a leading role in the Baltic intervention and continued to dominate the politics of the emigration. This was true outside Germany as well. But in Germany the Russian political right in emigration was especially strong, not only because of its traditional Germanophilia but also because it was warmly received by the political right in Germany, first in Berlin and later (after the Kapp Putsch) in Bavaria.

The "monarchist"[1] Russian emigration in Germany from 1919 to 1923 provides a story of increasing political frustration and despair, unpopularity with the Weimar government and much of German public opinion, and movement toward the far right in German politics. Hopeful at first of political support from the new Weimar government, the Russians were gradually forced to turn to those Germans who were themselves members of a powerless former political elite. These were the old leaders of the Second Empire in Germany who, like the Russians, had suffered the collapse of their old way of life by defeat in war and revolution. But by 1923 many Russians were interested in new and more extreme movements in European politics, notably Mussolini's fascism and Adolf Hitler's National Socialist German Workers' Party (NSDAP) in Munich. Many found in these groups an appealing antiliberal and anti-Semitic philosophy which they mistakenly felt stood for a restoration of the prewar European order of things and which they could utilize to further their own ends.

The Baltic Germans again proved important in putting right-wing Russians and Germans in touch with each other in these years.

[1] In its specific and narrow sense the term "monarchist" denotes those émigrés who, beginning in the spring of 1921, stood for the restoration of Romanov rule in Russia. In a broader sense the term will also be used to denote a conservative or reactionary political outlook characteristic of most such monarchists. When another shade of meaning is intended, a qualifying term will be employed, e.g., "constitutional monarchists."

Their own anti-Russian attitudes were reinforced now by German nationalism, and they in turn helped convey to German politics certain attitudes of Baltic Germans toward Russia and of Russians toward Jews. The colonial anti-Slav tendency in the German middle class and aristocracy of the Baltic area found once again, as it had before the war, a strong resonance in German nationalism. And once again the Russian Germans demonstrated their role as "marginal men," able to move freely in the political and cultural worlds of both Russia and Germany.

The political mood of the first wave of right-wing Russian aristocrats, politicians, and army officers who arrived in Berlin in 1918 and 1919 was one of desperation and bewilderment; they felt that they had survived a catastrophe brought on by deep and dark forces of change. War and revolution had broken their world into pieces, and they demanded an explanation. Like the medieval upheavals that had enveloped Europe in the form of the Black Death or the Tatar invasion in the thirteenth century, the First World War and the Bolshevik revolution induced in many people a feeling that the satanic forces of Antichrist were at hand and that the Jews were his agents. The traditional forces of evil—the Jews and the Mongols, the enemy within and without—were moving from the East to take revenge on the white race and Christian Europe.[2]

Such notions were common in the political literature of many countries in the wake of the war. But for the Russian émigrés they had a specific, concrete, and personal meaning. For them the "demonic servants of the prince of darkness" were indeed destroying the Russia in which they believed.[3] Did not the Jewish Bolsheviks now rule in Moscow itself? Were they not responsible for every insidious development in Russia since 1905, for the revolution of 1917, perhaps even for World War I? And was not the personal tragedy of every émigré a harbinger of things to come for Europe too? Were not the Jews and the Mongols plotting to take over the world from its European masters? The conspiracy theories of émigré right-wing periodicals in these years might be easy to dis-

[2] A. Castiglioni, *Adventures of the Mind* (New York, 1946), p. 361.
[3] Nikolai Talberg, *Kara bozhiia* (Berlin, 1920), p. 29.

miss were they not so widespread. Moreover, behind the extreme and sometimes ludicrous attempts to prove that the Rothschilds or Asiatics were behind every upheaval in world history lay a deep-seated fear on the part of many Europeans that their dominant role in the world was coming to an end, that new forces from the East were emerging, and that Europe was declining. It was a fear that many Balts were willing to cultivate.[4]

It was hardly surprising that the most politically active Baltic Germans in emigration were found on the political right. If their German nationalism had generated Russophobia before the war, their upper- and middle-class backgrounds now asserted themselves in their conservative anti-Bolshevism. Often they had experienced firsthand the loss of family, friends, and property during the Baltic intervention of 1918–1919. Even if they had not, they soon found that in Germany little was known about events in Russia during and after 1917. It was not surprising, therefore, that the Balts and the Russian Germans in general were among the first to warn of the dangers of Bolshevism in Germany. Familiar with Russia and fluent in German, journalists like the *Berliner Tageblatt's* Hans Vorst emerged everywhere as "Baltic Russian experts" who began by providing information and often ended by becoming prophets.

The Russian Germans were particularly bitter about their fate.[5] Many were visible in the several German propaganda organizations which sprang up in 1918 and 1919 to warn the German public against the dangers of Bolshevism in the wake of the November

---

[4] The fantastic notions of the Russian political right found their way to countries other than Germany in the 1920's. For an extreme version see Major-General Count Cherep-Spiridovich's *The Secret World Government or "The Hidden Hand,"* (New York, 1926) which describes a Jewish-Mongol plot to take over the world from Christianity and the White race and concludes that "the study of history proves indisputably that all the revolts and wars since 1770 were started by the Rothschild Jews" (p. 41). The author claimed to be a direct descendant of Riurik, and thus of true "Nordic origin." The *Protocols of the Elders of Zion* was also available in many countries at this time. See Walter Laqueur, *Russia and Germany* (London, 1965) and Norman Cohn, *Warrant for Genocide* (London, 1967), *passim*.

[5] On the Russian Germans see Johannes Schleuning, *Aus tiefster Not: Schicksale der deutschen Kolonisten in Russland* (Berlin, 1922) and F. Epp, *Mennonite Exodus* (Altona, Manitoba, 1962).

1918 turmoil in Berlin and the Bavarian Soviet Republic of April 1919. The most important such organization was the Anti-Bolshevik League of Eduard Stadtler, a former Catholic journalist from Düsseldorf who had been a prisoner of war in Russia since 1915.[6] The real danger of Bolshevism, Stadtler felt, lay not in the amount of territory under Bolshevik control but in its ideological appeal. Upon his return to Germany after the Armistice, he joined Heinrich von Gleichen, former head of the wartime propaganda agency known as the Union of German Scholars and Artists in organizing a new Union for National and Social Solidarity to wage intellectual war upon Germany's enemies at home and abroad. Through Gleichen and the "solidarists," Stadtler met a circle of Balts who had come to Germany before the war and who reinforced his own ideas concerning the "Bolshevik danger" in the East; among them were Max Boehm, Caesar von Schilling, and Paul Schiemann, Theodor Schiemann's nephew. With the expertise of these men and the financial backing of German industrialists, Stadtler in December 1918 formally established his General Secretariat for the Study and Combating of Bolshevism, and its journal, *Anti-Bolshevik Correspondence* (*A.B.C.*). Beside the Balts, Stadtler recruited for his staff Siegfried Dorschlag, a German colonist from South Russia whom he had met while interned near Kiev; Heinz Fenner, a former journalist for the *St. Petersburger Zeitung;* and Ernst Jenny, the "Russian expert" of the conservative *Deutsche Tageszeitung.*[7]

The pamphlets turned out by Stadtler and his Russian-German entourage in 1919 were overtly propagandistic and claimed a first-hand knowledge of the horrors of Bolshevism. The titles alone conveyed their message: "In the Bolshevik Insane Asylum," "The Asiatization of Europe," "The Imperialism of the Bolsheviks," "The

[6] On Stadtler and his Anti-Bolshevik League see the second and third volumes of his memoirs, published in Düsseldorf in 1935 and entitled respectively *Als politischer Soldat, 1914–1918* and *Als Antibolschewist, 1918–1919;* a brief account of the League's activity is also given in H. Schwierskott, *Arthur Moeller van den Bruck und der revolutionäre Nationalismus in der Weimarer Republik* (Göttingen, 1962), pp. 47–54.

[7] Stadtler, *Antibolschewist*, p. 13; Otto Schüddekopf, *Linke Leute von Rechts* (Stuttgart, 1960) pp. 104–105. Scattered issues of *A.B.C.* for 1919–1920 may be found in the Hoover Library, which also has pamphlets published by the Generalsekretariat intermittently during these years.

Despots of the Soviet Republic," and so on. Stadtler himself was apparently genuinely fearful of the implications of the Bolshevik revolution for Germany and felt a keen sense of duty to warn the German people about a danger with which they were only vaguely acquainted. The Baltic Germans, however, found anti-Bolshevism— like prewar Russophobia—to be a popular theme in Germany which had infinite possibilities for establishing them as political experts. Whatever their motives, the Balts found it easy to slip into the role of anti-Bolshevik informants at a time when alternative sources of information were unavailable.

Other Balts were active in their homeland and in East Prussia in 1918–1919 as anti-Bolshevik propagandists. Most notable among them was Max Erwin von Scheubner-Richter, the head of Oberost's press section in Riga which included a number of other Balts.[8] Like his friends Arno Schickedanz and Alfred Rosenberg, Scheubner-Richter had been a member of the aristocratic Rubonia student fraternity in Riga. In 1905 he defended the Imperial government against the forces of revolution as a cavalry officer before emigrating to Munich, where he became a Bavarian citizen. During World War I he fought gallantly both on the western front and

[8] The only full-length account of Scheubner's life is the biography by his fellow Nazi and wartime friend Paul Leverkuehn, *Posten auf ewiger Wache: Aus dem abenteuerreichen Leben des Max von Scheubner-Richter* (Essen, 1938). For a more recent account, see Laqueur, *Russia and Germany*, especially pp. 52–68. A laudatory sketch of Scheubner's life which appeared in *Völkischer Beobachter* in 1935 may be found in HA, roll 53, folder 1263. It is customary to mention Scheubner in various studies of the Nazi movement: H. H. Hofmann, *Der Hitlerputsch* (Munich, 1961); Alan Bullock, *Hitler: A Study in Tyranny* (rev. ed.; New York, 1961); Georg Franz-Willing, *Die Hitlerbewegung; Der Ursprung, 1919–1922* (Hamburg, 1962); Ernst Deuerlein, *Der Hitler-Putsch* (Stuttgart, 1962). There is also an account of Scheubner's role in the 1923 putsch by his chauffeur, Johannes Aigner, "Als Ordinanz bei Hochverrätern: Ein Beitrag zur Geschichte der nationalen Erhebung im November 1923" (Munich, n.d.). Bullock (p. 54) has confused Scheubner's story by describing him as a "German from East Prussia, who had acted as a wartime Russian agent in Constantinople before coming over to the Germans," a mistaken identity repeated by Hofmann. It was probably Konrad Heiden who first drew attention to the role of Scheubner and Alfred Rosenberg in the early years of the Nazi party in his *Der Führer* (Boston, 1944), pp. 183–185, and *A History of National Socialism* (New York, 1935), p. 42.

in the Middle East, joining Oberost as a Russian expert in the summer of 1917. Through Max Boehm and Paul Schiemann, Scheubner in 1919 became aware of the activities of Stadtler and Gleichen in Germany. Driven out of Riga in January 1919 by the Bolsheviks, Scheubner returned to Germany convinced by both personal upbringing and wartime experience not only that Bolshevism was a danger but that anti-Bolshevism was profitable. It was Scheubner's shrewd and cynical purveying of the anti-Bolshevik line in the coming years that would make him an important link between the Russian monarchists and the early Nazi movement.

In Königsberg in 1919 Scheubner became the political adviser of August Winnig, the Reichskommissar for the eastern territories still under German occupation. He also involved himself more deeply in anti-Bolshevik politics as head of the propaganda agency known as the Home Office for Eastern Germans (Ostdeutsche Heimatdienst), which disseminated warnings against the dangers of Bolsheviks and Poles, and as business manager of a right-wing parliamentary group in Danzig. Like the Free Corps, these groups were strongly anti-Bolshevik and heavily staffed by Balts and other Russian Germans. Many of these men, including Scheubner-Richter, became involved in the Kapp Putsch after Kapp himself visited Königsberg in early 1920. Scheubner's presence in Berlin and his position as Kapp's "press chief" was sufficient to implicate him in the Putsch, and he fled to Munich where he involved himself again in the politics of the Russian Civil War.[9]

In the wake of the Kapp Putsch a number of right-wing Russians also sought refuge in Bavaria. Botkin reported in July 1920 that both Markov II and Vinberg were there, along with Skoropadsky, Biskupsky, and others. These men were joined at the end of the year by other like-minded émigrés who had come to Germany from the Balkans after evacuation of Wrangel's army from the Crimea, among them G. V. Nemirovich-Danchenko, Wrangel's press secretary, and Ivan Poltavets-Ostranitsa, another Russian

[9] Leverkuehn, *Posten*, pp. 178 ff.; Adolf Eichler, "Max von Scheubner-Richter," *Deutsche Post aus dem Osten*, XI, No. 2/3 (February/March 1939), 24–27; Max Boehm, "Baltische Einflüsse auf die Anfänge des Nationalsozialismus," *Jahrbuch des baltischen Deutschtums*, XIV (1967), 58.

guards officer who had served on Skoropadsky's staff in the Ukraine in 1918. By the winter of 1920–1921 Munich was the center of activity for right-wing Russians still in Germany. The daily affairs of the colony were handled by F. F. Ewald through the Munich police president, completely independently of Botkin's Russian Delegation in Berlin. Ewald and Biskupsky managed to control matters through a five-man Russian Committee which registered new arrivals, represented the colony before the Bavarian government, and collected funds for the needy. The Munich colony, according to one of its members, was one marked by "gray intellectual mediocrity, dreams about returning to an unforgettable past, intense inbreeding with its petty gossip—cursing the Bolsheviks, the Jews, and the Yid-Masons and looking for tomorrow's money." [10]

As in Berlin the Baltic Germans were prominent as intermediaries for the Russian colony. Ewald was a Balt; so were some right-wing converts to Adolf Hitler's Nazi party: Gertrude von Seydlitz, Schickedanz, Rosenberg, and Scheubner-Richter. It was Scheubner-Richter's fond hope that these Balts would provide a bridge not only between the Munich Russian colony and the Bavarian right, but between a future monarchist Russia and Germany.

Scheubner himself initiated relations between the Munich Russians and their German friends in the summer of 1920 in connection with the attempts to support Wrangel. Having interested a group of South German industrialists in the possibility of trade relations with the Wrangel government, Scheubner went to the Crimea on what was to prove a futile mission. His Europe-Asia Firm was little more than a collection of Scheubner's Munich friends; the talks held with Wrangel and Nemirovich-Danchenko in the Crimea by Scheubner, two German businessmen, and a Hungarian army officer brought only negative results. What began as the first phase of Scheubner's proposed cooperation between the

---

[10] Nikolai Snessarev, *Kirill' Pervyi: Imperator . . . Koburgskii* (n.p., 1925), p. 47. On the Munich colony see Botkin to Giers, May 8 and July 12, 1920 (GA, folder 32), and Biskupsky's 1923 memorandum entitled "Polozhenie o Kolonii russkikh bezhentsev v Bavarii" (GA, folder 33).

forces of "national Russia" and "national Germany"—the exchange of German war-surplus weapons for Ukrainian wheat—cost the Europe-Asia Firm 70,000 marks and led to no concrete results.[11]

The Kapp debacle, the failure of the Crimean mission, and Wrangel's subsequent collapse were all sharp blows to Scheubner's plans for an anti-Bolshevik front. Yet he still preserved the vision of continued cooperation between like-minded Russians and Germans against the usurpers of legitimate authority in Berlin and Moscow. It was at this low point in Scheubner's career that Rosenberg suggested he attend a Nazi gathering in Munich. The platform of the party—its virulent anti-Semitism, anti-Bolshevism, and Francophobia—all made a deep and favorable impression. In October 1920 he met Hitler for the first time, and on November 22 heard him speak in public. It was enough. A few days later Scheubner joined the party and received membership card number 2414.[12]

Scheubner-Richter's entry into the Nazi party was a significant first step in what was to become an important ideological and financial contribution of right-wing Russian émigrés to the Nazis. Each group recognized in the other not only an anti-Semitic ideological companion but a potential source of funds. The Russians contributed the *Protocols of the Elders of Zion* to the Nazis, identifying Bolshevism in Russia with the Jews, and donated valuable funds during the party's early years; the Nazis and their allies encouraged the Russian monarchist movement and provided it with a successful example of a mass movement with anti-Bolshevik overtones. For a brief moment the lines of the dying Russian right and the rising Hitler movement intersected, and at the point of intersection stood the Balts: Scheubner-Richter, the economic middleman and administrator, and Alfred Rosenberg, the anti-Semitic ideologue.

The roots of political anti-Semitism in Munich antedated the Russian Revolution but were nurtured by it. Before the war the

[11] G. V. Nemirovich-Danchenko, *V Krymu pri Vrangele* (Berlin, 1922), pp. 80–81; Lampe to Wrangel, August 5, 1921 (LA, folder 53).
[12] Leverkuehn, *Posten*, p. 191.

Politics of Adjustment

Germanen Orden of Theodor Fritsch and Guido von List had engaged in Jew-baiting, which it found equally profitable after the
Armistice when it changed its name to the Thule Gesellschaft.[13]
What was new was the emphasis on the *Ostjuden* as the greatest
danger to Germany and their association with the Russian Revolution. Even before the war, one-quarter of the Munich Jewish community had come from Russia, Poland, or Austria-Hungary. Now
it turned out that two of the leaders of the Bavarian Soviet Republic of 1919 were prewar Russian émigrés to Germany, *Ostjuden*
who had joined a radical socialist group known as the Spartacists:
Evgeny Leviné and Tobia Akselrod. (Max Levien, a Russian
German, was also assumed to be a Jew.) The connection between
domestic revolution and Russian Jews seemed obvious to many
Germans and it was no accident that the eighth point of the Nazi
platform called for an end to the future immigration of such "non-
Germans." In the aftermath of the Soviet Republic many Jews were
brutalized in Bavaria, threatened with expulsion, and interned in
Fort Prinz Carl near Ingolstadt. The worst thing that the *Münchener Beobachter* could say about the socialist leader Kurt Eisner at
the time was that he was probably a "Russian Jew."[14]

If Scheubner was to become the urbane and personable contact
between the Nazis and the right-wing Russians in Munich, Alfred
Rosenberg was the writer who gave the Nazis a picture of Russia
based on a mixture of traditional Baltic Russophobia and upper-
class Russian anti-Semitism. Rosenberg also absorbed a substantial
amount of his anti-Semitism in Munich from writers such as Dietrich Eckart, the poet, playwright, and beer-hall intellectual in
whose scurrilous weekly *Auf gut deutsch* Rosenberg made his
first appearance. Rosenberg linked his anti-Semitism with events
inside Russia, on which he could claim some authority. Konrad
Heiden's story of Rosenberg's arrival in Munich with a copy of
the *Protocols* under his arm is largely imaginary, but it conveys

[13] R. Sebottendorf, *Bevor Hitler kam* (Munich, 1934), p. 53.
[14] *Ibid.*, p. 49; H. Lamm, *Von Juden in München: Ein Gedenkbuch* (Munich,
1958), pp. 41, 318–322; Norman Baynes, *The Speeches of Adolf Hitler, 1922–
1939* (Oxford, 1942), I, 104.

168

most dramatically the central role of Rosenberg in transmitting to the Nazis a new variation on political anti-Semitism and an entire attitude toward Soviet Russia.[15]

Born into a merchant family in Reval in 1893, Rosenberg had gone to Riga in 1910 to study architecture at the Technical High School. He belonged, like Scheubner, to the Rubonia student society and traveled to Germany to visit the art galleries of Berlin, Dresden, and Munich. It was the Bohemian atmosphere of Munich and Schwabing, rather than the "huge, gray, strange" world of Berlin which attracted him. But unlike Scheubner, Rosenberg did not come to Germany permanently; he lived in Riga and Moscow during the war and finally received his architectural degree in 1918 for the design of a Reval crematorium. Despite being a resident of Moscow during the stormy days of 1917, Rosenberg did not engage in political activity until his arrival in Germany in November 1918. Like many Russian émigrés, his subsequent political expertise on Russia was acquired only when he realized the effect of his opinion in Germany. After working for Oberost as a German instructor in Reval in 1918, Rosenberg fled to Germany at the time of the Armistice and settled in Munich. "I left my homeland," he recalled later, "in order to acquire a fatherland." In fact, his sudden flight from Russia had little if any political or nationalist overtones at the time; the attraction of Munich was cultural, artistic, and Bohemian, nothing more.[16]

Failing to find a job as an architect, Rosenberg had soon exhausted what little money he had brought with him and was forced to turn to a Baltic German refugee aid committee for rooms and food. With little else to do, he pored through books at the Bavarian State Library—Indian philosophy, Jewish history, art history— and was drawn into the sordid world of intellectual and middle-

[15] Heiden, *Der Führer*, pp. 1 ff.; on Rosenberg see especially his own memoirs, *Letzte Aufzeichnungen* (Göttingen, 1955); G. Schubert, *Die Anfänge der National-sozialistischen Aussenpolitik, 1919–1923* (Berlin, 1961), pp. 77–98; and Laqueur, *Russia and Germany*, pp. 68–78. There are also short biographies of Rosenberg in *Führerlexicon 1934/1935* (Berlin, 1935), p. 394, and in HA, roll 53, folder 1259.

[16] Rosenberg, *Aufzeichnungen*, pp. 32, 66; Schubert, *Aussenpolitik*, p. 79.

class anti-Semitism. He was soon earning money by contributing anti-Semitic articles on Russia to two Munich weeklies: Rudolf Gorsleben's *Deutsche Republik* and Eckart's *Auf gut deutsch.* Until this point Rosenberg had shown no inclination for politics whatsoever. In fact it was his German anti-Semitic friends who made him realize how much weight his words could carry on matters concerning Russia. It was a role he took up with enthusiasm.

The picture of Russia that Rosenberg introduced in Munich right-wing circles in the early 1920's was a curious amalgam of Baltic German hatred and fascination for Russia and right-wing Russian and German anti-Semitism. He played a shifting role in these years—now the Russian intellectual, now the embittered émigré, now the German anti-Semite—and one which contrasted sharply with his pallid personality and generally unorthodox appearance, which often included the wearing of purple shirts. Yet his views had a tremendous impact on the young Nazi party and its leader, Adolf Hitler, and, because of his "Russian" background, carried a certain authority. "Rosenberg," testified one party member later, "who spoke Russian better than he did German, wielded tremendous influence on Hitler and his associates when it came to propagandizing this anti-Bolshevist, anti-Russian line. Anyone who could claim to be a Russian expert was able to sing this sort of song in the party all day long and Rosenberg was the most adept at it." [17]

It was a simple and unoriginal message which ran through Rosenberg's writings in these years. Behind every evil in the world stood the Jew, who had killed Christ and now sought to run the world through a consortium (not unlike the British Empire). The Zionist Jews, closely allied with the Masons, had organized and carried out both World War I and the Russian Revolution. The devious means by which the Jews planned to take over the world were illustrated by the fact that not only most Bolsheviks but also most businessmen were Jews. The Weimar Republic was also run by Jews, and thus defended their interests. The Jews were the force of destruction for Europe, an Asiatic disease from the East, and only through an alliance of Russia and Germany under anti-

[17] Ernst Hanfstaengl, *Unheard Witness* (New York, 1957), p. 66.

Bolshevik leaders could the final mastery of the white race over the rising tide of Asia and Africa be assured.[18]

The Bolshevik revolution was an integral part of this Jewish plot, carried out by men like Braunstein (Trotsky) and Apfelbaum (Zinoviev), which aimed at destroying the "entire Russian intelligentsia." The German was a man of heroic proportions, a man of action, while the Russian was brooding, passive, and introspective, but endowed with a soul of infinite depth; both were now being destroyed by the Jew within. But Rosenberg's mentality was not entirely a colonial and "anti-Eastern" one; like Scheubner-Richter, he absorbed from the Nazis a certain "anti-Western" and even quasi-socialist attitude which hated the Jew above as well as the Jew below, the capitalist and revolutionary, the Entente and Soviet Russia. Hence for Rosenberg the Rapallo treaty became both "the binding of the German people to endless drudgery for Western high finance and the support of the rotten and decaying Jewish republic to the East." [19] But in the end the colonial outlook predominated and Rosenberg remained a staunch opponent of left-wing trends within the Nazi party. For Germans who knew him he was always "the typical Balt, overbearing and filled with hate against Russia," [20] and rarely the Russian intellectual he sometimes imagined himself to be.

In late 1919 Eckart introduced Rosenberg to Hitler and both became members of the German Workers' party in Munich, organized by Anton Drexler, a locksmith, and Karl Harrer, a journalist. Through Eckart and Harrer, Rosenberg also joined the more aristo-

[18] Beside his articles, Rosenberg turned out a number of pamphlets in the early 1920's: "Die Spur des Juden im Wandel der Zeiten" (1920); "Das Verbrechen der Freimaurerei" (1921); "Der staatsfeindliche Zionismus" (1922); "Pest in Russland" (1922); "Die Protokolle der Weisen von Zion und die jüdische Weltpolitik" (1923). His philosophy was expressed in the following articles in *Auf gut deutsch* in 1919: "Christus in Talmud," March 28, pp. 153–156; "Judenheit und Politik," June 13, pp. 263–277; "Jüdische Zeitfragen," October 23, pp. 531–542; "Corpora delicti," November 21, pp. 597–612; "Asiatische Pest," December 12, pp. 673–675.

[19] "Die russisch-jüdische Revolution," *Auf gut deutsch*, February 21, 1919, pp. 120–123; "Russe und deutscher," *ibid.*, April 4, 1919, pp. 185–190; "Pest in Russland," p. 87.

[20] Prussian Minister of the Interior to the Berlin police president, March 27, 1931 (HA, roll 53, folder 1259).

cratic Thule Gesellschaft. Rosenberg had no position of leadership in the German Workers' Party, yet he now began to consider himself the party "theoretician." In fact he was already beginning to have some influence on the pre-Nazi *Völkischer Beobachter,* particularly on its views toward Russia.[21] For *Völkischer Beobachter,* of course, all socialists from Marx to Trotsky were Jews, or half-Jews. Particularly dangerous were the *Ostjuden,* swarming into Germany, engaging in speculation, making crowded housing conditions worse, and infecting the country with tuberculosis, syphilis, homosexuality—and Bolshevism.[22] In the spring of 1920, *Völkischer Beobachter* first discovered the *Protocols,* recently published in *Luch sveta,* and was noticeably impressed and enthusiastic. "One can only be amazed," it wrote, "that this book, which appeared in 1919, has not yet circulated to every German in millions of copies and that there are still *deutschvölkisch*-thinking men and women who do not own it." [23]

In the winter of 1920–1921 the recently formed Nazi party purchased *Völkischer Beobachter.* With Eckart as editor and himself as assistant, Rosenberg now had an audience for his views on Russia even broader than that provided by *Auf gut deutsch.* Once again he reiterated the equation of Jews and Bolsheviks so popular in right-wing Russian circles; both were undermining the "national Russian intelligentsia." [24] By March 1923 Rosenberg had risen to the position of the chief political editor of the journal, now a daily newspaper whose views on Russia were in essence those which Rosenberg wished to propound. He had also become a German citizen. But if Rosenberg had been the one to make available to the Nazis and Hitler a watered-down version of right-wing Russian émigré thinking, it was Scheubner-Richter who proved to be the real go-between for the Bavarian Russians and the Nazi party.

[21] Bullock, *Hitler,* pp. 42–43; Franz-Willing, *Die Hitlerbewegung,* pp. 83–86.
[22] This theme appeared frequently in *Völkischer Beobachter* in January and February 1920.
[23] *Ibid.,* February 25, 1920, and April 22, 1920, p. 1.
[24] See Rosenberg's articles in *ibid.,* for February–March and August–November 1921.

The fall of 1920 marked the beginning not only of the end to the Russian Civil War but also of a genuine monarchist movement among the Russian émigrés. Until this time a number of people who stood for a restoration of the old regime had been living in Berlin, from former Octobrists to members of the Union of the Russian People. But as yet there had been no attempt to unite the forces of the right around a single journal or leader. With the appearance of another monarchist organ, *Dvuglavyi orel'* (The Two-Headed Eagle), under the leading representative of the Russian monarchists in Berlin, Markov II, it became obvious that if such a unified movement were to develop it would be dominated by the Germanophile extreme right, rather than by the moderates.[25]

Toward the end of 1920 Markov II and General Biskupsky began sending letters to right-wing Russian military and political leaders throughout Europe inviting them to attend a general gathering of monarchists in Berlin sometime in early 1921. At the beginning of January 1921 a preliminary meeting was held under the chairmanship of former Senator A. A. Rimsky-Korsakov to discuss the formation of a "national monarchist center" in Berlin. Then on February 26 some two hundred Russian conservative leaders met again, this time under A. V. Belgard, to work out a common program; but except for agreeing that the White armies had been defeated because they lacked a monarchist ideology, and reiterating the usual slogans about uniting tsar and people, restoring a Romanov to the throne, and encouraging individual peasant landholding, nothing specific was accomplished. And already there were signs of disagreement between moderates and extremists within the monarchist camp.[26]

One substantial outcome of the February 26 meeting, however, was the establishment of a temporary Russian Monarchist Union,

[25] The message of *Dvuglavyi orel'* was simple: the Entente, working closely with Jewish-Masonic organizations, had initiated World War I, which in turn led to revolution and civil war in Russia; only an alliance between some future monarchist Russia and Germany could avert the collapse of Western civilization at the hands of the Jewish Comintern. The issues of September 27 and December 28, 1920, and March 31, 1921, provide examples.

[26] *Rul'*, January 5, 1921, p. 5, and March 1, 1921, p. 3.

whose main task was to organize a congress. The leaders of the Union were Markov II, Baron M. A. Taube, and A. M. Maslennikov, a moderate, with Biskupsky as usual hovering in the background as "military adviser." Also involved briefly during his visit to Berlin in early March was Grand Duke Dmitry Pavlovich, a political nonentity who quickly proved himself unable to speak for the Romanov family with any authority. Nevertheless, plans went ahead for the meeting. Taube was sent off to Paris to organize support, and Nikolai Dmitrievich Talberg, Skoropadsky's former Minister of Internal Affairs, left for Yugoslavia and Bulgaria on a similar mission.[27]

But in the end the real initiative and organization for the monarchist congress came not from the Russians but from sympathetic Germans. Under pressure from the left-wing press and the Berlin police, it was decided now that the congress would be held not in Berlin but in the Bavarian resort town of Bad Reichenhall. A circle of German army officers, politicians, and businessmen undertook local arrangements for their Russian friends. The starting point was a meeting between Biskupsky and General von der Goltz in late April or early May 1921, during which Biskupsky was introduced to the nationalist writer Ernst Reventlow and to Scheubner-Richter, who now played the most important role in establishing relations between Russian and German right-wing circles and in bringing to fruition the plans for the Reichenhall congress of monarchists.[28]

In the winter of 1920–1921 Scheubner turned to Russian circles in Munich, now involved with their Berlin friends in planning for the monarchist congress, with a new project in mind: the organization of a society of Russians and Germans of similar views who recognized the complete impossibility of liberal-democratic regimes in either Russia or Germany and agreed that the only alternative

[27] The Grand Duke's visit is recounted in Wipert von Blücher, *Deutschlands Weg nach Rapallo: Erinnerungen eines Mannes aus dem zweiten Gliede* (Wiesbaden, 1951), pp. 59–60 and, less candidly, in *Dvuglavyi orel'*, March 28, 1921, pp. 41–48.

[28] E. A. Efimovsky, "Sorokaletie reikhengall'skago obshchemonarkhicheskago s"ezda," *Vozrozhdenie*, No. 130 (1962), p. 108.

to "Jewish Bolshevism" was restoration of the prewar monarchies. Scheubner gave the name *Aufbau* (*Vozstanovlenie*, "Reconstruction") to his society, which included, among others, Rosenberg, Arno Schickedanz, and General Biskupsky as head of the "Russian Section." Aufbau, working closely with Colonel Ewald of the Russian Committee in Munich, began to make arrangements for the Reichenhall congress of monarchists.[29]

The goals of the Aufbau circle envisioned the restoration not only of the Russian and German monarchies but also of German influence in Russia. "We wanted to save Russia from anarchy," Scheubner told a reporter shortly after Reichenhall, "and the only way to do this is to replace the collapsing dictatorship of the Soviets with another system which is so strong that it can unite all forces. . . . Russia can only be reconstructed by means of surplus intellectual and technical power which we have in Germany." There must be revived the "stream of emigration to Russia" from Germany to help with such reconstruction—in the interests not of German heavy industry, but of both German and Russian workers. It was the colonial dream of a Balt tempered by the antibusiness tone of the early Nazi party.[30]

Through Biskupsky's friendship with Ludendorff the Russian monarchists were able to persuade a group of South German business and industrial leaders to finance their long-awaited congress at Reichenhall in the spring of 1921. For the moment the interests of German nationalists and Russian monarchists coincided. Those émigrés sympathetic to the Allies, mainly liberal politicians and businessmen, were now on their way to Paris to attend another "national unity" meeting of émigrés, and the atmosphere at Reichenhall was decidedly anti-Versailles. There was some fear in the minds of Markov II and others, however, that if German support were too obvious, the movement would lose its appeal at the start by taking on a Germanophile coloring. With this in mind, Avalov had not been invited to the congress. The suspected recruitment

[29] *Der Kampf*, June 7, 1921; *München-Augsburger Abendzeitung*, May 31, 1921. There is a clipping file on Reichenhall in HA, roll 51, folder 1197.
[30] *Der Kampf*, June 7, 1921.

of his troops by German officers for the fighting in Upper Silesia that spring would hardly promote the appearance of an independent monarchist movement.[31]

Bad Reichenhall is a fairytale mountain resort town nestled on the Bavarian border some twenty kilometers southwest of Salzburg. Here in the Austrian Alps a remarkable collection of Russians began to gather during the last week in May 1921, about two hundred self-proclaimed monarchists ranging in prerevolutionary political affiliations from Octobrists to former Black Hundreds members. From twenty-three countries they came, mainly by personal invitation of Markov II or Biskupsky. For the next week, from May 29 to June 6, they took over the main hotel in town, the Deutscher Kaiser, as well as the surrounding villas, to participate in an endless round of "speeches, speeches, speeches, committees, committees, committees" which inevitably lasted well into the small hours of the morning.[32]

The leaders of the Berlin colony were all here—the curly-haired Markov II, Senator Rimsky-Korsakov with his deep bass voice and snow-white beard, the stern former Procurator of the Holy Synod, A. A. Shirinsky-Shikhmatov, and the tall, handsome Biskupsky. A. F. Trepov led a ten-man delegation from Paris. Scheubner-Richter was also in attendance with his entourage of anti-Semitic friends from Munich: Vinberg, Shabelsky-Bork, Colonel Ewald, and G. V. Nemirovich-Danchenko. Prince Lieven was there too, nursing his wounds, along with the former Okhrana official General Paul Kurlov. From Prague came E. A. Efimovsky, a former Kadet and now editor of the monarchist *Slavianskaia zaria* (Slavic Dawn), and from the Balkans, Metropolitans Antony and Evlogy. There were a number of non-Russian representatives as well. The Ukrainian contingent included Skoropadsky and one of his former ministers. One Bokhanovsky claimed to represent the "Belorussian Rada." A. N. Krupensky, chairman of the congress, was previously the Bessarabian representative at the Paris Peace Conference. Even

[31] *Der Kampf,* June 3, 1921; *Poslednie novosti,* July 13, 1922, p. 1; General Fürst Awaloff, *Im Kampf gegen den Bolschewismus* (Glückstadt and Hamburg, 1925), pp. 471–472.

[32] I. F. Nazhivin, *Sredi potukhshikh maiakov: Iz zapisok bezhentsa* (Berlin, 1922), p. 186.

Ataman Semenov, still holding out against the Bolsheviks in Siberia, had his representative to the congress. But in general the tone of the Reichenhall meetings was definitely Great Russian.[33] The center of activity at Reichenhall was the main hall of the hotel Post, where the speeches were given to the assembled delegates. At the front of the hall stood a green-garlanded podium flanked by two flags: the red-white-blue Imperial Russian banner and the white-yellow-black pennant of the monarchists. A large oval photograph of Nicholas II looked down on the proceedings as elegantly dressed wives of the delegates discussed over *schnappes* the possibility that he was still alive. The doors of the hall were generally kept closed, to the puzzlement of the non-Russian hotel guests.[34]

Scheubner-Richter had publicized the Reichenhall meeting as a "congress on the economic reconstruction of Russia." In fact, the tone was political and the mood was monarchist. The planning of the speeches and committee work had been in the hands of the Berlin monarchists' "organization bureau" since early May. The various sessions were to be devoted to such topics as the future reorganization of the Russian government, the church, the army, foreign affairs, propaganda, the organization of "monarchist work" within the emigration and, as an afterthought, economic matters.

The Reichenhall congress opened on May 29 with a benediction by Metropolitan Evlogy and the election of Krupensky, then living in Paris, as chairman. After a short report by Markov II on the work of the "organization bureau," Scheubner-Richter rose to welcome the delegates as the representative of Aufbau, the sponsor of the congress. In a brief address he pointed out the hospitality of the Bavarian government and hoped the meeting would prove an auspicious beginning to future Russian-German cooperation. E. A. Efimovsky then gave the main speech of the day. But it was Markov II who set the tone in his opening remarks:

[33] *Ibid.*, pp. 185–186; *Volia Rossii*, June 23, 1921, p. 3; Efimovsky, "Soroka-letie," p. 107; *Süddeutsche Presse*, June 4, 1921; *Münchener neueste Nachrichten*, June 4, 1921.
[34] Nazhivin, *Sredi*, p. 194; *Münchener neueste Nachrichten*, June 4, 1921.

The re-establishment of Russia is impossible without the resurrection of the monarchy. Resurrection of the monarchy is impossible unless the monarchists revive themselves. The monarchy fell not because its enemies were too strong but because its defenders were too weak.[35]

This basic theme ran through most speeches in the following days. Only a restoration of the monarchy could save Russia from Bolshevism (and the Jews); the old union of tsar, church, and people must be restored; the land must be distributed to the peasantry on the basis of individual holdings; and Russia must base her foreign policy on the cornerstone of close ties with a monarchist Germany.

The main activity of the congress turned out to be continuous meetings and social gatherings which produced little in the way of concrete results. On May 30 a telegram of good wishes was sent off to the Dowager Empress Maria Fedorovna in Copenhagen. More speeches followed. A. M. Maslennikov again called for a "stable" monarchist political system in Russia. E. K. Nozhin urged the creation of a monarchist propaganda organ, blaming their unwillingness to fly the monarchist banner for the failures of Denikin and Wrangel. T. V. Lokot spoke on the land question and again urged a return to smallholding. But there was a distinct unreality about all the grandiose schemes for a restoration of the monarchy which became most apparent when the final resolutions of the congress were adopted on the last day. It was solemnly pronounced that the restored monarch would be the legal heir from the Romanov family. But who would that be? Tsar and people would be united. But what did that mean? The new Russia would feature local self-government and national autonomy. But was this consistent with a multinational autocracy? Five out of fifteen resolutions dealt with the primacy of the Orthodox church, none with the question of non-Russian religious or national groups. On economic questions, however, there was clarity: "All property should be denationalized and freedom of trade restored."[36]

When the congress ended on June 6 it was clear that however improbable the eventual success of its program, the monarchist

[35] *Dvuglavyi orel'*, June 28, 1921, p. 8. For the proceedings of the congress see the accounts in the same journal for June 10, June 14, and July 14, 1921.

[36] The resolutions passed at Reichenhall are printed in *Dvuglavyi orel'*, June 14, 1921, pp. 7–10.

movement was now a real factor in émigré politics. On the recommendation of the former Black Hundreds leader V. P. Sokolov-Baransky the congress had taken its only substantial step: the creation of a permanent Supreme Monarchist Council (Vysshii monarkhicheskii Sovet), consisting of Markov II, Shirinsky-Shikhmatov, and Maslennikov, to continue the work of the monarchists. The Council would be centered in Berlin and would use Markov II's *Dvuglavyi orel* as its organ. For the first time in emigration the Russian monarchists seemed to have an idea of who they were, if not of precisely what they hoped to achieve. Signs of future doctrinal divisions were for the moment lost in the enthusiasm of mutual discovery.

Another significant result of the Reichenhall congress was that it opened further contacts between the right wing of the Russian emigration and German monarchist and nationalist circles. In particular, through Scheubner-Richter the Russians now heard about the growing Nazi party in Munich, and there began a mutual flirtation between many Russians and their German anti-Semitic friends, based not only on common political hatred of Jews, liberals, and Bolsheviks, but also on a desperate need for money and political support which each thought the other might supply. It was this potential alliance between the Russian and German political right, moreover, which quickly antagonized German liberal and left-wing public opinion.

Until Reichenhall the German press had not really noticed the number of Russians in Germany or the nature of their political activity. The Baltic intervention of Avalov and Von der Goltz had drawn some attacks in the leftist papers, as had the attempts to send Russian officers to Wrangel in 1920. But it was only in the spring of 1921 that German public opinion awakened to the activity of this new group of "undesirable aliens" among them. The general reaction was one of shock. The *Münchener Post* considered that the Bavarian government had made a "grave political mistake" in permitting the congress to be held.[37] But the South German newspapers which carried daily accounts of the congress were not nearly as critical as the left-wing press in Berlin.

Already in May 1921 the SPD daily *Vorwärts* pointed out that the

[37] June 4, 1921.

real "Russian danger" to Germany was not the *Ostjuden,* as German nationalists had claimed since before the war, but the right-wing Russians:

We certainly don't want to bait the Russian émigrés the way the Pan-German newspapers handle the *Ostjuden.* But the sympathies of our Pan-Germans for the former seem sufficiently strong to produce enough supporters of Kolchak, Denikin and Wrangel among them to form a permanent human reservoir for monarchist conspiracies.[38]

For *Vorwärts* the Reichenhall congress was a "New Bavarian–Old Russian Alliance" of "Russian Pan-Germans" and "German Pan-Russians" which was directed at the colonization of Russia by Germans along the lines suggested by Scheubner. The threat to the Weimar Republic from these forces was clear. Only in Bavaria could the congress have been held, where Munich was becoming a "new Coblenz" for the émigrés. "The Russian emigration," *Vorwärts* complained, "finds its support not only from Herr Pöhner [the Munich police president] but also from Ludendorff and his adventurous palladins. The Bavarian witches' cauldron of German nationalism has now received from the outpouring of Russians a new ingredient of fermentation." [39]

The Communist *Die rote Fahne* condemned the congress even more severely as a "fresh mockery of the political affairs of the German government." The meeting was described as a "Black Hundreds Congress" held with the tacit consent of the Wilhelmstrasse, and there was a steady campaign to have monarchist Russians expelled from Germany altogether. "Berlin," *Die rote Fahne* admitted with some resignation and disgust in late July, "is now known as the central point for all Russian reactionaries and the headquarters for all enemies of the Soviet Republic." [40]

In Munich itself the Reichenhall congress also came under fire, with violent results. In the June 21, 1921, session of the Bavarian Landtag, an Independent Socialist deputy rose to protest the holding of the congress as something which could "endanger German-

[38] *Vorwärts,* May 19, 1921 (*Morgenausgabe*), p. 3.
[39] *Vorwärts,* June 9, 1921 (*Morgenausgabe*), pp. 1–2.
[40] *Die rote Fahne,* May 14, May 31, June 1, June 7, and July 27, 1921.

Russian relations." He was promptly told by the state secretary that Reichenhall "only dealt with the business of economic relations" and had no political consequence. Another USPD deputy named Gareis, a critic not only of Reichenhall but of all right-wing activity in Bavaria, was less fortunate. A few days after the Landtag interpellation on the congress he was shot dead in the street in broad daylight by a young German nationalist.[41]

There was equally loud criticism from the left-wing and liberal émigré press. The Social Revolutionary *Volia Rossii* in Prague warned of the existence of a "monarchist international" which planned to kill Kerensky and Miliukov in Paris that summer. "The flag of anti-Bolshevism being waved by the present Black Hundreds people," wrote Vladimir Burtsev in his Paris daily *Obshchee delo*, "should not deceive us. It is worth no more than the eulogistic nationalism of the Bolsheviks, their red nationalism." The major émigré daily in Berlin, *Rul'*, termed the Reichenhall congress "definitely reactionary" and at the same time ineffective; "even if the basis for a dictatorship is to be created in Russia," wrote *Rul'*, "the work of the Berlin monarchists will hardly facilitate the development of monarchist ideas." [42]

The Liberals

On the political left of the Russian emigration the key intermediaries between Russians and Germans usually were not Russian Germans but Jews. This is not to say that there was some sinister connection between national origin and political position, but only that those driven into opposition and exile by the Imperial Russian government before the war were in a position to help the émigrés who left Russia after 1917. Both Alexander Stein, who had emigrated to Germany after the revolution of 1905, and I. V. Gessen, who remained in Russia until 1918 but had visited Germany before the war, provided such mediation. The fact that assimilation demanded deeper ties, however, is indicated by the collapse of the

---

[41] *Verhandlungen des bayerischen Landtags. I Tagung 1920/1921, 66 Sitzung*, p. 211; *Vorwärts*, June 22, 1921 (*Morgenausgabe*), p. 2.

[42] *Volia Rossii*, July 16, 1921, p. 2; *Obshchee delo*, November 10, 1921, p. 1; *Rul'*, May 31, 1921, p. 1, June 10, 1921, p. 1.

liberal Kadet faction within a few years and the persistence of the Mensheviks as friends of the German socialist movement for another decade.

Of all the prewar Russian political parties represented in Berlin in these years which could accept neither Bolshevism nor the monarchists, the Constitutional Democrats (Kadets) played the most vital role in the life of the émigré community. This was not true of the Kadet party as a political entity, which declared itself defunct in Berlin in late 1922, but rather of its individual leaders, most notably Vladimir Dmitrievich Nabokov and Iosif Vladimirovich Gessen. Both of these men were active in the "official" life of the emigration, where they participated in political and literary organizations side by side with the monarchists. Unlike the Mensheviks, the Berlin Kadets found no resonance in German political life for their own views. And whereas Berlin was the center of Menshevik life in emigration, it was on the fringe of Kadet politics, centered first in London and later in Paris around the historian P. N. Miliukov. In the end the Berlin Kadets did not serve their own political party as well as they served the Russian colony in Berlin, a civic role for which they deserve no small amount of credit.

The center of Kadet life in Berlin was the daily newspaper *Rul'* (The Rudder), by far the best Russian newspaper in the colony and rivaled outside Germany only by Miliukov's *Poslednie novosti* (Latest News). The leading figure behind *Rul'* until his murder in March 1922 was Nabokov, respected throughout the Russian community for his moral force, shrewd judgment, and moderation.[43] The second editor and business manager of the paper was Avgust Isaakovich Kaminka, but it was the third editor, Gessen, who pro-

[43] Vladimir Dmitrievich Nabokov, the son of a former Minister of Justice, was born in St. Petersburg in 1870. From the university there he embarked in the 1890's on a study of criminal law. A founding member of *Pravo*, along with Gessen and Kaminka, he used its pages to attack the notorious Kishinev pogroms of 1903, an act of some courage. He also wrote for *Rech'*, helped organize the Kadet party, and in 1917 drafted legislation for the Provisional government. Arrested by the Bolsheviks, he was soon released and fled to Kiev with his family in 1918. In London in 1919 he edited the journal *The New Russia* before coming to Berlin in the autumn of 1920. See *Rul'*, March 31, 1922, pp. 1–2.

vided the journalistic expertise for *Rul'* and the necessary contacts with German publishers.

Gessen was born in 1865 into the well-to-do family of a Jewish merchant in Odessa, and by 1914 he had achieved a reputation as one of Russia's leading legal experts and journalists. From 1893 until 1903 he worked for the Ministry of Justice, where he wrote several books on the law. In 1898, together with Nabokov and Kaminka, he founded *Pravo*, which became the leading juridical periodical in Russia. All three men were also active members of the Kadet party before World War I, and co-workers of Miliukov on the leading party daily, *Rech'*. During the war Gessen headed the All-Russian Society of Newspaper Editors, a position he maintained until 1918, when the organization and *Rech'* were closed by the Bolsheviks. Like his fellow Kadets, Gessen remained throughout his life a staunch supporter of the growing spirit of liberalism in Russian political life, with its axioms of economic progress, a strong middle class, the rule of law under a constitution, and democratic parliamentary representation. In January 1919 Gessen fled to Helsinki to begin life anew in emigration.[44]

Politically and culturally the Kadet party was drawn to England, and it was not surprising that both Miliukov and Nabokov emigrated to London after the Armistice, where they argued the case of Russian liberalism and anti-Bolshevik intervention in the pages of their English-language weekly, *The New Russia*. But in London, Miliukov and Nabokov found their political differences were greater than they had anticipated. While Miliukov favored a political "opening to the left," uniting Kadets and Social Revolutionaries in a common effort, Nabokov found this to be an unwarranted compromise of Kadet policies. Their mutual political animosity in fact reflected the growing tension between the conservative and liberal-interventionist wings of the Kadet party in general. By the autumn of 1920 this tension assumed geographic dimensions. When Miliukov left for Paris to participate in the formation of liberal-socialist

---

[44] I. V. Gessen, *V dvukh vekakh: Zhiznennyi otchet* (Berlin, 1937); on Kadet journalism see also Thomas Riha, " 'Riech': A Portrait of a Russian Newspaper," *Slavic Review*, XXII (1963), 663–683.

émigré coalition supporting General Wrangel, Nabokov decided to accept the invitation of Kaminka and Gessen to come to Berlin and assume the editorship of a new émigré daily, *Rul'*.[45]

It was Gessen who was largely responsible for preparing the way for Nabokov's arrival in Berlin and the founding of *Rul'*. After his flight to Helsinki in January 1919, Gessen had spent several months in Copenhagen and Stockholm, where he acted as a legal adviser for White circles involved in shipping weapons and supplies to the armies inside Russia. In late 1919 he came to Berlin to help the Ullstein Verlag organize a Russian book-publishing operation, for which some 500,000 marks had already been set aside. Like most Russians, Gessen found Berlin in the winter of 1919–1920 to be in sharp contrast to the city he had visited before the war. The economy seemed to be at a standstill, railroad service was bad, food prices were high, and the Germans, while not complaining, seemed to him strangely indifferent to life. Nevertheless, he reported to *The New Russia*, "Russians are everywhere greeted with exceptional kindness and hospitality." Gessen soon discovered that there was no respectable anti-Bolshevik Russian newspaper in Berlin (he discounted politically both *Prizyv* and *Golos Rossii*). He himself thus took advantage of a two-hour interview with the *Berliner Tageblatt* in February 1920 to warn that Bolshevism could mean "the destruction of Western culture" and that the Germans should help provide "rich financial material support for the Russian anti-Bolshevik movement with the help of the Western democracies." [46]

Gessen soon attracted the attention of a number of leading German political and journalistic figures. Dr. Wolff of the *Berliner Tageblatt* and Professor Bernhardt of the *Vossische Zeitung* arranged a dinner for him and the Octobrist leader A. I. Guchkov, which was also attended by Walther Rathenau and a group of

[45] *Poslednie novosti*, March 28, 1923, pp. 2–3. Much of the following section is based on the unpublished second volume of Gessen's memoirs, "Gody skitanii" (typescript, Hoover Library).

[46] Gessen, "Impressions from Berlin" and "More Berlin Impressions," *The New Russia*, I (1920), 183–186, 217–219; "Gody," pp. 21, 26–27. The interview was summarized by Hans Vorst in the *Berliner Tageblatt*, February 11 and 20, 1920, pp. 1–2.

German businessmen. Otto Hoetzsch, the noted Russophile, historian, and politician organized another social evening, followed by yet another occasion for Gessen during which he met Hermann Müller, Gustav Noske, Eduard Bernstein, and Hugo Preuss.[47] There were also the expected visits to the Wilhelmstrasse. But most of Gessen's time was now taken up by the negotiations with Ullstein over the details of an agreement to start a Russian-language publishing operation. The outcome was the establishment of the Slovo firm, subsequently the most important Russian book-publishing company in Berlin not supported by the Soviet government. Out of the Slovo negotiations, too, grew the idea of a Russian-language daily newspaper for Berlin.

The origins of *Rul'* dated from the spring and summer of 1920 when Avgust Kaminka arrived from Finland to join Gessen in Berlin. The two men soon decided to set up the daily. Gessen would handle the technical editing functions, as he had for *Rech'*, and Kaminka would be the business manager. Both agreed that Nabokov should be invited from London to lend "moral authority" to the newspaper. Initially the intention had been to publish *Rul'* through the Rudolf Mosse publishing house in Berlin. But Ullstein seemed more receptive, made it clear that they considered Nabokov a "good man," and had already established a working relationship with the Russians for Slovo. Within a short time the necessary funds had been collected—almost 700,000 marks in 1920 alone, thanks mainly to the donations from well-to-do Russians. By the agreement signed on November 5, 1920, Ullstein became not a corporation controlling *Rul'* but only the contractor responsible for printing and distribution. Although two directors of Ullstein also sat on the board of *Rul'*, their main concern was with the commercial success of the paper and they exerted no influence on editorial policy.[48]

Just as the first issue of *Rul'* was going to press, the news of Wrangel's defeat in the Crimea reached Berlin. But if the end of the Russian Civil War symbolized the political and military failure of

[47] "Gody," pp. 24–30. Hoetzsch had succeeded Theodor Schiemann as Professor of East European History at the University of Berlin in 1920, was a member of the Prussian Landtag from 1919 to 1930, and the Russian expert of the Deutschnationale Volkspartei (DNVP).

[48] *Ibid.*, pp. 124–129.

the émigrés, it also marked the beginning of that remarkable cultural, literary, and journalistic flowering of the Berlin colony which would continue until late 1923. For *Rul'* it signaled a career of journalistic success for its editors and publishers. At its highest point, the combined subscriptions and sales of *Rul'* numbered over twenty thousand copies in every area of the world. For Ullstein this meant an influx of foreign currency, especially valuable during the German inflation, and the firm was constantly working on improved layout, wider distribution facilities, and, in 1923, a photographic supplement. But when the mark stabilized in late 1923 and many Russians left Berlin, sales dropped off sharply and the value to Ullstein of foreign currency was no longer so great. Impressed by the stability of the Soviet regime, the Ullstein house in 1924 voided its contract with *Rul'* with a payment of fifty thousand marks, and the newspaper was then forced to operate on its own as an independent émigré daily. Nor would Gessen's friend Otto Hoetzsch cooperate in finding new sources of support. Through the 1920's *Rul'* dragged on, now dependent mainly on its subscribers, advertisers, and donors, with an occasional contribution from the Union of German Industrialists. It died in 1931 for lack of financial backing.[49]

During the early 1920's, however, *Rul'* was undoubtedly the best Russian daily newspaper in Berlin. *Golos Rossii* and the pro-Soviet *Nakanune* were much inferior in quality, and only Alexander Kerensky's *Dni*, which appeared in Berlin in the autumn of 1922, could compare with *Rul'*. From the beginning *Rul'*, like most émigré papers, declared itself a "nonparty" organ, urging that the emigration unite for its own good and cease the internecine struggles based on prerevolutionary issues and political alignments.[50] In its pages appeared extensive and objective coverage of newsworthy events and of items of common interest to the Berlin colony: the comings and goings of émigré leaders, banquets, balls, cultural events, and German life and politics. Its several pages of advertisements in themselves were a mirror of Russian life in Berlin with its theaters, typists, lawyers, doctors, German teachers, piano teachers,

[49] *Ibid.*, pp. 152, 154, 160–161, 165.
[50] *Rul'*, December 18, 1920, p. 2; December 25, 1920, p. 1.

pawnbrokers, bookstores, and shops. Its commentaries on the cultural life of the emigration were second to none; its reviews of art exhibitions, new books, and concerts were concise, moderate, and at a consistently high level. The Moscow Art Theater, Oscar Wilde's "Salome," Cossack and Ukrainian choral concerts, Karl Stählin's lectures on Russia at the University of Berlin, Chekhov and Turgenev at the "Kleines Theater," annual New Years' balls—*Rul'* reported them all.

Politically *Rul'* reflected the increasing isolation of the Berlin faction of Kadets, who dominated its editorial staff. Constantly critical of the Soviet regime, the Mensheviks, the Social Revolutionaries, Miliukov's circle in Paris, and the monarchists, *Rul'* gradually came to speak for the emigration as a whole precisely because it spoke for no politically important segment of it. The SR's, *Rul'* claimed, had romantic dreams of a popular uprising in Russia and overestimated the historical role of the peasantry. The Mensheviks either did not understand the evils of Bolshevism when they urged recognition of Soviet Russia or were hypocrites; moreover, they refused stubbornly to cooperate with the "propertied" classes in emigration. The members of Smena Vekh, like the Mensheviks, were practically Bolsheviks; the Kadet faction in Berlin expelled one member who began to write for their organ *Nakanune*. Concerning the monarchists, *Rul'* found the Reichenhall congress to be "definitely reactionary." Unable to accept either the monarchist right or the socialist left in emigration, the Kadets suffered continual individual defections to both.[51]

If *Rul'* represented the outlook and interests of any single émigré group, it was the liberal business community. Daily stock market figures were prominent features of the newspaper and there was steady reportage of the meetings of Russian and German businessmen. The Kadets had no illusions about a restoration of the old regime in Russia, but neither would they accept the lack of concern for lost property on the part of émigré socialists and fellow travelers. When the British government began trade talks with the

[51] *Rul'*, December 24, 1920, p. 1; February 8, 1921, p. 1; June 14, 1922, p. 5; May 31, 1921, p. 1. The Kadet expelled from the Smena Vekh group was A. S. Gurovich.

Bolsheviks in early 1921, *Rul'* warned against Western plans to "use" the Bolsheviks in their own interest.[52] Like both the left and right among the Berlin émigrés, it recognized the basic need for close economic ties between Germany and Russia. But such common interest was a threat as well as an opportunity, if Germany should decide to deal with the Bolsheviks, and in 1922 *Rul'* became a bitter opponent of the Genoa Conference and Germany's Rapallo policy.

Like Scheubner-Richter, Gessen found that his familiarity with Germany and the German language was extremely useful in establishing political contacts and organizing an émigré journal. It was not sufficient to encourage émigré political unity, however, and the Kadets, like the monarchists, found themselves deeply divided and frustrated in the spring of 1922 when the opening up of full-scale relations between Germany and Soviet Russia sharply worsened the legal position of the emigration. Moreover, the Kadets never shared the ties to Germany that characterized the right-wing monarchists or the Mensheviks. The Mensheviks, too, grew increasingly hostile to developments in Soviet Russia in the 1920's but were able to find sympathetic support from German socialism and journalistic opportunities to shape socialist opinion on Russia. That they could do so was a result not only of their prewar ties to the SPD but to the mediation of a prewar émigré, Alexander Stein.

The Mensheviks

One of the most vital political circles in Russian Berlin in the 1920's was that of the Mensheviks, the non-Bolshevik wing of the old Russian Social-Democratic Workers' Party (RSDRP). The Mensheviks were revolutionaries without a revolution. For them the Bolshevik revolution was a historical accident; a small group of clever men led by Lenin had usurped the natural Marxist historical progression toward a socialist revolution which would have come as Russia developed industrially and socially along Western lines. Thus the Mensheviks were the eternal optimists of the emigration, who analyzed every fissure and weakness in the structure of Soviet Russia with the prescience that history was ultimately on the side

[52] *Rul'*, January 16, 1921, p. 1.

188

of democratic socialism. Their revolution had not happened yet, but it would.

The Mensheviks were émigrés, but they were not part of the emigration. In their eyes there was no reason to wallow in the swamp of anti-Semitic generals, bourgeois liberals, and historically atavistic royalty which to them made up the bulk of the colony. Conversely, other émigrés viewed the Mensheviks as only a slightly milder version of the Bolsheviks themselves. Unlike most émigrés the Mensheviks came to Germany with deep roots in the German labor movement and German social democracy. With the help of prewar exiles like Alexander Stein and Paul Olberg they moved easily into positions as anti-Bolshevik critics in the German socialist press. Like the extreme right, and unlike the Kadets, they found a home in German politics. For the Mensheviks, too, Russia's future lay with the West, not the East, in a European revolution along Marxist lines whose path Russia would also follow. In the end their message was heard in Germany primarily because there existed from the beginning anti-Bolshevik socialists who wished to hear it.

In Germany the socialists most receptive to the Mensheviks were in the Independent Socialist Party (USPD). Its founders were all members of the SPD during World War I who formed their own Reichstag faction in March 1916 and a few months later constituted themselves as a separate antiwar socialist party, led by Hugo Haase, Arthur Crispien, Georg Ledebour, Wilhelm Dittmann, and Karl Kautsky. In Russia, with the exception of Georg Plekhanov's small circle of pro-war socialist "defensists," most socialists opposed the war from the start; in Germany the antiwar socialists formed a distinct minority.[53]

Similarly reversed positions appeared with respect to the Bolshevik revolution in Russia. In Germany only the small Spartacist faction of radical socialists led by Karl Liebknecht and Rosa Luxemburg greeted it with enthusiasm; it was met with suspicion not only

[53] On Russian socialism during World War I see Boris Dvinov, *Pervaia voina i rossiiskaia sotsialdemokratiia* (New York, 1962); B. Nicolaevsky, ed., *A. N. Potresov: Posmertnyi sbornik proizvedenii* (Paris, 1937); Peter Garvi, *Vospominaniia sotsial-demokrata* (New York, 1946).

by the majority SPD but by many Independent Socialists as well, and most vocally by Kautsky. Only a small minority of the USPD around Ledebour was immediately responsive. In Russia, however, most socialists accepted the demise of the "bourgeois" Provisional government, if not the Bolshevik takeover, and only a minority stood in direct opposition to the Bolsheviks at first. The Mensheviks in their December 1917 party congress voted for a policy of "co-operation" (*soglashenie*) with the new government, although a minority of "revolutionary defensists" led by Potresov objected to this and refused to enter the Menshevik central committee.[54]

In the months following the Armistice in Germany the USPD faced the choice of cooperation with the new majority socialist "Establishment" of the Weimar Republic or of potentially destructive subjugation to Moscow and the Comintern, of cooperation with or radical opposition to a new and partly socialist government. The party center of Haase, Crispien, Kautsky, and Rudolf Hilferding did its best to moderate these two centrifugal forces within the party. To this end it was decided in the spring of 1920 that a delegation should be sent to the second congress of the Comintern to talk with Lenin and other Bolshevik leaders and assess the implications of membership. The involvement of certain majority socialists in the suppression of workers' uprisings in the Ruhr that spring had confirmed the USPD leaders in their unwillingness to join a coalition government with the SPD.[55] It was thus a certain mood of belligerence that prompted the June 1920 USPD party congress to vote to send Crispien, Ernest Däumig, and Helene Stocker to Moscow to investigate the terms of admission to the Comintern.

The man largely responsible for arranging the dispatch of this delegation and for establishing contacts between the Mensheviks in Moscow and the USPD leadership in Germany was Alexander Stein, a Jewish socialist from the Baltic. Born in Wolmar in 1881 to a family of the lower middle class, Stein (he was born Rubenstein)

[54] This refusal to cooperate with the Bolsheviks in late 1917 probably marked the origin of the so-called right Menshevik faction. Grigory Aronson, *K istorii pravogo techeniia sredi Men'shevikov* (New York, 1960), p. 8.

[55] G. D. H. Cole, *A History of Socialist Thought*, IV, part I (London, 1958), pp. 166–167.

experienced at an early age the national complexity of the region, first as a student in a German private school, then as one of two Jews allowed to attend a *Gymnasium* of Russian and Latvian students in Mitau. Immersed in the German classics of his aunt's library and the Russian books of his school, Stein soon became adept at both languages and knowledgeable in the literature of both countries. He also became painfully conscious of his own identity as a Russian Jew:

I saw the need, the poverty, the backwardness in which we lived. Instead of the romantic illusions of childhood came a sober recognition of the economic inequality which I myself had experienced. I felt more sharply now than before the absence of rights, the discrimination, the intolerance, the persecution to which the Jewish masses in Russia had been especially subjected. . . . Without clearly recognizing the political and economic origins of social grievances I became instinctively and by intuition more and more opposed to my surroundings.[56]

By the time Stein arrived in Riga in the autumn of 1899 as a young man of eighteen to study chemistry at the Politekhnikum he was ready to be drawn into the radical movement.

The means for Stein's conversion was the Jewish student society in Riga, the Anatolika. Just as the German student society Rubonia was becoming a center of German nationalism and upper-class conservatism in these years, so Anatolika provided for Stein an entrance into the growing socialist movement in Riga and the Jewish socialist Bund. In fact it was a member of the Bund, Rafael Abramovich, who first introduced Stein to the writings of Karl Marx in the summer of 1900.[57] During the next five years Stein was gradually drawn out of the Jewish cultural movement (he had founded a Jewish lending library in Riga) and into the broader horizons of the Russian socialist movement as a Bund discussion leader, a student strike agitator, and an assistant to Maxim Litvinov in smuggling copies of *Iskra* into Russia from Germany via Libau.

[56] Alexander Stein, "Erinnerungen eines Staatenlosen, 1881–1906" (1945; typescript, International Institute of Social History, Amsterdam), p. 11. See also Stein's obituary written by Abramovich for *Sotsialisticheskii vestnik*, February 15, 1949, p. 28.

[57] Stein, "Erinnerungen," p. 21.

Politics of Adjustment

The variety of Stein's own national and cultural associations was both an advantage and a barrier in these years. His fluency in Russian and German helped him earn a living by translating; coupled with his facility in Yiddish and Latvian, it made him an ideal agitator among the workers of Riga. In 1905 Stein's multilingual talents served him again as a reporter in Moscow on the socialist movement in Riga. But for the young Latvians who were beginning to dominate the socialist movement in the Baltic after 1905, Stein's involvement with the RSDRP made him seem more a "Russian" and less a native of Riga.[58] Nor was Stein happy with the new trend toward radicalism among the younger activists—the expropriations, the robberies, the violence and conspiracy of the professional revolutionaries. Pursued by the police, unwilling to become a member of the revolutionary underground, Stein in early 1906 decided to assume yet another identity of temporary political exile in Germany.

In prewar Berlin Stein soon entered the mainstream of German socialism. A sensitive man, gentle, introspective, with a distaste for violence in any form, Stein with his fine literary sensibility might very well have preferred the life of a scholar or writer. But a deepening commitment to the workers' movement and European socialism drew him into political life in Germany. In 1907 he translated his first Russian article for the German socialist press—a critique of Ibsen by Plekhanov—and soon was a regular contributor to *Vorwärts*. With Parvus he edited for a few years an information bulletin on events inside Russia entitled *Russische Korrespondenz* and later helped Wilhelm Bucholtz bring out the *Russisches Bulletin* of the Berlin Mensheviks.[59] By 1914 Stein had found a second home in the German socialist movement.

During World War I, Stein remained in Germany, where he joined the antiwar minority within the SPD which included Kaut-

[58] *Ibid.*, pp. 55–56.
[59] *Sotsialisticheskii vestnik*, February 10, 1941, p. 39. *Russisches Bulletin* was published in Berlin from 1906 to 1914 with the help of Karl Liebknecht and *Vorwärts* and carried news of the labor movement in Russia. Like *Russische Korrespondenz*, it was funded mainly by private SPD donations. See P. Lösche, *Der Bolschewismus im Urteil der deutschen Sozialdemokratie, 1903–1920* (Berlin, 1967), pp. 49–50.

sky, Eduard Bernstein, and the future leaders of the Independent Socialists—Haase, Crispien, and Hilferding. Yet his Russian identity still haunted him. An alien, Stein was kept under police surveillance during the war as a "civilian prisoner," meaning that he could live at home but had to report at specified intervals to the local authorities. More than being an inconvenience it was a reminder to Stein that he was not quite a German. As the "eastern expert" for *Vorwärts*, Stein continued to watch developments inside Russia with a feeling of involvement.[60] Released from house arrest at the time of the Armistice, Stein immediately resumed his journalistic activities as Rudolf Hilferding's assistant on the new USPD daily *Freiheit*, as co-editor with Rudolf Breitscheid of the journal *Der Sozialist*, and as the editor of another bulletin on Russia. More significant than Stein's journalism, however, was his experience with both Russian and German socialist movements, experience which now enabled him to facilitate relations between the Mensheviks and the USPD.

It was through Stein that Kautsky and other German socialists learned of events inside Russia in 1919–1920. His correspondence with Menshevik friends also helped to open up relations between Menshevik and USPD leaders even before Martov's trip to Germany in the autumn of 1920.[61] Martov and the Mensheviks, like many USPD members, were disturbed at being forced to choose between a thoroughly discredited Second International and subordination to the Comintern. In a letter to Kautsky of January 28, 1920, Martov rejected both these alternatives and proposed instead some kind of "spiritual and political union of Marxist parties and groups" which might avoid either "Bolshevist communism" or "nationalistic opportunism." [62] Could not Mensheviks and Independent Socialists join in creating a truly international socialist organization?

---

[60] Friedrich Stampfer, *Erfahrungen und Erkenntnisse: Aufzeichnungen aus meinem Leben* (Cologne, 1957), p. 209.

[61] Grigory Aronson, ed., *Martov i ego blizkie; Sbornik* (New York, 1959), pp. 106–107.

[62] S. Volin, *Men'shevizm v pervye gody NEP'a* (New York, 1961), pp. 41–42. Stein had already argued for the creation of a new International shortly after the founding of the Comintern in 1919. See his *Das Probleme der Internationale* (Berlin, 1919).

Politics of Adjustment

Stein in his correspondence with Martov had become increasingly interested in such an alliance. But both men realized that it would be almost impossible to obtain a USPD majority which would oppose joining the Comintern. Stein suggested to Martov that he might contact the USPD delegation to Moscow that summer and sound out their opinion. Thus when Crispien and Dittmann arrived, they immediately began private talks with the Menshevik central committee, much to the dismay of the pro-Soviet wing of the delegation. Martov had already suggested to Stein that relations with the right wing of the USPD might be initiated independent of the party majority. Now, in Moscow, Crispien and Dittmann proposed a way by which the Mensheviks could not only extend relations with sympathetic USPD members but even turn the tide of party opinion in their favor: they could send representatives to the impending USPD party congress at Halle to be held in October 1920 and expose Bolshevism's true nature before the entire party.[63]

Martov himself was highly in favor of such an expedition. Other Mensheviks feared that with their leader out of the country repressions against the party would no longer be restrained. In the end the Menshevik central committee voted to send Martov and Abramovich to Halle, and Lenin granted his permission. Although the Menshevik application to the Council of Peoples' Commissars had hinted at the need to organize a "foreign delegation of our party," Martov and Abramovich probably did not realize when they set out for Berlin in late September 1920 that they would never return to Russia.[64] Their departure marked the beginning of the Menshevik emigration.

Another motive behind the Halle expedition was the increasingly anti-Bolshevik position being publicized abroad by one of the founders of Russian Marxism, Paul Akselrod. Akselrod, too, had

[63] *Sotsialisticheskii vestnik*, February 15, 1949, p. 28; Boris Nicolaevsky, "K pred"istorii 'Sotsialisticheskii vestnika'," *ibid.*, February/March 1956, p. 41; A. Stein, "Pamiati druga i tovarishcha (K smerti tov. A. Krispina)," *ibid.*, March 12, 1947, pp. 51–52.

[64] Nicolaevsky, "Pred"istorii"; Israel Getzler, *Martov* (Cambridge, 1967), pp. 207–208.

long-standing ties with the German socialists, particularly Bernstein and Kautsky. As early as 1903 he had pointed out to Kautsky the "bonapartist-bureaucratic" characteristics of Bolshevism and Lenin's "organizational fetishism"; Kautsky himself had complained at the time of the "sectarianism" within the Russian socialist movement.[65] Thus by 1917 Kautsky and the Austrian socialist Otto Bauer were already suspicious of the "Jacobin" nature of Bolshevism and receptive to the views of Akselrod, then living in Stockholm. Akselrod urged that a policy of "socialist intervention" be adopted against the Bolsheviks and that an international delegation be sent to Russia to investigate reports of terror and political persecution. In April 1920 the Mensheviks denied him the right to speak for them abroad. But Akselrod's voice remained a powerful one in European socialist circles. Many Mensheviks agreed that it should not be the only one.[66]

Martov's attack against the Bolsheviks at Halle in October 1920 solidified the anti-Bolshevik minority, although he ultimately failed to turn the USPD majority against the Comintern. The issue facing the USPD, Martov argued in his speech (read by Stein), was not so much whether or not to accept the twenty-one conditions of the Comintern but rather the "basic principles which should guide the workers' movement in a revolutionary epoch, the basic tactics of revolutionary socialist parties." Social reformism, discredited by the war, and Bolshevik demagogery were now competing for control of the labor movement in every country. To join the Comintern would mean to become one of a "united series of Communist parties and sects around the Russian soviet state," not a member of any truly international socialist movement. The effect of Martov's criticism of the Bolsheviks—the first public attack in Europe by a Russian socialist of such stature—and his factual account of Bolshevik terror and intimidation was electric. While it did not swing a majority behind the anti-Bolshevik wing of the USPD, it strongly

[65] Lösche, *Bolschewismus*, pp. 34, 44–45.

[66] Aronson, *K istorii*, pp. 106, 109–111. A useful collection of materials on Akselrod is his *Die russische Revolution und die sozialistische Internationale* (Jena, 1932). See also the sketch by Kautsky, "Was uns Axelrod gab," *Die Gesellschaft*, II (1925), 117–125.

reinforced their determination to let the majority secede rather than be forced to accept Bolshevik domination.[67]

In the end the Menshevik hope for a new International came to nothing. The Vienna Union (or Second and a Half International), established in early 1921, succeeded in bringing together representatives of all three Internationals in Berlin in April 1922. But the divisions between Bolsheviks and anti-Bolshevik socialists were too deep to be bridged. After the September 1922 merger between the USPD and the SPD, the Vienna Union also moved toward the right, joining with the old Second International in a new Labor and Socialist International (LSI). The Vienna Union, as one historian put it, "antagonized the reformists, but failed to attract the revolutionaries." [68]

More important than the Halle debacle was the fact that the first anti-Bolshevik socialists had now joined the ranks of the emigration in Berlin. In the winter of 1920–1921 Martov and Abramovich established the Foreign Delegation of the party. Hardly an émigré organization, its function was to revive the prewar channels for the publishing and smuggling of illegal literature into Russia and to establish connections between the Menshevik centers there. With the help of Stein, its journal *Sotsialisticheskii vestnik* (The Socialist Messenger) first appeared as a biweekly on February 1, 1921. Co-edited by Martov and Abramovich, it was registered in the name of Stein, a German citizen now, and published on the presses of *Vorwärts*. Within a few months it became the main organ of the Mensheviks inside Russia, as well as the small group already in exile. Its pages were filled with the facts and figures of Bolshevik dictatorship and Menshevik suffering inside Russia; only in October 1922, when the bulk of the party leadership

[67] J. Martov, *Bol'shevizm v Rossii i v Internatsionale* (Berlin, 1923), pp. 9, 12; Aronson, *Martov*, p. 83; Frïedrich Stampfer, *Die ersten 14 Jahre der deutschen Republik* (Offenbach-am-Main, 1947), pp. 212–217; Getzler, *Martov*, pp. 208–212; about 300,000 former USPD members joined the German Communist Party (KPD), another 300,000 joined other parties, mainly the SPD, leaving only 200,000 in the reconstituted USPD.

[68] Cole, *History*, I, 342. See also the report of the 1922 conference entitled *The Second and Third Internationals and the Vienna Union* (London, 1922).

had left Russia for Berlin, did it cease to be the foreign organ of a Russian party and declare itself to be the "central organ of the Russian Social Democratic Workers' Party." [69]

From the start the Mensheviks were outspoken in their critical view of the Soviet regime. They attacked the "economic bankruptcy of the present bureaucratic government apparatus, its complete inability to cope with the tasks of running a planned economy in Russia" and, in general, the "Bolshevik dictatorship . . . , the dictatorship of a minority organized in a strictly centralized political party" which would only widen the "break between the Communist Party and the masses." Yet with regard to foreign policy the Mensheviks argued that Western governments should recognize the Soviet regime, and that European socialists should support it abroad. For a time there was still hope of "agreement" with the Bolsheviks, of the "re-establishment of proletarian, socialist unity" on the international level. [70]

As Marxists, the Mensheviks were also optimists. Not armed intervention but historical pressures would destroy the Bolsheviks. Economics would triumph over politics. The New Economic Policy, wrote Martov, "had been from the very first day in irreconcilable contradiction with the political superstructure . . . , the terrorist regime of a revolutionary-utopian dictatorship." "Any dictatorship," added David Dallin, "is a constraint on economic development— military or monarchist, as well as Bolshevik"; "the crisis can end only with the complete liquidation of the NEP phase, i.e. the Bolshevik dictatorship." The Bolshevik repression of the labor movement in Russia was not only evil and tragic; it was historically self-defeating. [71]

Critics of the Bolsheviks at home, supporters of Russia abroad, the Mensheviks remained intentionally isolated from the rest of the Berlin colony. They considered Gessen, Miliukov, Kerensky, and the Kadet and SR émigrés little different from Kolchak and Wrangel. The Berlin Kadets in particular were described as the "reactionary

[69] Volin, Men'shevizm, p. 28.
[70] Sotsialisticheskii vestnik, March 18, 1921, p. 2; February 3, 1922, p. 5; December 2, 1921, p. 4.
[71] Ibid., October 15, 1921, p. 4; August 2, 1922, p. 3.

'flower of the Russian intelligentsia'," and any socialists who advocated collaboration with the liberals were severely chastized. The monarchists, of course, were beyond the pale. Yet they were not as dangerous as the "right" socialists, who distinguished between democracy and socialism, or the pro-Soviet émigrés, such as the *smenovekhovtsy*, who proved better defenders of the Soviet regime abroad.[72] In the spring of 1922 the tiny circle of Mensheviks in Berlin was joined by the rest of the party leadership from Russia, released from jail on condition that they emigrate. They too became émigrés outside the emigration.

It can hardly be argued that monarchists, Kadets, or Mensheviks were "assimilated" into German life in 1920–1921. Their rapid adjustment to life in Berlin and to like-minded political circles in Germany, however, was greatly facilitated by the technical knowledge, German citizenship, or language skills of a few men who were hardly typical "Russian émigrés." Enemies of the Bolsheviks, they found it relatively easy to disseminate their message in Germany and to find ways for other Russians to do the same. What none of them could do, however, was to prevent the process of political decay too characteristic of emigration in general. To add to their problems in 1922–1923, closer relations between Weimar Germany and Soviet Russia and factional disputes combined to weaken and divide virtually every émigré party in Berlin.

[72] *Ibid.*, June 5, 1921, p. 10; November 1, 1921, pp. 4–7.

-—◦◦{ **V** }◦◦—

Politics of Frustration

When the Weimar cabinet of Julius Wirth was formed on May 10, 1921, it immediately accepted the reparation terms imposed by the Treaty of Versailles and initiated a policy of "fulfillment." This entailed not only a willingness to deal with France, but also a cooling-off of relations with Soviet Russia almost before they had begun. The pro-Soviet elements in the Wilhelmstrasse suffered accordingly; Maltzan was named ambassador to Greece and attempts were made to remove both Schlesinger and Hilger from their jobs in Moscow on the prisoner exchange. In September 1921 a man firmly opposed to any alignment with Soviet Russia, Kurt Wiedenfeld, arrived in Moscow as the new representative of the German government. Then in November the League of Nations' decision to give Poland the richest part of Upper Silesia, former German territory, abruptly reversed the trend toward fulfillment. The Wirth cabinet resigned, Wirth himself took over the Foreign Ministry, and Maltzan—who had not left for Athens—was reinstated as head of the Eastern Section. Thus the stage was set for a new pro-Russian mood in German foreign policy which within a few months would culminate in the Treaty of Rapallo.

The growing rapprochement between Germany and Soviet Russia had two serious consequences for the Russian émigré colony in Berlin. First, it meant that the German government was more responsive to the wishes of the Bolsheviks, who naturally wanted to reduce any political or legal privileges enjoyed by the émigrés and to control their affairs where possible. Second, it marked the final stage in the erosion of émigré claims to Russian political authority and in the eyes of the German government completed their transformation from potential political leaders to political refugees. Both consequences were visible in the changing status of the émigré community as a whole and in the frustrations of émigré politics.

To the Wilhelmstrasse and to official Germany in general, the Russian emigration offered little political promise from the very beginning. The Germans watched the émigrés closely, maintained cordial relations with their leaders, and quietly paid them for information on the affairs of the colony and on events inside Soviet Russia. They never placed much stock in them. The exiles had no real political power, they were hopelessly divided among themselves, and their primary goal was to find new sources of income. Their main value to the Wilhelmstrasse was that they provided information on émigré politics not only in Germany but throughout the diaspora. But in the end they were politically significant mainly in a negative sense, as a potential or actual barrier to the development of warm Soviet-German relations before and after Rapallo.

As early as the spring of 1920 the Wilhelmstrasse was convinced that the Bolsheviks were firmly in power and talks had already begun with Leonid Krassin over possible economic concessions for German firms in Russia. Balts like Rohrbach submitted memoranda to the contrary; Bolshevism was a transient phenomenon, a "Muscovite-Great Russian" movement directed against the borderlands whose *Volkspsyche* was quite distinct and would ultimately overcome its Russian conquerors. Such theories carried no more practical weight, however, than the activities of the émigrés. The Russian Committee in Berlin was viewed as a strictly private organization and Botkin's Russian Delegation as merely a branch of the Entente-oriented Paris émigré groupings. Reports from the German embassy in Bern were equally skeptical: the right-wing émigrés represented "only a small minority of the population and of public opinion"; the Mensheviks and SR's had "no real influence on the masses or the Russian proletariat" and were too friendly to the

Entente powers; the only way out of the Versailles settlement lay in close relations with the new Soviet government.[1]

In the winter of 1920–1921 the Wilhelmstrasse expressed a certain interest in the right-wing émigrés. While refusing to support Wrangel at the end of the Russian Civil War, the Germans were impressed by Scheubner-Richter's long report on his travels to South Russia and Behrendt noted that the right-wing Russians were friendly to Germany and should be supported in some way, secretly if not publicly. In general the Germans perceived the various émigré political groupings in terms of their orientation toward either Germany or the Entente. In this sense the liberals and socialists appeared unworthy of consideration, leaving the extreme right and left of the Russian political spectrum as possibilities. For this reason the Germans showed a great interest in the émigré monarchist movement at the very time they were pursuing closer relations with Soviet Russia preparatory to Rapallo. Through Wipert von Blücher and Maltzan's Baltic German informant, Baron L. K. Knorring, the Wilhelmstrasse kept a close watch on the Reichenhall monarchist congress of June 1921. What they learned was that the monarchists were long on "great words and empty phrases" and very short on money, unity, and reliability. To the Germans, the Russian right had learned nothing from 1917 and consequently had nothing to offer politically.[2]

The Reichenhall congress thus confirmed the political impotence of the émigrés except as useful informants. Here again the vital role was played by Balts such as Rohrbach and Knorring, rather than the Russians themselves. Knorring, who described himself as "an outspoken Baltic German" with "well-known pro-German views" was particularly useful to Maltzan in following the twists and turns of émigré politics. The Wilhelmstrasse also kept in touch with the émigrés after Rapallo, maintained a clipping file on their activities,

[1] AA IV Russland, Politik (Po.) 2, Vol. 1 (March–August 1920), p. 97; Vol. 2 (August–October 1920), pp. 10–30; AA IV Russland, Po. 5, Vols. 1a, 1b, 1c.

[2] AA IV Russland, Po. 2, Vol. 3 (October–December 1920), pp. 256–257 (citing Scheubner's report); Vol. 4 (January–April 1921), pp. 46–53 (report on the émigrés); Po. 5, Vol. 6 (May–July 1921) on Reichenhall.

and worried about attacks against Soviet officials in Germany. Otherwise they were unimpressed. In July 1922 Maltzan wired the German embassy in Budapest regarding Scheubner-Richter's plans to organize another monarchist congress there: "Our experience with Scheubner-Richter here recommends the greatest care and caution." [3] It was an attitude which extended to the Russian emigration in general in these years.

The Monarchists

If the Reichenhall congress had succeeded in bringing a large group of émigré "monarchists" together for the first time, thanks to the organizational help extended by their German friends, it failed to provide a basis for unity in the months that followed. The Supreme Monarchist Council held its first meeting in Munich in mid-June and shortly afterwards began to publish a weekly monarchist bulletin in Berlin, edited by N. D. Talberg. But the Council's activity that summer showed little promise of holding together the diverse forces present at Reichenhall: constitutionalists, army officers, churchmen, Cossacks, former Black Hundreds members, and so on. The disintegration of a single monarchist movement was apparent in its very formation.

A number of more moderate monarchists had opposed the control of the movement by the extreme right from the beginning. Even during the preparations for the Reichenhall congress it became clear that Markov II and Biskupsky would not have everything their own way and that some concessions would have to be made to the "constitutionalists," led by two former Kadets, E. A. Efimovsky and A. M. Maslennikov. In the spring of 1921 there was even talk of establishing a second monarchist newspaper in Berlin to counter the influence of *Dvuglavyi orel*. During the summer, preparations were made to effect this plan and on September 1, 1921, the first issue of the "constitutional-monarchist" weekly *Griadushchaia Rossiia* (The Coming Russia) appeared in Berlin under the editorship of Efimovsky.[4]

[3] Maltzan to Budapest, July 27, 1922 (AA IV Russland, Po. 5A, Vol. 3 [July–September 1922], p. 37).

[4] *Rul'*, March 1, 1921, p. 3; April 19, 1921, p. 5. Scattered issues of *Gria-*

Efimovsky was a disillusioned liberal who had fled from Kiev to Prague in 1918. Like the Berlin monarchists, Efimovsky was sharply opposed to Bolshevism and local nationalism in Russia and hoped for some kind of reconciliation between Russia and Germany in the future. But he also hoped for a political program broad enough to attract mass support—in emigration or in Russia—and considered casting his lot with the congress of Kadet, Social Revolutionary, and Octobrist leaders which was to meet in Paris at the same time as the Reichenhall congress. In the end he chose Reichenhall, but not without misgivings.[5]

After attending the congress and several meetings of the Supreme Monarchist Council in the summer of 1921, Efimovsky had become increasingly disturbed by the narrow reactionary and Germanophile attitudes of most monarchist leaders. On the surface the program of *Griadushchaia Rossiia* appeared to differ little from that of Reichenhall. The plans for a Romanov restoration, local and national autonomy, private property, peasant smallholding, and a state-supported Orthodox church were the same. Nor was there any formal break with the Supreme Monarchist Council, whose announcements appeared regularly in the journal. But there was a new emphasis on establishing popular support for any future monarchy and on broadening the monarchist movement itself. The monarchists should face up to the land question, gain the support of the peasantry, and plan to establish a representative assembly to share some legislative authority with the monarch. Tactically, they should cooperate with any friendly elements in the emigration to the right of Miliukov's Kadet faction and should give up political anti-Semitism.[6]

In October the constitutional monarchists formed their own organizational bureau in Berlin and contacted sympathetic friends in Paris and Constantinople. The three leaders on the bureau were Efimovsky, Maslennikov, and Taube. The Berlin group now began

---

dushchaia Rossiia, which lasted only a few months, are available at the Hoover Library.

[5] E. A. Efimovsky, "Sorokaletie reikhengall'skago obshchemonarkhicheskago s"ezda," *Vozrozhdenie,* No. 130 (October 1962).

[6] *Poslednie novosti,* August 12, 1922, p. 1; *Griadushchaia Rossiia,* September 29, 1921, p. 2.

to call itself the Union to Resurrect the Fatherland and to make plans for holding its own monarchist congress sometime in early 1922. The appropriate letters of invitation were dispatched and a friend of Biskupsky was sent to arrange with Scheubner-Richter and Ernst Reventlow the details of the congress, which they hoped this time to hold in Berlin.[7]

Along with the incipient revolt of the constitutionalists, the monarchist movement was suffering from other ills in the winter of 1921–1922. Six months had now passed since the enthusiasm of Reichenhall, and *Dvuglavyi orel'* warned of "insufficient funds at the disposal of monarchist organizations" and began to solicit contributions from the Berlin colony.[8] Then there was still the question of who would be a suitable Romanov candidate for the throne. "Where," asked *Griadushchaia Rossiia*, "is the future monarch?"[9] Reichenhall had left the question unanswered, hoping for a claimant or a family decision. But neither of the two most likely heirs to the throne—Nicholas II's cousin, Grand Duke Kirill Vladimirovich, and the grandson of Nicholas I, Grand Duke Nikolai Nikolaevich—had yet come forward. The right-wing monarchists had formally ignored the issue; the constitutionalists now evaded it by deciding to leave it up to some future popular assembly (*zemskii sobor*) to decide.

The army in exile had also become a factor in monarchist politics. Avalov appeared in military parades with Ludendorff and Von der Goltz that summer and was now back in Berlin editing his journal *Rodina* (Fatherland). Many monarchists were happy to have him expelled from Prussia once again in December 1921 for his activity and to see him in relative seclusion in Hamburg. But some of Wrangel's officers in Berlin were now proving susceptible to monarchist propaganda, despite their talk of being above émigré party politics. The monarchists reciprocated, hoping to gain Wrangel's support for their cause. He was even cheered *in absentia* by the constitutionalists during their December 13 meeting at the Rosegartensaale. But no serious cooperation was forthcoming.[10]

[7] Efimovsky, "Sorokaletie," p. 111.   [8] November 14, 1921, p. 2.
[9] October 6, 1921, p. 1.
[10] Botkin to Giers, August 27, 1921 (GA, folder 33); *Rul'*, January 7, 1922, p. 5; *Golos Rossii*, December 16, 1921, p. 3; V. K. Davatts, *Gody: Ocherki piatiletnei bor'by* (Belgrade, 1926), p. 57.

The new monarchist congress, like Reichenhall, enjoyed at least
the moral support of German nationalist circles, and Scheubner-
Richter subsequently arranged to publish the proceedings. But even
more important at this time was Ernst Reventlow, whom Efimovsky
had met during the preparations for the Reichenhall congress and
who had proposed to him a number of schemes for future cooperation between "national Russia" and "national Germany." Indeed, it
was Reventlow who gave the welcoming address to the assembled
delegates when the congress finally began in late March 1922. In his
weekly publication *Der Reichswart* Reventlow had shown considerable interest in the right-wing émigrés, reprinting in its pages
both the pro-German Durnovo memorandum of 1914 and parts of
the *Protocols*. Most of the Bolshevik leaders were duly revealed to
be Jews, although Lenin escaped as only "mostly Jewish." "The
future is dark," Reventlow mused in the autumn of 1921:

but nevertheless it is certain that the Bolshevik regime will not last long
and it is probable that—after a brief period of anarchy—the monarchy
will take its place in Russia once again. It is enough to point out that
of the tens of thousands of politically active and important Russians
who have fled Russia, the overwhelming majority have been won over
to this conviction.[11]

Reventlow also wrote warmly about Reichenhall and pointed out
that until now the pro-German sentiments of the Russian political
right had been kept hidden from sight by the "indefatigable propaganda of Jewry within German liberalism and German social
democracy." His anti-Semitism was unflagging. Not only were the
Bolsheviks all Jews, but so were the liberals in emigration. Kadet
leaders like P. I. Novgorodtsev and I. V. Gessen were part of an
"Ostjudeninvasion," along with most Russian intellectuals. As for
Blücher and Maltzan, the two main émigré contacts at the Wilhelmstrasse, they were "the men with whose permission the eastern
Jewish train uncoupled in Berlin and whom the eastern Jewish colony in Berlin can thank for their existence." [12]

[11] Hans Von Rimscha, *Russland jenseits der Grenzen, 1921–1926* (Jena,
1927), p. 71; *Der Reichswart*, 1921, No. 44, p. 6; *Verhandlungen des Reichstags, I: Wahlperiod 1920*, 354, p. 6904.

[12] *Der Reichswart*, 1921: No. 14, p. 7; No. 22, pp. 1–3; No. 50, pp. 5–7.

But Reventlow was a fair-weather friend to the émigrés. Like other German nationalists in the early 1920's, he also saw the efficacy of developing relations with the Soviet government against Versailles. While he recommended that German patriots show "understanding, support and sympathy" for émigré right-wing Russians, he had little faith in their future political success. Germany must develop ties with Soviet Russia. "National Rusian circles," he confidently and mistakenly predicted, "are sober enough and judicious enough to understand that Germany cannot pull back from such relations and that with correct handling they will not harm national Russian interests." [13] Hence it was not without some wariness that the constitutional monarchists heard Reventlow speak at the second major monarchist congress on March 25, 1922, in Berlin.

It was a much smaller group than Reichenhall which assembled for their new series of meetings at the Rotes Haus restaurant; present were some thirty-five delegates from Germany, France, the Balkans, and the United States. The congress was "monarchist" in the sense that all recognized the desirability of putting a Romanov ruler back on the throne and accepted the authority of the Supreme Monarchist Council. But in fact it was dominated by the moderates. This by no means allayed the fears of either the German or émigré liberal and left-wing press. The USPD daily *Freiheit* warned that "just like last year at Bad Reichenhall in Bavaria, German and Russian monarchists at the Berlin congress demonstrated again their common goals and interests." For *Poslednie novosti* it was merely a meeting of monarchist "dreamers," not nearly as ominous a sign as Reichenhall.[14]

After an invocation by Metropolitan Evlogy and a welcoming speech by Reventlow, Efimovsky opened the meetings with a talk that emphasized the "liberal" policies which had been carried out in

[13] *Der Reichswart*, 1921, No. 44, p. 6.

[14] *Freiheit*, March 30, 1922 (*Morgenausgabe*), p. 3; *Poslednie novosti*, October 15, 1922, p. 1. The proceedings of the congress were later published by Scheubner's Aufbau Society as *Trudy uchreditel'noi konferentsii russkago narodno-monarkhicheskago soiuza (Konstitutsionnykh monarkhistov) s 25 marta po 5 aprelia 1922 goda* (Munich, 1922). See also I. F. Nazhivin, *Sredi potukhshikh maiakov: Iz zapisok bezhentsa* (Berlin, 1922), pp. 217–224.

the past by the Russian autocracy, particularly the Stolypin agrarian reforms. The proceedings which followed featured the usual speeches, intrigues, and slogans that characterized most monarchist gatherings. There was a sketch of the international scene and the machinations of liberals, Jews, Masons, and the Comintern, the standard argument that Bolshevik rule in Russia was "artificial," and the claim that monarchism still had a tremendous appeal both inside Russia and in emigration. An article on the conference in the pro-Soviet newspaper *Nakanune* produced a suitable suspicion of Bolshevik intrigue.[15] But there was also a new element which had been absent at Reichenhall.

The constitutionalists, it has been pointed out, recognized the need for popular support for any successful monarchist movement. Efimovsky in his second speech to the conference now argued that some type of constitutional government must be established in any future Russia, popular support for the regime must be encouraged, considerable autonomy must be granted to the non-Russian nationalities, and any future monarch must expect to share legislative authority with a representative assembly.[16] S. S. Oldenburg stressed the need to reduce the economic role of the state, and M. I. Goremykin spoke of the need for land reform which would guarantee a minimum acreage to every smallholder. The conference also resolved to broaden the base of the monarchist movement in emigration to include any groups "to the right of Miliukov," as well as the remnants of Wrangel's army in Bulgaria and Yugoslavia. There were even signs of a growing interest in the labor movement as a potential source of support.

The March 1922 conference was neither as large nor as well publicized as Reichenhall. Yet it revealed two important facts about the monarchist movement in emigration: first, that any unity of the movement was going to be difficult to achieve without a single leader and a strong compromise platform; second, that many monarchists had now recognized a fact of political life which had eluded both the Imperial Russian government and the political right before 1914—the need for mass support. But it was at this point that the movement was rocked by an event which discredited it

[15] Nazhivin, *Sredi*, p. 221.   [16] *Trudy*, p. 17.

even further in the eyes of the emigration as a whole: the murder of Vladimir Nabokov, the editor of the Berlin daily *Rul'*, leader of the conservative wing of the Kadet party in emigration, and one of the most respected members of the Berlin community. Nabokov's murder brought the Berlin police into the Rotes Haus to arrest the bewildered delegates and bring the conference to a sudden and unexpected close.

The spring of 1922 marked a crisis not only for the monarchist movement but also for the émigré community in general. A Soviet delegation arrived in Berlin on its way to the Genoa conference to meet with Western leaders as representatives of the new Russia. "In recent months," Botkin complained to Giers in February 1922, "Berlin has become little by little the center of Soviet Russia's delegation abroad." [17] German businessmen were becoming interested in Soviet trade, German nationalists in alignment with the new Russia against Versailles. More pro-Soviet émigrés were appearing in Berlin, and a group of Social Revolutionaries had just purchased *Golos Rossii*, the Russian daily in Berlin. There was also the threat that control of the affairs of the colony might soon pass into the hands of the Bolsheviks or pro-Soviet Germans.

These developments all served to heighten the sense of impotence and frustration in right-wing émigré circles, especially in Munich. Among others, F. V. Vinberg and two young army officer friends, Shabelsky-Bork and Taboritsky, helped spread the word that the liberals and the Jews had betrayed Russia and that true Russians must seek their revenge. Vinberg tried to prove in his book *The Crusade* that every social and political upheaval beginning with the French Revolution was the work of "Jewish-Masonic organizations." [18] The focus of their hatred soon became concentrated on an old enemy, the Kadet party leader Paul Miliukov, who had

[17] Botkin to Giers, February 18, 1922 (GA, folder 33).

[18] Published in Russian as *Krestnyi put'* (Munich, 1921) and translated as *Der Kreuzweg* (Munich, 1922). Vinberg, Shabelsky-Bork, and Taboritsky lived together in a pension on the Theresienstrasse in Munich. In the winter of 1921–1922 they were joined by Harald Graf, a Finnish naval officer and supporter of Grand Duke Kirill. Police reports on the affair are in BHSA, MInn 71624.

208

long stood for everything they despised: liberalism, democracy, and close ties with France and England. In the minds of the three right-wing fanatics the logic of political revenge now led to the conclusion that they must kill Miliukov.

On the evening of March 28, 1922, Miliukov was delivering a lecture to a large and enthusiastic émigré audience at the Philharmonia Hall in Berlin. He had come from Paris especially for this purpose, and the audience noted that political quarrels had not prevented two of his fellow Kadets, Nabokov and Kaminka, from attending the lecture as hosts. After the first half of the lecture, as Miliukov stepped down from the podium amid warm applause, a young man suddenly appeared between the front row of seats and the stage, shouted "for the tsar's family and for Russia," drew a revolver out of his pocket, and fired a series of shots in the general direction of Miliukov. As the first shot was fired, Miliukov was thrown to the floor by a member of the audience who sensed what was happening and was thus saved from almost certain death.

Nabokov was not so fortunate. Seated on a stool to the right of the stage and taking notes, both he and Kaminka had jumped up and started toward Miliukov as the first shot rang out. Grabbing the would-be assassin, they attempted to disarm him and all three fell struggling to the floor. In the meantime a second young man had begun emptying his revolver into the crowd, now streaming toward the exit in panic. A bullet from one of their guns—it was never clear which one—killed Nabokov almost instantly, passing through his spine and lodging in his heart. Kaminka and several others were wounded in the melee. The two men were arrested by the Berlin police as they tried to leave the hall.[19]

The two young men who had committed the shocking murder of Nabokov turned out to be none other than Taboritsky and Shabelsky-Bork. Vinberg, who had helped plan the attempt on Miliukov by his fanatical protégés, had also come to Berlin, but left for Munich on the night of Miliukov's lecture to avoid suspicion. As it turned out, this was not their first experiment with political murder. A few months earlier Taboritsky had tried without success to kill the Octobrist leader A. I. Guchkov (considered an "English

[19] *Rul'*, March 30, 1922, p. 3; *Golos Rossii*, July 14, 1922, pp. 4-5.

spy") as he stood in the Nollendorfplatz subway station, but had been arrested on the spot by the Berlin police and then set free. The whole affair fit not only the growing wave of political violence in Germany—such as the murder the previous August of Finance Minister Erzberger by nationalist hoodlums in the Black Forest— but also the growing frustration of the right-wing Russians. "There is reason to believe," conjectured *Poslednie novosti* a few days after the murder, "that Markov II's group, dissatisfied with the mood of the more moderate monarchists, finally decided to embark on terrorist activity."[20]

Nabokov's murder naturally was a tremendous shock to both German and émigré Russian public opinion. Nabokov had been greatly respected within the Berlin colony as a moderate journalist and a man of high moral standing and convictions, tactful in his dealings with others to the right or left of his own positions. The Council of United Russian Institutions and Civic Organizations in Germany made a formal apology to the Wilhelmstrasse for the affair, and Maltzan in return sent his condolences to the Council.[21] *Vorwärts* rightly placed the blame on the "Munich nest" of Russian, German, and Hungarian reactionaries and called for the expulsion of all right-wing Russians from Germany. Nabokov's murder seemed to be not an isolated incident but another "link in the chain of a long-prepared and extensive worldwide criminal organization." The only sympathy for the murderers in the Berlin press came from the *Lokal-Anzeiger,* which grumbled that "if Miliukov had not been around, the tsar would have made peace with Germany." In Paris *Poslednie novosti* also blamed "Munich" for the murder, which it claimed was perpetrated by a "Black International" of Russian and German monarchists.[22]

In the Reichstag there was an immediate outcry against the Russian monarchists. As the Reichenhall congress had, Nabokov's murder provided the catalyst for the more general hatred of right-wing Russians among the German left parties. The Communist

[20] April 1, 1922, p. 1; see also July 16, 1922, p. 2.

[21] Botkin to Giers, April 6, 1922 (GA, folder 33).

[22] *Vorwärts,* 1922: March 29 (*Abendausgabe*), pp. 1–2; March 30 (*Morgenausgabe*), p. 3; April 2 (*Morgenausgabe*), p. 3; *Poslednie novosti,* June 27, 1922, p. 1.

delegate Paul Frolich placed the blame for the murder on the "shameless patronizing of the Russian counterrevolution by the German government since the end of the war."[23] Another delegate spoke of the existence of a Russian "Murder, Incorporated" (*Morderzentrale*) in Germany and chided the government for allowing the monarchists to hold their conference in Berlin in March. "What would the commissioner for public safety do," he complained, "if a congress of Russian Bolsheviks were to be held in Berlin?"[24]

Nor was the importance of Baltic Germans like Scheubner-Richter in the Russian monarchist movement lost on the delegate Koenen, who argued that "if a German national is a Communist, he will be expelled, but if he is an active monarchist, he will be tolerated." Koenen went on to elaborate on the close relationship, thanks to Scheubner, between German and Russian right-wing circles, and claimed to have documents offering

striking proof, naturally not investigated by the German police, of how— not only at Reichenhall, not only in the Aufbauverein Ost in Munich, but also in various other organizations close to the main monarchist group of Markov II and within the Russian-German business community —a group of monarchist forces has been united which strives openly for a resurrection of the monarchy in both Russia and Germany.[25]

Koenen also attacked Ernst Reventlow's friendship with the Russians, and again concluded that Nabokov's murder was part of a pattern of monarchist violence, not an isolated case.

Reichstag pressure, along with the general outcry over the Nabokov murder, did at least bring Shabelsky-Bork and Taboritsky to trial that summer. During the proceedings, conducted from July 3 to July 7 in the Berlin criminal court, both of the accused denied that there was any broad plot behind their deed and claimed not to be interested in politics. In a perverse way they were correct. But those present at the trial continued to suspect a broader movement. The defense was undertaken by a Balt, Baron Foelkersham, later a leading supporter of Grand Duke Nikolai Nikolaevich in Germany. Foelkersham argued throughout that the right-wing Rus-

[23] *Verhandlungen des Reichstags, I: Wahlperiod 1920*, 354, p. 6696.
[24] *Ibid.*, p. 6970.   [25] *Ibid.*, p. 6904.

sians were Germany's only friends among the émigrés and that
Miliukov had consequently proved himself a Germanophobe. For
the prosecution another Balt, Hans Vorst, appeared as a witness to
the murder and claimed that Taboritsky had fired the fatal shot
while Nabokov grappled with Shabelsky on the auditorium floor.
Taboritsky repeatedly denied this, and said he had come to the
lecture only to lend "moral support" to his friend Shabelsky. In the
end the court found both men guilty and sentenced Taboritsky to
fourteen years in prison, Shabelsky to twelve. Neither, however,
served out his sentence, and both were active assistants to Biskupsky and Alfred Rosenberg after the Nazis came to power.[26]

Nabokov's murder signified the increasing weakness, rather than
strength, of the Russian monarchist movement in Germany. Berlin
was a dangerous place for monarchist activity, and many right-
wing Russians who had not already gone to Munich were now on
their way to Paris. Moreover the next congress of monarchists, held
in Paris in November 1922, revealed the existence of strong
"Francophile" sentiment: an unsuccessful attempt was made to remove Markov II as chairman of the Supreme Monarchist Council
and opinion was strongly in favor of supporting Grand Duke
Nikolai Nikolaevich, rather than the Germanophile Grand Duke
Kirill Vladimirovich, as claimant to the throne and leader of the
"national movement." There was also a widening split between
Wrangel's officers and the Supreme Monarchist Council in the
autumn of 1922; many officers were avid supporters of Grand Duke
Nikolai Nikolaevich. Wrangel himself considered Biskupsky to be
a "Germanophile spy" and his representative in Berlin, A. A. von
Lampe, in early 1923 refused Markov II's invitation to head the
military section of a new monarchist organization.[27]

Thus the year 1922 saw a deep fissure open between the majority
of monarchist émigrés intent on finding a legitimate pretender and
gaining popular support and the Germanophile extreme right.
Many of the latter now left Berlin not for Paris but for the Balkans,
where Wrangel's army provided fertile ground for monarchist ac-

26 *Poslednie novosti*, 1922: July 5, p. 1; July 6, p. 1; July 7, p. 1; July 9,
pp. 1–2; July 16, p. 2. *Golos Rossii*, July 14, 1922, pp. 4–5.

27 "K.", *Mit oder gegen Moskau* (Dresden, 1927), pp. 61–62; Davatts, *Gody*,
pp. 73–75; *Poslednie novosti*, April 11, 1922, p. 2 and November 21, 1922,
p. 1; Lampe to Markov II, April 3, 1923 (LA, folder 46).

tivity, or for Bavaria, where they found friends among the equally despondent, frustrated, and anti-Semitic Germans living there. Bavaria now became the center of the monarchist movement in Germany.

Beginning in 1922 the Russian monarchist movement in Bavaria centered itself around the person of the Grand Duke Kirill Vladimirovich, then living at Coburg. In 1920 Kirill and his family had left Finland for Switzerland; in 1921 they had moved on to the south of France and in late 1922 to Coburg and the Villa Edinburgh, where they had lived before the war. Here they lived in relative seclusion, cloistered in familiar surroundings and concerned largely with Kirill's two favorite hobbies: sports cars and monarchist politics. In the latter arena Kirill was urged on by his aggressive wife Viktoria and a small, curious group of supporters, adventurers, and opportunists.[28]

The Coburg circle of Kirill's followers was small and isolated. Even Kirill's most loyal publicist in Munich, Nikolai Snessarev, often had trouble getting to see Kirill himself, since his friends formed a private wall between the would-be ruler and the outside world. Kirill's closest confidante was his wife, probably the real driving force behind his reluctant candidacy for the Imperial throne, who managed to obtain funds for the movement from the United States. Among his supporters were his personal secretary, Captain Harold Karlovich Graf, a former follower of Purishkevich, and Count A. A. Bobrinsky, a wartime Minister of Agriculture who had helped recruit army officers for the German-sponsored Southern Army in Kiev in 1918. The tone was naturally Germanophile, with Bobrinsky and General Biskupsky writing manifestoes which proclaimed Kirill's right to the throne and the need for future cooperation between monarchist agricultural Russia and industrial Germany. It was also accepted as a political fact of life that the émigrés could achieve their aims only with strong German support.[29]

Until the winter of 1921–1922 Kirill had not been involved in

[28] There is a brief account of these years by Kirill's son Vladimir in Grand Duke Cyril, *My Life in Russia's Service—Then and Now* (London, 1939).

[29] Rimscha, *Russland*, pp. 74–76; *Arkhiv russkoi revoliutsii*, No. 15 (1924), 30; Nikolai Snessarev, *Kirill' Pervyi: Imperator . . . Koburgskii* (n.p., 1925), pp. 47–54.

monarchist politics to any degree. But a request by Ataman Semenov from Siberia that he come to the Far East and proclaim himself the Romanov "ruler of the Amur" apparently inspired visions of himself as a legitimate pretender to the throne and leader of the monarchist movement in emigration. This he declared, first in a letter to Markov II and then in a manifesto "to the Russian people" of August 8, 1922, probably drafted by none other than Scheubner-Richter.[30] In fact Kirill's legal right to the throne was doubtful, because his mother, Maria Pavlovna, a Princess of Mecklenburg, had converted to Orthodoxy only after Kirill was born, and because his wife Viktoria was a divorcee who had never converted to Orthodoxy. The equally sound claims of Grand Dukes Dmitry Pavlovich and Nikolai Nikolaevich, however, did not stop Kirill's followers from asserting his sole right of succession to the Imperial throne.[31]

Kirill's appearance as a pretender in the summer of 1922 received a generally cold reception within the emigration. Markov II and the Supreme Monarchist Council in Berlin were uneasy about supporting Kirill without prior consent from Nikolai Nikolaevich and it was rightly felt that Kirill was backed mainly by "Bavarian and Hungarian monarchist groups, among others General Biskupsky in Bavaria." [32] A three-week trip to Bavaria that summer only further convinced Markov II of Kirill's political insignificance. Efimovsky's new organization, the Popular Monarchist Union, however, resolved on September 3, 1922, to give Kirill at least "moral support," perhaps because of subsidies offered by Biskupsky. But in general sentiment within the monarchist movement was now running strongly in favor of Nikolai Nikolaevich. The Council of Ambassadors and most of the rest of the Paris colony rejected Kirill's candidacy, and even a family gathering of Romanovs held there in November thought it at best premature.[33]

[30] Rimscha, *Russland*, pp. 66–68; Paul Leverkuehn, *Posten auf ewiger Wache: Aus dem abenteuerreichen Leben des Max von Scheubner-Richter* (Essen, 1938), p. 186.

[31] Rimscha, *Russland*, p. 69; Kirill's claim to the right of succession was pronounced by G. K. Graf in *Gosudar' velikii kniaz' Kirill' Vladimirovich, avgusteishii bliustitel' gosudarstva prestola* (Munich, 1922).

[32] "Obzor politicheskago polozheniia v Germanii s 5-go po 20-oe avgusta 1922 goda," (LA, folder 36), pp. 15–17.

[33] Rimscha, *Russland*, pp. 68–69; *Dni*, December 21, 1922, p. 5; see also

Kirill's support was largely limited to the Germanophile far right in emigration and concentrated in Bavaria. He had his enemies there too—notably Duke Georg of Leuchtenberg and General Krasnov—but received substantial backing from the Munich colony. Biskupsky was a vocal supporter of Kirill, more out of his love for adventure and money than any personal friendship or serious political hopes. As Scheubner's assistant in Aufbau he was continually looking for possibilities to organize "anti-Bolshevik" paramilitary operations from Hungary or Poland, and when such projects proved abortive turned to Kirill. But Biskupsky was not trusted any more by Kirill and his supporters than by other émigré circles. In the eyes of Snessarev, Biskupsky was nothing more than a selfish plotter who, as he put it, cared no more for Russia than for Abyssinia.[34]

It was during the winter of 1922–1923 that a serious movement to support Kirill as pretender to the throne first appeared in Bavaria. The Russian Legitimist-Monarchist Union in Munich, however, turned out to be a tiny circle of right-wing Russians with slight hopes for political success within the emigration as a whole. Mainly Balts, they hoped that Bavaria would be the center of the new movement only "temporarily" and had visions of carrying on the work of the Reichenhall congress by replacing the Supreme Monarchist Council as the main émigré monarchist organization. The Union's program to restore the monarchy in Russia and reunite tsar and people offered little that was new aside from its specific support of Kirill.[35]

In the spring of 1923 Kirill's supporters in Munich also organized their own monarchist journal. The editor was Snessarev, a seventy year-old former journalist of the St. Petersburg daily *Novoe vremia*. The journal was called the *Vestnik russkago monarkhicheskago ob"edineniia v Bavarii* (Messenger of the Russian Monarchist Union in Bavaria) and was published with the help of the *Münchener neueste Nachrichten* through the facilities of the Oldenburg publishing house. If the journal was new, the message was old:

Lampe's political surveys for August 25–September 15 and September 28–October 18, 1922, in LA, folder 36.

[34] *Poslednie novosti*, August 22, 1922, p. 1; Snessarev, *Kirill'*, p. 10.

[35] See the "Memorandum vremennago komiteta russkago legitimnomonarkhicheskago soiuza" (Munich, 1923) which describes the goals and activities of this group.

Monarchies must be resurrected not only in Russia but throughout Europe to stem the tide of parliamentarism, liberalism, materialism, and socialism; Kirill was the legal heir to the Imperial Russian throne; and behind the evils of the modern world stood the "mercantile morality" of the Jews.[36]

Kirill, working in his study at Coburg, was at best lukewarm toward the movement now being organized in Munich on his behalf. At the end of May 1923 he did finally go there to meet with the Legitimist-Monarchist Union and was surprised by the extent of Snessarev's journalistic activity. But in the following months he continued to live in seclusion at Coburg, where he became more of a political object to be used by Biskupsky and interested Germans for their own purposes than an exiled political leader. In the company of Mathilde Scheubner-Richter, Viktoria still dominated her husband's activity and it was she, not Kirill, who was seen at Nazi gatherings and parades. Even now, as one Nazi emissary to Kirill later complained, "politics had become for these landless ladies and lords merely a pastime, not a matter of life and death." [37]

The interest in the Nazis shown by right-wing Russians in 1922 and 1923 is a complex matter. The upper-class and aristocratic circles of the emigration doubtless were convinced by the association of *salonfähig* Germans with the movement that the Nazis were a party of order: conservative, anti-Semitic, or even reactionary, but certainly not radical or socialist. It was a common mistake, and one made by a generation of German upper-class sympathizers. But there were also Russians who grasped the new meaning of the Nazi party: an alliance not of the privileged classes but of the masses, drawing on the hatreds and frustrations of the demobilized officer, the hungry peasant, and the unemployed worker or civil servant.

During the winter of 1922–1923 a number of Russian monarchists in emigration were beginning to appreciate the tactics of the new right-wing parties in Europe. Markov II now urged the adoption of slogans like "land and freedom," designated to appeal to the working

[36] *Vestnik russkago monarkhicheskago ob"edineniia v Bavarii,* April 20, 1923, and May 5, 1923. Also Snessarev, *Kirill',* pp. 47–54.

[37] Kurt Ludecke, *I Knew Hitler* (London, 1938), pp. 216–217; mention of Viktoria at a Nazi parade is made in HA, reel 53, folder 1263.

classes, along lines suggested by Kemal Ataturk and Mussolini. In Berlin in the summer of 1923 V. V. Shulgin lectured to a large audience of Russians on "Italian Fascism." Professor Alexander Baikov, one of Kirill's followers, wrote in *Völkischer Beobachter* that Russia too needed a "national socialism" which would use the power of the masses to overthrow Bolshevism and free the country from the "red and gold internationals." [38]

But even those Russians who recognized the potential appeal of Nazism and Fascism continued to assume that the end result would be a restoration of monarchies. Snessarev attacked the reactionary "bears" among the monarchists and praised the virtues of Fascism in Italy; but he too assumed that in the end Fascism would depend on a monarchy as the most popular form of government. If men like G. V. Nemirovich-Danchenko became avid supporters of the Nazis and contributors to *Völkischer Beobachter,* they tended to oppose precisely that radicalism within the party which gave it such mass appeal. The Russian monarchists were drawn to the Nazis as a vocal domestic right-wing political party which seemed to share their disillusionment with the modern world, their anti-Semitism, and their profound hatred for the Soviet government in Russia. The Nazis seemed to show an interest in the Russians as staunch anti-Bolsheviks and potential donors. Finally, the Russians saw in the Nazis a kind of "last chance" against Bolshevism in Germany and in *Völkischer Beobachter* another platform for their own views.[39]

The last act in the story of the relationship between the Bavarian Russians and the Hitler movement was the organization and carry-

[38] *Dni,* December 21, 1922, p. 5; February 7, 1923, p. 6. See Baikov's article "Die Krise der Räteherrschaft und die Zukunft Russlands," *Völkischer Beobachter,* September 1, 1923, p. 2.

[39] Nikolai Snessarev, *Provokatsiia monarkhizma* (Berlin, 1923). See Rodionov's fantastic anti-Semitic panorama of the Russian Revolution in *Völkischer Beobachter* beginning October 2, 1923, and Nemirovich's support of Kirill in the issue of October 19, 1923, p. 2. Nemirovich-Danchenko was Wrangel's former press chief, a friend of Skoropadsky in emigration, and a part-time employee of Scheubner in Aufbau. Like Rosenberg, he fought the pro-Russian socialist wing of the Nazis throughout the 1920's. In 1925, when Gregor Strasser called for Germany to join with Soviet Russia, Turkey, and China in a war against Versailles colonialism, Nemirovich led the campaign against him. See Otto Schüddekopf, *Linke Leute von Rechts* (Stuttgart, 1960), pp. 198, 424–425.

ing out of the Beer Hall Putsch of November 9, 1923, in Munich. Scheubner-Richter, in fact, turned out to be a leading actor in the whole affair, the all-important "contact man" between the still little-known Hitler and the "respectable" elements of Bavarian society. And it was the abortive putsch which revealed more than ever the fact that Scheubner was the tenuous thread holding together disparate forces of revolution and reaction behind the party. With his death the most important link between the Munich Russians and the Nazi party was broken.[40]

In the autumn of 1923 Germany was undergoing a severe economic and political crisis precipitated by the French occupation of the Ruhr area in retaliation for Germany's failure to meet expected reparations payments. Prices skyrocketed, the value of currency was deflated, and food became increasingly scarce. Agitation against the Weimar Republic was mounting on both left and right. In Bavaria and the Rhineland, local separatism had gone so far that Berlin could exert little authority. In Bavaria, too, the activity and mass meetings of the Nazis and right-wing paramilitary groups known as the Kampfbund were increasing, and on September 26 the head of the Bavarian government, Gustav von Kahr, assumed dictatorial powers to deal with it. His first act was to ban all further meetings of the Nazi party.[41]

For several months Hitler and his military friends in Bavaria had toyed with the idea of a march on Berlin, hoping to repeat more successfully the Kapp Putsch. The main deterrent to such a plan was not so much the central German government as the local Bavarian authorities, Kahr and General Lossow, Reichswehr commander for Bavaria. After September 26 Lossow enjoyed extraordinary executive powers conferred on the army by President Ebert's invocation of Article 48 of the Weimar constitution. Kahr himself was not so trusted by Berlin, however, and may even have had

[40] H. H. Hofmann, *Der Hitlerputsch* (Munich, 1961), pp. 95–96; Georg Franz-Willing, *Die Hitlerbewegung: Der Ursprung, 1919–1922* (Hamburg, 1962), p. 191.

[41] On the 1923 Hitler Putsch see Hofmann, *Hitlerputsch;* Alan Bullock, *Hitler: A Study in Tyranny* (rev. ed.; New York, 1961), pp. 73–85; R. G. L. Waite, *Vanguard of Nazism: The Free Corps Movement in Postwar Germany, 1918–1923* (Cambridge, Mass., 1952), pp. 254–263.

some separatist plans of his own. Hitler deplored these as counter to his own ideas.

In early November 1923 Hitler decided that the only way to bring Kahr and Lossow into his scheme for a march on Berlin was to force their hand by carrying out a successful putsch in Munich before they themselves could act. The original plan, drawn up jointly by Scheubner-Richter and Rosenberg, was to arrest Kahr, Lossow, and Crown Prince Rupprecht during a Munich parade scheduled for November and to proclaim a national German revolution under Hitler's leadership. But, this plan was soon discarded.[42] On November 6, Hitler and Scheubner, meeting in Scheubner's Munich apartment, began to work out a new plan of action involving a full-scale march on Munich on November 11 by troops of the Kampfbund, of which Scheubner was the "business manager." But when Kahr announced that he would speak at a meeting in the Burgerbrau Keller, a local beer hall, on the evening of November 8, Hitler decided to move up the date of the putsch.

Throughout November 7 and 8, Hitler and Scheubner frantically arranged not only for a march on the Feldherrnhalle in Munich by the Kampfbund and the Nazis on the 9th but also for a dramatic personal appearance by Hitler at Kahr's meeting. It was also decided that Scheubner would himself drive to Ludwigshohe that evening to pick up General Ludendorff, persuade him of the importance of the affair, and bring him to the Keller. Ludendorff was furious at not having been informed of the plan in advance, but he urged those present at the meeting to go along with Hitler's plan for a march the next day and temporarily erased even the resistance of Kahr and Lossow.[43]

On the morning of November 9, Hitler and several thousand followers began their fateful march on the Feldherrnhalle. In the front row marched Ludendorff, Hitler, and Scheubner-Richter, the latter resplendent in his old cavalry uniform, arm in arm with Hitler. Back in the column were Scheubner's friends Rosenberg and Schickedanz. At the Odeonsplatz the column of marchers encountered its first resistance, a detachment of police standing with

---

[42] Bullock, *Hitler*, p. 78.
[43] Hofmann, *Hitlerputsch*, pp. 156–157, 161; Bullock, *Hitler*, p. 81.

drawn rifles. Suddenly someone opened fire, a fusillade swept down the narrow street, and Scheubner fell to the ground, mortally wounded and dragging Hitler down with him. The marchers fled in terror, among them Schickedanz and Scheubner's chauffeur, Johannes Aigner, to whom fell the task of breaking the sad news to Scheubner's widow Mathilde.[44] The Beer Hall Putsch was over.

With the death of Scheubner-Richter and the temporary collapse of the Nazi movement, the relationship of right-wing Russians and the Nazis fell into abeyance. Schickedanz now took over Aufbau, which soon disintegrated into squabbling "Russian" and "Ukrainian" factions, presided over respectively by Biskupsky and Ivan Poltavets-Ostranitsa. While many right-wing Russians and Balts retained their ties with Hitler's movement and rose to positions of authority after 1933, the temporary phase of Nazi collaboration with the émigrés was over, and in later years the role of Scheubner-Richter was almost forgotten. Perhaps the most balanced assessment of his work was that of Sergei Botkin in a report to M. N. Giers of December 12, 1923:

My dear Mikhail Nikolaevich,
    During the recent unsuccessful coup in Munich there was killed one of Ludendorff's co-workers and a close assistant of Hitler, von Scheubner-Richter, editor of the publication *Economic-Political Aufbau-Correspondence*, published in Munich, about whom I have already written. Mr. Scheubner-Richter, who lived in Russia for a long period, was also very close to Russian monarchist circles in Munich and for a time helped them significantly by organizing the Congress at Reichenhall. In his writings he often sharply attacked the Bolsheviks and the Third International and considered an alliance of Russian and German conservative circles a necessity. However, as an implacable enemy of France he saw in many of our countrymen adherents of a Franco-Russian alliance and, especially in recent days, attacked any policy among Russian émigrés which would have led to the participation or cooperation of France. In this respect one should also mention several highly critical articles directed against Grand Duke Nikolai Nikolaevich, whose tone was becoming a bit more mild recently. With his death the

[44] Bullock, *Hitler*, pp. 83–85; Hofmann, *Hitlerputsch*, pp. 212–213; Johannes Aigner, "Als Ordinanz bei Hochverrätern; Ein Beitrag zur Geschichte der nationalen Erhebung im November 1923" (Munich, n.d.), pp. 29–30.

publication of *Aufbau* will probably cease, but it seems to me that in view of, first, its over-extreme and one-sided direction, but mainly its small distribution, Russian affairs will have lost little.

Respectfully and devotedly yours,

S. Botkin [45]

Culturally, the Russian monarchists represented probably the most discontinuous element within the emigration, politically Germanophile but with few ties to Germany. For them the political, spiritual, geographic, and social displacement which the Bolshevik revolution and emigration entailed were all severe. For many it produced a bitter and sometimes vicious type of catastrophic thinking which found in the Jews the scapegoats for every evil in the modern world. As with many upper-class Germans they thought they found in the early Nazi party fellow conservatives who might yet help them in the eternal campaign against Bolshevism. But the impact of their own brand of anti-Semitism on right-wing German attitudes toward Russia might have been far less significant without the ideological and organizational contacts provided by Scheubner-Richter, Rosenberg, Duke Georg of Leuchtenberg, and others with ties to both Russia and Germany.

Because of such men the traditional anti-Semitism of the Russian and Baltic German upper classes now was absorbed into the German attitude toward Russia. "The East" was something Asiatic, barbaric, and Jewish, a threat to the old Europe; this was the central message of Balts and Russian monarchists in emigration. But even within the Nazi party they were sometimes hard pressed to defend themselves against a rising tide of pro-Russian sentiment in Weimar Germany, on the right as well as on the left. By the mid-1920's Rosenberg's capitalist, anti-Eastern, and colonial view of Russia was being challenged by a socialist, anti-Western, and anti-colonial view popular in the North German wing of the party which romanticized both Russia and Germany as part of the coming East, the new, less developed nations in revolt against the old Europe.

While the right-wing Russian émigrés opposed any such interpretation, the left wing of the emigration—particularly the intellec-

---

[45] Botkin to Giers, December 12, 1923 (GA, folder 34).

tuals—did not. If the monarchists were a source of anti-Soviet attitudes in Germany, the intellectuals helped to encourage strong sympathies for "the new Russia." But the left also had its anti-Bolsheviks, liberal and socialist politicians who disliked the Soviet government and the monarchists alike. For them "the West" meant not a return to the old Europe but the creation of a new one: liberal, democratic, and even socialist.

The Liberals

Rapallo was a sharp blow to the Kadets, as to the emigration in general. Growing Western trade and recognition of the Soviet regime meant that émigré businessmen now had little hope of recouping their economic losses. The murder of Vladimir Nabokov at about this time was a further blow and led within a few months to the collapse of the Berlin Kadet faction as a political party.

From the beginning the Kadets in Berlin were almost as hostile to Miliukov's left wing of the party in Paris as they were to the monarchists and the Bolsheviks. The first meeting of the Berlin group, held under Gessen's chairmanship in December 1920 and attended by only ten men, was immediately hostile to Miliukov's proposal for a "democratic anti-Bolshevik front" in emigration which would include the SR's. On the basis of Kaminka's report of his recent conversations with Miliukov, they refused to recognize the authority of the Paris faction to take any action independent of Kadet groups in other European capitals. Moreover, they concluded that the recent activity of the SR's "does not leave room for any hopes of forming a united front with them." [46] The idea of reviving the abortive Constituent Assembly as a coalition émigré "national committee" also seemed vague and premature.

It thus came as no surprise when the Berlin Kadets declined to participate in a January 1921 meeting in Paris called to organize a

[46] "Zasedanie gruppy chlenov partii narodnoi svobody nakhodiashchikhsia v Berline," (KDA, I, 197). The December 19–25, 1920, meeting of the Berlin Kadets was attended by Gessen, Nabokov, Kaminka, O. E. Buzhansky, V. L. Gershun, L. M. Zaitsev, I. G. Kogan, I. O. Levin, P. I. Novgorodtsev, and S. I. Rozenfeld. The meeting was reported in *Rul'* on December 29, 1920, which noted that the Berlin group would not attend the January 8, 1921, Paris gathering of the émigré "Constituent Assembly."

united front of liberal and SR forces in emigration. The meeting's preliminary statement on future tactics was no more satisfactory than its final report, entitled dramatically "What Is to be Done after the Crimean Catastrophe?" *Rul'* doubted that anything substantial could come of such an attempt at émigré unity when its authority was questionable, its support minuscule, and its SR proponents too far to the left for most liberals. Nevertheless Miliukov sent off a report of the meeting to Berlin in an attempt to persuade Nabokov and Gessen to change their position.[47]

But once again the Berlin Kadets found the whole idea of a "new tactic".—cooperation with the SR's in an émigré "national" government—to be "internally false, a misunderstanding and the inevitable embryo of future decay." [48] The political reconstruction of Russia, they felt, must follow rather than precede the collapse of the Bolsheviks. And were the majority of the SR's even willing to cooperate with the liberals? Both Nabokov and Gessen agreed that it was time for the Kadets themselves to work out a new program, but one based on political principle, not on the opportunism of possible tactical success. The interests of Russia must be put above the interests of party. This the SR's had never been willing to do.

The reticence of the Berlin Kadets did not slow down the preparations in Paris now for a full-scale congress which would represent all "national" political and social groups in emigration, an émigré "parliament." But in the end the "national unity" conference, organized by Vladimir Burtsev, the SR editor of the Paris daily *Obshchee delo,* and held in Paris from June 5 to June 12, 1921, came to nothing.[49] Representing primarily business and professional circles, it featured long speeches on the need for unity, talk of maintaining the "White idea" of anti-Bolshevik intervention using the remnants of Wrangel's army, and considerable pro-French sentiment. But the tensions among those attending the conference—army officers and socialists, anti-Semites and Jewish liberals, Ger-

---

[47] *Rul'*, 1921: January 4, p. 5; January 11, pp. 1, 5. On the Paris meeting and its impact on Kadet politics see Rimscha, *Russland*, pp. 26–27, 35–37.

[48] "Zamechaniia Berlinskoi gruppy chlenov partii narodnoi svobody na zapisku Parizhskago komiteta 'Chto delat' posle Krymskoi katastrofy'" (KDA, I, 209).

[49] Rimscha, *Russland*, pp. 87–93.

manophiles and Francophiles—were obvious from the beginning. As an attempt to unite "old Russia" and the Russian "intelligentsia," as one historian put it, the success of the conference and its seventy-four man National Committee was only temporary.[50]

In May 1921 the Berlin Kadets had agreed to participate in the Paris conference, but warned that they felt Russia could be resurrected politically only by a new and truly representative national party in emigration and not by a coalition of old parties. "The basic condition for re-establishing the Russian state," read their resolution of May 21, "is the unification of social forces in a common national progressive-democratic program, putting aside narrow party slogans and formulas." [51] But it was clear that there was no unanimity within the Berlin faction after the conference. Nabokov now urged support of the National Committee, of which he had been elected a member, and noted with satisfaction that the Paris conference had rejected Miliukov's "new tactic" of collaboration with the SR's. But when he delivered his July 9 report on the Committee's work in Paris, Nabokov found himself faced with vocal criticism within the Berlin faction which was cut short only by the customary police curfew imposed on evening meetings.[52]

In short, Burtsev's Paris conference, while outwardly a demonstration of unity among émigré intellectuals and politicians, only widened the schism within the Kadet party. Although nineteen of the twenty-eight members of the old Kadet central committee in emigration had attended the Paris meeting, they were unable to resolve their own differences over the question of collaboration with either socialists or monarchists. *Rul'* was overly optimistic in its hope that the Kadet party might become the "center around which will grow the statist elements necessary for Russia's rebirth." [53] In fact on July 22, 1921, Miliukov announced his own secession from the Paris Kadet faction, which had failed to support his "new tactic." There now began a long polemic between *Rul'* and Miliukov's *Poslednie novosti* which only accentuated the fact that the liberals were now politically bankrupt, if journalistically solvent.

[50] *Ibid.*, p. 93.   [51] *Rul'*, May 24, 1921, p. 4.
[52] *Rul'*, June 8, 1921, p. 1; July 12, p. 5.   [53] *Rul'*, June 7, 1921, p. 1.

Since early 1921 Nabokov had been using the pages of *Rul'* to criticize Miliukov's policy of cooperation with the SR's. "Between the nonsocialist and the socialist parties," he wrote in March, "there is now no unity, and if the fantastic plan of cutting out the 'moderate socialists' to fit their own pattern does not succeed, then unity can be achieved only by surrendering all the positions of nonsocialist democracy." [54] Such criticism continued into the summer and fall of 1921, when the Berlin Kadets formally broke off ties with both Paris factions and declared themselves to be the "democratic group" of the Kadet party. [55] Nabokov now charged that Miliukov deliberately distorted Nabokov's position in 1919 in *The New Russia* to make it agree with his own "new tactic," while Miliukov continued to attack *Rul'* for its vague and unproductive middle-of-the-road position. [56]

Nabokov's tragic death at the side of his political opponent in the spring of 1922 reduced the intensity of the polemic between *Rul'* and *Poslednie novosti* for a time. But in late 1922 and early 1923 Miliukov returned to the attack, labeling *Rul'* an "antirepublican" newspaper with the slogan of "let us ignore" (*"ignoramus"*) and its editors men unable to adopt a "democratic" position because they still hoped to return to Russia as "masters." He was beating a dead horse. On December 14, 1922, Gessen and the tiny Berlin Kadet faction met and agreed that the Kadets no longer existed as a political party, that only liberal individuals could now be found either in Russia or in emigration, and that the entire basis of the party's program—the old intelligentsia, a legal order, constititionalism— were gone; by mutual agreement they declared themselves politically dissolved. [57]

The collapse of the Kadet faction in Berlin symbolized the collapse of Western-oriented liberalism both in Russia and in exile. Like the monarchists, the liberals saw Bolshevism and Russian socialism in general as something non-Western and non-European. *Rul'*

[54] *Rul'*, March 16, 1921, p. 1. [55] *Rul'*, September 13, 1921, p. 4.
[56] *Rul'*, August 16, 1921, p. 2; *Poslednie novosti*, September 16, 1921, p. 1.
[57] *Poslednie novosti*, December 3, 1922, p. 1; February 13, 1923, p. 1. On the last meeting of the Berlin Kadets see the minutes in KDA, I, 241–251.

complained that "the whole Russian intelligentsia is completely cut off from Western Europe's business practices and theory"; and Miliukov noted that "our Russian experience has shown that Russian socialism has not been penetrated by the wisdom of the West."[58] Gessen, too, questioned the romantic hopes of the Eurasians that a new revolutionary Russia would bring a new message to the world and predicted that "the result of war and revolution will be the triumph of the individual over the collective."[59] But neither could the liberals accept the restoration of the old Russia or the old Europe, a revival of the old West against the new East. Supporting close economic ties between Russia and Germany, they were unwilling to adhere to the anti-Bolshevik colonialism of German businessmen. Liberalism, like democratic socialism, could hardly compete in emigration with the broad appeal of either monarchism or pro-Sovietism.

The Mensheviks

Among the Menshevik newcomers in Berlin in 1922 were Fedor Dan (F. I. Gurvich) and his wife Lidia, Boris Nicolaevsky, Solomon Schwarz, Boris Dvinov, Peter Garvi, Mikhail Kefali, and Grigory Aronson. Together with the earlier émigrés—Martov, Abramovich, Stein, and David Dallin—they formed the remarkable Menshevik "circle" in Berlin which would survive for a decade as a vital political center in exile. In a sense they were a family more than a political faction, *nasha partiia* (our party), a group whose personal, emotional, political, and ideological ties went back twenty years or more. Partly as a result of the common past of conspiratorial political activity in Russia, the Mensheviks shared with the Bolsheviks a certain *Kto-Kogo* (who gets whom?) psychology which divided the world into those with us and those against us, good guys and bad guys. The years of exile deepened this trait, in both ideological and personal relations.

From the beginning the strongest Menshevik personality in Berlin was Dan, a member of the Union of Struggle for the Emancipa-

[58] *Rul'*, September 17, 1921, p. 1; *Poslednie novosti*, February 15, 1923, p. 1.
[59] *Rul'*, September 19, 1921, pp. 2–3.

tion of the Working Class in St. Petersburg, an old friend of Kautsky, and an experienced organizer of illegal circles before the revolution. Married to Martov's sister, Dan also exhibited a certain
"Great Russian" bias in his views akin to that of Dallin and Nicolaevsky. If Akselrod was the pope of Russian socialism, it was said,
then Martov was its tribune and Dan its organizer. Rafael Abramovich, although an excellent speaker, was always considered somewhat of an outsider as a former Bundist; the same was true of
I. Yudin (Aizenshtat). Boris Nicolaevsky, the historian and archivist of the group, was a passionate man with strong likes and
dislikes who was never able to surround himself with disciples.
Dallin had an excellent command of both the spoken and written
word, and was more open-minded, as was Grigorii Bienstock, who
later became intrigued by religion and the idea of the demonic in
Russian history. The only genuine worker in the circle was Kefali,
a former soviet and trade-union leader. The one man capable of
sustained cooperation with other political factions outside the
"family" was Grigory Aronson. Diverse as its personalities were,
the Menshevik circle retained its personal, if not ideological, unity
for a remarkably long time. But in the end it too suffered the factionalism of exile, particularly over the question of relations with
dissident socialists and liberals. For most Mensheviks men like
Potresov and Stepan Ivanovich were beyond the pale as anti-
Bolshevik liberals, and reconciliation proved futile.

The Mensheviks were thus very different people and they sought
out diverse socialists to admire in Europe as well. For Nicolaevsky,
the great man was Hilferding; for Garvi it was Kautsky; for Dan,
Otto Bauer, and so on. There were political divisions too. Since
1920 there had been among the Russian Mensheviks a steady trend
away from the "left" policy of cooperation with the Bolsheviks (for-
malized in the so-called "April theses") toward a general anti-
Bolshevik stance. The Kronstadt uprising of March 1921, the Soviet
invasion of Georgia, and the persecution of the Mensheviks themselves all contributed to this turn to the right. Whereas the leftists—
including the Foreign Delegation in Berlin—continued to hope for
the evolution of Bolshevism toward some form of democratic social-

ism, the rightists felt this could occur only with the removal of the Bolsheviks from power.[60] The arrival of the new émigrés in Berlin in 1922 marked the appearance not only of new personalities but of new disputes.

One source of opposition to the Foreign Delegation was Akselrod, who had moved to Berlin and begun writing his memoirs and who continued to argue in the press for some kind of socialist intervention against the "superhuman amoralism" of "Asiatic" Bolshevism; this contrasted sharply with Martov's view that the Bolsheviks could not be overthrown by force, since they commanded the loyalty of a "significant minority" of workers in Russia and would evolve into something better if left alone.[61] In addition several of the "right" Mensheviks in Berlin joined the circle of Stepan Ivanovich (S. O. Portugeis), a journalist and former Defensist who had come to Berlin in early 1922.[62] Ivanovich's journal *Zaria* urged all social democrats to unite behind the revived Second International in a common anti-Bolshevik front. And like both the Foreign Delegation and Akselrod, Ivanovich sought the legitimacy of approval from Kautsky.[63]

The rivalry between Ivanovich and the Mensheviks was a bitter one. While *Zaria* agreed that the NEP was a "red counterrevolution" directed against the real interests of Soviet workers, it sharply opposed Martov's hope for a "single proletarian front" which could include the Bolsheviks. Instead Ivanovich urged cooperation with

[60] S. Volin, *Men'shevizm v pervye gody NEP'a* (New York, 1961), p. 19.

[61] Paul Akselrod, *Die russische Revolution und die sozialistische Internationale* (Jena, 1932) pp. 180–205 (letter to Martov, September 1920) and Grigory Aronson, ed., *Martov i ego blizkie: Sbornik* (New York, 1959) pp. 52–61 (Martov's reply).

[62] Ivanovich (1881–1944) had been a Menshevik since 1903 and wrote for trade-union, Menshevik, and left-Kadet journals before the war. In 1918–1920 he was active trying to unite socialist and democratic anti-Bolshevik circles in South Russia. In 1925 he left Berlin for Paris, where he wrote for several "right" socialist and liberal journals, and was thus ostracized by *Sotsialisticheskii vestnik* until 1940. See Aronson's obituary of him in that journal for March 17, 1944, pp. 66–67.

[63] *Zaria*, 1922, No. 1, p. 2; see also the letter of Ivanovich to Kautsky of November 19, 1922, asking for support (KA, D-XVIII, pp. 652–654). *Zaria* appeared in Berlin biweekly from 1922 to 1925.

anti-Bolshevik liberals and socialists in the war on Bolshevism. This most Mensheviks refused to countenance, with the exception of Aronson, who associated with both circles. Martov described Ivanovich as one of the "marauding swine who try to profit off the ruins and corpses sown by the civil war and vowed that "we will remain on different sides of the barricades." In 1923 a few Mensheviks, led by Garvi, tried to reconcile the two warring socialist factions in Berlin by expanding the membership of the Foreign Delegation. This came to nothing, however, and in April 1923 the Foreign Delegation resolved that "the *Zaria* group is neither organizationally nor ideologically a part of the RSDRP." Only in 1924, when a new party program was being worked out, was there a move toward reconciliation, and even then a number of rightists were not allowed to participate.[64]

Akselrod and the *Zaria* circle were not the only rivals of the Foreign Delegation in Berlin. There was also a group of Georgian Mensheviks, bitterly anti-Bolshevik as a result of the conquest of Georgia by the Red Army in early 1921, who sought to re-establish their ties with their friends in the Second International. Several of them had come to Berlin in the summer of 1918 not as émigrés but as representatives of the independent Georgian government seeking loans and recognition in return for manganese concessions to German industry. Cordially received, they found no concrete support, either from the Germans or, after the Armistice, from the Allied Supreme Council in Paris. The Georgians who stayed on in Berlin were given their own passport office in 1920 under Dr. Lado Akhmeteli, a journalist who had studied in Germany before the war. But the Germans had no illusions concerning the political future of the Georgians. A Foreign Office memorandum of January 13, 1922, noted that while they "might play a political role" in the end, "Soviet power in the Caucasus will fall only if it falls in the rest of

---

[64] *Zaria*, 1922, No. 2, pp. 55–57; 1922, No. 3, p. 64; S. Ivanovich, *P'iat let bol'shevizma: Nachala i kontsy* (Berlin, 1922), p. 21, 44; Grigory Aronson, *K istorii pravogo techeniia sredi Men'shevikov* (New York, 1960), p. 116; Martov's letters to S. Shchupak (June 8, 1921) and E. Anan'in (March 8, 1921) cited in Volin, *Men'shevizm*, p. 36.

Russia as well, or if Soviet Russia through military catastrophe on other fronts is forced to pull its troops out of the Caucasus."[65]

Among German socialists the Georgians found a much warmer reception. Kautsky and Bernstein had known several of them through the prewar International and in 1918 had conducted conversations with Akhmeteli and Akaki Chenkeli, the head of the Georgian delegation to Berlin, about the situation in their country. Many German socialists also had fond hopes regarding the success of the Georgian experiment in socialism in 1918–1920. Kautsky, who had traveled there in 1920, argued that "it is the duty of the Social Democrats of all countries to assist Menshevism to the utmost extent of their power. This is the same thing as working for the triumph of the methods of little Georgia." In his private correspondence he also encouraged the exiles in the 1920's in their struggle against "Communist terrorism and Russian domination." The Labor and Socialist International was also receptive to the attack on "Bolshevik imperialism" leveled by Irakli Tsereteli in these years; like Abramovich for the Mensheviks, Tsereteli enjoyed the status of representative of an "affiliated party" in the 1920's, and found in the remnants of the Second International a willing audience for Georgian anti-Bolshevism.[66]

Like many anti-Bolshevik émigrés, the Georgian Mensheviks portrayed Bolshevism as an Eastern and Asiatic phenomenon. If Akselrod and the Mensheviks represented the "European, Western element" in Russian socialism, wrote Tsereteli, then Lenin and the Bolsheviks formed only its "eastern branch." According to Noi Zhordaniia, Bolshevism was a legacy of Russian Jacobinism, the Blanquist wing of Populism in the 1870's, and the terror was an inheritance from Ivan the Terrible. Russian Bolshevism "has nothing in common with Western European Communism, the Communism

[65] AGFM, T-120, reel 3298, K282/KO98375–391. For the story of Georgian Menshevism and the establishment of Georgian autonomy in 1918–1920 see Richard Pipes, *The Formation of the Soviet Union* (Cambridge, Mass., 1957), pp. 17–18, 99, 210–214, 233–240. On Georgian pursuit of German support in 1918 see Z. Avalishvili, *The Independence of Georgia in International Politics, 1918–1921* (London, 1940), pp. 61–113.

[66] N. Jordania, *Marxismus und Demokratie* (Berlin, 1921), pp. 8–9; K. Kautsky, *Georgia: A Social-Democratic Peasant Republic* (London, 1921), p. 111; see also Kautsky's letter of encouragement to Georgian "comrades" dated March 16, 1923 (KA, G–XVII, pp. 35–36).

of a developed industrial proletariat" and the Bolshevik revolution was a "specifically Russian-peasant phenomenon" which bore "certain features of Asiatic revolutions, the revolutions of Turkey, Persia, and China." But in the long run Russia would follow the path to socialism laid down by industrial Europe, not agrarian Asia. Concluded Zhordaniia: "Although Russia is not Europe, she must in the end become Europe." [67]

Like the Russian Mensheviks, the Georgians were able to write for the German socialist press and to put their case against the Bolsheviks in public view in the 1920's. But whereas the Mensheviks were drawn to the USPD, the more anti-Bolshevik Georgians found a voice in the SPD and *Vorwärts*. In part this was simply because the majority socialists found authentic anti-Bolshevik reports useful. But the Georgians also had their middleman in Paul Olberg, a prewar Jewish émigré who had been a member of both the Bund and the Menshevik faction. Like Alexander Stein, Olberg came to Germany after the revolution of 1905 as a journalist writing on Russian affairs and a specialist in smuggling illegal literature into Russia. After a year in Russia in 1917–1918, Olberg returned to Germany where he became a journalist for *Vorwärts*.[68]

In the early 1920's Olberg wrote frequently on Russian matters and, like Kautsky, was a proselytizer for Menshevik Georgia, which they had visited together in 1920 as part of a European Socialist Study Commission. He also served as a useful go-between for the "right" émigré socialists, Russian and Georgian, and the SPD leaders.[69] *Vorwärts* was never as receptive to the émigrés as *Freiheit* and the USPD, however, and it was Stein and the Foreign Delegation who were able to find a more willing outlet for their views in Germany.

The case against the Bolsheviks presented in the pages of *Freiheit* by Stein, Martov, Abramovich, and Dan in 1921–1922 was the

---

[67] Akselrod, *Russische Revolution,* p. xvii; N. Zhordaniia, *Bol'shevizm* (Berlin, 1922), pp. 12, 20, 58, 80–84.

[68] On Olberg see *Sotsialisticheskii vestnik,* 615, 12, p. 234; 725, 1, p. 24; 741, 5, p. 100. Also P. Olberg, "Georgien im Not," *Vorwärts,* March 5, 1921 (*Morgenausgabe*), pp. 1–2; and his *Briefe aus Russland* (Stuttgart, 1919) and *Die Bauernrevolution in Russland* (Leipzig, 1922).

[69] Aronson, *K istorii,* pp. 115–116.

same as that which appeared in *Sotsialisticheskii vestnik.* Martov wrote about the "Blanquist-Jacobin tendency in socialism, recently revived in Bolshevik neocommunism" and predicted after the Kronstadt uprising that there was not only "tension among the leaders of the Communist party" but the beginning of a "process of disintegration from within for Bolshevism." The NEP was "the program of a Bonapartist military-bureaucratic dictatorship" which revealed the "economic impossibility of the further existence of the dictatorship of the Communist party." Abramovich too predicted a "fearful economic crisis" in Russia, warning that "the existing governmental system as organizer of Russia's planned economy has completely broken down." What was so remarkable was not that Menshevik predictions of imminent Bolshevik collapse proved incorrect, but that Marxist optimism enabled them to reiterate them so relentlessly.[70]

If the NEP did not lead to a Bolshevik collapse, was it not at least a regression to capitalism? Dan developed the theme that Bolshevism was now only a "utopian dictatorship" which was destroying Russia's "productive powers" by its "deeply reactionary" economic policies, not to mention its "complete lack of elementary political freedom." Stein, too, characterized the NEP as the "reconstruction of capitalism" and feared that improving trade relations with the outside world would make Russia a "colony of West European capital." "The masses in Russia," Abramovich told a big USPD rally in Berlin in January 1922, "must be given back their freedom to organize, or it will be impossible to save the Russian Revolution, and Russia will become the prey of the Entente." [71]

With the merger of the SPD and the USPD in the autumn of 1922, *Freiheit* was closed down and the Mensheviks found themselves without "their" organ. But they had now established themselves in Berlin as articulate and authoritative socialist spokesmen against the Soviet government, and would subsequently continue in their role as anti-Bolshevik experts for the German socialist press.

---

[70] *Freiheit,* 1921: February 12, p. 2; April 1, pp. 1–2; April 2, pp. 1–2; July 17, pp. 1–2; March 8, pp. 1–2.

[71] *Freiheit,* 1922: January 16, p. 2; February 19, p. 9; February 26, pp. 1–2; March 12, pp. 1–2; March 13, p. 1.

Like other anti-Bolshevik émigrés the Mensheviks never influenced German policy toward Soviet Russia, as the collapse of the idea of "socialist intervention" and of reconciliation through the Vienna Union indicated. Like them, too, they found life in exile tolerable only in the belief that the Soviet government would soon collapse before the forces of mass discontent. Unlike them, they found it possible to assimilate with relative ease into life in a new land.

Social Revolutionaries and Anarchists

The émigré representatives of the Social Revolutionary Party, (PSR) Russia's major peasant party, also suffered factional decay in the wake of Rapallo. Already divided between prewar "minimalists," who advocated participation in the political process through democratic channels, and "maximalists," who favored illegal tactics of terror and assassination, they were fragmented further in 1917 into the majority faction willing to work with the Provisional government, led by Alexander Kerensky and Viktor Chernov, and a dissident left wing which supported the Bolsheviks. The participation of SR's in the All-Russian Provisional Government established at Ufa in 1918 with the blessing of Admiral Kolchak provided a further source of division.

In emigration most SR's preferred the Allied capitals of London, Paris, or Prague, although a tiny group existed in Berlin beginning in the spring of 1919 around the first émigré newspaper, *Golos Rossii*. The PSR did not actually buy the paper until 1922, but its leading contributors were all party members. Like other factions, the Berlin SR's claimed to speak for "the Russian people" against the machinations of minorities such as émigré "imperialists," "liberals," and "militarists." [72] But they were never an important group in Berlin until the party purchased the newspaper with Czech support in early 1922.

SR interest in Berlin as a party center began in the summer of 1921, when they started to distribute party literature in the Russian POW camps with the cooperation of Zemgor and to seek out means

---

[72] For example, *Golos Rossii*, February 14, 1920, p. 1, and February 22, 1920, pp. 1–2. In 1920–1922 the newspaper was variously under the editorship of G. Shumakher, M. Ter-Pogossian, and the Kadet leader Paul Miliukov.

of "socialist intervention" against the Bolsheviks. In 1922 that city became an important SR listening post in connection with the trial of forty-seven party members in Moscow on charges of treason. They urged the conference of European socialists held in Berlin that April to form a "united front" against Soviet Russia and sought assistance from German socialists and Martov's Menshevik circle. Despite the talk of "socialist moral intervention" there was little to do but await the outcome of the trial and criticize it in the pages of *Golos Rossii,* Kerensky's journal *Dni,* and the literary organ *Sovremennye zapiski,* temporarily moved from Paris to Berlin in 1922–1923.[73]

Like the Kadets, the SR's suffered the pangs of internal party fissures at this time. For them the question was whether the PSR should remain a "peasant party" or whether it should join in a broad "democratic" front in emigration. It was a choice common to many of the old parties in emigration: to retain old ideological consistency or to seek new tactical successes in the changed conditions of émigré life. The leftists among émigré SR's (not the Left SR's) around V. V. Sukhomlin felt that the PSR should retain its old platform in preparation for some eventual coming to power in Russia. The rightists in Paris sought a broader émigré coalition and agreed with Miliukov that the emigration was not all "Black" and monarchist but also contained "democratic" elements.[74] By 1922 the rightists had been expelled from the Foreign Delegation of the PSR.

In Berlin in 1922–1923 the transformation of the PSR from a party in exile to a party of exiles was equally apparent. In the spring of 1922 Viktor Chernov attempted to launch a party "peasant" journal *Nuzhdy derevni* (Village Needs)[75] which argued that the PSR as

[73] On the trial see *Dvenadtsat' smertnikov: Sud nad sotsialistami-revoliutsionerami v Moskve* (Berlin, 1922). On SR agitation among Russian POW's in Germany see Holmsen's report to Paris of August 2, 1921 (MiA, folder 17).

[74] *Poslednie novosti,* September 24, 1922, p. 2.

[75] *Nuzhdy derevni* was described as a "monthly scientific economic and public affairs journal" and lasted from April through September 1922. Edited by Grigory Shreider and featuring frequent articles by Viktor Chernov and Sergei Maslov, it was a last attempt to revive the "thick journals" of the 1890's in the tradition of *Otechestvennye zapiski* and *Syn otechestva.* Its main message was that the peasant village must be revived as a basic unit in society if it were to survive the pressures of industrialization and urbanization.

a peasant party could and should now direct its attention away from industrial Europe to the agrarian East. Both capitalism and Bolshevism were basically rooted in the urban West and had an "industriomorphic" outlook which would prevent them from having a strong appeal in the "liberation movements of the colonial countries." The postwar era was "a new era in the history of humanity" marked by the decline of Europe and the rise of the colonial non-European world. "The anti-imperialism of the colonial countries and peoples is not proletarian but agrarian anti-imperialism," wrote Chernov, and since Bolshevism was directed against the peasantry inside Russia, "how can it provide an ideology for the liberation movement in the agrarian countries?" [76]

In emigration few SR's were willing to follow Chernov's logic and to rethink old assumptions. Rather than revitalize party orthodoxy, many chose to turn away from politics to literary and journalistic efforts or simply to appeal to the amorphous "democratic" layers of the emigration. By the autumn of 1922 *Nuzhdy derevni* had closed down and several months later few SR's would defend the idea of a peasant party.[77] The collapse of *Nuzhdy derevni* coincided with the closing of the newspaper *Golos Rossii* and the unfortunate ending of the Moscow trials. SR revitalization, it seemed, could only be purchased at the cost of ideological consistency.

In the autumn of 1922 it was decided to establish a new SR-sponsored daily newspaper in Berlin under Alexander Kerensky. Like *Golos Rossii* before it, the new daily—entitled *Dni* (Days) and subtitled "a Russian daily for politics, economics, and literature" —was financed from Prague and published in the *Vorwärts* building. But unlike its predecessor, *Dni* made no claim to be an SR organ:

The journal *Dni* was founded by a group of persons not connected by publishing obligations with any political party or organization existing either in Russia or abroad, united only by the independence of demo-

[76] Viktor Chernov, "Gorod i derevnia (mirovoe znachenie agrarnogo voprosa)," *Nuzhdy derevni*, 1922, No. 1, pp. 24–26.

[77] The debate as to whether the SR's should remain a peasant-centered party or move toward a broader "democratic" position took place between Maslov and A. V. Peshekhonov in the pages of *Dni* in the winter of 1922–1923.

235

cratic thinking, an awareness of the need to fight for the rebirth of a free Russia, and a belief in her sacred future.[78]

The driving force behind *Dni* was in fact the personality of Kerensky, who was forced to live a conspiratorial existence in Berlin in these months out of fear of physical attacks by right-wing Russians or Germans similar to those on Rathenau and Nabokov. It was a sad existence for the former Provisional government orator and leader. Dressed in shabby suits and depending on occasional subsidies from Prague, Kerensky on his walks to and from the *Dni* offices never went alone, often changed the times of his arrivals and departures, and even established passwords for those desiring to pass through the several doors leading to his inner office.[79]

As a democratic newspaper, *Dni* would not countenance extremism on the right or the left, "neither a return to monarchy nor, even less, cooperation with the tyranny of Russia's present rulers." Throughout the years 1922 and 1923 in Berlin, *Dni* was particularly attentive to these anti-democratic circles and even to possible links between them, such as the cooperation between *Nakanune* editors and German army officers in the pages of the Berlin military journal *Voina i mir* (War and Peace). It attacked Bolshevism as "the enemy of Russia" and émigré monarchism as a "Black Dream" with equal fervor. During the summer of 1923, when there were signs of temporary collaboration between German Communists and Nazis, *Dni* warned that German right-wing circles should never try to "use" the Bolsheviks, as Ludendorff had done in 1917. The Beer Hall Putsch seemed to *Dni* part of this right-left conspiracy: "Ludendorff and Hitler—the old protector of Zinoviev and Lenin and the new friend of K. Radek and Bukharin—overthrew the insufficiently 'revolutionary' von Kahr and proclaimed the dictatorship of the 'national-socialists' (surely 'national-bolsheviks')." It was a premature and erroneous judgment. But at the time the fear of a combined right-left alliance was extreme.[80]

[78] *Dni,* October 29, 1922, p. 1. *Dni* ran as a daily newspaper from October 29, 1922, to June 30, 1928, when it became a weekly, moving from Berlin to Paris in 1924. The Hoover Library has a virtually complete file.

[79] A. F. Damanskaia, "6 otryvkov iz vospominanii Avgusty Filippovny Damanskoi" (typescript in the Columbia University Russian Archive, folder 7 ["Berlin 1920–1923 gg."]), pp. 12–13.

[80] *Dni,* October 29, 1922, p. 1; January 6, 1923, pp. 2–3; March 25, 1923,

In the language of the times, *Dni* identified with the West against the East, with the European liberal-democratic tradition against the political extremism described as something barbaric and Eastern. For E. D. Kuskova, communists and right-wing circles alike shared a political outlook resembling oriental despotism: "Two brother allies. . . . And both of them—are they not from Asia? Would anyone listen to such slave language in a democratic state, this conferring on a few people of the right to say good-bye, to take a bath, to punish those who are recalcitrant?" [81] Culturally, *Dni* liked neither the optimism of those who hoped for new winds from the East nor those who spoke of the "decline" of the West. Europe was still very much alive. True, the war had produced a shift in global political power away from Europe to the former colonial areas, "but the decline of Europe is not the 'collapse of civilization,' any more than its economic depression is a 'crisis of capitalism.' It is only a crisis inside capitalism, the beginning of growth." [82]

Like the Kadets, *Dni* found it easier to criticize the two extremes of monarchism and Bolshevism in emigration than to produce a meaningful alternative. There was constant talk of a "third front" of émigré democrats and the "unity of a liberal-democratic republican movement" which eventually would establish a "republic" in Russia ("the only historically possible form of popular government in Russia").[83] But in practice *Dni* was unable to bring together any of the many liberal and socialist factions in the emigration. Its call for *Rul'* and *Poslednie novosti* to reconcile their differences and join in a single democratic movement went unheard. To *Rul'*, *Dni* remained a "moderate socialist" daily, despite its claim to be "republican-democratic." The vague slogans like "the Russia of Labor and Freedom" were hardly sufficient to overcome old differences or to command the respect of many émigré intellectuals or politicians.

Nor did *Dni* have any strong ties with German circles. Most SR's came to Berlin simply because life was cheaper and publishing op-

---

p. 1; June 6, 1923, p. 1; July 17, 1923, p. 1; November 10, 1923, p. 1. *Voina i mir* was a Soviet military-technical journal published in Berlin from 1922 to 1924 under the editorship of Paul Kosmel.

[81] *Dni*, December 22, 1923, p. 1.   [82] *Dni*, October 5, 1923, p. 1.
[83] *Dni*, December 6, 1922, p. 1.

portunities greater. German socialists did extend technical aid to the Berlin SR's but there was no collaboration such as that which occurred between the Mensheviks and the Independent Socialists. Friedrich Stampfer, Heinrich Ströbel, and Eduard Bernstein did contribute an occasional article to *Dni* on German life, but the relationship between Bernstein and such Russians as Kerensky, S. N. Prokopovich, and E. D. Kuskova was more personal than political. Kerensky was as isolated from the Germans as he was from Menshevik and Kadet circles, and his few meetings with Bernstein were devoted largely to the latter's investigation of German support for the Bolsheviks in 1917.[84]

In brief, the role of Kerensky and the SR's in Berlin in 1922–1923 was transitory and insignificant. Unlike the Kadets, they played no particular role in the life of the colony, although *Dni* became for a time a haven for writers. Nor did they have any success in maintaining party unity; the time and the place were inadequate for either a specifically peasant or a vaguely democratic party. Finally, the SR's, like the Kadets, lacked the strong ties to political circles in Germany which might have facilitated their assimilation as indivduals. Both found no more real support in Germany than within the emigration.

The Mensheviks and the SR's were joined on the left by a tiny faction of Russian anarchists. In the winter of 1922–1923 anarcho-syndicalists from several countries met in Berlin and established a new International Workingmen's Association as their own successor to the First International, headed by Rudolf Rocker of the London Anarchist Federation. One Russian faction, the Group of Russian Anarchist-Communists Abroad, headed by Peter Arshinov, established the journal *Anarkhicheskii vestnik* (The Anarchist Messenger) there from 1922 to 1925 before moving on to Paris. Like the Mensheviks, they saw the Bolsheviks as purveyors of false doctrines which sooner or later would be exposed before the sentiments of

---

[84] Prokopovich and Kuskova, husband-and-wife economists with a long-standing enthusiasm for Bernstein's reformism, arrived in Berlin in the autumn of 1922 but soon moved on to Prague, where Prokopovich had an opportunity to set up his "economic cabinet." In 1923 he edited *Ekonomicheskii vestnik*, a monthly journal of economic analysis in Berlin devoted to Soviet Russia.

the masses inside Russia, as social reactionaries who had arrested the process of revolution, and as the Loyolas, Machiavellis, and Robespierres of 1917. The NEP was a chimera; rises in industrial productivity were false indicators of prosperity. To oust the Bolsheviks, the anarchists must unite and acquire the very organizational capabilities that had given Lenin and his party their success.

Yet the anarchists could not even unite successfully with the left SR's and the faction of Grigory Maksimov and Alexander Shapiro in Berlin, which published the journal *Rabochii put'* (Labor's Path). In the end the formation in 1923 of a United Committee to Defend Arrested Revolutionaries in Russia and the existence of a common anarchist tradition based upon the theories of Michael Bakunin and the Ukrainian anarchist Nestor Makhno proved insufficient to hold the anarchists together. For them, as for the other political groupings of the Russian diaspora, emigration only served to widen already existing factional differences. Rocker's Association stayed on in Berlin until the 1930's, when it was moved to Amsterdam and then to Madrid, and the Left SR's continued to publish occasional issues of their journal *Znamia bor'by* (The Banner of Struggle) there until 1929. But most of the anarchists moved out of Germany in the late 1920's, in search of a satisfactory revolution that had proven as elusive in Germany as in Russia.[85]

If the anarchist dream of a unified "workers' front" directed against the Bolsheviks proved futile, the anarchists themselves found friends in Germany. Like the Mensheviks, they viewed Germany as a place to maintain contacts with the underground inside Soviet Russia and the homeland of like-minded Germans, in this case a "strong and healthy anarchist-syndicalist movement." The Free Workers' Union of Germany (Syndicalists), claiming a membership of 120,000 in 1919, was particularly helpful to the Russians. The Union not only extended aid to the Russian anarchists and their families who arrived in early 1922 but also provided them with a publishing outlet in the pages of *Der Syndikalist*. Exiles

[85] On the Russian anarchist movement before and during the Russian Revolution see Paul Avrich, *The Russian Anarchists* (Princeton, 1967), especially the brief section on the emigration, pp. 238–243; *Anarkhicheskii vestnik*, Nos. 1–4 (1923), *Rabochii put'*, No. 1 (1923), and *Znamia bor'by*, Berlin, 1924–30.

found Rocker and his circle particularly receptive to their anti-Bolshevik views, and urged their German anarchist friends to "marshall all our forces in a struggle against the Knouto-communist regime which wants to revert to the capitalist order." [86] Like the Mensheviks, they offered their German comrades an authoritative anti-Bolshevik voice. Like them, too, they were well received because their anger provided a welcome confirmation of an anti-Soviet mood.[87]

In the early 1920's the liberal and socialist parties in exile in Berlin suffered a political fate common to their countrymen in other European capitals. Speaking neither for the restoration of the Imperial regime nor for open accommodation with the Bolsheviks, they failed to unite on a democratic or democratic-socialist platform which might have offered a third alternative. In criticizing the "Eastern" despotism of the Bolshevik rulers, they were outdone by the monarchists; in attacking the "colonialism" of the Versailles system, they played into the hands of the pro-Soviet intellectuals. Generally reasonable men, they became either increasingly divided over old issues and new tactics or increasingly bitter in their anti-Bolshevism.

The Kadets, the SR's, and the Mensheviks all considered themselves linked to "the West" and its democratic-liberal or socialist traditions. But only the Mensheviks assimilated as a group into a Western political movement—German socialism—which shared with them and reinforced in them their Marxist optimism and anti-Bolshevik criticism. Only they were able to enjoy such a role in Berlin long after the rest of the old parties had either collapsed or moved on.

Internecine disputes and factionalism are a familiar feature on

[86] *Vmesto programmy* (Berlin, 1922), p. 4.

[87] On the Russian anarchists in Berlin see especially Rudolf Rocker's unpublished memoirs "Revolution und Rueckfall in die Barbarei" (International Institute of Social History, Amsterdam), pp. 243–276. Rocker had already expressed his anti-Bolshevik views in *Der Bankrott des russischen Staatskommunismus* (Berlin, 1921). Two revealing Russian anarchist pamphlets are "Goneniia na Anarkhizm v Sovetskoi Rossii" (Berlin, 1922) and G. P. Maksimov, "Za chto i kak Bol'sheviki izgnali anarkhistov iz Rossii?" (Berlin, 1922).

the landscape of political emigrations. With regard to the Russians in Berlin, neither left nor right was immune from them in 1922–1923. The fact that Germany recognized Soviet Russia in 1922 was one source of their frustrations; the worsening political and economic situation inside Germany was another. Equally important was the arrival in Germany of a "second wave" of émigré intellectuals in 1922 who, as recent victims of Lenin's Russia, could speak with more authority of events inside their homeland. The fact that some were not without enthusiasm for the Soviet experiment deepened further the cracks in émigré unity already opened by the passage of time. Those who had fled to the West now mingled with those who had remained in the East.

⟶⟨ VI ⟩⟵

The Way Out to the East

The story of the political life of the Russian emigration to Germany is largely one of despair and ultimate defeat; the story of its cultural life is one of intellectual ferment and literary productivity.[1] If Paris became the political capital of Russia-in-exile in the early 1920's, Berlin became, beginning in the winter of 1921–1922, its cultural center. The reasons for the sudden and remarkable flowering of Russian intellectual, literary, and artistic activity in Berlin in these years were coincidental and temporary: a relatively cheap standard of living, a flourishing publishing activity which spawned innumerable books and periodicals, and the existence of a large Russian colony. But the forms which Russian cultural life in Berlin took on in these years were marked by a traditional obsession with the problem of Russia's identity—her relationship to West and East —common to Russians in Germany before the war. The fact that World War I and the Russian Revolution appeared to many to have broken down the old European-centered world of 1914 served, moreover, to accentuate a problem that had tormented Russian in-

---

[1] There is no single work of substance on the intellectual life of the Berlin colony in the 1920's, and materials are widely scattered. The best secondary works are by Gleb Struve: *Russkaia literatura v izgnanii* (New York, 1956) and his "The Transition from Russian to Soviet Literature," in M. Hayward and L. Labedz, eds., *Literature and Revolution in Soviet Russia, 1917–1962* (London, 1963), pp. 1–27. In addition see the memoirs of Ilia Ehrenburg, *Men, Years, Life,* Vol. III: *Truce: 1921–1923* (London, 1963) and Nina Berberova, *The Italics are Mine* (New York, 1969).

tellectuals since the late eighteenth century: Russia's relationship to Europe. The "cultural despair" of the prewar and postwar era in Germany, the feeling that the entire edifice of Western civilization was weak and crumbling, was well received by many émigrés who had long harbored the earlier Slavophile sentiments about the "rottenness of Europe." So, too, many émigrés were willing to engage in discussions about Russia only at a high plane of abstraction. But these two tendencies—the acceptance of the "decline" of Europe and the rise of "the East," including Russia, and the maintenance of a vague, general, and idealistic level of debate—represented potential weakness insofar as it encouraged, both in Germany and within the emigration, the acceptance of Soviet Russia as a new culture, a way out of the old Europe. These themes made the Russian intellectual colony in Berlin a cultural center of great vitality, but they also contributed to its political collapse.

The émigré intelligentsia, of course, brought its own cultural baggage with it. This included not only the mixture of admiration and disdain for Europe and European thought and the search for a Russian national identity, but the passion for social justice which burst forth in the nineteenth century. The Russian intelligentsia had always lived "on the margin of the West," to use Wladimir Weidle's term, and even its national consciousness was formulated with the help of European thought and shaped by the experience of exile, travel, or study in the West. It had also indicated a certain propensity for selecting and taking to extremes currents or ideas within European culture and giving them an almost religious dimension. Until the 1880's Russian thought had thus been characterized by extensive "borrowings" from the West, extreme statements about the national or social superiority or inferiority of Russia, and a general frustration born of the social suspension of the intelligentsia midway between the autocracy and the peasant, between state and society. It had also moved away from the sentimental and romantic philosophy of the 1820's and 1830's toward more action-oriented movements such as Populism and Pan-Slavism. The ultimate meaning of ideas lay in the moral deeds that followed, deeds judged by their service to some social entity—state or people—outside the intelligentsia itself.

After the murder of Alexander II in 1881 there was a general fragmentation of the intelligentsia into a spectrum of movements too complex to be lumped together as fathers, sons, or grandsons. Driven underground for a time, the movement for social change soon re-emerged with the growth of radical, liberal, and conservative political parties, the moral preachings of Tolstoi, the bombs and robberies of the revolutionary lower depths, and the general distrust of the government after 1900. But there was also a strong counter-movement which set itself against the radical traditions of the nineteenth-century intelligentsia and declared itself for culture and religion independent of any yardstick of social or political utility. Religious thinkers such as Nikolai Berdiaev and Sergei Bulgakov moved "from Marxism to idealism," to Christian communalism, and to an attempt to create a genuine philosophy of religion. Mikhail Artsybashev's novel *Sanin* (1907) symbolized the turn toward eroticism, Fedor Sologub dabbled in black magic, Igor Stravinsky and the *Ballets Russes* of Sergei Diaghilev alternatively scandalized and thrilled the audiences of European capitals, the journal *World of Art* (1899–1904) filled its pages with the innovations of European and Russian art. Stanislavsky brought to the Moscow Art Theater not only the psychological immersion of the actor in his role but the lavish fusion of sets, music, and sound effects into an integrated whole both realistic and symbolic. It was a time of intellectual experimentation, and art was not only its own justification, but a religion.

The tone of intellectual life after 1900 was set by the symbolist poets, most notably Viacheslav Ivanov, Andrei Belyi, and Alexander Blok. In their poetry they sought to express by the use of symbols the presence of a mysterious world of the spirit behind, within, and beneath the apparent material reality of the visible world. Returning to the works of Neo-Platonists, medieval mystics, German romantics, and French symbolists they developed their own ill-defined millenarianism, a feeling that the world was about to come to an end but that this end would herald a new world, a Second Coming, a rebirth. And like many European intellectuals of their generation they began to feel a mixture of hope and fear concerning vague forces moving on Europe from the East, forces which could both destroy and revivify a world on the wane.

The most dramatic statement of the dangers coming from the "East" was made by the religious philosopher Vladimir Soloviev (1853–1900). In his remarkable essay *Three Conversations on War, Progress, and the End of World History* (1899–1900), Soloviev described a vast Asiatic invasion of Europe under the banner of "Pan-Mongolism" which was only driven back after some years under the leadership of a young superman—an ascetic, spiritualist, and vegetarian leader claiming to be Christ. In the end he turns out to be not Christ but Antichrist. Only after he has conquered the world is he overthrown and the thousand-year rule of Christ finally established. Soloviev's vision of an impending clash between Europe and Asia had an enormous effect on the next generation in Russia. But very few of them sought a way out through a resolution of East and West in the ecumenical sense which Soloviev intended.

The Russian intellectual currents which preceded the 1917 revolution—symbolism, decadence, and futurism, among others—continued to draw intellectual sustenance from European culture at the very time they were critical of "the West" in general. The constant intellectual traffic between Paris and Munich, on the one hand, and Petersburg and Moscow, on the other, played a crucial role in the fertilization of art forms which European audiences took to be peculiarly Russian. In this way emigration to Germany after 1917 was more of a return to familiar ground for many Russian intellectuals than a flight to a new land. At the same time, the ambivalent feelings toward Europe persisted. Just as Europe could mean the boredom and dehumanization of industrial life or the joys of German idealism, so the East could offer the mystique of Indian philosophy or the fear of hostile "Mongol" forces. In the minds of many intellectuals the scales could tip toward either East or West. Further evidence was required to indicate that Europe had played out its historical role and that the East, the non-European world, could provide a "way out" of Europe's crisis. World War I, the Russian Revolution, and exile provided such evidence.

The Berdiaev Circle

Until 1922, when the Treaty of Rapallo indicated the warming of Soviet-German relations and a new wave of intellectuals was ex-

pelled from Soviet Russia, there was little sympathy in anti-
Bolshevik Berlin for "the East" in general or Soviet Russia in particular. An exception was the small circle of intellectuals gathered
around Vladimir Stankevich and his journal *Zhizn'* (Life). The
message of *Zhizn'* was that the Russian intelligentsia in emigration
must turn away from the White movement seeking to intervene in
Russia's affairs and rejoin the Russian people in the common enterprise of reconstructing the country. "It would be a tragedy," wrote
Stankevich, "if the Russian intelligentsia set off for foreign countries
to seek support against its own people." Both West and East now
needed peace in order to rebuild their shattered economic life and
Europe should throw off its colonial legacy and use its material advantages to help revive the "spiritual" forces of Russia and the East:

> Russia is now an enormous, inexhaustible force, despite its material
> devastation. By approaching Russia peacefully, Europe will help put
> this spiritual force to work, re-establishing what has been destroyed,
> creating a new life. But it would be most unfortunate if Russia's spiritual
> force and the remains of Europe's material resources were spent on an
> armed conflict between themselves.

Russian intellectuals ("close to both West and East") had an opportunity and a responsibility to "turn back to the people" and
facilitate such a peaceful reconciliation between the imperialist
West and the colonial East.[2]

But the sympathies of *Zhizn'* lay much more with the East than
with the West. The colonial heritage must be undone, for Europe
can no longer expect to master the world. "Would it not be more
correct to expect that, on the contrary, the center of political life
will now pass from its ruins to other parts of the globe?" Throughout the pages of *Zhizn'* ran the theme of a rising East, the new influence which countries such as Japan, China, and India would soon
enjoy on the world scene. The wartime triumph of the Allied
powers was only temporary. Russia and Germany, the defeated
powers, would join the new forces in the East in resisting the
hegemony of the West, not militarily or economically but spiritually, with new ideas. "Culturally," wrote Stankevich, "Germany,

[2] *Zhizn'*, No. 1 (April 1, 1920), pp. 8–9.

Russia, and Hungary will not retreat before the victors, as is obvious from the spiritual influence which the ferment in Russian political life is now exerting over the whole world." [3]

In its July 1, 1920, issue *Zhizn'* printed a public statement critical of both Russian Bolshevism and the White movement.[4] Arguing that "the struggle against Bolshevism and for the unity of the country is only possible by peaceful means," the statement went on to demand an end to armed intervention, lifting of the blockade against Russia, the dispatch of food, clothing, and medicine to the Russian people, and the revival of trade between Russia and the West. The statement was signed by most members of Mir i Trud, including Stankevich, Goul, Ofrosimov, G. N. Breitman, editor of the popular weekly *Vremia,* and A. S. Yashchenko, the former professor of law at Perm University and later editor of the literary journal *Novaia russkaia kniga.* It was a futile gesture. The mood of the colony was still one of belligerence toward the Soviet regime and attention was now concentrated on Wrangel in South Russia. By the autumn of 1920 Mir i Trud, which had proved a useful outlet for many writers in Berlin, had dissolved.

Among the several hundred scholars and intellectuals expelled by the Soviet government in 1922 was a small circle of men who had chosen to turn their backs on the radical traditions of the Russian intelligentsia. Nikolai Berdiaev, Sergei Bulgakov, S. L. Frank, and Alexander Izgoev were four of the six surviving contributors to the remarkable prewar collection of essays *Vekhy* (Landmarks) which had urged Russian intellectuals to turn away from revolutionary socialism to individualism, the rule of law, and religion—from Marxism to idealism.[5] They were joined by a number of other intellectuals who had shown an interest in religious and philosophical themes in their writings and who hoped for a "way out" of the crisis of modern man not through social revolution and violence but by a turning inward to man and outward to God; among them were

[3] *Zhizn'*, No. 3 (May 1, 1920), pp. 28–29.   [4] No. 7, pp. 1–3.
[5] The other two surviving contributors to *Vekhy* were Peter Struve, then living in Paris, and Mikhail Gershenzon, who lived in Germany from 1922 to 1924 but returned to Soviet Russia.

The Way Out to the East

L. P. Karsavin, N. O. Lossky, A. A. Kizevetter, and Fedor Stepun. Berdiaev and his friends in their collection of essays *Iz glubiny* (De Profundis, 1918) and numerous other writings since the Bolshevik revolution had articulated two main themes: first, that world history in the beginning of the twentieth century had reached a crisis, a dilemma from which man could free himself only by a return to religion and the sense of a power greater than himself acting in history; second, that the impetus for such a renewal would come not from the decrepit West but from the East, the world beyond Europe.[6] Spengler's *Decline of the West*, not surprisingly, had been a focal point of Moscow intellectual life in these years.[7] But Spengler had neither accepted the "religious meaning of culture" nor recognized the role that a technically backward but spiritually superior nation like Russia might play in reviving Europe. Berdiaev wrote:

> For a long time we [Russians] have recognized the distinction between culture and civilization. . . . Beneath their hostility to the West many Russian writers and thinkers revealed not a hostility to Western culture but to Western civilization. . . . Russian easternism (*vostochnichestvo*), Russian Slavophilism was but the open struggle of the spirit of religious culture against the spirit of irreligious civilization.[8]

Was it not possible, asked Berdiaev, that the Russian Revolution symbolized the beginning of a new epoch? Was it not, like the birth of Christ, "the incessant eruption of eternity into time" with the message that "the Eastern peoples will once again join the torrent of history and that they will once again play a role of world importance"? "In our epoch," he noted, "Western civilization has turned East and the cultured people of this civilization look for light from the East." Was not Russia the logical source of that light, particularly since "the Russian consciousness is more acutely and

---

[6] The religious meaning of the Russian Revolution was the theme of "*Iz glubiny*": *Sbornik statei russkoi revoliutsii* (Moscow-Petrograd, 1918). Five of the *Vekhy* contributors (Berdiaev, Struve, Frank, Bulgakov, and Izgoev) were also involved in "*Iz glubiny*".

[7] Fedor Stepun, *Byvshee i nebyvsheesia* (New York, 1956), II, 268–281.

[8] Nikolai Berdiaev, "Predsmertnye mysli Fausta," *Shpengler i zakat evropy: Sbornik statei* (Moscow, 1921), pp. 65–66.

deeply aware of the cultural crisis and tragedy of historical destiny than that of the more fortunate people of the West"? [9]

When Berdiaev and the other refugee intellectuals arrived in Berlin in November 1922, they were already well-known figures both within the colony and in Germany. Otto Hoetzsch organized a gala evening reception for the group at which Frank, Stepun, and I. A. Ilin grew effusive about the need to revive once again those "spiritual connections" between Russian and German intellectual life which had been "very close before the World War." [10] Some of the older émigrés were suspicious of the new arrivals; at best they were men who had chosen life under the Bolsheviks for four years, at worst Soviet agents. But in general the German government was helpful and the Russian colony receptive.

Through F. T. Pianov the new group of émigrés soon made contact with the YMCA in Berlin. Paul Anderson and others had been for some time aware of the "religious revival" going on in Russia under the aegis of Berdiaev's Academy of Spiritual Culture. Anderson soon invited Berdiaev, Frank, and some others to his apartment and asked them what the YMCA might do to help them continue this work abroad. Berdiaev knew nothing of the YMCA until this time, but quickly proposed that that organization might be able to help him rebuild his Academy in Berlin. [11]

In fact there already existed in Berlin a Russian Philosophical Society, formed only two months before Berdiaev's arrival by V. V. Zenkovsky, another philosopher. Zenkovsky had first come to Berlin from Belgrade in the summer of 1921, where he met Pianov, learned of the work of the YMCA, and told him in turn of his own work with émigré young people in the Balkans. [12] In 1922 Zenkovsky returned to Germany to attend an émigré Christian Youth Conference organized by Pianov. Here he met Paul Anderson for the first time. The YMCA at this point showed no particular interest in sup-

[9] Nikolai Berdiaev, *The Meaning of History* (New York, 1936), p. 124; "Predsmertnye mysli Fausta," p. 68; *The Meaning of History*, pp. 223–224.

[10] *Dni,* November 17, 1922, p. 6.

[11] Donald Lowrie, *Rebellious Prophet: A Life of Nicolai Berdyaev* (New York, 1960), pp. 164–165.

[12] V. V. Zenkovsky, "Moe uchastie v russkom studencheskom khristianskom dvizhenii," p. 5 (ZC).

porting Russian religious activity abroad outside of the student movement and Zenkovsky was forced to turn to an émigré Russian banker to finance a philosophical society in Berlin. With the arrival of Berdiaev, however, Zenkovsky's circle soon broke up, and Zenkovsky himself, who had no particular ties with the new émigrés, left Berlin for Belgrade and then Prague to devote himself to the Russian Student Christian Movement, also under YMCA auspices.[13]

Within a short time Berdiaev had his Religious-Philosophical Academy in Berlin. Anderson and Pianov found rooms in a former French private school on the Reichstagsufer for the Academy's offices and classrooms, and on November 26, 1922, there was a formal opening ceremony attended by hundreds of interested émigrés, YMCA staff members, and Germans. Berdiaev himself held forth at length on the catastrophic nature of the epoch, the common guilt of the Russian intelligentsia for the sins of the revolution, and the need now to unite around the banner of Christianity for a renewal of life on a spiritual level. "Only a religious resurrection," read the program of the new Academy, "can save Russia and revivify Europe and the whole world." [14]

On December 1, 1922, the Religious-Philosophical Academy opened its full schedule of lectures to the public. Until 1924 it remained one of the most interesting intellectual centers of the Berlin colony and continually atracted crowds to its series of courses, lectures, and evening meetings. Some of the best minds of Russia contributed: Berdiaev on religious philosophy, Stepun on romanticism, Aikhenvald on Russian intellectual history, N. S. Arseniev on early Christianity, I. A. Ilin on the philosophy of art, L. P. Karsavin on the Middle Ages, and Frank on Greek philosophy. Many of the

[13] The Russian Student Christian Movement originated in the winter of 1922–1923 in Prague and became a permanent organization financed by the YMCA and directed by Zenkovsky a few months later. Its function was to promote religious, educational, and recreational activities among émigré young people. See Nikolai Klepinin, "Survey of North American YMCA Service to Russians in Europe" (YMCA), pp. 123–208 for a summary of the Movement's work in the 1920's and 1930's. See also ZC, folders 4 and 5, entitled respectively "Moia rabota na pedagogicheskom poprishche" and "Moi vstrechi s vydaiushchimisia liud'mi."

[14] *Sofiia: Problemy dukhovnoi kul'tury i religioznoi filosofii* (Berlin, 1923), p. 136.

Academy's lectures appeared as articles in Berdiaev's short-lived journal *Sofiia,* of which only one volume appeared in 1923.[15]

The common theme of *Sofiia* and the Academy was that to save himself man must turn away from his worldly concern with political and economic life and recognize the primacy of spiritual and cultural forces. The contemporary crisis produced by war and revolution made this even more urgent:

We must turn inward, go deeper, find a more spiritual and wiser relationship to life, free from the spirits of the evil and the commonplace, from the bloody nightmare. We are living in an epoch of deep world crisis. . . . A deep spiritual reaction is needed against this external, political relationship toward life which has predominated for so long.

In this respect Russia's fate was intimately tied up with that of Europe:

The world is entering an epoch when a greater unity of all positive spiritual forces will be needed. Russia's problem, like that of the spirit, cannot be completely separated from the problem of Western Europe and its peoples. The Christian spirit around the world must be creatively resurrected and renewed, or the world will be threatened by collapse and spiritual death, whose symptoms are already too obvious.

But the way out for the West was not only through a return to religion but through acceptance of the new spiritual forces of the East. "The old world, central Europe," wrote Berdiaev, "is being conquered by the new world, the Far West, America, and the Far East, Japan and China, to us mysterious and even fantastic." But was not Russia also of the East, the potential leader of a new Christian revival which would free Europe from its present crisis? Berdiaev thought so.

The theme of political despair also ran through the pages of *Sofiia:* a complete rejection of the divisions of class and nation as well as the give and take of democratic politics. Democracy was no solution to man's problems but merely "a crossroad, a relativistic system, a system of open doors branching off in unknown directions from the corridor." Nor were the authors agreed among themselves

[15] Lowrie, *Prophet,* pp. 165–166; *Sofiia,* pp. 136–138; Klepinin, "Survey," pp. 80–88.

politically. On the one hand, Karsavin wrote of the "deep truth of monarchist trends within the church itself"; on the other hand, N. O. Lossky urged a "synthesis of the valuable aspects of the individualistic economy of contemporary capitalism with the valuable aspects of the socialists' ideal." But in general the way out was spiritual, not political, internal, not external. Man must change within himself. A political revolution, after all, was but an outward reflection of a deeper internal spiritual sickness.[16]

Berdiaev's Religious-Philosophical Academy was in Berlin for too short a time to have a significant impact on German intellectual life, although Berdiaev's writings were widely read. Berdiaev himself managed to meet Oswald Spengler and the phenomenologist Max Scheler—two of the German thinkers who proved so attractive to Russians in the postwar era—but found them much less exciting in person than their ideas had been at a distance. Scheler was persuaded to give a lecture at the Academy, attended by the young theologian Paul Tillich, but the Academy established no strong ties to German intellectual circles. By the time Berdiaev left Berlin in 1924 his closest intellectual companion in Germany was not a German but a Balt, Hermann Keyserling, now operating his Wisdom School in Darmstadt and considered by Berdiaev to be a brilliant "intuitive philosopher." It was Keyserling who translated Berdiaev's *The New Middle Ages* into German, wrote an introduction to his *The Meaning of History,* and arranged to publish these works in Germany. Their meeting in Berlin marked the beginning of a lifetime of friendship, intellectual respect, and personal correspondence.[17]

Scythians and Eurasians

Berlin in the 1920's was also the temporary center of the intellectual movement known as Scythianism (*Skiffstvo*). The leader of the Scythians, a group which first appeared in Russia in the months following the November revolution, was a Left-SR intellectual,

[16] *Sofiia,* pp. 3, 4, 21, 46, 103, 60 (Karsavin), 92 (Lossky), 126 (Berdiaev).
[17] Lowrie, *Prophet,* p. 164; *Novaia russkaia kniga,* 1923, No. 3, p. 45; the later personal correspondence between Berdiaev and Keyserling is contained in the Berdiaev Collection of the Columbia University Russian Archive, folder 5.

R. V. Ivanov-Razumnik, but the movement became significant not because of Ivanov-Razumnik or his followers but rather because the
well-known Russian poets Alexander Blok, Andrei Belyi, and Sergei Esenin became for a time his devotees. Blok's famous poems
"The Scythians," from which the movement took its name, and "The
Twelve" appeared in 1918 in the pages of the Left-SR journal
Znamia truda. Scythianism was one of those currents of political
and intellectual life in Russia after the revolution which helped
channel the Messianic enthusiasm of Russian intellectuals for "the
East" into political support for the Soviet regime. In Berlin in the
early 1920's the Scythians were neither émigrés nor a well-defined
group. Rather, they represented a loose coalition of intellectuals
sympathetic to the new Russia who found in Berlin more advan-
tageous conditions for writing and publishing than they had found
in Russia.

Ivanov-Razumnik's ideas may be summarized as follows: The
revolutions of 1917 in Russia represented an event of global significance superseded in historical importance only by the birth of
Christ, to which it was not dissimilar. Russia thereby has become
"the country where out of the blood and torments of the revolution
has been completed the birth, the birth not of a bare, abstract idea
but of the flesh of a new world." Russia, not Europe, was the bearer
of glad tidings. "The new ecumenical idea now incarnated into the
world through 'backward,' 'uncultured,' 'dark' Russia resembles the
birth of Christianity twenty centuries ago in dark, uncultured and
backward Judea, rather than in advanced, cultured, brilliant
Rome." This new idea was "socialism," not in its postivistic and
materialistic nineteenth-century form but as a new doctrine which
recognized the essential meaninglessness of history and the need for
each individual to impose order upon it. This "Imminent subjec-
tivism" combined "a recognition of the supreme value of the human
personality with great social activity." [18]

Ivanov-Razumnik did not thus excuse the excesses of Bolshevism.
In a vague and romantic way, however, he articulated the view that
the Russian Revolution represented a beginning in the creation of

[18] R. V. Ivanov-Razumnik, *Rossiia i inoniia* (Berlin, 1920), pp. 8, 15 and
his *O smysle zhizni* (Berlin, 1920), p. 22.

some new order that "we must continue to the very end."[19] But except for the elimination of "zoological" nationalism and "bourgeois" socialism as alternatives, the end was never clear. Scythianism became more of a mood than a doctrine, a vague, mystical, religious left-wing enthusiasm for a revolution which it interpreted to suit its own needs. If Vladimir Soloviev had conceived of the barbaric East as a dangerous force of darkness in his *Three Conversations*, Belyi, Blok, and Esenin led the way in transforming this image into a vital and primitive force which could lay waste the hated banality of Europe. The work of the three Scythian poets, wrote Ivanov-Razumnik, "poses with new force the old eternal question about East and West, Russia and Europe" and raises in a new form the query of whether Russia could fulfill her "eternal universal mission in Europe," in this case "to blow apart the old Europe with its Scythianism,' its spiritual and social 'maximalism.' "[20]

In 1919, Belyi, Blok, and Ivanov-Razumnik had organized in Petrograd a Free Philosophical Association, a circle of writers, artists, and other intellectuals interested in the fate of Russian and European culture. Within a year of its founding, a series of lectures on anthroposophy, Dostoevsky, Goethe, modern art, and religion had become so popular that a branch opened in Moscow under Berdiaev and Gershenzon. In the autumn of 1921 it was decided to organize yet another branch in the Berlin Russian colony. In the end, it turned out to be Andrei Belyi, despondent over the recent death of his friend Blok, who made the trip west.[21]

Representatives of the Scythians had first appeared in Berlin in 1920 to negotiate an arrangement for publishing their works with the German publisher Otto Elsner.[22] Nor was it without some irony that Russia's self-proclaimed barbarian intellectuals made use of German technology to propound their doctrine. The leading Scythians then in Berlin were actually three Left-SR's who had unsuccessfully tried to coexist with the Bolsheviks until 1919 when they were

[19] Ivanov-Razumnik, *Svoe litso* (Berlin, 1918), p. 10.
[20] Ivanov-Razumnik, *Ispytanie v groze i bure* (Berlin, 1920), pp. 23, 26, 37.
[21] Andrei Belyi, "Vol'naia filosofskaia assotsiatsiia," *Novaia russkaia kniga*, 1922, No. 1, pp. 32–33.
[22] A. S. Yashchenko, "Skify," *Golos Rossii*, December 23, 1920, pp. 3–4.

arrested and forced to leave the country. The most important was I. N. Steinberg, who was one of the main figures within the Left-SR faction and for a time Commissar of Justice under the Bolsheviks.[23] In Berlin he had been joined by two other Left-SR friends: Alexander Shreider, his deputy at the Ministry of Justice and a writer of some talent, and Ilia Bakal.

Steinberg, Shreider, and Bakal, along with Ivanov-Razumnik and the writer E. G. Lundberg, made up the core of the Berlin Scythians. But the term "Scythian" was loosely applied in those days to a number of intellectual émigrés who had no direct contact with the formal publishing operations of the Scythians or with Ivanov-Razumnik, among them Nikolai Minsky, Aleksei Remizov, Lev Shestov, and Ilia Ehrenburg.[24] Andrei Belyi also had connections with the movement, but he was a major writer independent of Scythianism.

Belyi's rather bizarre behavior in Berlin in these years was more a result of his personal problems than any conscious attempt to shock Berlin as a Scythian. With his fluffy white hair, his constant drinking, and his compulsion to write, Belyi was a tragic figure who had returned to a Germany he had known before the war, tried without success to resurrect his love affair with Asia Turgenev and his prewar relationship with the anthroposophist leader Rudolf Steiner, and ended by throwing himself into literary work. "The Russian emigration," Belyi had complained when he left Russia, "is just as foreign to me as the Bolsheviks; in Berlin I will be alone." After two years of furious activity Belyi did indeed return to Russia, but not without leaving his mark on the literary life of the Berlin colony through his many articles and his own journal, *Epopeia*.[25]

[23] Steinberg resigned as Commissar of Justice along with the other Left-SR ministers the day after the signing of the Treaty of Brest-Litovsk. Arrested in February 1919, he tried without success to negotiate with Lenin for a return of the Left-SR's to the status of a legal political party. At the end of the year he fled to Germany with Alexander Schreider. See his *In the Workshop of the Revolution* (New York, 1953).

[24] As an example of this confusion see the long list of "Scythian" writers in *Golos Rossii*, December 4, 1921, p. 1.

[25] Konstantin Mochulsky, *Andrei Belyi* (Paris, 1955), p. 222. *Epopeia*, published by the Gelikon house, appeared four times from April 1922 to June 1923 and included pieces by Belyi, Remizov, Pilniak, Tsvetaeva, Khodasevich, and Tolstoi.

Belyi's writings in this period echoed the sentiments of other émigré intellectuals. Following Spengler, he argued that the twentieth century was a historic turning point that heralded the breakdown of the European "West." Likewise he distinguished between technical "civilization" and "culture" and concluded that Russia— Soviet Russia—might prove the source of precisely that spiritual and cultural revival needed in Europe. Unlike the Scythians, however, Belyi thought in terms of a return to Renaissance humanism rather than a spiritual invasion from the East. So too he followed the pro-Soviet Smena Vekh writers in criticizing the emigration for its isolation from the new Russia which had inherited the traditions of prerevolutionary culture, but he could not accept their adherence to the spirit of the NEP. In the end he remained, as he had feared, quite alone.[26]

In general Scythianism remained an ingredient in the thought of many émigré intellectuals rather than the recipe of a few. This was true of Belyi and also of Ilia Ehrenburg, whose short-lived journal of "leftist" art in Berlin, *Veshch*, was also linked with the Scythians. In fact Scythianism was a label which both Ehrenburg and the Left-SR Scythians disavowed, and *Veshch* remained a cosmopolitan journal of art and literature without ideological baggage, Soviet or émigré.[27] The true visage of Scythianism, if such existed, appeared in Berlin but for a brief moment in the spring of 1922 in the person of the young Sergei Esenin, the gifted peasant poet whose writings urged a return to animism and the primitive.[28]

Esenin did not come to Berlin as an émigré but merely as a traveler accompanied by the American dancer Isadora Duncan. Miss Duncan was one of many Westerners caught up by the magic of the new Russia in these years, a country which for her represented "an entirely different world . . . a New World . . . the future for

[26] *Golos Rossii*, December 21, 1921, p. 2; *Epopeia*, 1922, No. 1, pp. 7–17; "O 'Rossii' v Rossii i o 'Rossii' v Berline," *Beseda*, 1923, No. 1, pp. 211–236; "Kul'tura v sovremennoi Rossii," *Novaia russkaia kniga*, 1922, No. 1, pp. 2–6.

[27] Ehrenburg, *Truce*, p. 23; Struve, "Transition," p. 26; *Literaturnye zapiski*, 1922, No. 2, pp. 5–6.

[28] On Esenin's poetry see Renato Poggioli, *The Poets of Russia 1890–1930* (Cambridge, Mass., 1960), pp. 269–275.

Artists and the Spirit." [29] Since Isadora's arrival in Russia in the summer of 1921 to open a school of the dance, Esenin had become her tempestuous plaything, a surrogate son and lover. For Esenin, the leading poet in Moscow's Bohemia, Isadora was a companion and lover. For Isadora, Esenin was the eternal Russian, a childlike peasant in whose earthy behavior seemed to lie some powerful spiritual force.

When Esenin and Miss Duncan alighted from their airplane in Berlin on May 9, 1922, they had no intention of leaving Russia but merely of traveling in the West. Esenin expected to return at the end of the summer with a full report on the activity of the Berlin Scythians and, in the meantime, to sell a small volume of his poems to Grzhebin for publication.[30] For a time Esenin became a center of intellectual ferment in Russian Berlin. He visited his friends there —Gorky, Ehrenburg, Belyi—and made the rounds of Berlin's literary cafés in his blue suit, cap, and white tennis shoes. He drank, he read his poems, he smashed furniture. At the Leon café on the Nollendorfplatz he found the price of vodka excessive, told all who would listen that life was better in Moscow, and again marched off to the bank to exchange Isadora's dollars for German marks.[31]

For Esenin himself, life in Berlin was an appalling experience. In late June 1922 he wrote to a friend from Wiesbaden that he was "completely run down" from his experiences and promised that he had "stopped drinking and begun to work." Older émigrés suspected that Esenin had been sent to Berlin "on Bolshevik money" as at best a propagandist and at worst a police agent. Esenin in turn reviled "the West" in typically Scythian clichés:

Here one really finds the slow, sad descent of which Spengler wrote. Let us be Asiatics. Let us smell evil. Let us scratch our backsides shamelessly

[29] Isadora Duncan, *My Life* (New York, 1927), pp. 160, 358–359.

[30] Letter to N. A. Kliuev, May 5, 1922, and to A. B. Mariengof, Ostend, July 9, 1922, in Sergei Esenin, *Sobranie sochinenii* (Moscow, 1962), V, 155, 161. A volume of Esenin's poems appeared in Berlin in 1922 as *Esenin: Sobranie stikhov i poem.*

[31] Z. Arbatov, "'Nollendorfplatskafe' (Literaturnaia mozaika)," *Grani*, No. 41 (1959), pp. 109–110.

in front of everyone. But we will not stink like corpses, as they stink, inside. There can be no revolution here. Everything has come to an *impasse*. Only an attack by barbarians such as ourselves can save and rebuild them. We must march on Europe.[32]

Esenin continued his march to Wiesbaden, Paris, and then the United States, stopping only briefly in Berlin again in late August on his return to Moscow. For Isadora, his antics had become less than amusing. Within a short time of their return to Moscow they separated, Esenin to his poetry and ultimate suicide in 1925, Isadora to the Riviera and her tragic death in an automobile accident two years later. The *affaire Esenine* had been but an episode in the complex life of Berlin's Russian colony, but a symbolic one. For a brief moment a true Scythian had appeared, living and breathing the anti-European message of the Russian Revolution. And in Berlin he had found the West wanting.

The Scythians were a small circle of intellectuals who found Berlin a useful place to publish their writings in these years. Eurasianism, on the other hand, was an émigré movement originating in Sofia in 1920 which had less of an impact on the Berlin Russian colony. The initial assumptions of the Eurasians, however, set down in their first collection, *The Way Out to the East* (Sofia, 1921), helped contribute to that romanticism about the East and Russia's cultural mission which was to prove a divisive force within émigré opinion. The postwar era was an era of catastrophe and crisis in which one of the few stable elements was "culture"; history, however, had reached a turning point marked by the end of "Romanogermanic" culture and the beginning of a new dominant culture from "the East"; this culture, like culture in general, was not a superstructure of society dependent on economic and social twists and turns but an independent variable, individualistic and opposed to the collective; in this cultural sense, Russia was neither Asiatic nor European but a uniquely "Eurasian" fusion of Near Eastern and

[32] Letter to I. I. Shreider, Wiesbaden, June 21, 1922 (*Sobranie sochinenii,* V, 156–157).

Central Asian cultures whose appearance as a force in the world was marked by the revolutions of 1917.[33] Like Spengler and the Scythians, the Eurasians accepted the cultural decline of Europe and felt that 1917 marked the start of a new epoch in world history which would be dominated by "the East," in this case "Eurasia." To these assumptions were added the ideals of a planned, corporate society, the state as the driving force for economic development, and the role of an intellectual minority (presumably the Eurasians themselves) as the dictatorial rulers of the new society. Some of the Eurasians admitted a certain similarity to Mussolini's Italian fascism in these views. But Eurasianism in the end was no more successful than any other émigré political or intellectual movement and did more to turn the attention of émigrés toward Soviet Russia than to create an independent movement.[34] Its achievements were scholarly, not political.

Germany was never a center of Eurasianism, but German romanticism had influenced the Eurasians, who in turn were a subject of great debate within the Berlin Russian colony. Much of Eurasian thinking may have matured even before the war. Nevertheless the language of Spengler struck a responsive note within the movement, which borrowed from him such concepts as the Europeanization of Russia since Peter the Great as a "pseudomorphic" transformation of Russian life.[35] Keyserling's *Reisetagbuch* also appears to have had an influence on the Eurasians' association of Russia with China, India, and "the East."[36] The only Eurasians liv-

---

[33] *Iskhod k vostoku* (Sofia, 1921), pp. iii–vii. The original Eurasians were Peter Savitsky, Prince N. S. Trubetskoi, G. Suvchinsky, and George Florovsky. Savitsky moved to Prague in 1922 and lived briefly in Berlin in 1923. Prince Trubetskoi moved to Vienna in 1922 and lived there until his death in 1938. Florovsky moved to Paris, taught at the St. Sergius Theological Institute from 1926 to 1948, and then came to the United States. The original Eurasians were later joined by a number of other intellectuals, the most notable convert being L. P. Karsavin. See Otto Böss, *Die Lehre der Eurasier* (Wiesbaden, 1961); Nicholas Riasanovsky, "Prince N. S. Trubetskoy's 'Europe and Mankind,'" *Jahrbücher für Geschichte Osteuropas*, XII (1964), 207–220, and "The Emergence of Eurasianism," *California Slavic Studies*, IV (1967), 39–72.

[34] Böss, *Lehre*, pp. 67–83.   [35] *Ibid.*, p. 53, n. 226.

[36] I. Bunakov, "Puti Rossii," *Sovremennye zapiski*, 1920, No. 2, pp. 141–177; 1921, No. 4, pp. 228–284.

ing in Berlin in these years, however, were Peter Savitsky, who gave a course on the "economic geography" of Russia at the Russian Scientific Institute in 1923, and L. P. Karsavin, who did not declare himself a "Eurasian" until 1926. The Eurasians did make use of Berlin publishing facilities in 1922 to bring out four issues of a journal, but otherwise their relationship to Berlin was indirect.[37]

Many Russians in Berlin were lukewarm or even hostile to the Eurasians from the beginning. V. D. Nabokov found Prince Trubetskoi's *Europe and Mankind,* an anticolonial Eurasian essay identifying Russia with "mankind" in opposition to "Europe," to be a tract of misguided cultural relativism. European civilization was in fact a unique achievement, he argued, and "in spite of the author's opinion, objective criteria for the superiority of one culture over another (ethnographic) exist and can be demonstrated." Another *Rul'* reviewer found *The Way Out to the East* to be too vague and general to be of any significance, although he admitted that the Eurasians were "one of the most interesting trends within Russian neonationalism." Savitsky promptly rose to the defense. In a lead article in *Rul'* he denied that the Eurasians rejected all of European civilization out of hand but only its "fetish of technical 'progress'"; such progress had led to the current crisis of war and revolution and must now be replaced by "faith." Savitsky spoke of Russia's impending "world cultural influence" and observed that the Bolsheviks had already recognized that the culture of the future would be Eastern and religious.[38]

The Eurasians in their many writings continued to argue that Russia was neither Eastern nor Western but a single cultural unit of Turkic and Iranian origins—in short, Eurasia, which fused elements from both Europe and Asia.[39] But like the Scythians, they leaned more toward the East than the West. Like them, too, they contributed to a transformation in the Russian view of "the East"

[37] *Novaia russkaia kniga,* 1923, No. 3, p. 45. Their journal, *Evraziiskii vremennik,* appeared in 1922 and was edited by Savitsky, Suvchinsky, and Trubetskoi.

[38] *Rul'*, April 4, 1921, p. 6; September 4, 1921, p. 7; November 5, 1921, pp. 1–2; January 10, 1922, pp. 2–3; January 11, 1922, pp. 2–3.

[39] For example, N. N. Alekseev, "O kharakter i osobennostiakh russkoi filosofii prava," *Novaia russkaia kniga,* 1923, No. 2, pp. 5–8.

from the dangerous threat of Soloviev's "Pan-Mongolism" to a potential ally in the cultural war against the West.[40] It was a romantic notion widespread in European intellectual circles in the wake of the war, one which émigré Russian intellectuals both absorbed and reinforced in their own writings. From the point of view of the Russian emigration, however, Eurasianism did represent an attitude of "self-consolation" (*"samouteshenie"*), as Grigory Landau put it.[41] By interpreting the Bolshevik revolution as a cultural or religious event, rather than a political one, the Eurasians made it seem not only logical and earth-shaking, but even worthwhile.

Bolshevism and the Emigration

Two dominant themes stood out in the intellectual life of the Berlin colony in these years. One was the essentially religious and ahistorical significance of recent world events, a theme characterized by a general distrust of "politics" and old value systems which had helped bring on the war. Man must completely transform himself to survive, to create new values. "After the fire test of the revolution," wrote one émigré, "these values had to be of an absolute nature, as all purely humanitarian ideals failed in the trial. In other words the new values had to be religious." [42] The second dominant theme was the breakdown of Western civilization and the feeling that Russia and the other "non-European" areas of the world might yet provide for Europe a new culture to replace the old.

Both these ideas owed a great debt to German idealism with its critique of "civilization" and idealization of "culture." [43] Both German and Russian intellectuals had engaged in various forms of cultural nationalism since the eighteenth century, stimulated by a feeling of the inferiority of their own countries with respect to the West. For Germany "the West" meant France and England; for Russia it meant Germany as well. Since Herder there had been con-

[40] Riasanovsky, "Trubetskoy," p. 219.
[41] *Rul'*, January 14, 1922; February 12, 1922.
[42] Klepinin, "Survey," p. 2.
[43] A. G. Meyer, "Historical Notes on Ideological Aspects of the Concept of Culture in Germany and Russia," in A. Kroeber and C. Kluckhohn, eds., *Culture: A Critical Review of Concepts and Definitions of Culture* (Cambridge, Mass., 1952), pp. 207–212.

siderable ink spilled by writers in both countries concerning the "rottenness" or "decline" of the West and the coming role of the less developed nations of the world on the cultural scale, perhaps even to a level superíor to that of the West. Russian intellectuals had long nourished such hopes; study in Germany before the war had often stimulated them, and the apparent postwar collapse of Europe completed the process. If Russian intellectuals had long hovered on the margin between admiration for the creative elements in Western civilization and pride in Russian culture, the Russian Revolution and emigration convinced many of them that the "way out" lay not West but East. It was an emotion which the Bolsheviks were able to cultivate with considerable success.

Initially the Bolshevik attitude toward the political émigrés was one of reconciliation based on the weakness of the new government. "The times of the Tsars and of Kerensky and Miliukov have passed," Trotsky promised several weeks after the Bolshevik revolution, "and every Russian citizen, be he a political émigré or a revolutionary soldier in France, now enjoys the protection of the State power of the Russian revolution." [44] With the civil war, however, and the involvement of many émigrés on the White side, the Bolshevik attitude toward the emigration became one of irreconcilable opposition. "The experience of past years," Foreign Minister Chicherin observed in the summer of 1921, "has shown that the organizations of the Russian emigrants abroad constitute wholly counterrevolutionary groupings which use the means at their disposal to provoke attacks on the territory of the Soviet Republics." [45] Even at this time the Bolsheviks had already begun a campaign to undermine those groups within the emigration, particularly the monarchists, that might prove dangerous. To this end they created a bogus monarchist organization inside Russia, known as the Monarchist Union of Central Russia, or "Trust," which continued through-

[44] Speech to the Petrograd Soviet, November 30, 1917, cited in Jane Degras, ed., Soviet Documents on Foreign Policy, Vol. I: 1917–1924 (London, 1951), p. 13.
[45] Ibid., pp. 248–249.

out the 1920's to seek out, infiltrate, and disarm monarchist and military elements within the diaspora.[46]

With respect to the left wing of the Russian emigration, particularly the intellectuals, the Bolsheviks initiated a crude campaign of propaganda which sought to capitalize on the hardships of the émigrés and encourage the view that Soviet Russia represented a new society free of the fetters of bourgeois Europe and, at the same time, a culture in the tradition of nineteenth-century Russia. "The 'Scythians,' the Eurasians, the Smena vekh group," Ilia Ehrenburg recalled, "had one thing in common: they contrasted Rusia with the decaying West." [47] It was this cultural optimism which the Soviet leaders now sought to exploit. To this end they subsidized pro-Soviet émigré intellectual circles, engaged in extensive book publishing abroad in competition with émigré publishing houses, and made it known to sympathetic émigré intellectuals that if they returned to Russia they would be given amnesty and the freedom to continue their work.[48] The height of the campaign was reached in 1922 and 1923 and its center abroad was in Berlin.

The primary object of the Soviet campaign to interest émigré intellectuals in returning to Russia was the movement known as Smena Vekh or "changing directions." [49] Initially Smena Vekh was the product of a small circle of émigré intellectuals in Harbin, Prague, and Paris who urged support for the Soviet regime as the patriotic heir to the national Russian tradition. Subsequently it became a powerful tool in the hands of the Bolshevik leaders for enrolling "bourgeois" intellectuals inside and outside of Russia in support of the new government. In time it coincided roughly with the

[46] See G. Bailey, The Conspirators (New York, 1960) for a history of "Trust" and other Soviet-émigré intrigues in the 1920's and 1930's; also Richard Wraga, "Trest'," Vozrozhdenie, No. 7 (1950), pp. 114–135.

[47] Ehrenburg, Truce, p. 26.

[48] Z. Arbatov, "Vstrecha s Maksimom Gor'kim," Grani, No. 42 (1959), p. 111.

[49] Useful sketches of the Smena Vekh movement are given from the émigré side in Struve, Literatura, pp. 30–35 and in a Soviet article by I. Ia. Trifonov, "Iz istorii bor'by kommunisticheskoi partii protiv smenovekhovstva," Istoriia SSSR, 1959, No. 3, pp. 64–82. See also E. H. Carr, A History of Soviet Russia: Socialism in One Country, 1924–1926, I (London, 1958), 56–59.

period of the New Economic Policy, originating in the summer of 1921 and surviving inside Russia until the winter of 1925–1926, when the last of the Smena Vekh journals were closed down and further public lectures were forbidden. In emigration the central organ of Smena Vekh was the newspaper *Nakanune* in Berlin, although there were other journals as well: *Novaia Rossiia* in Sofia, *Novosti zhizni* in Harbin, *Put'* in Helsinki, and *Novyi put'* in Riga.

Although Smena Vekh began as an émigré movement, it soon had wide support in intellectual circles inside Soviet Russia as well. For the Bolsheviks the movement was a useful means of encouraging middle-class support for the regime, and a number of Smena Vekh journals were allowed to appear in Russia in 1921–1925, among them *Novaia Rossiia, Rossiia,* and *Ekonomist.* In March 1922 Lenin acknowledged that Smena Vekh was a "very useful thing" since its members and followers "express the mood of thousands and tens of thousands of various bourgeois individuals and Soviet white-collar workers, participants in our new economic policy." [50] An August 1922 Bolshevik resolution noted that Smena Vekh "has played an objectively progressive role up to now and can continue to do so," although it warned that "it is impossible to forget for a moment that even in the *smenovekhovstvo* movement there are strong bourgeois-restorationist tendencies and that the *smenovekhovtsy* hope along with the Mensheviks and SR's that after the economic concessions will come political ones favorable to bourgeois democracy, etc." [51] Nevertheless the movement was generally tolerated as a useful supplement to the NEP. Even as late as 1925 Stalin described it as "the ideology of the new bourgeoisie, which is flourishing and gradually joining the kulak and the white-collar intelligentsia," but added paternally with respect to the leader of the movement, N. V. Ustrialov: "let him dream about a rebirth of our party. We do not forbid dreaming." [52]

[50] V. I. Lenin, *Sochineniia* (Leningrad, 1951) XXXIII, 256–257. From Lenin's March 27, 1922, speech to the eleventh party congress.

[51] *KPSS v rezoliutsiiakh i resheniiakh s"ezdov, konferentsii i plenumov TsK* (Moscow, 1954), I, 671.

[52] I. V. Stalin, *Sochineniia* (Moscow, 1947), VII, 341–342. From Stalin's December 18, 1925, speech to the fourteenth party congress.

The leaders of Smena Vekh, however, were all émigré intellectuals, many of whom later returned to Soviet Russia to work. Most
were former Kadets or Octobrists who had participated in various
White movements during the civil war and had later reconciled
themselves to support for the Soviet regime. The leading member of
the group, and its most original thinker, was N. V. Ustrialov, a
former teacher in Moscow and Perm whose political sympathies
had been with the Kadet party before 1917. In 1918 Ustrialov had
been chairman of the "eastern section" of the Kadet central committee in Siberia, contributed anti-Bolshevik articles to the journal
Russkoe delo, and supervised Admiral Kolchak's press and propaganda section before emigrating to Harbin. The two other leaders
of Smena Vekh were Yu. V. Kliuchnikov, a former follower of the
religious philosopher Prince E. N. Trubetskoi and later Kolchak's
Minister of Foreign Affairs, and A. V. Bobrishchev-Pushkin, a member of the conservative wing of the Octobrist party who had
worked for A. I. Denikin and the Volunteer Army.[53]

The immediate origin of the Smena Vekh movement was a small
collection of essays by the same name published in Prague in July
1921. The contributors were Ustrialov, Kliuchnikov, Bobrishchev-
Pushkin, and three other repentant intellectuals: S. S. Lukianov,
S. S. Chakhotin, and Yu. N. Potekhin. Throughout the book ran
the theme that the Bolsheviks must now be accepted by Russians
everywhere as the heirs of Imperial Russia. Campaigns against
them must henceforth be rejected as useless and antipatriotic. The
Russian Revolution was not the seizure of power by a small faction
of revolutionaries but the logical outcome of the whole tradition of
the Russian intelligentsia. Moreover, that intelligentsia now possessed the weapon by which it could transform Russia according to
its prerevolutionary ideals: state power. The revolution of 1917,
wrote Ustrialov, was something "genuinely Russian," a national phenomenon and not a foreign importation, which must be accepted
and preserved if Russia's status as a European great power were to
be maintained. "Progress is unthinkable without cataclysms," added
Bobrishchev-Pushkin, and "there will be no third revolution." Rus-

[53] Trifonov, "Bor'by," pp. 65–66.

sian intellectuals must not only accept the responsibility for the Bolshevik revolution, but support it as Russian patriots.[54]

Ustrialov, as a refugee in China, had already pursued these ideas in various articles in the Harbin journal *Novosti zhizni* in 1920. By the beginning of that year he had decided that the civil war was over and that the various White movements, by tying themselves to the support of foreign powers, had abdicated their claims to be Russian patriots. The main task was now the "reconstruction of Russia as a powerful and unified state"; any further attempts at anti-Bolshevik intervention would necessarily be an "anti-Russian enterprise." "Since the power of the revolution, and only that power, is now capable of reviving Russia as a great power with international prestige," he concluded, "our duty in the name of Russian culture is to recognize its political authority." [55]

Ustrialov had known both Kliuchnikov and Potekhin from civil war days and had corresponded with them afterward. In the summer of 1921 Kliuchnikov and Potekhin, along with Lukianov, Bobrishchev-Pushkin, and another member of their circle, P. A. Sadyker, were all living in Paris. Ustrialov, in Harbin, remained the leader of the group, although it had been Kliuchnikov who had conceived of the first collection of essays and its title.[56] In the months following the appearance of *Smena vekh*, Paris remained the center of the tiny movement. Still few in numbers, they hoped to accomplish a remarkable task. "We must paralyze the emigration," wrote Ustrialov to Potekhin, "and reconcile the emigration to the Soviet government." [57]

In the autumn of 1921 the Smena Vekh circle in Paris began to issue its first periodical, which was designed to propagandize the line of reconciliation laid down in the original collection. The new journal, a weekly also entitled *Smena vekh*, was regarded by its participants as "the next step in the reconciliation of the émigré Russian intelligentsia with Russia and the Russian revolution" and a "bridge between the Russian intelligentsia abroad and the Rus-

[54] *Smena vekh* (Prague, 1921), pp. 49, 79, 96, 135. In 1922 a second edition appeared simultaneously in Berlin and Smolensk.

[55] N. V. Ustrialov, *V bor'be za Rossiiu* (Harbin, 1920), pp. 5, 17, 55.

[56] UA, folder 2, p. 17.

[57] Ustrialov to Potekhin, Harbin, February 14, 1922 (UA, folder 2, p. 32).

sian intelligentsia in Russia."[58] Bolshevism, Ustrialov argued in response to sharp criticism of the movement by Peter Struve in *Rul'*, was a Russian movement in the tradition of the radical intelligentsia; to accept the Bolsheviks as Russia's present rulers was not to become a Marxist or an advocate of political terror but simply to recognize the "tremendous creative value of the very principle of state organization as such" and to work with that state.[59] Not only were the Bolsheviks obviously in power for the foreseeable future, but the NEP indicated a trend toward moderation, "from utopias to a healthy spirit." It was the duty of all émigrés not only to accept the Bolshevik regime and to return to Russia, but also to "reconcile the 'civilized world' to the new Russia."[60]

At first the reaction of the Russian emigration to the new movement was almost universally hostile. Nevertheless Smena Vekh caught the eye of the Soviet government at precisely the time when it desperately sought trade and recognition from various European governments and a voice in European matters, such as the upcoming economic conference at Genoa in the spring of 1922. Kliuchnikov had championed a conference on European economic and political problems which would bring the two pariah nations, Russia and Germany, back into the European community. The Italian-Soviet trade talks initiated by Chicherin in the winter of 1921–1922 were also warmly applauded. Kliuchnikov even attended the Genoa conference as the "legal adviser" to the Soviet delegation, a step which he announced to Ustrialov constituted "the first practical application of *smenovekhovstvo*."[61] From the émigrés, however, came only a stony silence.

In the spring of 1922 the circle decided to expand *Smena vekh* into a daily newspaper and to move operations from Paris to Berlin. Until now there had been little contact with Berlin. Bobrishchev-

---

[58] *Smena vekh*, October 29, 1921, p. 2; the journal appeared weekly in Paris from October 29, 1921, to March 25, 1922, when it moved to Berlin as the daily newspaper *Nakanune*. The Hoover Library has a complete file of the journal.

[59] *Smena vekh*, November 12, 1921, p. 4.

[60] *Smena vekh*, January 7, 1922, pp. 10–12.

[61] *Smena vekh*, December 24, 1921, pp. 1–4; December 31; Kliuchnikov to Ustrialov, Genoa, April 17, 1922 (UA, folder 2, p. 39).

Pushkin had written some articles for the Soviet journal *Novyi mir* there, and a Berlin émigré, Roman Goul, had already begun to contribute to *Smena vekh*. But other than this their arrival in Berlin in early 1922 was largely unexpected. Nor were Kliuchnikov and his friends welcomed in any way by the Russian colony there.

On March 26, 1922, the first issue of *Nakanune* (On the Eve), the new Berlin daily, appeared and began its campaign to enroll émigré intellectuals in support of the Soviet regime. Kliuchnikov and G. L. Kirdetsov were the editors. From the beginning the newspaper was particularly attentive to the first successful Soviet gamble in international politics—the Genoa conference and the resultant Rapallo treaty with Germany, the fruit, as *Nakanune* had predicted, of "the next struggle between young Russia and the old West." [62] The use of such language and of the image of Russia under the Bolsheviks as the political incarnation of culture, youth, the future, and the East soon became the most powerful weapon of *Nakanune* in the campaign to convert the émigrés' cultural optimism into political fellow-traveling. Berlin, Potekhin snapped at the Kadet leader Paul Miliukov, was closer to "Russia" than Paris, not only geographically but spiritually.[63] Ustrialov was particularly aware of the need to appeal not only to revolutionary romanticism, as the Scythians had done, but also to national, religious, and cultural pathos, to disseminate the idea of a Russian "national-bolshevism." [64] "Has the time not come," he asked N. N. Alekseev in November 1922, "to synthesize our revolution with the old Slavophilism?" [65]

[62] *Nakanune*, March 26, 1922, p. 1. *Nakanune* appeared as a daily in Berlin from March 26, 1922, until June 1924. Kliuchnikov and Kirdetsov were assisted in the editing by Lukianov, B. V. Diushen, and Potekhin. By the autumn of 1922 Kliuchnikov and Potekhin had left for Moscow, leaving Diushen and Kirdetsov as editors with Lukianov, Sadyker, and Chakhotin as associates.

[63] *Nakanune*, April 20, 1922, pp. 2–3.

[64] Ustrialov to Bobrishchev-Pushkin, Harbin, April 25, 1922 (UA, folder 2, p. 44). The term "national-bolshevism" was probably coined by Ustrialov in 1920. The *smenovekhovtsy* were aware of movements in Germany by the same name in the 1920's but had no formal ties with them.

[65] Ustrialov to Alekseev, November 4, 1922 (UA, folder 2, p. 74).

In 1922 and 1923 *Nakanune* became the main weapon of Smena
Vekh and its columns were full of slogans designed to appeal to the
émigré intellectuals. Like most other journals of the movement, it
received Soviet subsidies. Life in Russia was getting better and life
in emigration worse; was not the only "way out" now to return to
Russia? "The bridge between Russia and Europe will be difficult
to build," it proclaimed, "but it is a necessity and it will be built."
The entire political structure of "the West," announced Ustrialov,
was going through an "indisputable crisis" and a "new epoch" in
world history had arrived which would be marked by the "worldwide influence of Russia and Russian culture." The Russian emigration belonged to the "old world," whereas inside Soviet Russia a
"new world" was being built.[66]

Russia was clearly identified with the East against the West. "At
an earlier time," Yashchenko observed, Russia was "a European
state with Asiatic colonies, but it is now a Eurasian state without
colonies, whose main part lies in Asia." *Nakanune* was full of talk
about the decline of Europe and the rise of the East, "the beginning
of a new cultural-historical period." That this was not mere Soviet
propaganda is evidenced by the voicing of similar themes in the
correspondence of Ustrialov and his friends. Ustrialov predicted in
late 1924: "The awakening of colonial peoples may be considered
already formulated in the schemes of N. Ya. Danilevsky and
Spengler, even before Orthodox Marxism. National revolutionary
movements signify in themselves a change of races, nations, and
cultures, not an international. Russia's role in this will undoubtedly
be tremendous and world-historical." Bobrishchev-Pushkin also
wrote enthusiastically to Ustrialov of "the inevitable process of decline of the 'rotten West' ":

From a national Russian point of view we can now say: 'We are now
the most revolutionary country in Europe. So we will lead the revolution.' . . . Faith, but not orthodoxy. Firm authority, but not autocracy.
Nationalism, not in opposition to other nations but fusing with them,

[66] N. A. Ukhtomsky to Ustrialov, Berlin, June 30, 1924 (UA, folder 5);
Nakanune, 1922: May 4, p. 1; July 13, p. 5; November 14, p. 3; November 26,
pp. 2–3.

leading them. Blok's Christ leads the Red Army men on with a bloody banner—the only Christ in which one can still believe is the new Rus', if one can believe in any Christ at all.

The *smenovekhovtsy* were of value to the Bolsheviks precisely because they were not mere propagandists but true believers, seeking to convert others.[67]

The question of how independent Smena Vekh could remain in the face of Soviet acceptance and support was a pressing one. From the early summer of 1923 on there were signs of differences within the movement over the issue of how much to criticize the excesses of Bolshevik domestic policy. One member had already written to Ustrialov in June of "worsening relations among certain members of the group" over the question. Most agreed in their support for Soviet policy abroad. But Bobrishchev-Pushkin, for one, insisted on the right to criticize Soviet policy at home when deemed necessary. By the summer of 1922 *Nakanune* was becoming more and more enthusiastic in its support of Bolshevism and Kliuchnikov, who had hoped to keep *smenovekhovstvo* a "neo-Kadet" émigré party, complained that "any chances of connections with émigré circles have rapidly disappeared." Chakhotin's assertion in *Nakanune* in September that "there is essentially no differentiation within *smenovekhovstvo*" could not have been further from the truth. Privately Bobrishchev-Pushkin reported continued "friction between rights and lefts" in *Nakanune,* "a difference in ideology . . . as well as personal frictions." [68]

When Kliuchnikov and Potekhin left Berlin in the summer of 1922 to accept teaching positions in Moscow, *Nakanune* began a period of steady decline. The original tone of its articles gave way to a propaganda style and content closer to *Pravda.* By October 1922 Ustrialov himself was concerned about the growing differences between his own "national-bolshevism" circle in Harbin and the

[67] *Nakanune,* December 22, 1923, p. 3; January 22, 1924, p. 1; Ustrialov to I. G. Lezhnev, Harbin, October 23, 1924 (UA, folder 3, p. 33); Bobrishchev-Pushkin to Ustrialov, Monte Carlo, June 10, 1922 (UA, folder 2, pp. 51–53).

[68] UA, folder 2, p. 59; *Nakanune,* September 16, 1922, p. 2; Bobrishchev-Pushkin to Ustrialov, Monte Carlo, July 30, 1922, and August 22, 1922 (UA, folder 2, p. 65).

Berlin *smenovekhovtsy*, who appeared more and more to be imitators of the Soviet line. Yet he was afraid of provoking further a split that could destroy the movement altogether.[69] His conviction that Bolshevism was becoming less and less compatible with his own aims and should not take *Nakanune* into its own hands was tempered by the warning of Bobrishchev-Pushkin that the "lefts" now occupied the "dominant position" in the Berlin circle.[70] To investigate the situation there he persuaded his friend N. A. Ukhtomsky to go to Berlin in early 1923.

Ukhtomsky's reports only confirmed the dismal prognostications of Bobrishchev-Pushkin. The "moral prestige of *Nakanune*," he wrote Ustrialov in March 1923, was now "very low." The departure of Kliuchnikov and Potekhin had left the journal in the hands of lesser men: Kirdetsov, Diushen, Lukianov, Chakhotin, and Sadyker. The pro-Soviet pronouncements of *Nakanune* had convinced few émigrés of the advisability of returning to Russia. "As far as ideology is concerned," Ustrialov was forced to admit, "it is certainly impossible to deny that *Nakanune* has seriously undermined the prestige of *smenovekhizm*." Diushen, Ukhtomsky complained, was now receiving money from the American YMCA in Berlin and was involved in their émigré correspondence school; moreover, he had succeeded in driving from the Berlin circle several prominent émigré intellectuals.[71]

During the summer of 1923 there was talk of bringing Ustrialov himself to Berlin to take over *Rul'* from the Kadets and to transform it into a pro-Soviet journal of "Russo-German cooperation." *Nakanune* was now read hardly at all in Berlin, and Kirdetsov and Chakhotin left the journal in July. But in Germany nationalists and Communists were allied against the French occupation of the Ruhr. Was there not room in Berlin for a new "national-bolshevik"

---

[69] Ustrialov to Lukianov, Harbin, October 1922 and October 19, 1922 (UA, folder 2, pp. 67–68).

[70] Ustrialov to Bobrishchev-Pushkin, Harbin, October 20, 1922; Bobrishchev-Pushkin to Ustrialov, Monte Carlo, November 9, 1922 (UA, folder 2, pp. 70–73).

[71] Ukhtomsky to Ustrialov, Berlin, March 8, 1923 (UA, folder 5, p. 55); Ustrialov to I. G. Lezhnev, Harbin, March 15, 1923 (folder 3, p. 3); Ukhtomsky to Ustrialov, Berlin, June 15, 1923 (folder 5, p. 65).

organ for the Russian community? Plans for such a journal never reached fruition. "In Berlin," Ukhtomsky had warned Ustrialov, "you would find things more difficult than in Harbin." By the time I. G. Lezhnev, another friend of Ustrialov, had investigated the possibility of opening a new journal in Berlin, conditions for publishing and distributing literature had become much worse; not only had costs risen, but the number of émigré readers was declining. "To print a journal there for importing into Russia," Lezhnev wrote Ustrialov in October, "has become impossible." [72]

By the end of 1923 *Nakanune* itself was ready to admit a deep schism within Smena Vekh between those who hoped for an evolution of Bolshevism into a more moderate political system and those who still hoped for an independent "third revolution." [73] Most of its space until its closing in June 1924 was taken up by steady support for Soviet foreign policy and little else. Backed by Soviet subsidies throughout its career, *Nakanune* now seemed to its sponsors to have outlived its usefulness. Trotsky, Bukharin, and other Bolshevik leaders had long considered it superfluous as a Soviet propaganda organ abroad. Its sales had dropped to almost nothing, its editorial board was inferior and divided, and their wives were reportedly living too well off the newspaper's funds. By mid-1923 Ukhtomsky had turned to Paris as the possible center for a new organ.[74] But within the emigration *smenovekhovstvo* was now dead. Only inside Russia did it survive for a few more months before being suppressed by the government.

In its attempt to persuade Russians abroad to support the new regime and return to Russia, Smena Vekh enjoyed only moderate success. Among the peasant and Cossack remnants of Wrangel's army in Czechoslovakia and the Balkans its message did help convince several thousand émigrés to return to their homes in 1922–1923.[75] But in Berlin it was far less successful. A few pro-Soviet in-

[72] Ukhtomsky to Ustrialov, Berlin, June 15, 1923; July 1923; August 29, 1923; Ustrialov to Ukhtomsky, Harbin, July 15, 1923 (UA, folder 5); Lezhnev to Ustrialov, Moscow, October 15, 1923 (folder 3, p. 17).

[73] *Nakanune*, December 16, 1923, p. 1.

[74] Ukhtomsky to Ustrialov, Berlin, June 30, 1924 (UA, folder 5, pp. 82–83).

[75] G. Cherniavsky and D. Daskalov, "Sud'by russkoi beloemigratsii v Bolgarii," *Istoriia SSSR*, 1961, No. 1, p. 116.

tellectuals—Vladimir Stankevich, Alexander Drozdov, Roman Goul, Yashchenko, Diushen, and Aleksei Tolstoi—did become involved in *Nakanune* for a time, although not all returned to Russia. Diushen and Yashchenko also influenced some of the YMCA-sponsored student organizations.[76] But in general the Berlin Russian colony ignored *Nakanune* and looked on Smena Vekh as a Soviet, rather than émigré, movement.

The best-known convert among émigré intellectuals was Aleksei Tolstoi, the novelist who had lived in France from 1919 to 1921 and gradually decided to "change directions" and return to Russia.[77] Tolstoi had become involved in the Smena Vekh circle in Paris in the summer of 1921 and had gone to Berlin at the end of that year for the usual reason: Berlin was less expensive. In Berlin Tolstoi became an eager member of the intellectual community, a friend of Esenin and Maiakovsky, and a contributor to *Nakanune*, for which he soon became the literary editor. Tolstoi's conversion to *smenovekhovstvo* was a significant event in émigré life and a controversial one. In April 1922 he received a letter from the former Populist leader N. V. Chaikovsky demanding that Tolstoi justify his conversion. He replied with a long "open letter" in *Nakanune* on April 14, 1922, in which he praised the Soviet government because it "defends Russia from attacks by its neighbors, supports the unity of the Russian state and at the Genoa conference was the only one to come out in defense of Russia against possible enslavement by other countries."

Tolstoi was undoubtedly the most important convert to the ranks of *smenovekhovstvo*, and his voice was heard both inside and outside

[76] On pro-Soviet movements within Russian student organizations see the letter of F. T. Pianov to E. T. Colton, Berlin, December 17, 1926 in YMCA, World Service Box 8, folder D.

[77] Born in 1883 in the province of Samara, Tolstoi had established himself as a writer of note even before World War I. In July 1918 he moved with his family to South Russia and then to France, where he lived until the autumn of 1921. During this time he wrote a great deal and became increasingly disenchanted with the ideals of the emigration and the White movements. His first venture into politics with Smena Vekh and his final decision to return to Russia probably date from the winter of 1921–1922. See V. Shcherbina, *A. N. Tolstoi: Tvorcheskii put'* (Moscow, 1956); M. Charnyi, *Put' Alekseiia Tolstogo* (Moscow, 1961); I. Rozhdestvenskaia and A. Khodiuk, *A. N. Tolstoi: Seminarii* (Leningrad, 1962).

Russia. Russian intellectuals at home and abroad must once again become "a single family," he urged, and must realize that European culture "is beautiful but it is a mausoleum." Russia must play a decisive role in the life of Europe. "From here, from Russia, must come salvation from the oblivion of death. If there is any rationality to history, then I believe it is in the fact that everything which originates in Russia is meant to save the world from the folly of being conscious of death." [78] It was an old theme, and one which Tolstoi was eager to spread among his fellow writers. Emigration and life in the West had only convinced him further, he wrote to a friend in Russia, that Europe suffered from a cultural disease for which the new Russia might yet provide the cure:

Except in Germany, Russia is hated and feared throughout Europe. Russia can count on no one—only on her own strength. And Russia's main strength now (it would seem that this is not understood yet inside Russia) is that she has passed through the fire of revolution, she breathes fire. One can feel this only by sitting here, in the West, where there has not been the shock of revolution but where life is on the decline. Here the catastrophe is inevitable. And here in general are the reasons which compelled me to write my letter to *Nakanune*. I shall sever my ties with the emigration.[79]

✓ For Tolstoi, cultural despair had inspired political conversion.

For Tolstoi, too, Berlin was a way station on the road back to Russia. Besides his work as literary editor of *Nakanune,* he wrote stories, read revolutionary poetry with Maiakovsky, and visited Maxim Gorky at his seaside retreat at Heringsdorf; in the summer of 1922 Tolstoi saw his comedy "Love—the Golden Book" performed by the Moscow Art Theater. He also worked for the Soviet book outlet in Berlin, Russkoe Tvorchestvo, and had ideas of starting his own journal which would publish both Soviet and émigré writers. Gorky was also interested in such a journal, not so much to reconcile émigré writers to the Soviet regime as to escape the censorship inside Russia, and he tried to lure Tolstoi away from *smenovekhovstvo* to his own project. For Gorky, the *Nakanune* circle was

[78] *Literaturnye zapiski,* 1922, No. 1, p. 4.
[79] Tolstoi to A. Sobol, Berlin, June 12, 1922 (quoted in Shcherbina, *Tolstoi,* p. 193).

a group of "bourgeois" writers who knew nothing of realities inside Soviet Russia. But after hinting to Gorky that he would be interested in his journal, even on Gorky's condition that he break off his relations with *Nakanune*, Tolstoi continued his association with Smena Vekh until his own return to Russia in the end of July 1923.[80]

Tolstoi's conversion was one of the few notable successes of *smenovekhovstvo*. As an attempt to transform émigré intellectuals' cultural passion for "the East" into political reconciliation with Soviet Russia, Ustrialov's movement converted mainly its own adherents. Kliuchnikov, Potekhin, Bobrishchev-Pushkin, and Tolstoi all had returned to Russia by the autumn of 1923. Kirdetsov became a Soviet press attaché in Rome and later returned to Berlin to work for the Soviet embassy there. Lukianov left for Paris in early 1924, where he worked for Soviet cultural organizations for a few years before returning to Moscow in 1931. Ustrialov himself remained in Harbin as an employee of the Soviet government.

As an attempt to persuade the émigré professional classes to return to Soviet Russia in the 1920's, Smena Vekh was a failure. To the degree that it echoed the Soviet line after 1922, it alienated the émigrés. It was more important as a factor in the erosion of émigré claims to legitimate sovereignty in Russia. For the first time a number of articulate refugees had admitted that the national heritage of Russia still lay within its territorial boundaries, not outside them. Although the movement failed to convert a large number to its support for the Soviet regime, it introduced yet another note of political division and factionalism into an already crumbling facade of émigré unity. Finally, even those who rejected Tolstoi's solution often moved toward a personal position of psychological acceptance, or at least neutrality, with respect to the Bolshevik regime. Anti-Bolshevism remained a powerful current in émigré affairs and would be revived in a new form after 1930 when the "Stalin revolution" sent another wave of refugees into Europe. But under the NEP a number of émigré intellectuals were willing to "change directions" spiritually, if not politically or geographically.

[80] Shcherbina, *Tolstoi*, pp. 193–195; Rozhdestvenskaia and Khodiuk, *Tolstoi*, pp. 145–147.

Toward the end of 1920 the writer Maxim Gorky approached his friend Lenin about the possibility of supporting the publication of Russian books in Germany. Not only could such a program make use of the more developed German book publishing industry and import books back to Russia, Gorky argued, but it would prevent the emigration from monopolizing the business of Russian publishing abroad. I. V. Gessen had just announced the formation of the Slovo house in Berlin. Why not, asked Gorky, allow private Soviet book publishers, in particular his friend Z. I. Grzhebin, to organize a rival operation there? Lenin agreed, thus beginning the Gorky-Grzhebin "Universal Literature" project—the printing of Russian books in Berlin in the early 1920's and their reimportation into Russia.[81]

The Grzhebin operation in Berlin, begun in 1921, initiated the movement of a number of other Soviet book publishing houses to Berlin in the next few years, much to the dismay of the young Soviet State Publishing House which sought to monopolize the printing of all Soviet books. Grzhebin and Gorky came to Berlin to supervise their own operation, and were followed by the Moscow house Vozrozhdenie, Petrograd's Epokha firm, and the Kniga house of I. P. Ladyzhnikov.[82] The Ladyzhnikov operation was a semi-official one; Ladyzhnikov and his German representative, Alexander Stein's brother Boris, were in charge of the entire Soviet book trade under the Soviet trade representative in Berlin, and Kniga (renamed Mezhdunarodnaia Kniga in 1923) was the official Soviet book company abroad.

Ladyzhnikov himself had been in charge of Bolshevik foreign publishing since 1905, first in Geneva and then in Berlin, and had known Gorky since the 1890's. His prewar output had included primarily Bolshevik and Marxist pamphlets, illegal in Russia, and Gorky's own writings, most of the income from which went into the

[81] V. D. Bonch-Bruevich, "Lenin i Gor'kii (Iz vospominanii)," *Voprosy literatury*, 1963, No. 4, pp. 81–84; *V. I. Lenin i A. M. Gor'kii: Pis'ma, vospominaniia, dokumenty* (Moscow, 1958). Zinovy Isaakovich Grzhebin (1869–1929) was an old friend of Gorky who had opened a Bolshevik publishing house in Petrograd in 1919. After coming to Berlin in 1921, he decided to remain abroad, where he died in 1929.

[82] *Novaia russkaia kniga*, 1922, No. 1, p. 35.

Bolshevik treasury. After 1917 he seemed the logical man to direct Soviet publishing abroad and returned to Berlin for this purpose in 1921.[83] He also brought out a literary periodical there (*Russkaia kniga*, renamed *Novaia russkaia kniga* in 1922), which resembled *Nakanune* in that it attempted to bring Soviet and émigré writers into a common pro-Soviet enterprise that was ostensibly nonpolitical. But it was of a higher literary level than *Nakanune*, devoted itself primarily to literature and publishing, inside and outside Russia, and declared its goal to be to "gather and bring together information on Russian foreign publishing and literary activity" independent of political divisions.[84]

For a time *Novaia russkaia kniga* was a first-rate literary journal whose authors included Belyi, Aikhenvald, Ehrenburg, Remizov, and Pilniak. Like other Berlin journals, it asserted the essential unity of Russian culture apart from political divisions and hinted at some vital role for Russia in Europe's future. Its editor, A. S. Yashchenko, spoke of a "general world crisis in the spiritual foundations of life" and noted that "it is a time for prophets, but there are no prophets." But the answer provided in the pages of *Novaia russkaia kniga* was not the cultural pessimism of the Spenglerians, not the Slavophile nationalism of the Scythians or the Eurasians, but a return to the Populist tradition of the nineteenth-century Russian intelligentsia. Russian intellectuals must once again "lead the people along the road of enlightenment from their condition of barbarism and a primitive way of life they have hitherto led, and which has been the main cause of the toil and trouble which have struck Russia." "Either Russia will cease to exist," predicted Yashchenko, "or she will travel new roads." [85]

Novaia russkaia kniga was in fact close to the Berlin Smena Vekh circle. Many of its contributors—Yashchenko, Alexander Drozdov,

[83] *Perepiska A. M. Gor'kogo s zarubezhnymi literatorami* (Moscow, 1960), p. 75; *Arkhiv A. M. Gor'kogo, Tom VII: Pis'ma k pisateliam i I. P. Ladyzhnikovu* (Moscow, 1959). Ladyzhnikov, a lifelong friend of Gorky, later returned to Russia where he became Gorky's literary executor after his death.

[84] *Novaia russkaia kniga*, 1922, No. 1, p. 1. The journal ran as a literary monthly in Berlin from January 1922 until mid-1923.

[85] A. S. Yashchenko, "Krizis intelligentsii i novaia ideologiia," *Novaia russkaia kniga*, 1923, No. 1, pp. 1–5; "O novykh put'iakh i 'novom' iskusstve," *ibid.*, 1922, No. 3, p. 1.

Roman Goul, Gleb Alekseev, Yury Ofrosimov—had been connected with the early Stankevich group and now with *Nakanune*. Similarly, it represented that muddied ground where émigré and Soviet writers contributed to a common enterprise without knowing whether they would be future émigrés or Soviet writers themselves. But Yashchenko and others around *Novaia russkaia kniga* were not as pro-Soviet as they appeared to the rest of the Berlin colony. The censorship inside Russia, which prevented *Novaia russkaia kniga* from reaching there after a few issues, was one of the first sources of disillusionment.[86] It was to circumvent this censorship that Gorky, at about the time *Novaia russkaia kniga* was forced to close down in mid-1923, decided to institute his own literary journal in Berlin.

When Gorky arrived in Germany, in December 1921, he went immediately to the St. Blasiend spa in the Black Forest for his health—one of the usual reasons given by Soviet writers for emigration—and began through correspondence with Grzhebin and Ladyzhnikov to work out the details of Soviet book publishing. Until this time Gorky's only ties with Germany had been his prewar negotiations with the Cassirer house over translation of his writings. Being unfamiliar with either the German language or German life in general, Gorky depended a great deal now on his close family friend and personal secretary Maria Ignatevnia Budberg, a Baltic German baroness whose German and English far surpassed her Russian, to Gorky's constant amusement. It was she who acted as his interpreter in meetings with German writers; "without her," Gorky wrote to V. F. Khodasevich, "it is as if I were without hands. And especially—without a tongue." [87]

Until the winter of 1922–1923 Gorky was concerned mainly with Soviet book publishing operations in Germany. But in early 1923 he began work in earnest on a journal of his own in Berlin, *Beseda* (Colloquy). Since the spring of 1922 Gorky had nurtured the idea of a periodical which would acquaint Russians with developments in European intellectual life, and vice versa, and provide an outlet for Soviet writers free of Bolshevik censorship. On April 16, 1922,

---

[86] Struve, *Literatura*, pp. 35–38.
[87] "The Letters of Maksim Gor'kij to V. F. Xodasevič, 1922–1925," *Harvard Slavic Studies* (Cambridge, Mass., 1953), I, 288, n. (5); 299.

Gorky had written H. G. Wells of his high hopes for such a journal which would be printed in both Berlin and Petrograd and would include not only Russians but also such European luminaries as Albert Einstein, Oswald Spengler, J. M. Keynes, and Thomas Mann. But little was actually done in the following months. In early 1923 Gorky wrote Wells again that he still hoped to establish a "literary-scientific journal of an informative type, the goal of the journal being to acquaint Russia with the intellectual life of Europe." [88]

In fact the idea behind *Beseda* was probably less grandiose—namely, to provide a foreign journal to which Soviet writers and their European friends could contribute free of censorship and which would then be imported back into Russia. The idea was probably Viktor Shklovsky's.[89] Gorky had planned to call the journal *Putnik* (The Traveler), but in the end the title suggested by Khodasevich was adopted. It was hardly a "Soviet" journal. Gorky was particularly hostile to *Nakanune* at this time and during the winter of 1922–1923 arrangements to publish *Beseda* were made not with Ladyzhnikov or Grzhebin but with the Epokha publishing house, then run by two Mensheviks, David Dallin and S. G. Kaplun-Sumsky.

The first issue of *Beseda* appeared in the spring of 1923, edited by Gorky, Khodasevich, Andrei Belyi, and two Germans: B. F. Adler and F. A. Braun. Braun was a Balt, a former professor of language and anthropology at St. Petersburg, now at Leipzig, who edited the "scientific" section of *Beseda* and informed Gorky of Soviet books he thought worth translating for German audiences.[90] *Beseda* ran from June 1923 until the beginning of 1925 in seven numbers, first directed by Gorky and later, after Gorky left for Italy in the autumn of 1923, by Braun. But from the start *Beseda* failed in its original function and purpose. Not only were Soviet writers unable to send material out of Russia for publication in the journal, but Gorky's continual requests for permission to import it into Russia were turned down.

[88] *Perepiska A. M. Gor'kogo*, pp. 71–72, 73.

[89] "Letters of Maksim Gor'kij," p. 286, n. (2).

[90] Born in 1862, Braun was a rare Baltic German of left-wing sympathies but typical Germanophilism whose works included *Die Urbevölkerung Europas und die Herkunft der Germanen* (Berlin, 1922).

Most of *Beseda* thus was made up of materials submitted by the editors and other émigrés. Viktor Shklovsky published a section of his widely read *Zoo* ("In Berlin the Russians live, as is well known, around the Zoo. . . . There are many subways, but there is no reason to travel about the city on them since the entire city looks the same").[91] Remizov, Braun, Gorky, and Khodasevich all contributed stories and articles; Nikolai Otsup published some poems; Belyi printed fragments of his memoirs. In subject matter, the focus of the articles was diverse, concentrating on science and literature and including articles on linguistics, anthropology, and relativity theory. There was no set pattern to the political tone of the articles. Together with Belyi's gloomy attack on the collapse of modern western culture was printed the remarkable article of Lev Lunts, the young member of the Serapion Brothers circle of poets, criticizing the modish romanticism about "the East" and urging that Russian writers must now "go West" to learn from the traditions of modern European literature.[92]

But the journal suffered a continual lack of contributors. Not only were Soviet writers now cut off by the censorship, but émigrés were leaving Berlin, and Gorky's tireless campaign to persuade outstanding European writers and scientists to contribute to *Beseda* met with little success: an article on Ghandi by Romain Rolland appeared, and a translation of a story by Stephan Zweig—but that was all. As an international literary venture, *Beseda* was a failure, its circulation confined to the emigration. Even before the second issue, in the summer of 1923, Gorky was sadly waiting for manuscripts that never came and talking of moving to Austria.[93] For the next few months he continued to hound Soviet officials with requests for permission to import *Beseda* into Russia, to no avail. In September 1923 both Gorky and Khodasevich had decided to move to Italy. By November they were in Prague and preparing for the move south. It was left to Braun to edit the remaining issues of *Beseda* and to oversee its final dissolution in the winter of 1924–1925.

[91] *Beseda: Zhurnal literatury i nauki*, 1923, No. 1, pp. 145–146.
[92] *Beseda*, 1923, No. 3, pp. 259–274.
[93] "Letters of Maksim Gor'kij," pp. 296–297.

The involvement of the Soviet government and individual Soviet intellectuals with the Berlin colony in the early 1920's did little to stem the tide of Russians flowing west. A few intellectuals, notably the *smenovekhovtsy,* were drawn home to the East. But the organized attempts to play upon the sentimental romanticism of émigré intellectuals toward "the new Russia" and "the East" were generally rebuffed. The causes of the dispersal of the emigration from Germany in 1923 were more economic than political; had Germany remained a comfortable place to live, Soviet writers might have stayed on. Gorky was among those who came to Germany to publicize the new regime in Russia and found life abroad more attractive than he had at first anticipated.

By 1924 the temporary community of Russians in Germany, living in limbo between East and West, home and emigration, was breaking up. Berlin was now replaced by many new centers of emigration—Paris, Prague, the Balkans—and the artificial unity of Berlin now gave way to new divisions, political and geographic. As a political and social community, the colony dispersed and moved on. Those who stayed in Germany were often drawn by more traditional forces than those that had made Berlin a center of Russian life in the early 1920's.

-...≪{ VII }≫...-

Shock of Permanence:
1923-1933

With the stabilization of German economic life and Soviet-German relations in the mid-1920's, the position of those Russians who continued to live in Germany became more difficult. The center of émigré life had shifted to Paris and Prague, the Foreign Office had lost interest in the plight of the exiles, and there could no longer be any pretense of a future return to Russia except as willing citizens of the Soviet state. Until 1923 it had still been possible for many Russians to think of emigration as a temporary condition; now it became obvious that it was permanent, that there was no going back and perhaps no hope of assimilation either. For the next decade those Russians who remained in Germany became increasingly frustrated in their search for a way out, for money, for a pretender to the throne, and for a cultural identity that would overcome the despair of political exile. Living in a Weimar Germany where cultural enthusiasm for Russia moved easily into political acceptance of the Soviet regime, they found themselves quite alone.

Weimar Germany turned out to be a mirror of the emigration itself. Politically, nationalist right and Communist left attacked the fledgling democratic center, the former for Weimar's "fulfillment" of Versailles and the latter for its failure to make a social revolution. Economically, inflation and depression struck again and again at the savings and purchasing power of the middle and lower classes. Culturally, the excitement and experimentation of art, music, and literature passed all too often into the boredom, sadism, and erotic abberations of the darker recesses of café and cabaret life. Like the Russians themselves, the Germans suffered the torments of the vanquished: political impotence, economic deprivation, and intellectual fantasies.

For the Russians who lived in Germany in these years, events and images flashed by with the jerky and confused motions of the early cinema: street barricades, breadlines, street-corner orators, wheelbarrows full of worthless marks, cabarets, Georg Grosz drawings, Bauhaus furniture, plays of Bertolt Brecht, Marlene Dietrich's legs, the Beer Hall Putsch, hungry children, Sunday walks in the Tiergarten, the rumble of the S-Bahn, the trees of Unter den Linden. All belonged to the German world in which the Russians lived and moved, but from which they remained in the end quite estranged.

The decade from 1923 to 1933 saw the final erosion of émigré institutions and political parties, but it also saw the emergence of the emigration as a transmitter of Russian culture in Germany. Tragically, the very enthusiasm for Russian literature or the Russian Revolution that the émigrés encountered among German intellectuals drove them further down the road toward both cultural and political alienation from their German environment. Only a few Russian-German intellectuals succeeded in bridging this gap.

Despair

Among émigré institutions Botkin's Russian Delegation, or Russische Vertrauenstelle, continued to deal with the juridical and economic problems of the Berlin colony. In 1923–1925 it issued some eight thousand passports to Russians leaving Germany; according to Botkin only the "weakest elements" now remained behind, mainly "those who had some kind of connection with the country, for example, persons of German origin," and those who —like the Jews—had no economic possibility of moving on.[1] Until the economic and political upheaval of 1923, life had been cheaper in Berlin than elsewhere in Europe; now it was more expensive.

[1] Botkin's report to the National Information Bureau in New York, 1929 (BA/RD, folder 58, p. 3).

Rents were higher, jobs were scarcer, publishing opportunities were fewer. For most Russians, Germany lost its appeal.

The erosion of émigré institutions was partly a result of the exodus of Russians from Berlin. By the summer of 1924 Botkin reported an end to the "epidemic of meetings" that had previously been so typical of émigré life, and a loss of interest in the affairs of the Council of United Russian Institutions and Civic Organizations in Germany. Maltzan and Hausschild were often "busy" when he called at the Wilhelmstrasse. In early 1925 the German government threatened to close the remaining refugee camps unless émigré organizations would pay for their upkeep. To add to his problems Botkin was pressured by Schlesinger to relinquish control of émigré affairs to the League of Nations. Money was increasingly in short supply; the Red Cross and Zemgor were now unable to fund the major welfare and army organizations in Berlin. There was also legal pressure from the Soviet government, as in the suit brought before German courts in 1928–1929 to recover the property of the old Vladimir Brotherhood. Beset from all sides, émigré organizations found it difficult to survive at all.

By 1929 the picture of the Russian emigration in Germany, as reported by Botkin, was vastly changed from the early 1920's. There were still nearly one hundred thousand Russians living in Germany, three quarters of them in Berlin and the rest scattered in other cities: 450 in Hamburg, 200 in Munich, 1,500 in Dresden and Saxony, 100 in Stuttgart, and so on. But the economic position of the émigrés, wrote Botkin, was now "extremely difficult," to say the least. In a Germany rocked by depression, where three million of its own citizens were unemployed, it was virtually impossible for Russians to find jobs other than as waiters, chauffeurs, and clerks. Botkin was not immune to these problems either. In December 1929 Giers wrote him from Paris that the monthly subsidy of the Russian Delegation would be reduced once more, and that further financial support was now impossible.[2] In the summer of 1930 Botkin filed his last report to Giers, although he continued to operate the Delegation on his own until forced out by the Nazis.

The depression and the rise of Adolf Hitler created yet another exodus of Russians from Germany between 1930 and 1933. By the

[2] Botkin to Giers, December 29, 1929 (BA/RD, folder 58).

spring of 1933 there were perhaps fifty thousand émigrés left in all of Germany, and only about ten thousand in Berlin.[3] The dominant political element was the extreme right, the dominant national element the Russian Germans. Few other émigrés could find in the Third Reich either a place of refuge or a center of culture in any way resembling that offered by Berlin ten years before.

In the decade after 1923 the number of *Ostjuden* in Germany also declined relative to the general population. The number of Jews in Germany was reduced from 564,000 in 1925 to 500,000 in 1933, the number of foreign Jews from 107,000 to 98,000.[4] Out of a German population of 63,000,000 in 1925 there were some 63,000 Jews from the territory of Imperial Russia, hardly an overwhelming number.[5] It was not the size but the supposed "influence" of the Jews in banking, commerce, industry, and the left-wing parties, of course, which fanned the flames of anti-Semitism in these years. In fact by 1925 Teitel's Union of Russian Jews had ceased to function in Berlin for lack of funds, and the Russian Zionist journal *Razsvet* had moved to Paris. Most of the Russian or Polish Jews who remained in Germany eked out a living as railroad workers or farmers, or joined the ranks of the unemployed. The legacy of the emigration of the Jews of eastern Europe to Germany before and after the First World War would have its tragic consequences soon enough. Leo Baeck brilliantly understated the problem in the spring of 1923:

The East, and along with it eastern Jewry, has migrated further West as a result of the war and postwar events, producing one of the historical phenomena of our time. The need to join this world amicably and to define its relationships has become for Europe and especially for Germany a very real problem.[6]

Beside Botkin's Russian Delegation a number of other émigré organizations continued to maintain themselves in the 1920's. After 1924 the Council of United Russian Institutions and Civic

[3] The estimate of the Nansen passport office in Berlin, as reported in *Nash vek*, No. 70 (1933), p. 2.
[4] S. Adler-Rudel, *Ostjuden in Deutschland, 1880–1940* (Tübingen, 1959), p. 147.
[5] *Ibid.*, p. 150.
[6] *Razsvet*, XIV, No. 51 (1923), p. 9.

Organizations ceased to be an active force in a community torn by internal disputes, and in 1925 I. V. Gessen formed a rival United Organization of a dozen émigré civic groupings to supplant it.[7] In contrast to the monarchist leanings of the Council, Gessen's group sought a closer relationship with Schlesinger and the League of Nations, accepted the Nansen passport system, and avoided involvement in émigré politics. The monarchists consequently drifted away into yet another organization, the Russian-German Club, which served in the late 1920's to maintain a working relationship between émigré and German businessmen. The Club's membership included a number of Balts, among them Freytag-Loringhoven, Lampe, Shlippe, Gamm, and Krüdener-Struve. Having friendly relations with Otto Hoetzsch's *Osteuropa* circle, the Club also enjoyed the company of such luminaries as Behrendt from the Foreign Office, Heinrich von Gleichen, and other German industrialists and bureaucrats eager only to use the emigration to open up knowledgeable business relations with Soviet Russia.[8]

Through Shlippe and the Russian Red Cross the German Red Cross continued to send limited funds to support the émigré veterans' organizations still active in Germany. These ranged from the Russian All-Military Union (ROVS) of Lampe to older organizations such as the Officers' Mutual Aid Society, the Central Union of Disabled Russian Veterans, and the Society of Russian General Staff Officers. But by the mid-1920's the membership in these organizations had been reduced to a few hundred individuals, many of whom lived the pathetic existence of welfare recipients or day laborers while meeting periodically to reiterate their loyalty to General Wrangel or Grand Duke Nikolai Nikolaevich. Wrangel's visit to Berlin in December 1924, intended to unite the exiles behind the political leadership of Nikolai Nikolaevich, was successful in undercutting any support which Kirill may have had in Berlin; it could not solve the problems of financial erosion closer at hand. As the center of army politics shifted from Berlin to Paris after 1924, even the drama of dispute disappeared from the daily life of the Berlin colony.[9]

---

[7] "Soveshchanie russkikh obshchestvennykh organizatsii i uchrezhdenii v Germanii" (BA/RD, folder 67).

[8] "Russisch-Deutsche Klub" (BA/RD, folder 57).   [9] LA, folders 12, 24.

The Catholic church was another supporting pillar of the émigrés in the late 1920's. In 1921 both Pope Benedict XV and the Catholic Caritasverband in Berlin had contributed substantial sums of money for refugee welfare work through the Committee for Aid to Russian Children in Germany. Then in 1924 the church decided to establish its own Emigré Welfare Office in Berlin, headed by Dr. Ludwig Berg, a Baltic German professor from Aachen. To provide food and medical care it operated a soup kitchen and hospital in Berlin for a few years. In 1928 several Catholic organizations were brought together in a single organization called Papal Aid for Russians in Germany. With the help of contributions from the United States and the Russian Red Cross, it continued to provide funds for needy émigrés until the end of the 1920's.[10]

Unlike the YMCA, the Catholic church had some ideological motives for its good works. Both Benedict XV and Pius XI were interested in a union of the Eastern and Western churches, as was Ludwig Berg. Berg edited several books in the late 1920's in both Russian and German that sought to convert Russian Orthodox émigrés to Catholicism. In them various contributors argued that the Russian church had preserved the original "collective feeling" (*Gemeinsamgefühl*) of Christianity, which offered a kind of mystical renewal to a Catholicism suffering from the headlong rush of Western man toward individualism, rationalism, and secularism. The mystical East and the realistic-individualistic West were not opposites but complements, and a union of the two branches of Christianity along lines previously suggested by the Bavarian philosopher Franz Baader and the Russian Vladimir Soloviev would join the best traditions of each. Feeling would be merged with logic, the "mysticism of the Russian soul" with the "realistic-individual life of Catholics," Russian nationalism with Catholic supranationalism.[11]

Berg's campaign was not highly successful. There were some Russian conversions to Catholicism in Berlin in the 1920's, and

[10] Hans-Erich Volkmann, *Die Russische Emigration in Deutschland, 1919–1929* (Würzburg, 1966), pp. 18–25.

[11] Ludwig Berg, ed., *Die römisch-Katholische Kirche und die orthodoxen Russen* (Berlin, 1926), *Novye religioznye puti russkago dukha* (Mainz, 1926), *Ex Oriente: Religiöse und philosophische Probleme des Ostens und des Westens* (Mainz, 1927).

Russian churchmen were invited both to Rome and to an ecumenical conference in Vienna in 1926. But most Russians either remained within the Orthodox fold or lost touch with religion entirely. If the desire for a firm faith drove some to conversion, the nostalgia for Russia prevented most from religious assimilation in the West.

The picture of the official life of the emigration in the late 1920's was a rather dismal one. Departures for other countries, financial problems, factional disputes, and pressure from both Moscow and Berlin had all sapped the vitality of émigré life. Similarly, émigré politics in these years degenerated into backbiting and intrigue which only accelerated the mood of hopeless bitterness that seemed to pervade the colony. The shock of permanence heightened political despair.

Polemics and Intrigue

With the temporary collapse of the Nazi party in the wake of the abortive 1923 Beer Hall Putsch in Munich, the Russian monarchists found themselves even more isolated from German political life. The Supreme Monarchist Council had long since moved to Paris, and many of the right-wing émigrés who had appeared at Reichenhall in 1921 were now scattered far beyond the borders of Germany. In his manifesto of August 31, 1924, Grand Duke Kirill formally announced himself to be "the oldest member of the Tsarist dynasty and the only legitimate heir to the Russian throne," adding the usual promises of a future Russia in which a benevolent tsar and Church would rule over a happy landholding peasantry. This only served to alienate the German government once again from the activity of the monarchists, however. The head of Kirill's Russian Legitimist-Monarchist Union, General Biskupsky, was expelled from Bavaria for a time, the Bavarian government forced Kirill to make a statement that he would give up political activity, and the Communist party introduced a bill in the Landtag calling for Kirill's expulsion as an "undesirable alien." Kirill wisely responded by taking a long winter trip to Paris and New York, where he hoped to gain financial support for his cause.[12]

[12] BGSA, folder MA 104351.

Biskupsky was hardly inactive in these years. Beside working for Kirill, he helped maintain what was left of Scheubner-Richter's Aufbau Society in Munich, campaigned against the supporters of Grand Duke Nikolai Nikolaevich as Freemasons, and dreamed of a war of intervention against the Soviet Union using the remnants of Wrangel's army in alliance with French and Polish troops. Biskupsky had his hand in so many schemes in these years that many émigrés considered him a double agent working for the Soviet government. He was outdone by his assistant, however, the Ukrainian adventurer Ivan Poltavets-Ostranitsa. An army officer with little formal education, Ostranitsa had unsuccessfully suggested himself to the Germans in 1918 as Hetman of the Ukraine, and remained an enemy of Skoropadsky in exile. In Germany he claimed to head an imaginary Ukrainian National Cossack Union of some 150,000 members both in the Ukraine and in emigration, proclaiming its fascist loyalties in a long letter to Hitler (the "national leader of the German people") in April 1923. In 1926 he attempted a similar ruse with the Reichswehr. Neither the Nazis nor the army were sufficiently gullible, however, and even the Ukrainian émigrés found Ostranitsa to be a "charlatan." The Bavarian police, too, recognized him only as a swindler seeking German money and political support from any possible source.[13]

In general, the government kept a close watch on the émigré politicians after 1923 but had few illusions concerning their political promise. The Wilhelmstrasse was aware of the complexities of émigré politics in both Berlin and Paris, held occasional talks with Russian, Georgian, and Ukrainian political leaders, and yet felt that men such as Ostranitsa were "imposters" and that the émigrés were "unreliable" in any political sense. The Ministry of the Interior was perfectly willing to expel right-wing émigrés when necessary, as in the case of Biskupsky or the émigré forger Alexander Gumansky in 1930. In the bitter years of exile for the Russians, official Germany proved to be tolerant, but never simple-minded.[14]

[13] Records, T-454, roll 19, 933–934; T-84, roll 5, 4088–4103; report of Ministerialrat Zetlmeier to the Bavarian Ministry of the Interior, February 22, 1927 (BHSA, folder MInn 71490).

[14] AGFM, T-120, roll 3942, K104657-674; BHSA, folder MInn 71644.

As in the early 1920's the Russian emigration continued to be important to the German government primarily as a danger to Soviet-German relations. The fact that so many émigrés had moved on was in this sense a relief. But it was still necessary to keep a watchful eye on adventurers such as Biskupsky with his plans for terrorist activity on the East Prussian border and his public charges that the Weimar government was "playing a dangerous and unacceptable game with the dictators of the Third International." The fact that such rumblings had little if any support did not make them less dangerous as potential sources of an anti-Soviet incident. The Soviet government was always worried about the activities of the "White Guardists," and was particularly nervous in 1929–1930 when the émigrés on trial for forging Soviet currency were given lenient sentences and the Russian-German exiles were clamoring for German intervention to help the German colonists inside the USSR brutalized by collectivization. For a time both of these affairs endangered the commercial negotiations between German firms and the Soviet government related to the First Five-Year Plan and produced visible uneasiness in both foreign offices. Once again, however, common Soviet-German interests proved too strong for the émigrés.[15]

In the late 1920's the politics of the Russian emigration took on a certain air of unreality. Since any possibility of influencing Weimar foreign policy against a profitable relationship with Soviet Russia had disappeared at Rapallo, the émigrés settled down to their own anti-Bolshevik campaigns in a world of fantasy, more literary than political. On the right and on the left, the émigrés now sought to make their views known through their writings—a conscious attempt to find foreign support for their cause, an unconscious attempt to relieve their own frustrations of political impotence.

The leading sponsor of monarchist literature in Germany in the 1920's was Duke Georg of Leuchtenberg, a Russian-German member of the Romanov family who, it will be recalled, had lived off

---

[15] AA IV Russland: Po. 2, Vol. 13, pp. 314–321 (Biskupsky) and Vol. 14, pp. 194–195; ORuss, Vol. 24 (Mennonites); ORuss, Vol. 25 (Chervontsy forgers' trial).

and on since before World War I at his ancestral castle of Seeon in Bavaria. At Reichenhall in 1921 Duke Georg had made the acquaintance of a number of right-wing Russians, some of whom had known him in Russia. In 1922 he began his career as sponsor of émigré Russian literary activity by financing a journal of "healthy national thinking" edited by Ivan Nazhivin, a former follower of Tolstoi, and called *Detinets* (The Fortress); he also published his own memoirs on the civil war in the Ukraine, and later edited with Lampe the journal *Beloe delo* devoted to civil war history.[16]

Better known than Nazhivin was the Cossack General Peter Krasnov, another friend of Duke Georg who lived with him at Seeon in the 1920's. Krasnov himself was not a Cossack but a Russian guards officer, military attaché, and war correspondent who became greatly intrigued by Cossack life after being made commander of a Siberian Cossack cavalry regiment shortly before the First World War.[17] During the Russian Civil War he had fought against the Bolsheviks in South Russia, first under Kaledin and then on his own with substantial German military and financial support, rendered with the aid of Duke Georg in Kiev. In emigration Krasnov was isolated from Cossack politics, then centered in Paris and the Balkans, and consequently spent most of his time at Seeon working on a series of novels and stories.[18]

Krasnov had shown unusual literary and artistic inclinations since before the war, when he produced his first novel and took art courses at the St. Petersburg Academy. Now in emigration he wrote voluminously, long novels and stories on Russian life, the Cossacks, and the culpability of Jews and Masons for Russia's troubles. His major literary effort was the panoramic novel of Cossack life entitled *From the Two-Headed Eagle to the Red Flag*, which first appeared in Berlin in 1921. Issued by the publisher Olga Diakova, and modeled after Tolstoi's *War and Peace*, Krasnov's four-volume

[16] G. N. Leikhtenbergsky, *Vospominaniia ob "Ukraine"* (Berlin, 1921). *Detinets: Sbornik pervyi* appeared in Berlin in 1922.

[17] See the biography of Krasnov by S. V. Denisov in *Kazachii sbornik*, 1922, No. 1, pp. 39–49, No. 2, pp. 47–53.

[18] *Volia Rossii*, 1926, No. 2, pp. 149–164; No. 3, pp. 127–143; G. N. Leikhtenbergsky, "Kak nachalas' 'Iuzhnaia armiia'," *Arkhiv russkoi revoliutsii*, No. 8 (1923), 166–182.

epic was immensely popular among the Russian colony and sold out its first edition of five thousand copies within a few months.[19]

Krasnov's political views were also revealed in his novel *Za chertopolokhom* (Beyond the Thistle), the tale of a group of Russian émigrés in the middle of the twentieth century who travel by Zeppelin to Russia to learn about a country which they know only second-hand. With their German *Wandervogel* friends, they soon discover that while Europe has degenerated into democratic party politics and materialism, Russia has restored the monarchy. About an émigré living in Berlin Krasnov writes:

He had been born in Berlin at a time when an old priest had been living at the embassy church and had been baptized. His identity papers listed him as Orthodox and his birth certificate was in order. But the old priest who had run the Russian church in Berlin died, its parish began to quarrel among themselves over the monetary value of church property and lands. The young democratic majority argued that in a state which rejected the Christian faith it was sinful to hold on to a church and that its property should be distributed among the "poor," that in general everything should go to the "poor." The minority, which turned out to be mainly toothless, taciturn old men who remembered better times, protested—but the party of free bicyclists who dreamt of building a racetrack on church land near the graveyard threatened to "ruin" them. Since to execute such a threat against former senators, governors and generals in a democratic state was possible, if somewhat risky—the minority was silenced and the church was closed. Its property was sold. The imperial gates and iconostasis were bought by a rich Jew and placed in a large restaurant at the entrance to the dining room. Religion was thrown aside and it would have been ridiculous to argue in court that these were sacred objects. The only things sacred and holy in Western Europe were the laws of the proletariat and the slogans of the revolution.[20]

But the old ties of the Russian and German people were too strong to be overcome by the forces of modern socialism and materialism. Thus when the returning travelers reported the existence

---

[19] On the background to the novel see *Ot dvuglavago orla k krasnomu znameni, 1894–1921* (2d ed.; Berlin, 1922), pp. 3–8.

[20] *Za chertopolokhom: Fantasticheskii roman* (Berlin, 1922), p. 162.

of a monarchy in Russia, there was an immediate favorable reaction:

Almost daily new publishing houses and newspapers appeared. The old books which talked about the past glory of Russia and Germany were dug up. Portraits of Emperor William and Bismarck appeared in the streets, and in the toyshops they began to sell metal soldiers over the protests of the Allied commissions.

A certain wealthy Bavarian bought the iconostasis of the old Russian church from the Jewish restaurant and resurrected the embassy church. The Germans sought out the ninety-year-old priest, Father Tikhon, who had been living alone in Bavaria, and invited him to consecrate the church.

Germany energetically prepared to recognize Russia and already during the evenings in Sans Souci park in Potsdam children who had escaped the surveillance of their tutors sang: "Deutschland, Russland über alles, über alles in der Welt!" [21]

Thus did Krasnov anticipate the erosion of the old Russia in emigration and dream of its revival in the future. But the novel's anti-Semitism, aristocratic attack on democracy, hatred for the Entente powers, and warm feelings for Bavaria bore a distinctly contemporary ring.

Although Krasnov told a *Rul'* correspondent in 1921 that "officers should remain outside politics," his interests were not only literary. "To be a Russian," Krasnov wrote in 1922, "means to be a Black Hundreds man, a participant in pogroms and surely a monarchist, a restorationist and an extreme reactionary." In fact, he had contributed numerous articles to both *Dvuglavyi orel'* and *Griadushchaia Rossiia* that were full of the usual patriotic and Germanophile sentiments. In his attempts to dabble in Cossack politics, however, Krasnov was notably unsuccessful, although he did edit a short-lived periodical devoted to Cossack affairs. In the end he proved a literary success and a political failure.[22]

[21] *Ibid.*, pp. 295–296.
[22] *Rul'*, February 5, 1921, pp. 1–2; *Kazachii sbornik*, 1922, No. 1, p. 50; *Dvuglavyi orel'*, February 14, 1922, pp. 1–32; *Griadushchaia Rossiia*, October 6, 1921, p. 2.

Krasnov's right-wing literary fantasies reflected the deeper malaise of the Russian colony in Germany in the 1920's. With the removal of monarchist and army politics to France, and the general hostility of German public opinion toward émigré Russians, life on the émigré right took on an air of desperation, unreality, despair, and intrigue. In the summer of 1924 Belgard's son Aleksei and his friend Alexander Gumansky amused themselves by forging the famous Zinoviev Letter with the help of another Balt, Edward Friede. This was a document purporting to instruct the British Communists in matters of revolution, and it had a profound impact on the British general elections.[23] The scheme probably originated with Vladimir Grigorievich Orlov, a former intelligence agent for the Volunteer Army who reported on Soviet affairs to Wrangel from Berlin in the 1920's. In the end the information he passed on to Lampe and Holmsen about Soviet police activity helped to indict him in 1929 as a Bolshevik agent, resulting in his expulsion from Germany.[24]

Another example of émigré intrigue in these years was the so-called Georgian affair of 1930. In 1929 the German police arrested the conservative Georgian émigré Alexander Karumidze on charges of forging Soviet currency with the intention of disrupting the Georgian economy and precipitating a revolution. Among the more sensational aspects of the case was Karumidze's revelation at his trial that summer that his project had been financed by Sir Henri Deterding, the anti-communist director of the Royal Dutch Shell oil company who had made numerous contributions to Russian émigré causes, and some eminent Germans, including General Max Hoffmann. Deterding apparently was willing to try anything to recover his nationalized oil wells, and Hoffmann had cultivated émigré support for armed intervention for years. In the end the court commuted the sentences of all the defendants and Karumidze

---

[23] L. Chester, S. Fay, and H. Young, *The Zinoviev Letter* (Philadelphia and New York, 1968). The recently discovered "Harvard text" of the letter suggests that the handwriting is that of Sidney Reilly, a British agent.

[24] Botkin to Giers, March 18 and July 15, 1929 (BA/RD, folder 60); *Rul'*, May 9, 1930, p. 1, and May 13, 1930, p. 3.

left Germany, but the affair served once again to draw attention to the fruitless machinations of the embittered exiles.[25]

The most famous case of émigré intrigue in Germany in the 1920's involved the appearance of a pretender to the Imperial heritage and its account in the Bank of England in the person of a young woman who claimed to be Anastasia, youngest daughter of Nicholas II.[26] On February 17, 1920, a girl was pulled out of the Landwehr Canal in Berlin after an abortive suicide attempt. Until May 1922 the "woman who rose again" was lodged in a mental hospital at Dallsdorf, where she suffered symptoms of deep depression and melancholia. Two "Anastasias" who appeared in France and the United States during this time had proven to be frauds, and the Russians who began to visit their German counterpart in the winter of 1921–1922 were skeptical. In the spring of 1922 she was taken from the hospital by a Baroness Kleist and brought to Duke Georg of Leuchtenberg's lair at castle Seeon. It was here that she revealed to visitors through her Baltic German interpreter, Mrs. von Rathlef-Keilman, an astounding knowledge of the intimate personal life of the last Romanov family.

Emotions surrounding the girl were heated. Kirill and his followers attacked her as a rival pretender to the throne. Other Romanovs felt that she was simply a demented woman with a good memory who had been fed information by Baroness Kleist and others close to the family. The German government through Duke Georg and his protectors, General Hoffmann and Wittelsbach Crown Prince Rupprecht, may have feared revelations of their insufficient concern for the rescue of the family in 1918. Botkin simply worried about another incident which could add to the

[25] On the Karumidze affair see the accounts of the trial in *Rul'*, June 12, June 14, and July 22, 1930; G. Roberts, *The Most Powerful Man in the World* (New York, 1938), pp. 304–311; Essad Bey, *Das Weisse Russland* (Berlin, 1932), pp. 197–202, and the materials in AA IV Russland, ORuss, folder 25.

[26] The best published accounts of the German "Anastasia" are Gleb Botkin's *The Woman who Rose Again* (New York, 1937) and Harriet von Rathlef-Keilman, *Anastasia* (New York, 1929). Botkin was the son of Nicholas II's personal physician and a cousin of S. D. Botkin. Unpublished materials are contained in TA.

existing tension between the émigrés and their German hosts. As late as January 1926 Botkin still felt that the real Anastasia had perished with the rest of the family in Ekaterinburg, and that the woman at Seeon was simply a well-trained puppet of Baroness Kleist.[27]

In March 1926 Botkin made his first visit to Seeon. The pretender's knowledge of Romanov family affairs now made him think that he might indeed be faced with the legitimate Anastasia. Duke Georg suggested that it might be wise to give the girl the protection offered by some German industrialists and nationalist politicians. Sympathetic to the girl's plight, Botkin began to send funds from Berlin to help in her upkeep. There was also a strong desire on the part of some influential émigrés to send the girl to America, something which Botkin did not want insofar as it meant losing control of a woman whose identity was more plausibly Anastasia's than they had previously thought.[28]

In 1927 the case broke into the public eye when the *Königsberger Allgemeine Zeitung* of March 7 charged that the woman of Seeon was simply primed by monarchist Russian émigrés to serve their political and financial goals. This report was substantiated by the authoritative account of von Rathlef-Keilman in a book which revealed that the woman was a Mrs. Tchaikovsky whose peculiar mental makeup had led her to believe she was in fact Anastasia and to absorb vast amounts of information given her by the Kleists and others. The resulting scandal made it imperative for the woman to leave Bavaria, and Botkin's cousin finally succeeded in procuring a six-month American visa and a refuge on a Long Island estate for her.

These foregoing events all highlighted the frustrations of the political right within the emigration. Forgeries, requests to the Wilhelmstrasse for funds to support imaginary armies of intervention, the dispatch of young émigré terrorists into the Soviet Union, the intrigues of rival claimants to the Imperial mantle were typical

[27] Botkin to Giers, January 8, 1926 (TA, folder 10).
[28] See Botkin's correspondence with Duke Georg of Leuchtenberg, TA, folder 6.

of the worsening status of the émigrés in these years in Germany.[29] Right-wing exiles like General K. V. Sakharov continued to foresee the imminent collapse of the Jewish-Bolshevik regime and to search for a nationalist line capable of reconciling the feuding émigrés and unleashing the real or imagined anti-Bolshevik powers of the Russian people.[30] Yet in the twilight years of the NEP preceding the Stalin revolution it was increasingly obvious that the emigration found no serious supporters at home or abroad.

On the political left the situation was equally desperate. The liberals had never enjoyed strong ties to German society, and since the murder of Nabokov they had turned increasingly to managing the affairs of the colony and engaging in the scholarly endeavors of the Russian Scientific Institute or German academic life. *Rul'* was forced to close down in 1931, and its short-lived successor newspaper *Nash vek* (Our Times, 1931–1933) confined itself to reporting the news of the day and the deteriorating life of the Russian colony during the depression.[31] The left-SR's who remained in Berlin continued to attack the Soviet government for its persecution of party members inside the USSR while maintaining a vague Scythian enthusiasm for revolution in the pages of *Znamia bor'by.*

The only political faction of any influence in Germany in these years was that of the Mensheviks. Through their contacts with German socialists and their diminishing, but still existent, ties with party members living in the USSR the Mensheviks were able to provide a running account of Soviet affairs in Germany until the coming of Hitler which was both informative and influential within the socialist community. They reached not only a Russian audience

---

[29] See, for example, the reports of Kutepov's attempt to elicit German funds for an émigré army in France in 1929 and of the activities of terrorists operating out of Finland in 1927: AGFM, T-120, roll 3942, K104676-685, and roll 5216, K483816-822.

[30] Sakharov published a short-lived journal *Put' pravdy* in Berlin in 1929 and later joined the Nazi camp. See his anti-Semitic works *Bolschewisierung der Welt* (1937) and *Judas Herrschaft im Wanken* (1937).

[31] The Hoover Library has scattered issues of *Nash vek* for the period October 1932–April 1933.

in the pages of *Sotsialisticheskii vestnik*, but a German one through their own weekly *Mitteilungsblatt der Russischen Sozialdemokratie* (1924–1932) and their articles in the main German-language socialist journal of the 1920's, Rudolf Hilferding's *Die Gesellschaft*.

The Mensheviks were also suffering the fissures and bitterness of factionalism in these years. In the spring of 1924 a Menshevik conference was held in Berlin to discuss issues raised by the arrival of the "right" faction and to hammer out a party program. Although differences among the Mensheviks were generally mild during the NEP, the rise of Stalin and his struggle against right and left oppositions in Russia proved more divisive. The "rights" were generally excluded from the pages of *Sotsialisticheskii vestnik*, and Garvi, Aronson and Kefali were more or less ostracized by the party's Foreign Delegation. The same was true of Potresov and Stepan Ivanovich, who criticized the Berlin Mensheviks in the pages of their Paris journal *Zapiski sotsial-demokrata* in the late 1920's. In addition there were widening divisions between Georgians and Russians over the nationalities question.[32]

In public the Mensheviks continued to pour out a stream of articles and books on Soviet affairs in which they evinced great optimism that the Bolsheviks would not outlast the inevitable economic crisis. In this they found a willing reception from Rudolf Hilferding, who served twice as Finance Minister of the Weimar Republic (in 1923 and 1928–1929) and who gave the Mensheviks a valuable platform in the pages of his journal *Die Gesellschaft*. It was in this journal between 1924 and 1932 that they reiterated their combination of political hostility and economic prediction concerning the USSR.[33]

As "Russian experts" the Mensheviks continued to make the familiar points which had appeared in *Freiheit* a few years before. The shortage of industrial goods and basic investment capital was

[32] Grigory Aronson, *Bol'shevistskaia revoliutsiia i men'sheviki* (New York, 1955), pp. 9–10.

[33] For several Mensheviks, Hilferding was the greatest European socialist after Marx; as editor of *Freiheit* he had welcomed them into the ranks of the USPD. See Alexander Stein, *Rudolf Hilferding und die deutsche Arbeiterbewegung* (New York, 1946).

at the heart of Russia's economic crisis in the 1920's; this shortage in turn determined the nature and direction of the political struggle between Stalin and his opponents. This struggle was not a clash of personalities or ideologies but a reflection of the underlying class struggle between peasant and worker. The threat of a new variety of "fascism" hung over Russia; only the resurrection of a strong, independent labor movement (led by the Mensheviks) and the establishment of democratic socialism could save the country from Bolshevik dictatorship.[34]

The Mensheviks also remained believers in the ultimate collapse of their enemies. "The Bolshevik dictatorship," prophesied Abramovich as late as 1931, "can never succeed in building a socialist society in backward Russia." Stalin's policy of forced industrialization through the First Five-Year Plan would prove neither economically productive nor politically stable. "Bolshevism," wrote Abramovich, "has a political form and method shared by Bonapartism but lacks its social basis, has no classes beneath it sufficient to reap fruits of revolution or erect a stable counterweight in society." "If Stalin's policy is pursued in Russia," he concluded, "a catastrophe, an economic breakdown is inevitable." [35]

The same kind of arguments appeared in Menshevik books published in Germany. The function of such publications remained, as Dan put it, to show the "broad masses of the western proletariat what the real situation in Russia is." The NEP was "nothing less than the rebirth of capitalism." The rights of workers were being violated in part because there was no independent labor organization. The growth of the Red Army was symptomatic of the general "militarization" of Soviet society, particularly of the trade unions. Peace and democratic socialism, not war and dictatorship, were the

---

[34] A. Jugow, "Die 'Sozialistische Akkumulation' und die Zukunft der Industrie in Russland," *Die Gesellschaft*, II (1925), 546–563; "Wirtschaftslage und Parteikrise in Russlands," *ibid.*, III (1926), 421–442; "Grundprobleme der russischen Volkswirtschaft," *ibid.*, IV (1927), 419–454; Rafael Abramovitsch, "Die Entwicklung Sowjetrusslands," *ibid.*, III (1926), 322–345; Theodor Dan, "Die Krise der Demokratie und die Krise der Diktatur," *ibid.*, III (1926), 235–250.

[35] Rafael Abramovitsch, "Revolution und Kontrrevolution in Russland," *Die Gesellschaft*, VII, 537, 541; "Stalinismus oder Sozialdemokratie," *ibid.*, IX (1932), 133–147.

only way out for modern man. But both were now going under in Russia, where the maxims of Bolshevik politics were simply "total authority from above, state slavery from below." [36]

In the spring of 1929 Kautsky promised Dan that "there is no doubt in my mind that Russia is headed for catastrophe (or a more extreme dictatorship in Russia)" and that "the collapse of Bolshevism will, I believe, be brought about by the peasantry, and Russia will become a peasant state." Dan was equally sanguine, although he found the notion of some future democratic-peasant republic in Russia to be utopian. The peasants might well bring down Stalin's party by their resistance to collectivization, but the future would still belong to the Mensheviks, whose function remained "propaganda work to clarify the basis on which a proletarian mass party can be constructed after the revolution." [37]

In private, however, Menshevik factional differences were more pronounced than in public, revealing the same "sectarianism" which Kautsky had noted among the Russian socialists well before the war. The basic question dividing the Mensheviks was now whether to wait out the internecine struggle going on inside the Soviet Union or to throw their support behind one of the rival groups. Dan's view was that the Mensheviks must somehow help organize the working class in Russia to facilitate the "democratic liquidation of the terrorist regime" behind the most desirable communist faction; they could not simply reject all groups indiscriminately. The right Mensheviks, including Garvi, Bienstock, Aronson, and Kefali, argued that no choice was possible, since the "opposition" might prove as much of a dictatorial force as Stalin. By 1928 Peter Garvi reported privately to Kautsky that there were "great differences of opinion" among the Berlin Mensheviks, and added somewhat wistfully "the smaller the party organization, the

[36] As examples of this literature see Theodor Dan, *Gewerkschaften und Politik in Sowjetrussland* (Berlin and Stuttgart, 1923) and *Der Arbeiter in Sowjetrussland* (Berlin and Stuttgart, 1923); Paul Olberg, *Die rote Gewerkschafts-internationale und die Europäische Gewerkschafts-Bewegung* (Stuttgart, 1930); Peter Garvi, *Der Rote Militarismus* (Berlin, 1928) and *Sowjetdeutschland* (Berlin, 1932).

[37] Kautsky to Dan, April 21, 1929, and Dan to Kautsky, May 5, 1929 (KA, G–XV, pp. 8–17, 122–127).

stronger the sectarian spirit." Kautsky reiterated his complaint of twenty years' standing that the Russian revolutionaries in general were masters of sectarian feuds who "can solve all problems, even the practical ones, only in theory." [38]

By 1929 Grigory Bienstock also complained of personal and ideological divisions, particularly the fissure between Dan and Potresov, and voiced his fears that Menshevism might well go the way of the DeLeon sect of socialists in America. Kautsky again warned Dan that signs of sectarianism had been "especially strong among the Russian socialists of all tendencies," and urged the Russian and Georgian wings of the party to cease their internal squabbling and work together. Nonsense, Dan replied, in effect: Any attempt to produce unity among the exiles would only stifle true proletarian discussion and debate; "unity in the emigration cannot improve the prospects of a mass proletarian movement, but, on the contrary, the existence of such a movement in Russia is a necessary precondition for socialist unity." But Abramovich, too, noted the widening gap between the Georgian enthusiasm for concessions to local nationalism and the "Great Russian" opposition to it on the part of Dallin and Nicolaevsky. The "centrist" group around Dan and Garvi could only try to hold the party together, an increasingly difficult task.[39]

Even more devastating to the Mensheviks was the arrest and trial of a number of economists who were former party members inside the Soviet Union in early 1931. The charge was that they worked as agents of foreign powers, European socialists, and the Menshevik Foreign Delegation in an effort to "wreck" the First Five-Year Plan. The Mensheviks themselves soon refuted the charges in public. The Soviet accusation of Menshevik "interventionism" was absurd, wrote Dan in *Vorwärts;* the economists Grohmann and Sukhanov had left the party a decade ago. Abramovich, speaking before 20,000 workers in the Berlin Sportspalaz, also

---

[38] Dan to Kautsky, December 19, 1924 (KA, G-XV, pp. 111–118); Garvi to Kautsky, September 18, 1926, and January 10, 1928 (D-XI, pp. 18–62).

[39] Bienstock to Kautsky, May 3, 1929 (KA, G-XVI, pp. 24–27); Kautsky to Dan, June 3, 1929 (G-XV, pp. 54–61); Dan to Kautsky, May 5, 1929 (G-XV, pp. 122–127); Abramovich to Kautsky, May 9, 1929 (G-XV, pp. 91–95).

denied any connection between those on trial and the Mensheviks abroad, and Hilferding charged that the Soviet accusation that Grohmann had received money from Dan and Abramovich was an "unthinkable lie." [40] In private Peter Garvi bemoaned the trial as a "comedy of Justice" and a "catastrophe" for the Mensheviks still left inside the Soviet Union. "Hard times are ahead for Russian social democracy," he noted sadly. "Such an unfortunate country! One generation after another fights for freedom—and we now have a tyranny unparalleled in human history." [41]

By 1932 the Mensheviks had turned somewhat abstractly to the working out of a new party program. There were the usual endless discussions on the impact of collectivization and the future of Russia, discussions which served to widen the division between the two Berlin factions—Dan, Yugow, Schwarz, Yudin, and Gurevich on one side, and Dallin, Abramovich, Nicolaevsky, Aronson, and Kefali on the other. Although the debate raged on in the usual atmosphere of Marxist dialectics, Garvi observed that "personal relations are not uninfluential." "Naturally," he wrote to Kautsky that spring, "we are only a tiny heap of émigrés who have been long banned from Russia." [42]

With the coming of Hitler, Berlin was no longer a possible place of refuge for the Mensheviks. "In the colony," wrote Abramovich in early 1932, "there is unfortunately a great deal of unemployment, need, and illness. But we cannot expect anything better than the millions of Germans who live around us." In early 1933 they left Berlin for other European cities, often in a last-minute flight before the Gestapo without personal possessions or archives. By April 1933 virtually all the Berlin Mensheviks were in Paris, with the exception of Vladimir Voytinsky, who was living in Zurich; Georg Denicke, who was in jail in Germany; and Nicolaevsky, who was still trying to salvage his archives from the clutches of the police in Berlin. Alexander Stein, who joined the German socialist colony in Prague in the 1930's, wrote that summer that he found himself with no other choice but to flee "the great concentration camp

[40] See the published Menshevik criticism of the trial edited by Alexander Stein, *K protsessu t.n. "Biuro Ts.K. RSDRP* (Berlin, 1931).

[41] Garvi to Kautsky, March 6, 1931 (KA, D-XI, pp. 18–62).

[42] Garvi to Kautsky, April 9, 1932 (*ibid.*).

Germany." Now the Mensheviks began their third flight to freedom, not from the tsar or the Bolsheviks but from a land transformed from a country of refuge to a chamber of antisocialist horrors. Bienstock's comment to Kautsky from Prague in the autumn of 1934 summed up the situation: "The older one gets the lonelier one becomes. Most of my Russian friends are now either dead or in Bolshevik prisons or scattered in exile." [43]

The Mensheviks' personal acquaintance with the Bolshevik leaders, their knowledge of economics and the labor movement, and their past experiences in the ranks of the Russian Revolution all made them natural experts on Soviet Russia at a time when a lack of information encouraged grotesque theories. In Germany they found other socialists they had known before, equally frustrated by their failure to make a socialist revolution in the wake of World War I. Yet throughout Menshevik writings ran a basic flaw, an unwillingness to accept the possible primacy of politics over economics in Soviet Russia; economic contradictions, they felt, must ultimately end in political collapse. "The tragedy of the November Revolution," wrote Stein, "was that the Bolsheviks saw only the problem of power and not of economics." [44] The tragedy of the Mensheviks in emigration was that, in criticizing the terror, economic contradictions, and absence of workers' rights inside Soviet Russia, they saw only the problems of economics and not of power. One must also add, however, that this same Marxist myopia provided the very optimism that saw them through so many years of exile and despair. In the end they, too, fell victims in 1933 to a second totalitarian revolution which overwhelmed the cause of democratic socialism. But in Paris and New York they remained believers in this cause.

Cultural Russophilia

The émigré intelligentsia, in contrast to the anti-Bolshevik politicians, remained under the spell of a kind of cultural Russophilia in these years. The Smena Vekh movement had died out by 1924

---

[43] Abramovich to Kautsky, February 19, 1932 (KA, D-I, pp. 7–40); Stein to Kautsky, August 12, 1933 (D-XXI, pp. 357–380); Bienstock to Kautsky, October 14, 1934 (D-VI, pp. 14–41).

[44] *Vorwärts*, November 7, 1922 (*Abendausgabe*), pp. 1–2.

and the more pro-Soviet exiles had either moved on or returned to Russia. But many of the great names of Russian culture—Kandinsky, Eisenstein, Prokofiev, Stravinsky, Rachmaninoff, Berdiaev—continued to live or perform in Germany in the late 1920's. The enthusiasm for Russia which they kept alive, however, was a mixed blessing. If it helped make life possible in a world of samovars, *piroshki,* Easter eggs, and concerts, it also contributed to a German fascination with Russian culture which worshiped not merely the tradition of Russian literature, art, and music but its gradual reappearance in Soviet Russia. Politically opposed to the excesses of the Russian Revolution, the émigré intelligentsia became, quite unconsciously in many cases, its representative symbols in Germany.

Within the colony itself intellectual life never recovered from the great exodus of 1923–1924. Berdiaev's Religious-Philosophical Academy did reopen in Berlin after having closed for a year, and the appearance of Russian musicians and artists was always greeted with enthusiasm by the émigré press. The Russian Scientific Institute also continued to offer courses to Russian students with funds provided by the Wilhelmstrasse and the League of Nations until 1932. But the number of students declined from six hundred in 1923 to less than one hundred in the late 1920's, and many of the faculty members were living abroad. Then, too, the number of concerts and art exhibitions was never again as spectacular as it had been in the early 1920's. Most of the intellectuals who stayed on in Germany lived in relative isolation now. The philosopher S. L. Frank knew only Max Scheler with any degree of intimacy, and later recalled from Paris that Germany remained a kind of wilderness for him. The same was true of the young writer Vladimir Nabokov. Few émigrés were able to assimilate easily into German intellectual life, and most remained quite alone.[45]

Those émigré intellectuals who did assimilate in some way were often caught up in the "anti-Western" mood of Weimar which drew from the emigration not its political Russophobia but its

[45] "Russisches Wissenschaftliches Institut in Berlin: Verzeichnis der Vorträge" (BA, III, folder 55); Volkmann, *Emigration*, pp. 129–134; V. S. Frank, "Semen Liudvigovich Frank, 1877–1950," in V. V. Zenkovsky, ed., *S. L. Frank, 1877–1950* (Munich, 1954), pp. 1–16.

enthusiasm for things Russian. Those who spoke in vague terms of a new era in a Europe revivified by spiritual forces from the East were listened to; those who had close cultural ties to Germany going back to the prewar period found it easier to speak. Any "influence" which the émigrés had in Germany, however, only linked them ever more closely with a Russia whose political life they rejected. Cultural Russophilia bred political isolation.

The artists within the emigration were particularly important in transmitting to émigrés and Germans alike the sense of a new era. The postimpressionist revolution in art, of course, was a European phenomenon which had preceded the Russian Revolution by a decade or more. But movements such as expressionism, futurism, and constructivism all had a substantial Russian contribution from such artists as Marc Chagall, Wassily Kandinsky, El Lissitsky, Aleksei Yavlensky, Naum Gabo, and Antoine Pevsner. All of these men also made significant contributions to art in Germany, particularly to prewar expressionism and the postwar Bauhaus circle. In the 1920's they helped generate a radical and apocalyptic view of art and society in Weimar Germany which made Germans associate them with the Russian Revolution, rather than with its émigré opponents.

Both Kandinsky and Yavlensky had lived in Germany before the war, first as students at the Azbé school in Munich and later as leading expressionists in the Neue Künstlervereinigung of 1909 and the *Blaue Reiter* circle three years later. Like Andrei Belyi, Kandinsky had been a devotée of the anthroposophist Rudolf Steiner, and it was under Steiner's influence that he was drawn to the view that only the artist and the mystic could reintegrate the chaos and disorder of the external world revealed most recently by the breakdown of classical physics. "The disintegration of the atom," wrote Kandinsky, "was to me like the disintegration of the whole world." [46] In his paintings before the First World War, Kandinsky wavered thematically between East and West, Russia and Europe, Moscow princesses and Murnau railroad trains, assimilating European ele-

[46] Will Grohmann, *Wassily Kandinsky: Life and Work* (New York, 1958), p. 54. On Yavlensky see Clemens Weiler, *Alexej Jawlensky* (Cologne, 1959).

ments but never being overwhelmed by them. Finally, because of the Baltic German background of his maternal grandmother, Kandinsky found assimilation to German life relatively easy. "I grew up half-German," he wrote in 1904, "my first language, my first books were German."[47]

World War I brought an end to the favorable conditions for the development of the new art in Europe. Both Kandinsky and El Lissitsky, a young architecture student at the Darmstadt Technical High School, now returned to Russia. Here they naturally became swept up in the artistic ferment which accompanied the 1917 revolution. In July 1918 Kandinsky joined Anatoly Lunacharsky's Commissariat for Public Instruction, taught at several government art workshops, and later helped found a Museum of Pictorial Culture (1919) and the Academy of Aesthetics (1921). Lissitsky joined Marc Chagall at the latter's Academy of Art in Vitebsk, where he became drawn into the world of Russian "constructivism" through two of its leading practicioners, Vladimir Tatlin and Kasimir Malevich.

Constructivism had its formal beginnings in Moscow in 1913 when Tatlin, Malevich, and two brothers, Naum and Antoine Pevsner, joined in condemning naturalism in art and moving away from painting to the construction of spatial objects out of steel and other materials. Both Naum (who later changed his name to Gabo) and Antoine had lived in Europe before the war, Naum as a medical student in Munich and Antoine as an artist in Paris, where he shared in the cubist discovery of space, distance, and time as elements of art. Returning to Moscow in the spring of 1917, they assisted Tatlin, Malevich, and Kandinsky a year later in the organization of Vchutemas (Higher Art and Technical Workshop). Here they began to move from the world of sculpture into more socially useful tasks such as the design of aesthetically pleasing radio stations and Tatlin's famous monument to the Third International.[48]

[47] Grohmann, *Kandinsky*, pp. 16, 43, 46.

[48] On constructivism see: Hans Richter, *El Lissitzky: Sieg über die Sonne* (Cologne, 1958); pamphlet of the New York Museum of Modern Art, "Gabo-Pevsner" (1948); George Rickey, *Constructivism: Origins and Evolution* (New York, 1967); S. Lissitzky-Küppers, *El Lissitzky* (Dresden, 1967).

The shift from abstract art to a kind of state-sponsored engineering design program split the movement in two. On the one hand were those who, like Tatlin, could subordinate their art to the ideological desires of the new government. On the other hand were those criticized as "pure" constructivists (including Gabo, Pevsner, and Lissitsky) who continued to accept Tatlin's aesthetic doctrines but not his subordination of art to the needs of engineering, politics, popular enthusiasm, or other social requirements. "To realize our creative life in terms of space and time: such is the unique aim of creative art," ran their August 1920 Manifesto; "we shape our work as the world its creation, the engineer his bridge, the mathematician his formulas of a planetary orbit." [49]

As expected, the dissidents ultimately became the émigrés. In 1922 Gabo went to Berlin to supervise the constructivist section of the Soviet art exhibit at the Van Diemen Gallery and did not return to Russia. Lissitsky, who had been in Germany in 1920 and helped organize a constructivist circle in Düsseldorf, also emigrated. Pevsner followed in 1923, first to Germany and then to France. It was thus through the medium of emigration that the "pure" wing of constructivism became an element in the artistic revolution which would lead to the Bauhaus.

In 1921 Kandinsky came to Germany on a three-month visa and decided to stay. His hopes for a new start in painting were soon dashed, however, when he was unable to retrieve many of his prewar works which had been sold during the war, and when living conditions proved hard during the winter of 1921–1922. Nevertheless he was able to find employment at the Bauhaus in June 1922 with the help of Paul Klee. Chagall, too, had emigrated to Berlin that summer, noting that he had never before seen so many Russian constructivists as at the Romanic Cafe in Berlin that year.[50]

Thus the artists who arrived in Berlin from Russia in 1922 were exiles, but they were also products of the Russian Revolution, men who lived and worked for five years under the Bolsheviks and intellectually supported the revolution to one degree or another. The

[49] "Gabo-Pevsner," p. 54.
[50] F. Meyer, *Marc Chagall* (New York, 1964), p. 316.

sense of a sharp division between émigré and Soviet art hardly existed in these years. The Berlin colony had a lavishly illustrated art journal edited by A. E. Kogan, *Zhar-Ptitsa* (The Firebird), which published prewar, émigré, and Soviet art side by side along with the stories of Pilniak and Bunin, Tolstoi and Zaitsev, Balmont and Aldanov. In 1922 Kandinsky, Chagall, Gabo, and Pevsner, as exiles in Berlin, could see their own works displayed by the Soviet government in the Van Diemen exhibit. Even the artists sometimes did not know their own status, as with Lissitsky, who lived for seven years in Germany before deciding in 1928 that revolutionary art was only possible in a revolutionary society and returning to Russia.

Lissitsky had already established contacts with German artists in Berlin in 1921, among them the dadaist Hans Arp, the founder of the Stijl group Theo van Doesburg, the architect Mies van der Rohe, and the film maker Hans Richter. When Gabo arrived he, too, was introduced to this circle of friends, including the Hungarian Laszlo Moholy-Nagy, through whom many of the constructivist ideas of Lissitsky and Gabo later found their way to the Bauhaus. In 1922 Lissitsky joined with the writer Ilia Ehrenburg in editing an international journal of the new art, *Veshch/Gegenstand/Objet*, in Berlin. In it they proclaimed that the blockade of Russia had ended and that a "new epoch of creativity" would result from the free exchange of ideas between the "young forces of Europe and Russia which are creating new things." [51] The emphasis on things rather than ideas, on coming to grips with the machine in a machine age, was part of the constructivist message; it was not surprising that they were welcomed and listened to by the Bauhaus circle.

When Walter Gropius founded the Bauhaus in Weimar in 1919 he termed it "a guild of craftsmen without class distinction." The radical nature of the Bauhaus consisted in its fusion of art and technique, artist and worker. Workshops replaced classes, artists designed furniture, and cooperation with industry was welcomed. In a way, it was a dramatic attempt to eliminate the sense of alienation between self and product which the young Marx had

[51] *Veshch/Gegenstand/Objet*, Nos. 1–2 (1922).

noted in the nineteenth-century working class. Work should be the result of the inner man's creativity and spiritual search for meaning. "Mechanized work is lifeless, proper only to the lifeless machine." Artists must become "useful" to society by making useful things. They must master all the skills that go into the making of a final product. They must come to terms with the machine in order to liberate men from enslavement to machines. The Bauhaus, according to Gropius, would try to overcome "the loss of creative unity which has resulted from technological development" because of the "much too materialistic attitude of our times and . . . the loss of contact between the individual and the community." [52]

The ideological ties between the Bauhaus and Russian constructivism were evident. Art must not simply imitate the machine, but master it; it must become functional, spatial, and material, not merely to make things but to fuse artist and worker, brain and hands, into a more meaningful and creative individual; the artist, like the worker, must become a productive member of society. Within Germany the Bauhaus grew out of prewar expressionism and the Blaue Reiter movement. But it was also under the direct influence of Russian constructivism after 1917, at first through knowledge of the work of Malevich, Gabo, and Lissitsky inside Russia and later through the arrival of Moholy-Nagy in 1923 as a member of the Bauhaus. If constructivism did not dramatically alter the nature of the Bauhaus program, it reinforced the trend toward a revolutionary art which, among other things, made the artist feel useful to society.

Kandinsky always made it clear that he was not one of the constructivists, despite his work with them in Russia. At the Bauhaus he hoped to "work in space, i.e. with architecture" and to find a new spiritual meaning which had apparently remained unsatisfied by the anthroposophy of Steiner, the Orthodox church, or his own painting. "But in addition to synthetic collaboration," he wrote in 1924, "I expect from each art a further powerful, entirely new inner development, a deep penetration, liberated from all external purposes, into the human spirit, which only begins to touch

[52] Walter Gropius, *Idee und Aufbau des staatlichen Bauhauses* (Weimar and Munich, 1923).

309

the world spirit." [53] Such apocalyptic expectations were unlikely to be satisfied in any environment. In addition, in 1924 Kandinsky came under attack from German public opinion as the "red" Russian in the Bauhaus, part of a general campaign against it that forced a move to Dessau later that year. "I have never been active in politics," he wrote wistfully that September, "I never read newspapers . . . it's all lies . . . even in artistic politics I have never been partisan . . . this aspect of me should really be known." [54]

Kandinsky's artistic productivity at the Bauhaus was at any rate his best since 1914. Once again he began to rethink his ideas on art, culture, and religion in a manner which made him more sympathetic than hostile to the intent, if not the fulfillment, of the Russian Revolution. In his prewar memoirs and his essay *Concerning the Spiritual in Art* (1912) he developed his theory of nonobjective art as the artist's creation of his own reality rather than as a reflection of some external material reality which modern physics seemed to have destroyed for Kandinsky. Art was a spiritual experience, satisfying a psychic need, which moved beyond the "normal" world of three dimensions to a nonrational world in which space and time were indistinguishable.

In the 1920's urged on by the enthusiasm with which German artists had greeted the arrival of Russian constructivism through the Van Diemen exhibit, Kandinsky maintained his hope that his mystical view of art would be realized in Soviet Russia, if not in the West. Unlike Lissitsky, he chose not to return. But he foresaw the real possibility that the center of development in art would shift from West to East, from Europe to a Russia where "spiritual values" seemed more dominant. Only Germany had a comparable reservoir of romantic artistic creativity within her, of which she was somewhat afraid; "on this point, at least, the somewhat hidden affinity between the two nations emerges." [55]

In 1926 the German interest in constructivism revived when

---

[53] Grohmann, *Kandinsky*, p. 174. In his *Point and Line to Plane* (Munich 1926) Kandinsky also developed his idea that art must reflect the "inner life behind the appearance of things—the soul."

[54] Grohmann, *Kandinsky*, p. 175.   [55] *Ibid.*, pp. 179–180.

Malevich arrived at the Bauhaus to arrange for the publication of his *Non-Objective World*. Naum Gabo and Kandinsky maintained their connection with it until the Nazis closed it down in 1933, at which point both moved on, Gabo to London and Kandinsky to Paris. Probably for Kandinsky the emigration of 1933 from a country in which he had lived and worked for nearly thirty years was more traumatic than his departure from Russia in 1922. "We are not leaving Germany for good," he wrote from Paris that December; "I couldn't do that; my roots are too deep in German soil." [56]

The relatively easy assimilation of Kandinsky and the constructivists in Germany was a consequence of both prewar experience and postwar intellectual affinities. Kandinsky, Lissitsky, and Gabo had all lived in Germany before 1914 and spoke fluent German. Moreover, the message of constructivism coincided with the thrust of the Bauhaus, which was also under the influence of Dutch nonrepresentational art through Piet Mondrian and the De Stijl group. But in a sense they were never really émigrés. Indeed, their voices represented an echo of the Russian Revolution, not a condemnation of it.

The mournful and ecstatic sounds of Russian music were yet another source of cultural Russophilia in Weimar in these years. What German audience could resist an émigré concert which might feature Rachmaninoff or Heifetz as the soloists, conducted by Stravinsky or Prokofiev? From 1925 on Stravinsky appeared annually at Paul Hindemith's chamber music festivals in Donaueschingen and Baden-Baden, where he was lionized. The young and penniless cellist, Gregor Piatigorsky, became the first-chair performer under Fürtwangler at the Berlin Philharmonic, and found brilliant company in a trio with pianist Vladimir Horowitz and violinist Nathan Milstein. Prokofiev lived in Bavaria in 1922–1923 while writing the score for *The Flaming Angel;* in the autumn of 1926 he returned to Berlin to hear a performance of his *Love of Three Oranges* before returning to the Soviet Union. While émigré groups such as the Don Cossack Choir of Sergei Jaroff appealed to the nostalgia of the older Russians, the brilliance and innovation of other world-

[56] *Ibid.,* p. 221.

famous musicians contributed to that general enthusiasm for Russian culture which characterized German intellectual life in the Weimar years.[57]

The lure of the new Russia also reached Germany through the media of theater and cinema. In 1922, along with the Van Diemen exhibit, the Moscow Art Theater made its first postwar appearance in Berlin and was received by Germans and émigrés alike with enthusiasm. Its arrival was no surprise to the colony, since Nabokov, Sergei Gornyi, Alexander Drozdov, and others had kept the émigré reading public well informed of Soviet theatrical events in the pages of the journals *Teatr* and *Teatr i zhizn'* in 1921–1922. As in art and literature there was a sense that the theater was also a way to find a "new and personal ideology" and a new "world view." Soviet film making created an even greater stir in Berlin in the 1920's. In 1923 and 1925 the productions of the Soviet producer Alexander Tairov and the Moscow Chamber Theater appeared in Berlin, followed by the first showing of Sergei Eisenstein's dramatic film *Potemkin* in 1925 and the arrival of Meyerhold's entire company in 1930. Like the constructivists, Soviet theater directors and film makers helped infuse German intellectuals not only with an enthusiasm for the wedding of machinery and art but also with the radicalism of the new communist aesthetics.[58]

The arrival of Eisenstein in Berlin in 1927 was thus an event of great importance in German art circles. The films *Potemkin* and *Strike* were not only innovative in their techniques but filled with the sense of revolutionary triumph in Russia which had eluded the German left in 1918–1919. Eisenstein for the Germans was not merely a director, but the prophet of a new revolutionary age. After attending a directors' conference in Switzerland with Hans Richter, he returned to Berlin where he was applauded by the left-wing press and intellectuals and interviewed on the radio for his views on art and politics. Like Esenin a few years earlier, however, Eisenstein found in Germany signs of decay rather than creativity.

[57] Gregor Piatigorsky, *Cellist* (New York, 1965), pp. 50 ff.; Victor Seroff, *Sergei Prokofiev: A Soviet Tragedy* (New York, 1968), pp. 122–137.

[58] *Teatr*, No. 14 (1922); *Teatr i zhizn'*, Nos. 5–6 (1921); *Kino-iskusstvo*, No. 1 (1922); J. Willett, *The Theater of Bertolt Brecht* (New York, 1959), pp. 110–112.

The German cinema was full of "mysticism, decadence, and dismal fantasy . . . showing a future as unrelieved night crowded with sinister shadows and crimes," and films such as *The Cabinet of Dr. Caligari* (1920) were part of some "barbaric carnival" reflecting the "chaos and confusion of postwar Germany." [59] The brothels, pornography, and perverse behavior of Berlin café life were shocking and decadent. The film industry was crass and commercial. Even his contacts with the poet Ernst Toller, the playright Bertolt Brecht, and the film director Erwin Piscator were not sufficient to convince Eisenstein that the German West was vital or revolutionary. When he left for Zurich he remained, as he put it, a working Bolshevik and not a capitalist bum.[60]

Assimilation

The cultural Russophilia of the émigrés in Weimar resonated with the anti-Western mood of many German intellectuals as well. For the émigrés Germany remained something more than a mere place of exile; it was "the West" with its mixed qualities of technological progress and cultural bankruptcy. Many Russians agreed with Spengler that Europe was clearly in a state of "decline"; even such a cultured enthusiast of Europe as Fedor Stepun found his faith shaken by his arrival in Germany in 1922:

here is what we Russians, the old "good Europeans," dreamed of and wrote about during the years of revolution. Now we have been banished from Russia to this Europe, toward which we have looked so fervently in recent years—odd, hardly conceivable, and yet it is so: our banishment to Europe is turning into our banishment from Europe. Apparently we "Russian Europeans" loved Europe only as a marvelous country seen through our "Peter's window"; the familiar windowsill on which we leaned disappeared beneath our hands, and so went the spell of the country.[61]

Many German writers expressed a similar sense of despair.

More than this, postwar Germans critical of Europe voiced a new

[59] S. M. Eisenstein, *Film Form* (New York, 1949), pp. 202–203.
[60] M. Seton, *Sergei M. Eisenstein* (New York, 1952), pp. 126–136.
[61] Fedor Stepun, "Das bolschewistische Russland: Gedanke und Bilder," *Hochland*, XXI (1924), 522.

optimism regarding the world beyond Europe of which Russia was a part. Thomas Mann in his *Reflections of a Non-Political Man* (1918) found in Russia the possible source of a new apolitical revolt of the individual against "the West," against politics, against civilization. The 1917 revolution for Mann represented "the end of the epoch of Peter [the Great], of the western, liberalizing European period" of Russian history, in opposition to which he now placed the "anti-Petrine, primitive Russian, opposed to civilization." Moeller van den Bruck found in Russia another "young" people with which Germany might align herself in a war against the capitalist West in the interests of German power abroad and national unity at home. Oswald Spengler, too, parroted the popular notion of Russia as a young, less developed nation of the future whose destiny would be different from that of Western Europe, a limitless expanse which might be either a source for a new spiritual revival of Western man or a destructive force linked with the Asiatic or "colored" peoples who now threatened the hegemony of Europe over the rest of the globe. "The ideal of the Karamazovs, an ancient, Asiatic-occult ideal," wrote Hermann Hesse, "is beginning to become European, is beginning to devour the spirit of Europe. This is what I call the decline of Europe." [62]

Yet to most German writers, "Russia," for all their rhapsodizing, remained largely an unknown quantity. Mann interpreted the Russian Revolution as some vague cultural upheaval and was generally unaware of its events or political significance. For Moeller, Russia meant Dostoevsky and little more, an abstract ideal upon which he could project his hopes for a German revival. Spengler knew no Russian and cared little about the details of a land which for him symbolized a child, half-mystical, half-intuitive, endowed with a simple and deep wisdom from which the West could learn a great deal. Hesse saw Russia primarily through

[62] Thomas Mann, "Goethe und Tolstoi," *Deutsche Rundschau*, XLVIII, No. 6 (1922), p. 239; Lili Venohr, *Thomas Manns Verhältnis zur russischen Literatur* (Meisenheim/Glan, 1959), p. 40; Fritz Stern, *The Politics of Cultural Despair* (New York, 1965), pp. 302–310; H. S. Hughes, *Oswald Spengler* (New York, 1962), pp. 147–149; Hermann Hesse, "Die Brüder Karamasoff oder der Untergang Europas," in his *Gesammelte Schriften* (Berlin and Frankfort, 1957), pp. vii, 162.

314

Dostoevsky and described the typical Russian as the Karamazov of the East, "the coming man of the European crisis, already upon us," who could point the way toward a new world by throwing off the repressions of the old Europe, revealing unconscious and healthy animal instincts so long unrecognized or unaccepted.[63]

In Weimar Germany there was a "Dostoevsky epidemic," as El Lissitsky's wife described it, which rivaled even the prewar enthusiasm for his work. The great writer remained not simply a novelist but often the source of most Germans' knowledge of Russia itself. During World War I the earlier German picture of him as a religious thinker, psychologist, and Russian nationalist gave way to a new attitude. Dostoevsky now became the hero of the intellectuals' struggle against "bourgeois" Europe, the prophet of a "way out" of the European frame of reference after 1918 to "the East." Dostoevsky to many intellectuals symbolized the world beyond Europe's geographic and mental horizons: Russia, India, China, Buddhism, anthroposophy, occultism, spiritualism. The meaning of this enthusiasm was not lost on the Bolsheviks, and the Ladyzhnikov publishing house in Berlin brought out parallel Russian and German editions of his works. But the most popular interpretation of Dostoevsky in Germany remained that of Dmitrii Merezhkovsky: Dostoevsky was "choas," the irrationality of the human soul, the antithesis to the order, form, and repression of the West.[64]

The Russian emigration, like Russian literature and the revolution itself, helped heighten German interest in Russia throughout the Weimar years. For many Germans the émigrés were not considered political refugees but the cultural heritage of a cultural revolution. "Thus it turns out," wrote one German theater critic, "that all these Russians who have fled the revolution bring it to us. Not the political one! The revolution in art which we have felt for a decade in our bones has already been achieved in painting and the

---

[63] Stern, *Politics*, p. 302; Oswald Spengler, *Briefe, 1913–1936* (Munich, 1963), pp. 45, 55–56, 224, 231, 237; Hesse, "Karamasoff," p. 164. See also Hesse's "Gedanken zu Dostojewskij's 'Idiot,'" *Gesammelte Schriften*, pp. 178–186.

[64] Lissitzky-Küppers, *El Lissitzky*, p. 24; T. Kampmann, *Dostojewskij in Deutschland* (Munster, 1931), p. 114.

plastic arts." [65] In early 1922, when the first wave of intellectual émigrés arrived in Berlin, *Die neue Rundschau* began to publish a large number of stories and memoirs by émigré Russians in its pages, among them Ivan Bunin, the Scythian Alexander Shreider, Maxim Gorky, E. G. Lundberg, and Aleksei Remizov. That July they devoted an entire issue to Russia. Caught up in the German enthusiasm for Russia, many émigrés also began to sound the note of the "cultural" or "spiritual" meaning of the Russian Revolution. Emigrés and Germans thus encountered each other well prepared with preconceptions. Just as Thomas Mann expected and found in his émigré friends "sympathy, solidarity and a kind of utimate *Kamaraderie*," so the Russians found Germany to be in precisely that state of decline they had long anticipated.[66]

The Russians living in Germany and the German intellectuals interested in Russia helped reinforce in each other the feeling that 1917 represented a cultural, rather than a political, apocalypse. Hence Berdiaev, following a view long popular in Germany, announced solemnly that "he who understands Dostoevsky integrally has assimilated an essential part of the Russian soul and has read in part the mystery of Russia." To show that Russia was "a world apart, mysterious and unintelligible to the European," he cited a very un-Russian source: Oswald Spengler. It was not Marxism that had created the Russian Revolution, but Russia's uniqueness: "The geography of the land coincides with the geography of her soul, a symbolic expression of its spirit. The evenness, the unending distances, the indefiniteness of the features of the Russian earth embody the nature of the Russian man and typify similar qualities in his soul." [67]

Berdiaev's view was shared by other émigrés, most notably Fedor Stepun, who also admitted his debt to Spengler for the pic-

[65] *Augsburger Allgemeine Zeitung,* May 5, 1923, p. 5.

[66] Venohr, *Manns Verhältnis,* p. 32. Most of the stories and memoirs appeared in *Die neue Rundschau* between January 1922 and 1923, when émigré literary activity in Berlin was at its peak. See also Georg Wlassow, "Bolschewismus und Geisteskultur," *Deutsche Rundschau,* LI, No. 1 (1925), pp. 17–32, and Dmytro Donzow, "Die Grundlagen der russischen Kultur," *ibid.,* No. 2 (1925), pp. 7–20.

[67] Nikolai Berdiaev, *Dostoevsky* (New York, 1957), pp. 16, 19, 161–162.

ture of Russia as chaos, infinitude, holiness, and barbarism—qualities Spengler himself had originally borrowed from Dostoevsky.[68] The Russian emigration was no exception to the general rule that the relationship between Russian and German thought was not so much one of "influence" as of resonance.

The writers and philosophers of the emigration were translated into German and readily available to German audiences in the 1920's. Belyi, Berdiaev, Ehrenburg, Stepun, Bunin, Remizov, and others were all men whose ideas could be gleaned from their books. But for general commentary on the meaning of the Russian Revolution, German readers were often dependent on the more popular exegeses, anthologies, and essays turned out by émigrés who were as much a product of German life and culture as Russian. The most prolific writers on Russia in Germany in the 1920's were Karl Nötzel, Fedor Stepun, Alexander Eliasberg, Hermann Keyserling, Arthur Luther, and Elias Hurwicz. All of them were either of Russian-German or Jewish origin, had lived in Germany before the war, and had an excellent command of both languages. All of them also helped convey the sense of drama and tragedy of the emigration and the revolution to a German audience eager for Russian authenticity. Not Russians themselves, they became Russian experts, combining the experience in their old homeland with the language of their new one. Neither Russians nor Germans, they became important interpreters of Russia in Germany.

Karl Nötzel, a Balt, was particularly influential in this respect. Beginning in World War I, Nötzel poured out a stream of books on Russia, most of which saw the complex events of recent Russian history reflected in Russian literature, particularly the writings of Tolstoi and Dostoevsky. In his translation of Danilevsky's *Russia and Europe* (1920), a book whose historiosophic message promised a great role for Slavs and Russians in the final stage of history, Nötzel described the book as a "completely Russian" picture of the

[68] Fedor Stepun, *Das Antlitz Russlands und das Gesicht der Revolution* (Bern and Leipzig, 1934); Stepun cites Spengler's *Decline of the West*, Nötzel's *Die soziale Bewegung in Russland*, (Stuttgart, 1923), and E. Rosenstock's *Die europäischen Revolutionen, Volkscharaktere und Staatenbildung* (Jena, 1931).

West. The Russian people, Nötzel wrote, "is the most revolutionary because it was the most religious"; Russia's "cultural mission" has just begun, and Danilevsky's book was a part of that mission.[69] Russia was distinctly different from the West, having no deep philosophical tradition but endowed with a primitive religious consciousness that had been expressed in the great works of Russian literature. In this respect Dostoevsky was the typical Russian writer. The essence of the Bolshevik revolution was its non-Western emphasis on the collective over the individual, its *Gemeinschaftsleben,* and its roots in Russian religious life—a theme developed elsewhere by Berdiaev.[70]

Another émigré of Baltic German background, Fedor Stepun, was equally important (if not as prolific as Nötzel) as an interpreter of things Russian. While living in Dresden, Stepun gave hundreds of lectures in the 1920's to audiences in Germany, Austria, and Switzerland. In them he developed the theme that Bolshevism was simply an "aberration" or "pseudomorphosis," to use Spengler's term, of the religious energy of the Russian people which manifested itself alternatively in holiness or barbarism, submissive religiosity and destructive revolution. What was Lenin but another revolutionary priest in the spirit of Avvakum? Berdiaev was right to compare the apocalyptic beliefs of the Third Rome and the Third International. Since Bolshevism was a religious phenomenon, concluded Stepun, only a new religious spirit was capable of opposing and replacing it. This would be found in the true meaning of the "Russian soul": Christian truth, humanist freedom, and democratic socialism. Only a new generation of Russians, a postrevolutionary generation "united in guilt before God," could

[69] N. Danilewskij, *Russland und Europa* (Stuttgart and Berlin, 1920), pp. 327, 329. Among Nötzel's other works are: *Das heutige Russland* (2 vols.; Munich, 1915–1918), *Die Grundlagen des geistigen Russland* (Jena, 1917), *Tolstoi und wir* (Munich, 1919), *Der russische und der deutsche Geist* (1920), *Dostojewskij und wir* (1920), *Einfuhrung in den Sozialismus ohne Dogma* (1920), *Vom Umgang mit Russen* (1921), *Das Leben Dostoewskis* (1924), *Die soziale Bewegung in Russland* (Stuttgart, 1923). Nötzel also translated Dostoevsky's *Sämtliche Romane und Novellen* (Leipzig, 1921–1922). His almost mystical fascination with "the East" is still visible in his later *Östliche Weisheit* (Starnberg-am-See, 1947).

[70] Karl Nötzel, *Die russische Leistung* (Karlsruhe, 1927).

achieve any meaningful triumph over Bolshevism "on the spiritual level." [71]

Both Nötzel and Stepun thus passed along to German readers the view espoused by the émigrés in Berlin in 1922–1923 that the Russian Revolution was not a political but a cultural and even religious phenomenon which was historically unprecedented and culturally distinct from anything experienced in the West. If they did not simply reiterate Berdiaev's ideas, they at least expressed the mood which had nurtured his own writings in these years. Hermann Keyserling, the philospher and prewar Baltic German émigré, also continued to act as an oracle on Russian matters from his Wisdom School at Darmstadt. But his views on Russia were not nearly as positive as before the war: Bolshevism was a materialist and collectivist doctrine, a "gospel for the masses of the Orient"; European civilization had nurtured individualism, whereas "the chaotic soul of the Russian again and again limits itself by calling forth, and submitting to, dictatorships"; Russia was not a part of Europe, which accounted in part for the mutual attraction between "German intellectuality" and the Russian "breadth of soul"; for Keyserling what was best in Russian life was her Westernized intelligentsia, now represented in the "tremendous influence exerted on the whole of Europe by the Russian emigration, i.e., by that part of the Russian intelligentsia which has remained European." [72]

The "tremendous influence" of the Russian emigration in Germany, however, must be qualified in two ways. First, one cannot say that the émigrés "influenced" German public opinion in the sense that they provided some totally new message. What interested German intellectuals was not so much the emigration but Russian literature and the Russian Revolution. Indeed, in some cases German enthusiasm for Russia influenced the émigrés, rather than vice versa. The émigrés were not political refugees but Russians, and that was enough. They helped provide German intellectuals

[71] Fedor Stepun, "Das Bolschewistische Russland," *Hochland*, XXI (1924), 539; Stepun, *Antlitz*; Fred Höntsch, "Fedor Stepun—Ein Mittler zwischen Russland und Europa," *Hochland*, XXXIV (1936–1937), 189–200.

[72] Hermann Keyserling, *Europe* (New York, 1928), pp. 368, 386, and his *The Recovery of Truth* (New York, 1929), pp. 71, 218.

with weapons for flailing away at the corpse of bourgeois Europe. But in the end their portrait of Russia as a unique non-Western culture only helped deepen their isolation in Germany as "Easterners" living in "the West."

Second, one must add that only a few of the émigrés ever became well known interpreters of Russia in Germany, and these were mainly the older prewar émigrés, Baltic German and Jewish. In addition to Nötzel, Stepun, and Keyserling one must also mention the translator and editor Alexander Eliasberg, the *Osteuropa* editor Arthur Luther, and the writer on Russian matters for *Hochland* and *Neue Rundschau*, Elias Hurwicz. All of these men were "influential" in providing translations and interpretations of Russian works, in popularizing the ideas of the emigration, and in characterizing the Russian Revolution as a revolt against the West. They also helped make a crucial distinction between the political and cultural dimensions of the revolution. Russian art, literature, music, and religion still offered the West a new spirit in an age of decline, whatever one might think of the Bolsheviks. Politically the Russian Revolution meant a collectivist dictatorship; culturally it offered a new spiritual message to the West.[73]

In his epic novel *The Magic Mountain*, published in 1924, Thomas Mann brilliantly summed up the appeal of Russia and the

[73] Eliasberg was a well-known Jewish translator who had popularized Russian literature since before World War I; see his *Russische Lyrik der Gegenwart* (Munich, 1907), *Russische Kunst* (Munich, 1915), *Ostjüdische Novellen* (Munich, 1918), *Ostjüdische Volkslieder* (Munich, 1918), *Russische Baukunst* (Munich, 1922). He also arranged for introductions to his collections by Dmitrii Merezhkovsky (*Russische Literaturgeschichte in Einzelporträts*, Munich, 1922), Thomas Mann (*Bildergallerie zur russischen Literatur*, Munich, 1922), and Hermann Keyserling (*Der russische Christ: Eine Auswahl aus russischen Erzählern*, Munich, 1922).

Arthur Luther, a Russian German who had lectured at Moscow University before emigrating to Germany in 1914, also edited a group of Russian stories under the title of *Meisterwerke der russischen Bühne* (Leipzig, 1922). In the 1930's he served as the Russian correspondent for several German newspapers.

Hurwicz came to Germany in 1905 as a young Jewish student to study law and decided to remain. His memoirs appeared in *Hochland*, XLV (1952–1953), 446–454; LVI (1963–1964), 438–448; LVIII (1965–1966), 513–518. See also M. Körling, *Die literarische Arbeit der Zeitschrift "Hochland" von 1903 bis 1933* (Berlin, 1958).

Russian Revolution for German intellectuals in the 1920's. Committed to a Swiss sanatorium, Hans Castorp finds himself drawn to both the enthusiasm for progress and European civilization of the Italian humanist Settembrini and the barbaric yet alluring qualities of the Russian Clavdia Chaucat. For Settembrini the Russians in the sanatorium mean Asia, the Tatars, "wolves of the steppe, snow, vodka, the knout, Schlüsselburg, Holy Russia. They ought to set up an altar to Pallas Athene, here in the vestibule—to ward off the evil spell." He urges Castorp as a "son of the godlike West" to avoid contact with the "barbaric lavishness with time" of the Russians. "Great space, much time—they say, in fact, that they are the nation that has time and can wait. We Europeans, we cannot." Germany, he warns Castorp, "placed as she is between East and West," must make a choice between the two.

Castorp is unconvinced. He finds Clavdia Chaucat initially Asiatic, "Kirghiz-eyed," and tainted within, "habitually late to table, without reason or excuse, solely out of a lack of order and disciplined energy." Ultimately, however, Castorp succumbs to her seductive appeal and "relations with the slant-eyed sufferer went beyond the limits prescribed by the traditions of the Occident." He in effect turns his back on Western civilization for a love affair with Russia. "For love of her, in defiance of Herr Settembrini, I declared myself for the principle of unreason, the *spirituel* principle of disease, under whose aegis I had already, in reality, stood for a long time back."

The role of the Baltic Germans in the novel is to convey to Castorp some of the distant excitement of Russia itself. Frau Engelhardt, a schoolteacher, assures him that "Russian women all have something free and large about them" and that the typical Russian official "is a very rough type, I assure you. I once saw one of them, with an iron-grey beard and a red face—they are all frightfully corrupt too, and drink quantities of vodka, you know." His conversations with Anton Karlovich Ferge are even more rewarding:

His talk was devoid of the "higher things," but it was full of facts, and interesting to listen to, particularly for Hans Castorp, who found it profited him to hear about Russia and life as it was lived there: about samovars and pirogues, Cossacks, and wooden churches with so many towers shaped like onion-tops as to look like a whole colony of mush-rooms. He led Herr Ferge to talk about the people, the strange and exotic northern types, with their Asiatic tincture, the prominent cheek-bones and Finnish-Mongolian slant to the eye, listening with anthropo-logical interest to all that he heard. At his request, Herr Ferge spoke Russian to him; the outlandish, spineless, washed-out idiom came pour-ing from under the good-natured moustache, out of the good-natured Adam's apple; and Hans Castorp enjoyed it the more, youthlike, because all this was, pedagogically considered, forbidden fruit he was tasting.

Thus did Mann mirror the dilemma of the émigré intellectuals, whose appeal lay in the very Garden of Eden which had rejected them.[74]

The great paradox of émigré intellectual life in the 1920's was that contact with German culture did not lead to assimilation but to estrangement. Most of the German intellectuals who appealed to the Russians were also engaged in a war upon the West, and hence upon the very Europe in which the émigrés were forced to live. On the positive side, the romantic enthusiasm for Russia and the East only served to heighten the sense of cultural nationalism which made the Russians proud to be alone. In the end their contact with Germans deepened their sense of isolation from Ger-many.

Isolation

For most émigrés life in Germany produced neither the Russo-philia of those who rhapsodized about "the East" nor the anti-Bolshe-vism of the political right but simply isolation from both Russia and Germany. Until the late 1920's most émigré literature described the events in Russia of the stormy years before, during, and after the revolution. Within a few years, however, the endless agonizing over the spiritual sickness of the West and the vitality of Russian culture seemed to have reached an impasse. The Russian emigra-tion had no identity of its own outside of Soviet Russia or Germany. It was in danger of losing its language, its past, and its mind.

Many Russian exiles exhibited traits of other survivors of extreme

[74] Thomas Mann, *The Magic Mountain* (trans. H. T. Lowe-Porter, New York, 1948), pp. 137, 227, 241, 242–243, 311–312, 517, 554, 610.

situations in the twentieth century, among them concentration camp inmates and those who lived through the holocaust of Hiroshima. Having brushed close to death, they remained alive as members of a new community, the source of whose shared guilt was its very survival. Imagery involving a coming end of the world was persistent. Individuals withdrew from each other, began to think of themselves as objects and not as persons, and demonstrated a "pervasive tendency toward sluggish despair." [75] Amnesia, daydreaming, belief in hopeful fantasies followed by extreme depression, the loss of a sense of time—all characterized the so-called survivor complex. Many individuals "behaved as if their old environment simply had not disappeared. They fantasied themselves in their old situations." [76]

A Russian émigré who lived in Berlin was also struck by some of these qualities in the life of the colony. Wrote Nina Berberova:

Many times subsequently this "concept of survival" came to me in its most diverse aspects, bringing with it a whole rainbow of overtones: from the conception "not to be devoured" of a beast, to the ancient "self-affirmation in the face of destruction"; from the instinctive "not to be caught by the enemy" to the lofty "deliver oneself of the final Word."

Her own sense of time, she recalls, was disjointed. "Past and present interweave, fuse into one another, pour over into one another." In others she began to see a mood of endless despair and imminent catastrophe:

In different people in different ways there began to appear the sense of a possible end—not so much a personal one but a kind of collective abstract one, which, however, did not practically impede one's staying alive; not a *physical* end certainly because NEP continued to play its role and the "pinkish shade" appeared in faces here and there, but perhaps some spiritual end.

Nor for most Russians was there a way out by assimilating to German life. "The German Berlin," Berberova recalled, "was only the background for these years, sickly Germany, sickly money, the

---

[75] R. J. Lifton, *Death in Life: Survivors of Hiroshima* (New York, 1967), pp. 481, 494, 504.

[76] Bruno Bettelheim, *The Informed Heart* (Glenco, Ill., 1960), p. 201.

sickly trees of Tiergarten, where we sometimes strolled in the morning." [77]

One of the problems was that between the older generation, writing stories and memoirs about the past, and the younger generation, which had left Russia too early to carry as much of its culture with it, there was no writer capable of describing the world of Russian émigrés in the language of Russian literature. Then in 1929 such a writer made his appearance in the form of the thirty-year-old Vladimir Vladimirovich Nabokov. For Nabokov revealed in his writings not only his Russian past but his émigré present, the world of Russian Berlin:

The Potsdam square, always disfigured by city work (oh, those old postcards of it where everything is so spacious, with the droshki drivers looking so happy, and the trains of tight-belted ladies brushing the dust—but with the same fat flower girls). The pseudo-Parisian character of Unter-den-Linden. The narrowness of the commercial streets beyond it. Bridge, barge, sea gulls. The dead eyes of old hotels of the second, third, hundredth class.[78]

Nabokov himself claimed that while the subjects of all his stories were inevitably Russian émigrés, usually living in Germany, his work had no autobiographical or social significance; he might just as well have written about "Norwegians in Naples or Ambracians in Ambridge," since he was "merely using materials that happened to be near." [79] For the émigrés themselves, however, the appearance of Nabokov as a writer and chronicler of their own despair marked a new stage in the intellectual self-consciousness of the emigration.

The issue of Contemporary Annals, with the first chapters of The Defense, came out in 1929. I sat down to read these chapters, and read them twice. A tremendous, mature, sophisticated modern writer was before me; a great Russian writer, like a phoenix, was born from the fire and ashes of revolution and exile. Our existence from now on acquired a meaning. All my generation were justified. We were saved.[80]

The emigration had found its chronicler.

[77] Nina Berberova, The Italics are Mine, pp. 143–144, 154, 167.
[78] Vladimir Nabokov, The Gift (New York, 1963), pp. 370–371.
[79] Nabokov, The Eye (New York, 1965), p. viii.
[80] Berberova, Italics, p. 319.

Some remarks on Nabokov's own background are relevant here. Born in 1899 he came, like so many Berlin Russians, from the upper class of the old regime, the child of a wealthy family of liberal and Anglophile leanings but also of aristocratic lineage with a mixed Russian and Baltic German ancestry. His grandfather was Minister of Justice from 1878 to 1885, and his father was a leader of the Constitutional Democratic party and editor of the most important liberal newspaper in Russia, *Rech'*. On his mother's side he was descended from a branch of the Korff family, one of those myriad Baltic German clans which since the time of Peter the Great had provided civil and military service for the Russian government all out of proportion to their number.

To Nabokov's German ancestry was added an English upbringing. In his autobiography Nabokov stressed the Anglophile aspects of his childhood, and admitted that it was only during his years at Cambridge (1919–1922) that he began to become a "Russian" writer. He says he learned English before he learned Russian. Until 1914 Germany for Nabokov was a pleasant stopping-place on the way to the Riviera on the Nord-express, the "land of music" where one could roller skate near the Kurfürstendamm in Berlin, a country with orthodontists superior to those in St. Petersburg.[81]

Thus prior to his emigration Gemany assumed a dim but favorable locus in Nabokov's memory through his own ancestry and his several trips there. The "good" Germany predominated over the "bad." Nabokov's Germanophobia (even his recent and adulatory biographer Andrew Field admits that "it is a reasonable deduction that Vladimir Nabokov cannot be counted among the most fervent admirers of German civilization and culture")[82] was a consequence of his political emigration. As Nabokov tells us, his existence in Berlin in the 1920's and 1930's was an isolated one within the Russian community. He recalls making no more than two good friends among Germans and Frenchmen in these years and remembers the time as "an odd but by no means unpleasant existence, in material indigence and intellectual luxury, among perfectly unimportant

[81] Nabokov, *Speak, Memory* (New York, 1966), p. 205.

[82] Andrew Field, *Nabokov: His Life in Art* (Boston and Toronto, 1967), p. 205.

strangers, spectral Germans and Frenchmen in whose more or less illusory cities we, émigrés, happened to dwell." Yet although Germany remained relatively unknown to Nabokov ("no real communication, of the rich human sort so widespread in our own midst, existed between us and them"), he felt qualified in his autobiography to personify Germany not as a musician or philosopher but as "a young German university student, well-bred, quiet, bespectacled, whose hobby was capital punishment." [83]

The experience of two selves permeates Nabokov's own life: the Russian past of his childhood and the German present of emigration, the good Germany of his youth and the bad of his manhood, the creative artist and the constrained refugee. Even as a writer Nabokov chose to create another self in the form of his pseudonyms—Vasilii Shishkov, Cantab, F. G.-Ch., Vivian Calmbrood, Vivian Darkbloom, and Vladimir Sirin. It was under all these names that Nobokov's poetry, stories, and novels appeared in the pages of *Rul'*, *Sovremennye zapiski,* and other émigré journals. Supported by his writing and by tutoring young Germans in English and tennis, Nabokov passed his years in Berlin in admiration—as he playfully tells us in his autobiography—of that wonderful writer Sirin who startled the emigration with his brilliant works from 1925 to 1940 only then to vanish "as strangely as he had come." [84]

In what sense do Nabokov's writings mirror his own émigré environment and personal background? That Nabokov's own life and the life of the Russian emigration provide frequent themes and images in his novels and stories is not surprising. "While a man is writing," observes Hermann in *Despair,* a short novel written in 1932, "he is situated in some definite place; he is not simply a kind of spirit, hovering over the page." [85] Virtually every one of Nabokov's characters is an émigré living in Europe or the United States. More interesting, however, is the pervasive appearance of the "double" motif in Nabokov, not simply as a repetition of the old *Doppelgänger* tool of modern European and Russian literature, but as a

[83] Nabokov, *Speak, Memory,* pp. 276, 278–279.   [84] *Ibid.,* p. 287.
[85] Nabokov, *Despair* (New York, 1965), p. 53.

reflection of that essential duality suggested by the life of a Russian émigré in Germany.

Nabokov's own denial notwithstanding, the double theme is present throughout his writings.[86] Sebastian Knight's brother is engaged in an endless search for the man who, in the end, may be himself. Hermann Karlovich, the Russian émigré hero of *Despair*, has his German double, Felix, who may be his brother, or even his dead self—"the flawlessly pure image of my corpse"; the confusion increases when Hermann ostensibly kills Felix but Felix continues the narrative in the first person. The narrator of the story "Conversation Piece" (1945) has a double, a "very White" Russian émigré of the "automatically reactionary" variety. Even the lovable Pnin thinks he sees himself in another man. "What made Nabokov choose the theme of the Double as most congenial to the truths he wanted to dramatize?" asks a recent critic.[87] The two answers usually suggested are that the double is a standard literary device, employed by Dostoevsky among others, and that it reflects the sense of alienation from society experienced by artists and writers in general. The Russian emigration suggests still another answer.

The Baltic German, a figure prominent in Nabokov's own ancestry, is an important double both in the emigration and in Nabokov's work. Like many of Nabokov's characters, the Balts suffered from an identity crisis of their own. Were they Russians or Germans? Pnin has a Baltic German aunt, and Luzhin, the hero of *The Defense*, marries a Russian-German girl in Berlin. Hermann Ivanovich Busch in *The Gift* is "an elderly, shy, solidly built, likeable gentleman from Riga, with a head that looked like Beethoven's" whose "farcical accent and bizarre solecisms were incompatible with the obscurity of his meaning." [88] And Hermann in *Despair* is the mirror image of Nabokov himself, a Baltic German on his father's side and "pure Russian" on his mother's.

[86] "An Interview with Vladimir Nabokov," *Wisconsin Studies in Contemporary Literature*, VIII, No. 2 (Spring 1967), 145.

[87] Claire Rosenfield, "*Despair* and the Lust for Immortality," *ibid.*, p. 175.

[88] Nabokov, *The Gift*, pp. 78 ff.

More generally the double motif is visible in the contrast between the Russia of Nabokov's past and the Germany of his present. The nostalgia for prewar Russia which infuses *Speak, Memory* is matched by constant Germanophobia in his writings. In his masterful short novel *The Defense*, where life in emigration becomes a chess game whose only foolproof solution is death, grandmaster Luzhin is surrounded by Germans who are drunk, suffer from constipation, and have one-track minds. In his other writings they kill cats for fun, collect birds and butterflies, play sadistic pranks, and are stupid dreamers. In "Cloud, Castle, Lake" (1937), Nabokov created a terrifying tale of the torments experienced by a young Russian émigré on a camping trip with members of the Hitler Youth. In *The Gift* he writes of "the hopeless, godless vacancy of satisfied faces . . . that renowned German good-naturedness which can turn so easily at any moment into frenzied hooting." [89]

The "bad" Germany also has its double. The Germany of his youth recalled in *Speak, Memory* is in marked contrast to the harsh portrait of Weimar and the Third Reich; in the story "Mademoiselle O" (1942), Wiesbaden before 1914 is remembered as a "gay, populous" town. So, too, those spectral figures Nabokov rarely met but often created in emigration are contrasted with the Germans he had known as a child in Russia:

(By the way: what has happened to those originals who used to teach natural history to Russian children—green net, tin box on a sling, hat stuck with pinned butterflies, long, learned nose, candid eyes behind spectacles—where are they all, where are their frail skeletons—or was this a special breed of Germans, for export to Russia, or am I not looking properly?)

But the "good" Germany is fading into the past with the "good" Russia. In its place Nabokov creates largely from his imagination and isolation a Germany of his own mind:

Generally speaking I'd abandon tomorrow this country, oppressive as a headache—where everything is alien and repulsive to me, where a novel about incest or some brash trash, some cloyingly rhetorical, pseudobrutal tale about war is considered the crown of literature; where in fact there

[89] *Ibid.*, p. 348.

is no literature and hasn't been for a long time; where sticking out of the fog of a most monotonous democratic dampness—also pseudo—you have the same old jackboot and helmet.[90]

Yet the "bad" Germany Nabokov would abandon is a Germany he has created out of the bitterness of exile, not the memory of youth. It is also the land which fostered his father's murder and Adolf Hitler. But Nabokov can never leave his Germany, not only because of the "personal circumstances" to which he alludes, but also because it travels with him.

The Russian colony within which Nabokov lived is in still another sense the "bad" mirror image of a "good" Russia left behind. Right-wing émigré circles are one obvious target, a "sunset behind a cemetery," "ludicrous but vicious organizations" at whose annual meetings "a bearded old rascal in a shabby cutaway coat, former member of the Holy Russ First, would take the chair and vividly describe what the Israel-sons and the Phreemasons (two secret anti-Semitic tribes) were doing to the Russian people." [91] The left is equally suspect, not only the Mensheviks—"perpetual" émigrés "exiled by both the Tsar and the proletariat"—but also writers such as Andrei Belyi and Aleksei Tolstoi, considered by Nabokov to be simply "pro-Soviet" fellow travelers.[92] Even the émigré intelligentsia with its fetishism of publishing newspapers, books, "thick journals," and bad poetry comes in for acid criticism.

One question constantly recurs: Why does a Russian émigré with a great distaste for both Germany and the emigration remain for fifteen years in Berlin? Perhaps, like Fedor in *The Gift*, Nabokov found "wonderful solitude in this country, the wonderful beneficent contrast between my inner habitus and the terribly cold world around me" which enabled him to maintain his distance from both his German environment and the Russian colony in Paris. Nabokov himself admits that his years in Germany provided him with "absolute mental freedom" to write, but also with "a certain air of fragile unreality." In this way isolation gave him the

---

[90] *Ibid.*, pp. 114, 362.
[91] Nabokov, "The Assistant Producer" (1943) in *Nabokov's Dozen* (New York, 1958), pp. 56–57, 60–61.
[92] "An Interview," *Wisconsin Studies*, p. 147.

gift of recalling his Russian past in the mirror of his German present. Hermann Karlovich in *Despair* finds a German fishmonger whose name is identical with a Volga German he once knew, a house resembling one seen in a St. Petersburg suburb, a street lamp with the same number as one outside his apartment in Moscow. For a moment the Germany in which he resides becomes the Russia in which he still lives.[93] Has Hermann killed Felix or has Felix killed Hermann? Is it the Russian or the German double who has survived the despair of exile?

Vladimir Nabokov's hostility to both the new political Russia and his German cultural environment revealed the central intellectual and spiritual dilemma facing the Russian emigration to Germany. On the one hand, it had become difficult, if not impossible, to maintain a position of cultural enthusiasm for Russian thought and literature as "Eastern" spirituality without also losing one's political identity as a refugee from Bolshevism. On the other hand, political hostility to Bolshevism drew one easily into receptive German circles which were generally anti-Russian and endangered one's identity as a Russian. To assimilate culturally meant to move toward political acceptance of revolutionary Russia as well; to assimilate politically meant to forsake one's Russian background for German language and culture. Thus Russian intellectuals who joined their German brethren were generally treated as "red Russians" politically; those political groups, such as the Mensheviks, who moved easily in German political circles were no longer considered "Russians."

Those who, like Nabokov, isolated themselves under Weimar could continue to do so under the Nazis. Those who sought assimilation now had to reject both Russian culture and Soviet politics. Only the extreme political right and the Russian Germans found that choice possible, given the shift from the Russophilia of Weimar to the Russophobia of the Third Reich.

[93] *The Gift*, p. 362; *Speak, Memory*, p. 280; *Despair*, pp. 78–81.

⸺⁘ VIII ⁘⸺

The Third Kingdom

With the coming to power of Adolf Hitler in 1933 the story of the Russian emigration to Germany circles back to its pre-World War I origins. The vast majority of Russians now fled the country, and only a few thousand remained. The only politically significant émigrés in the Third Reich were the Russian Germans, whose unhappy fate in Russia since the 1880's had been so often reflected in their writings and activities in Germany. Like the Second Empire, the Third Reich created an atmosphere of Russophobia in which those Russian Germans hostile to their adopted country could play a considerable role. The Rosenbergs, Schickedanzes, and their friends had played a major part in stimulating Hitler's own picture of Russia as a weak and Asiatic land controlled by Jewish Bolsheviks. Now they appeared as experts and policy executors, no longer the dregs of an embittered political party in Munich but the advisers on Russian matters to a German government. It was a role that would have tragic consequences for both of their homelands. For four decades, as one Russian German himself observed in the wake of World War II, Germany had deluded itself into considering the Russians a mere paper tiger largely because it came to believe the picture of Russia brought into Germany by the Russian-German émigrés. The Russians were not only hostile, but weak. In 1941, as in 1914, Germany would make the fatal mistake of going to war against a people it considered hopelessly inferior. And once again it would suffer the consequences of defeat.[1]

"Coordination"

The few thousand Russians left in Berlin in the spring of 1933 greeted the coming to power of Adolf Hitler and the Nazi party with a mood of tentative acceptance. Most émigrés who disliked the Nazis had already fled the country; those who chose to remain were a mixture of old monarchists, second-generation Nazi sympathizers, Ukrainian nationalists, and army officers. Botkin's Vertrauenstelle sent its congratulations to the new Reichskanzler in the name of twenty-eight émigré organizations and assured him of its anti-Bolshevik sympathies in stemming the "Red Flood" in Germany.[2] A few dozen left-wing Russians were arrested for a time, and it was announced that all Russians must apply to the police or the Nansen Office for permission to reside in Germany. But fears of expulsion were dissipated for most when Botkin and Lampe called at the Wilhelmstrasse and were promised that there would be no major shift in the legal position of the émigrés.[3]

The political groupings among the émigrés after 1933 present a bewildering assortment of Russian and non-Russian circles. The older monarchists were generally supporters of the Grand Duke Kirill. Through Biskupsky, Kirill's representative in Germany, they also had connections with the much younger right-wing émigrés around Alexander Kazem-Bek's Young Russia movement (Mladorossy) both in Germany and abroad. There was also a local Russian Nazi organization, the Russian National Socialist Movement (ROND), and a branch of the All-Russian Fascist Party, centered in Harbin, China. The Russian All-Military Union (ROVS) of Lampe also still had its branch in Berlin, as did the National Union of the New Generation, or National Labor Alliance (NTS), as it later became known. In addition there were several Ukrainian groups: the republican followers of Petliura, the supporters of Hetman Skoropadsky, and the Ukrainian National Union (UNO) of Colonel Eugene Konovalec. All of these groups shared a distaste

---

[1] Arthur Just, *Russland in Europa* (Stuttgart, 1949), p. 40.
[2] *Nash vek*, No. 69 (1933), p. 1.   [3] *Vozrozhdenie*, June 6, 1933, p. 6.

for their rivals, a desire for Nazi largesse, and a fervent anti-Bolshevism.[4]

In the first months after the *Machtergreifung* the most notable feature on the émigré landscape was mutual hostility. Biskupsky's initial attempt to represent himself as leader of a united monarchist emigration that spring came to nothing; he spent several months in jail, before turning again to the Wilhelmstrasse and the Nazis in early 1934 without success. A pact between ROND and the Mladorossy in September 1933 proved short-lived. The church was divided into supporters of Bishop Tikhon in Berlin and Metropolitan Evlogy in Paris. The Young Russians were at odds with both the army ROVS and the older Supreme Monarchist Council in Paris. The All-Russian Fascist Party competed with a rival All-Russian Fascist Organization in the United States. The Ukrainians, too, were hopelessly divided into pro-German and pro-French factions, Hetmanites and Republicans.[5]

All of these groups lost no time in making known their desire to benefit from the new Germany. Both Biskupsky and his friend Peter Shabelsky-Bork assured the Wilhelmstrasse of their anti-Bolshevism and German loyalties. Supporters of the old Directory government of the Ukraine bombarded the Foreign Office with requests for money and memoranda directed against both the Hetmanite Ukrainians and the followers of Petliura. One of Avalov's officers suggested to both Göring and the Wilhelmstrasse that the émigrés might prove useful in organizing anti-Soviet terrorist activities. Finally, there was the memorandum of a "Dr. Caligula" in the name of the "Russian people" to Hitler himself which promised that the bulk of the Red Army was ready to revolt and the émigrés were in the process of forming a new Russian government.[6]

---

[4] Vasily Biskupsky, "Bericht über die russischen monarchistischen Organisationen in der Emigration," (October 18,1935) (Records, T-175, roll 58, folder 148); *Germania*, October 2, 1934, p. 5; *Chasovoi*, No. 114–115 (1933), p. 8.

[5] AGFM, T-120, roll 3553, 9461/E667438-449; Erwin Oberländer, "The All-Russian Fascist Party," *Journal of Contemporary History*, I (1966), 166–168.

[6] AGFM, T-120, roll 2987, 6678/H095405-558; AA IV Russland, Po. 2, Vol. 20, pp. 515–529 and Vol. 21, pp. 386–387.

At first the Nazis were not impressed. The Foreign Office continued to consider the émigrés a completely unreliable political entity. The pro-Nazi ROND was soon broken up by the police for its political activity, and a successor group, the Party of Russian Freedom Fighters led by Avalov, was also kept under Gestapo surveillance. In August 1933 a certain Dr. Müller in Chemnitz, a Nazi, wrote a long memorandum to the Foreign Office in which he warned that there would be "nothing worse for the German people" than to support anti-Soviet adventures by the émigrés and that "just as the Bolsheviks are generally hated by the Russian people, so the émigrés—above all the aristocracy, especially the Baltic Germans, former army officers, big capitalists and great landowners—are no less hated." Most German officials probably shared this view.[7]

In the winter of 1933–1934, however, the new men in the Nazi leadership decided that rather than ignore or suppress the Russians they would "coordinate" their activities. At worst, the party would at least be kept informed as to the political machinations within the émigré camp; at best, the émigrés might even prove useful. The two branches of the government assigned to this task were the Propaganda Ministry and the Nazi party's Foreign Policy Office.

Within these two branches of the government the problem of coordinating and controlling the activities of the various émigré organizations soon fell to a group of Russian Germans who had found their way into the Nazi party in the 1920's. Foremost among them was Alfred Rosenberg. In the late 1920's he had continued to propound his Jewish-Bolshevik conspiracy theories in the pages of *Völkischer Beobachter* and his monumental, if unread, *Myth of the Twentieth Century*. Now he was given the post of chief of the party's Foreign Policy Office, from which he continued to put forth his anti-Soviet views in the 1930's. Rosenberg brought with him his old schoolboy friend and fellow anti-Semite, Arno Schickedanz, a man given more to intrigue than to originality of thought

7 AGFM, T-120, rolls 2987 and 3553, *loc. cit.;* report of the Bavarian Gestapo of May 11, 1934, typescript in the Institut für Zeitgeschichte, Munich; AA IV Russland, Po. 2, Vol. 19 (May–August 1933), p. 408.

who characterized the Jews as a "bastardizing herd" in his *Jewry as an Anti-Race* (1927). These two Balts were joined by a Black Sea German from Odessa, Georg Leibbrandt, head of the "eastern section" (Amt Osten) of Rosenberg's Office. A student in Dorpat during World War I, Leibbrandt had enlisted in the German army in 1918 and spent the 1920's in German, English, and American universities before returning to Germany in 1933.[8]

Rosenberg had his rivals. The Propaganda Ministry, headed by Joseph Goebbels, was also interested in making use of the anti-Bolshevik émigrés as propagandists, and one of Goebbels' assistants, Dr. Eberhart Taubert, was especially intrigued by this possibility. Shortly after Hitler's seizure of power Taubert revived the idea, popular in the party a year earlier, of organizing an anti-Communist "united front" of émigré and German organizations to do battle with Bolshevism. To this end he enlisted the services of two other Russian Germans: Adolf Ehrt, a Mennonite anti-Communist writer for the Deutsche Hochschule für Politik and the Evangelical church; and Ewald Ammende, a Baltic German émigré active in *Auslandsdeutschen* circles and later general secretary of the European Congress of Nationalities. During the winter of 1933–1934 Ehrt was put in charge of what Taubert called the Union of German Anti-Communist Societies (Gesamtverband Deutscher Antikommunistischer Vereinigungen), later abbreviated to Anti-Comintern. It was this organization which fought with Rosenberg's Foreign Policy Office for control of the affairs of those Russian émigrés whom they never really believed or trusted, but could not ignore.[9]

The rivalry between the two branches of Nazi propaganda was continuous from the beginning. First there were the bad feelings caused when an employee of Taubert's approached Amt Osten in

[8] Alexander Dallin, *German Rule in Russia, 1941–1945* (London, 1957), pp. 86–89; *Deutsche Post aus dem Osten,* XIV, No. 6 (June 1942), 25.

[9] "Querschnitt durch die Tätigkeit des Arbeitsgebietes Dr. Taubert (Antibolschewismus) des RMVP bis zum 31.12.1944," a Gestapo report on Taubert in the Yivo Institute for Jewish Research, New York. Also Records, T-81, roll 14, EAP 250-d-18-15/5 on Ehrt and *Deutsche Post aus dem Osten,* VIII, No. 5 (May 1936), 1–2 on Ammende. See also Walter Laqueur, *Russia and Germany* (London, 1965), pp. 176–195.

November 1933 urging a great propaganda effort among non-Russians and complaining that Taubert's plans for Anti-Comintern would not prove very effective. Then there was the continuing struggle for control over émigré activities, such as the publishing of the Russian-language newspaper *Novoe slovo* (*The New Word*). Finally, there was an ongoing personal clash between Leibbrandt at Amt Osten and Taubert at Anti-Comintern which was reflected in the in-house correspondence of Rosenberg's Office. It was a story of institutional rivalry and personal intrigue not unknown in other branches of the Third Reich.[10]

The jealousies of Amt Osten and Anti-Comintern can hardly be said to have stemmed from a great concern with the émigrés themselves. If anything, the Nazis looked on them as more of a nuisance than an ally. Hitler himself had never had much use for the right-wing Russians and Ukrainians who flocked to his side in Munich in the early 1920's, and in October 1934 the Reichskanzlei let Amt Osten know that the Führer was generally against "overestimating the political influence of émigrés." The attitude of Leibbrandt was not dissimilar: as long as the émigrés stayed out of mischief and worked "quietly" they were tolerated; on the other hand the Foreign Policy Office had "no interest in furthering or rejuvenating émigré organizations." In private Amt Osten characterized émigré political circles as "not worth much" and warned that "one must be very careful in dealing with them." [11]

Despite this cynical attitude both organizations spent an enormous amount of time hiring émigrés for propaganda work and keeping generally informed on the very Russians they held in such low esteem. Among the employees of Amt Osten were Harald Siewert, another of Rosenberg's Baltic boyhood chums; the Georgian émigré forger Alexander Nikuradze; Nikolai Talberg, a former member of the Supreme Monarchist Council who was now the Berlin correspondent for the Paris journal *Vozrozhdenie;* and the eminent Turkologist Gerhard von Mende who had his own

---

[10] Records, T-81, roll 11, *Aktennotiz* November 27, 1933 and Amt Osten *"Im Hause"* report dated August 25, 1936.

[11] Reichskanzlei to Amt Osten, October 16, 1935, and June 11, 1936 (Records, T-81, roll 11).

flock of Turkestani, Georgian, and Ukrainian assistants. A number of émigrés wrote for the propaganda mill of Anti-Comintern. Others were employed part-time as lecturers and experts in Rosenberg's anti-Bolshevik Foreign Policy School and at Ehrt's seminar at the Deutsche Hochschule für Politik. For every émigré employed, there were several others desperate for the income that a book, translation, or report might bring.

What were the ideas put forth in the writings of these organizations in the 1930's? Basically they were no more than a vicious and sensational updating of the old anti-Bolshevik accounts with which the émigrés had flooded Germany in the early 1920's. Most popular were Jewish conspiracy books, accounts by Russian Germans of Soviet brutality, and the fresher revelations of recent Soviet defectors. Ehrt led the way with several books which demonstrated clearly that all violence in Weimar Germany had been perpetrated by communists and socialists, that behind the "Bolshevik danger" lay the Jews and the Freemasons, and that the greatest danger to society lay in the infernal machinations of Stalin's Comintern.[12] Long reports were prepared for Anti-Comintern by its Russian specialists showing that the Soviet Academy of Sciences was run by Jews, that the origins of Bolshevism could be deduced from Dostoevsky's *The Possessed,* that no more and no less than 41,962,500 people in Russia and Europe had been killed by Bolsheviks since 1917, that the Bolsheviks were secretly in alliance with the Anglo-American plutocracy, and that the Russian revolutionary movement before 1917 was also dominated by the Jews.[13] Rudolf Kommoss, a German imprisoned in Russia for a time in the 1930's, gained fame with his *The Jews Behind Stalin* (1938), and the legal expert Reinhard Maurach defended the idea of the Pale of Settlement and promised that the "solution of the Jewish problem" in Europe was now in its "decisive phase." [14] Finally, the journal

---

[12] Adolf Ehrt, *Entfessellung der Unterwelt* (Berlin and Leipzig, 1932), *Bewaffneter Aufstand!* (Berlin, 1933), *Terror: Die Blutchronik des Marxismus in Deutschland* (Berlin and Leipzig, 1934).

[13] A, Groups I, II, and IIIb.

[14] See the articles by Maurach on Russian Jewry in *Volk und Reich,* November 1939, pp. 809–819 and *Der Weltkampf,* November 1939, pp. 469–475.

Contra-Komintern featured the latest anti-Bolshevik eyewitness accounts by escaped ship captains and defectors, as well as the usual anti-Soviet and anti-Semitic essays by other émigrés.[15] Through all of these channels the bitter recriminations of the Russians found their way into the wheels of the Nazi propaganda machine.

Most of the work of Anti-Comintern was directed toward German and other European audiences, utilizing the testimony of the émigrés as ammunition for its anti-Soviet artillery. In addition, the right-wing émigrés could also be counted on to authenticate the old story about the connections between the Russian Revolution and the Jews. An interesting example of the manner in which the Nazis made use of the Russians in the 1930's is the case of the *Protocols of the Elders of Zion,* the old Russian anti-Semitic forgery brought into Germany in the early 1920's by the émigrés. In 1934 in connection with the "trial" of the *Protocols* in Berne it was one of Adolf Ehrt's publishing operations, the anti-Semitic Weltdienst, run by a retired German Lieutenant Colonel Ulrich Fleischauer in Erfurt, which was asked to organize the defense. The logical "witnesses" were the Russian émigrés.

The Boris Tödtli Caper

The *Protocols* came under public scrutiny in the 1930's when a right-wing Swiss nationalist organization known as the National Front began distributing copies during a demonstration in Berne in June 1933.[16] A group of leading Swiss Jews promptly filed suit against the distributors, contending that the document describing a Jewish plot to take over the world fell under the ban on "indecent writings." When the court convened in October 1934 the plaintiffs had marshaled an impressive array of witnesses, including Chaim Weizmann, Vladimir Burtsev, and Boris Nicolaevsky, while the

---

[15] Typical articles in *Contra-Komintern* include: Bishop Seraphim, "Das religiöse Leben und die Christen Verfolgungen in der Sowjetunion," July 1937, pp. 151–166; Gerhard von Mende, "Der Bolschewismus und die Nationen in der UdSSR," January 1938, pp. 16–25; Yury Solonevich, "Zwangsarbeitslager im Lande der Illusionen," June 1938, pp. 241–246. The journal ran from April 1937 to December 1939 and was edited by Nils von Bahr, a Swedish army officer who had lived in Petrograd for a time in 1918.

[16] Norman Cohn, *Warrant for Genocide* (London, 1968), pp. 220–231.

defense had found not a single "expert" to defend the document's authenticity. For this reason the court adjourned until April 1935.

In November 1934, Ulrich von Roll, the gauleiter for Berne of the National Front, took the fateful step of appealing to the Nazi Brown House in Munich for aid in the defense of the *Protocols*. This decision led to the involvement of Fleischauer and his Weltdienst, which ultimately spent some 30,000 Reichsmarks on the trial. Von Roll, however, was soon disenchanted with Fleischauer's insistence that he subordinate his Swiss interests to those of the Third Reich. Looking for someone more pliable, Fleischauer discovered one of Von Roll's deputies in the Berne National Front, a man peculiarly suited to arrange for the defense of the *Protocols*: Boris Tödtli.

Like Rosenberg and Scheubner-Richter, Boris Tödtli was a man of two worlds, Russian and German, who could move with relative ease from the exotic politics of the emigration to the bureaucratic machinery of the Nazi party and back. Born in 1901 in Kiev of Swiss parents, Tödtli had just completed his first two terms as a medical student when the March revolution broke out. He volunteered for the White armies, was commissioned in the field, and in October 1919 lost his hearing as the result of a bomb explosion. Taken prisoner by the Red Army near the Rumanian border in early 1920, Tödtli contracted typhus and was sent to a hospital in Odessa. Afterwards, he lived with his parents until, in January 1922, he joined the ranks of the Russian emigration.[17]

As an embittered ex-officer with no trade skills, Tödtli wandered from one menial job to another in the 1920's. In 1923 he studied photography in Zurich, where he worked for two years before moving on to Paris, Geneva, Lausanne, and, finally in 1932, to Berne. There he became a dental technician. Until 1933, when he joined Von Roll's National Front, Tödtli apparently did not engage in any political activity. It was only in that year that this

---

[17] Biographical information on Tödtli comes from his two depositions before the Berne police of November 24, 1936, and February 26, 1937, TC, and the extensive summary of his background in FC, folder 6, entitled "Abschriften aus Hauptdossier: Bericht der Bundesanwaltschaft, Abhörungen Tödtli."

nondescript Russian émigré found a home in the Nazi movement and that his bilingual fluency and anti-Semitism made him a useful go-between for Russians and Germans.

When he joined the National Front, Tödtli began to establish contacts with Russian right-wing circles. In June 1933 the ROND group in Berlin gave Tödtli the high-sounding title "Leader of the Russian National Socialists in Switzerland," and it may have been through this channel that copies of the *Protocols* became available to the National Front for distribution. Approached by Markov II of *Weltdienst* in November 1934 to help arrange the defense of the *Protocols* in court, he immediately appointed himself "Chief of the Swiss Section of the Russian Imperial Union" and dispatched letters to dozens of right-wing exiles asking for expertise and testimony at the trial. By October 1935, Tödtli had dreams of being the head of an all-European Russian fascist party, and yet was still new enough at the game of politics to greet a personal letter from the Reichskanzlei with childish glee.

As far as the *Protocols* were concerned, Tödtli's efforts were not rewarded. It was not that his correspondents were not willing. ROND's publicly stated purpose was "to open the eyes of all our brothers to the true enemy," the Jews, and it defended the authenticity of the *Protocols* in the press.[18] Markov II, in his Jew-baiting *Zhidoved*, urged all "national-thinking" Russian émigrés to work for Russia's "emancipation from the Jewish-Masonic Comintern yoke."[19] Yet while correspondents such as General Krasnov, the former "Eurasian" N. N. Alekseev, and N. D. Zhevakov, the biographer of the *Protocols'* author Sergei Nilus, agreed on the authenticity of the *Protocols,* they balked at coming to Berne to testify unless supplied with money and visas, which Tödtli was unable to procure from his Weltdienst bosses.[20] More precisely, the 4,000 Reichsmarks it gave Tödtli in 1935 were apparently spent primarily on the latter's own personal and political needs. In the end

[18] *Deviatyi val'*, June and October 1935.

[19] *Zhidoved*, No. 1 (September 1935), p. 1.

[20] See the letters to Tödtli from Krasnov and Markov II, November 4, 1934; from Alekseev, November 13; and from Zhevakov, December 18 (FC, folder 1).

only Fleischauer was called to testify before the court, and his Russian witnesses never appeared.

More important for Tödtli, the trial had only whetted his political and financial appetite. As a result, he became so closely associated with the Russian émigrés and the Nazi bureaucracy that in November 1936 the Berne police arrested him and charged him under Article II of the Swiss Espionage Act of June 21, 1935. It was alleged that Tödtli, by his acceptance of funds from Fleischauer's Weltdienst, had in fact become a paid agent of the German government. Other political activities that the Berne police discovered in his correspondence with Russian émigrés were equally incriminating.

With respect to the Nazis, Tödtli apparently made the mistake of looking for support from two hostile camps within the German bureaucracy: Goebbels' Propaganda Ministry and Rosenberg's Foreign Policy Office. His relations with the former were established through Fleischauer, who after the trial asked Tödtli to handle the book distribution of the U. Bodung Verlag in Switzerland. Finding the income from this activity insufficient for his needs, Tödtli in the summer of 1935 took on the additional task of spying (for Rosenberg) on German émigrés in Berne. The intermediary in this case was Harald Siewert, a friend of Rosenberg who specialized in peddling forged documents to the German government in the 1920's.[21] Unfortunately for Tödtli, Siewert was not only unable to keep his promise of financial backing and of a personal meeting with Rosenberg, but Tödtli himself was naïve enough to inform Fleischauer of his new friends and potential supporters.[22] In addition he used his Weltdienst income to send his wife and child on a five-week vacation in Bavaria. Despite protestations to Fleischauer that he was a loyal agent of the Third Reich, Tödtli's intrigues made it quite unlikely by 1936 that he could count on German sympathy in the event of trouble with the Swiss authorities. He had made himself expendable.

[21] A. Norden, *Fälscher* (Berlin, 1959), pp. 122, 151, 159–162.

[22] See Tödtli's letters in TC of July 15, 1935 (to Fleischauer) and of August 26, 1935 (to his friend De Poterre) in which he mentions plans to visit Siewert and Rosenberg in Berlin and Siewert's promises that money was forthcoming.

That the Nazis kept Tödtli on their payroll as long as they did was probably due to the extensive anti-communist campaign launched by Goebbels in connection with the Anti-Comintern Pact (November 1936) and the outbreak of the Spanish Civil War. However politically inept the Russian émigrés might be, they retained a certain propaganda value as anti-Soviet experts and Goebbels planned to display several of them at the Nuremberg party rally in September.[23] Thus when, in April 1936, K. V. Rodzaevsky named Tödtli the "European leader" of the All-Russian Fascist Party he probably contributed unconsciously to Tödtli's political longevity among the Nazis.

It would appear that both Nazi friends and such foes as the Jewish Central Information Office in Amsterdam vastly overestimated the importance of Tödtli's activities and Russian connections. The letters confiscated by the Swiss police seemed to reveal a vast, international anti-Semitic network. They included grandiloquent instructions from Tödtli to K. P. Kondirev, head of the Russian Fascists in Bulgaria: "Your assignment is to gather reports and information concerning everyone who plays a role in the emigration and is close to the Jews and Freemasons." [24] Behind the ostensible "intelligence reports" from the Soviet Union, plans to send volunteers to Franco, and talk of an army of Russian Fascist supporters in Sofia, Paris, Harbin, Constantinople, and Warsaw lay a much more prosaic and pathetic fantasy world of embittered émigrés. Rodzaevsky's very appointment of Tödtli as his man in Europe was most probably part of the internecine feud with Vonsiatsky over control of the tiny Russian Fascist movement; the supposedly top-secret correspondence consists largely of insignificant exchanges: Tödtli promises Rodzaevsky that he will send material on Vonsiatsky to the Gestapo; he claims 2,500 "true friends of Germany" within the Russian diaspora; he sends a complimentary copy of Streicher's *Stürmer* to Harbin and receives in return a copy of *Nash put'*.[25]

[23] Z. A. B. Zeman, *Nazi Propaganda* (London, 1964), pp. 92–95.
[24] Tödtli to Kondirev, May 2, 1936 (TC).
[25] Tödtli to Rashchev, June 3, 1936, and to Peter Shabelsky-Bork, June 24, 1936 (TC).

It Tödtli's correspondence has a central theme, it is money. The Russian Fascists, he wrote in June 1936, should have close ties to Germany and establish a headquarters near Munich. The Propaganda Ministry, he promised, "will help us." [26] Two months later he was complaining that the Rodzaevsky party had given him no funds and warning that "we cannot remain independent for we are poor. The only hope is support from Germany." [27] For Tödtli, as for so many unfortunate émigrés, politics was often a function of indigence.

Tödtli's political naïveté became clear in his depositions before the Swiss police following his arrest in the autumn of 1936. On the one hand, he did not conceal the fact that his bitter experiences in Russia had drawn him into the politics of anti-Semitism. "I am an anti-Semite from personal experience," he told the police; "I sympathize with the NSDAP and the present German regime in general because I am a fanatic opponent of Bolshevism and Judaism, which in my opinion are responsible for the present world crisis." [28] On the other hand, Tödtli viewed anti-Semitism as revealed truth rather than as political expediency. He maintained throughout that his anti-Semitism and his "work against Bolshevism" were "nonpolitical" good works, and that Anti-Comintern and Weltdienst were international vigilante organizations rather than cogs in the Nazi bureaucratic machinery.

In part this was simply a defense against the charge of being a German agent, an accusation easily substantiated by his correspondence with Fleischauer. But it also reflected the general clumsiness of Tödtli's political behavior at every turn, which made him disappear from the political scene as rapidly as he had emerged. In 1937 he was sentenced to two months in prison, but fled to Germany. In May 1938, as the representative of Russian Fascists at a "unity" meeting of various right-wing Russian groups in Berlin, including ROND, ROVS, and NTS, Tödtli made his last appearance on the stage of émigré politics.[29] With the signing of

---

[26] Tödtli to Harbin, June 3, 1936 (TC).
[27] Tödtli to I. V. Richkov, Belgrade, August 3, 1936 (TC).
[28] Berne police depositions (TC).
[29] *Deutsche Post aus dem Osten*, X, No. 6/7 (June/July 1938).

the Ribbentrop Pact between Germany and the Soviet Union, the Russian exiles became a political liability for the Third Reich, and in December 1939 Tödtli was extradited to Switzerland, where he was promptly imprisoned. He died during the Second World War.

Tödtli was hardly a significant political figure, and yet his case is an interesting one. Like many other émigrés, businessmen, anti-Semites, and conservatives he made the mistake of thinking he could use the Nazis as they had used him. Indeed, for a time they gave him some badly needed money and prestige. Ultimately he was able to match their cynical anti-Semitism, but not their political acumen.

"The New Word" and General Biskupsky

Besides contributing to the Nazis' propaganda operations, the émigrés had one of their own directed at the colony itself. Like most supposedly "Russian" institutions and organizations, the newspaper *Novoe slovo* (The New Word) was firmly under the control of the Germans, at first through Anti-Comintern and later through Amt Osten. As such it served not only as the one newspaper of the Russian colony in the 1930's, but also as a means of disseminating Nazi propaganda within the emigration. Control of the paper therefore exacerbated and reflected the internal political squabbles of both the Nazi bureaucracy and the émigrés themselves.

The first issue of *Novoe slovo* in May 1933 pronounced its goal to be "a new free Russia" and added that "the enemy of yesterday—Germany—will be the best friend of tomorrow." The Young Russians were said to have ties with the Hitler movement dating back to 1923, the ROND movement was warmly applauded, and Colonel Avalov emerged from obscurity to declare that "we will succeed in overcoming the moral factionalism of the émigrés and in organizing them for a successful struggle to liberate the homeland." [30] During the next year the émigrés managed only two more issues of the paper, in which they made the usual optimistic claims that the Soviet Union was undergoing an economic crisis which would lead to a popular uprising, that Hitler was the "new great unifier" of the

[30] *Novoe slovo: Russkaia natsional'naia gazeta*, 1933, No. 1, p. 2.

anti-Bolshevik struggle, that Grand Duke Kirill was the legitimate heir to the Romanov throne, and that the future rulers of Russia would govern according to the principles of "recognition of the family, authority, hierarchy, and labor." [31]

Until the summer of 1934 *Novoe slovo* struggled along as the very occasional newspaper of the colony, whose vaguely monarchist or fascist views it reflected. Then on August 1, 1934, its fourth issue came out under the editorship of an old Baltic German Free Corps officer, Nikolai Hoerschelmann, and the paper became a regular biweekly. The real power behind it, however, was Anti-Comintern, whose man on the spot was the editor of a German-language supplement, Rudolf Kommoss. Kommoss had joined the Nazi party in 1932 and left for a trip to the Soviet Union shortly thereafter for study and travel. Arrested by the secret police, he spent his time in jail learning Russian and returned to Germany a professional anti-Bolshevik. It was through the bilingual facility of Hoerschelmann and Kommoss that the Nazis took over the financial and editorial responsibility of *Novoe slovo*. Then in September 1934 they added to the editorial board a Russian émigré of Greek origin, Vladimir Despotuli. It was under Despotuli that *Novoe slovo* became the willing anti-Semitic mouthpiece of the Nazis within the Russian colony.[32]

The message of *Novoe slovo* was not very distinct from the earlier rantings of the émigré right or the contemporary viciousness of Anti-Comintern. In reply to the Soviet embassy's formal protest against the paper as an "anti-Soviet" operation, Hoerschelmann promised that "our newspaper . . . does not have either a direct or an indirect relationship to the 'Russian National Socialists' (ROND) but is strictly a non-party organ" and Kommoss added that "we are fighting not against the Soviet Union but against the Communist International, which for us is the mortal enemy of all nations." [33] (The latter distinction would have greatly amused Stalin.) *Novoe slovo* frankly admitted its function as an anti-

[31] *Novoe slovo*, 1933, Nos. 2 and 3.
[32] Records, T-81, roll 14, EAP 250-d-18-10/11-13 and T-454, roll 86, frames 331–334.
[33] *Novoe slovo*, 1934, No. 5, p. 1.

communist propaganda organ, a function which some hoped would extend beyond the ranks of the emigration to the Soviet Union itself. As such the paper soon broke with the older generation of monarchists and White army officers. "The new generation," wrote Despotuli, "does not dream of liberating the homeland with foreign support"; the "White idea" was dead, stabbed in the back by the old "toothless governors" and pensioners now sunning themselves on the Riviera or the Adriatic, and must be replaced by "young forces." [34] Who these "young forces" were was never made clear, however, since Kazem-Bek's Young Russians were described as "children" who "think and spread rumors like old men." [35]

Many émigrés naturally accepted *Novoe slovo* for what it was—a "Hitlerite Russian organ"—and Despotuli's claim that it was "independent" never held water. For a time, however, in 1934–1935, its pages were enlivened by some interesting views of a right-wing journalist named I. I. Kolyshko who wrote variously under the names of Baian, Sovremennik, and N. Ermakov. Russia, he wrote, was a country with two wills, one Eastern and the other Western, Asiatic and European, whose main gift was its culture, a spiritual heritage which must in the future be re-established. The value of National Socialism in Germany was that it represented a kind of religious revival in the tradition of the Reformation, a "national religious mission" against the "irreligious domination of the world" by the Jews. This might be possible in Russia too, since the spiritual forces of the people had changed little in recent years despite the modernizing efforts of both the Imperial and Soviet government. What distinguished Kolyshko from so many writers on the right was that he saw in the Nazis not simply another anti-Bolshevik force for intervention but a model for a new nationalism. By the summer of 1935, however, his articles had disappeared from the pages of *Novoe slovo*, which devoted itself more and more to anti-Semitism.[36]

In late 1936 *Novoe slovo* was taken over from Anti-Comintern by Rosenberg's Foreign Policy Office and its Amt Osten. Leibbrandt was quite proud of the fact that the paper was now "under

[34] *Novoe slovo,* 1934, No. 10, p. 1.   [35] *Novoe slovo,* 1935, No. 8, p. 1.
[36] *Novoe slovo,* 1935, Nos. 3, 8, 14, 19, 24.

our political leadership" and succeeded in procuring the necessary funds from Rosenberg to operate it. Despotuli retained his position as editor, although in the late 1930's he was challenged by General Biskupsky, since 1936 the head of the official émigré Vertrauenstelle and ever eager for new intrigues. Biskupsky had approached both Taubert and Leibbrandt in the winter of 1937–1938 for funds and the editorship of *Novoe slovo* and had received vague promises of support from both rival organizations independently. In February 1938, however, Biskupsky was called into Taubert's office and told that he would receive help from neither and that Despotuli would remain editor.[37] In the final analysis it was not émigré intrigue but the Ribbentrop Pact which ended the career of Despotuli and his newspaper. For a time he had enjoyed Nazi largesse and public display at Nuremberg party rallies as a suitably anti-Soviet émigré; now the Nazi-Soviet agreement made him superfluous and inconvenient. In September 1940 the career of the newspaper which critical émigrés called "a German newspaper in Russian" came to an end. Despotuli's charges that Biskupsky was a Soviet secret agent did not revive it.[38]

Just as they had established firm control over the émigré press in these years, the Nazis kept a watchful eye on the church and the "official" organizations of the colony. The leading Orthodox churchman in Germany, Bishop Tikhon, had for some years supported the Paris diocese of Evlogy, and most priests in Germany followed suit. When Tikhon later turned away to join the more reactionary Balkan churchmen centered in Sremtsy Karlovtsy, he caused a split in the ranks of the Russian Orthodox church in Germany. Like every other political and social group in the emigration, the church was deeply split when the Nazis came to power. Not surprisingly the Germans decided to enforce support of the Sremtsy Karlovtsy church in a decree of October 28, 1935, which defined a new diocese. The "Russian Orthodox Diocese" in Germany was

37 Records, T-454, roll 86, frames 520–526; Amt Osten Aktennotiz (Schickedanz), August 22, 1939.

38 Amt Osten "*Im Hause*" reports of December 21, 1936, and January 27, 1937, and letters of Leibbrandt to Rosenberg, September 1, 1938, February 7, 1940, and June 6, 1940 (Records, T-81, roll 11).

now headed by a new bishop, Seraphim, a member of the Karlovtsy synod, who held forth from the new church on the Hohenzollerndamm in Wilmersdorf, a Berlin suburb. Although the émigrés were allowed to pursue their own religion in relative peace, the political limits of the church were now clarified by the strident anti-Bolshevik and anti-Semitic statements of its leaders.[39]

Similarly, the Nazis soon ousted older and more reasonable men such as Botkin from the émigré Vertrauenstelle and installed more pliable anti-Semites in their place. It was in this manner that Biskupsky finally emerged as nominal representative of the Russian colony in Germany. In October 1935 Biskupsky submitted a long report on the politics of the Russian émigré monarchists, naturally emphasizing the importance and legitimacy of Kirill's supporters, to the Nazis. He also enclosed various documents, such as letters from Kirill praising Biskupsky for his good works and some reminders of the good old days in Munich when Kirill and Scheubner-Richter had rendered financial aid to the party. To the dismay of many other émigrés, Biskupsky finally succeeded in May 1936 in getting himself appointed head of the Vertrauenstelle, assisted by none other than the murderer of Vladimir Nabokov, Sergei Taboritsky. It was from this new position that Biskupsky embarked on yet another series of intrigues.[40]

The Nazis viewed Biskupsky's position as harmless. He would issue a few identity cards, shuffle papers, and have "no political assignment," according to the Gestapo.[41] But the Germans underestimated the wily general. What Biskupsky now attempted to achieve over the next three years was no less than the recovery of what he claimed was a longstanding debt owed the Russian émigrés by the Nazi party for the money provided in the lean years before the 1923 Beer Hall Putsch. And as with most cases of émigré attempts to use the Nazis as they were using the Russians, he failed.

In the autumn of 1936 Biskupsky learned that the Mendelsohn

[39] W. Haugg, "Die Orthodoxe Kirche des Ostens in Deutschland," *Kyrios,* 1939/1940, No. 1, pp. 57–67.

[40] Biskupsky, "Bericht."

[41] Gestapo circular dated July 7, 1936 (Records, T-175, roll 423, frames 951216–7).

Bank in Berlin held an account valued at nearly 200,000 Reichsmarks in the name of Nicholas II. Whether the account belonged to the now nonexistent Russian crown or to the Romanov family personally was a thorny legal question. Opened in the summer of 1905 as protection against the revolutionary events of that year, the "Caisse du Ministére de la Cour Impériale de Russie" was a logical attraction for émigré intrigue after 1917. As the Mendelsohn directors themselves admitted, its current ownership was unclear. Biskupsky was promised fifteen per cent of whatever he could recover by Grand Duke Kirill in 1936, but had to contend with at least two other rivals—the Soviet government and Mrs. Tschaikovsky (Anastasia), now living in the United States and represented by a lawyer-friend of Scheubner-Richter, Paul Leverkuehn. Biskupsky, like most émigrés, lacked money; the Romanov account offered precisely that.[42]

Biskupsky lost no time in this matter. On May 17, 1936, he wrote the Reichskanzlei requesting an interview with Hitler, a request which he was forced to repeat one month later. On November 12 he was granted a half-hour interview, probably through the mediation of Harald Siewert, but no commitment. Not to be discouraged, he then turned to the SS some months later requesting Himmler to use his influence in the matter; it would mean for Biskupsky and his family, he noted, "a great lightening of our émigré burden." Once again he found no satisfaction. In 1938 Biskupsky's quest was further complicated by the death of his benefactor, Kirill, which was quickly followed by the appearance of both the Soviet government and Mrs. Tschaikovsky as rival claimants. But a Nazi court found none of these claims convincing, despite Biskupsky's attempt to produce Kirill's son Vladimir as the legal heir to the Romanov estate. After all, said Himmler, Vladimir lived in France, and Germany could use the money herself; when Biskupsky tried to arrange for him to move to Germany, moreover, Nazi Foreign Minister Ribbentrop refused on the grounds that it would mean more political trouble from the émigrés.

[42] The account of the intrigue surrounding the Mendelsohn money is taken from the material contained in the Records, T-81, roll 10, frames 18270–18317 and T-175, roll 58, frames 373958–374019.

Shortly after the German attack on Poland in the autumn of 1939 Biskupsky made one last attempt to obtain the money. This time he tried Arno Schickedanz at Amt Osten. His argument was that the Nazis were obliged to repay to the Russian émigrés, in particular to Kirill's supporters, the money provided by Kirill in Munich in the early 1920's:

Here I must note that the Grand Duke Kirill Vladimirovich and his wife gave General Ludendorff a sum of nearly half a million gold marks in 1922–1923 for German-Russian national matters. On the basis of the treaty of May 12, 1922, which I concluded with General Ludendorff at that time, he promised to repay this money at the first opportunity. But his plans were shattered and the money was lost.[43]

But the Nazis were not known for remembering past services rendered from any of the many political supporters they had cultivated over the years. Biskupsky was no exception. The money remained at Mendelsohn, and Biskupsky himself disappeared from sight during the war, possibly a victim of the Gestapo. Like the Tödtli affair, Biskupsky's futile attempts to lay claim to the Romanov bank account only revealed again that the Nazis were not about to be duped by the émigrés they were using.

The Russian Germans

The Nazis also kept lines of communication open with the non-Russian émigrés in the 1930's, particularly the Ukrainians, Georgians, and Russian Germans. The idea of using the anti-Russian sentiments of the non-Russian borderlands against their central government, of course, was an old German scheme dating back before the First World War. Under Weimar the Wilhelmstrasse had also kept open channels to the non-Russian émigrés, always skeptical of their political future but thoroughly informed as to their activities. In the late 1920's German intelligence circles in the Reichswehr had even allowed the formation of the Ukrainian Military Organization of Colonel Eugene Konovalec, a Ukrainian émigré paramilitary force whose aim was to conduct terrorist activity

---

[43] Biskupsky to Schickedanz, October 23, 1939 (Records, T-81, roll 10).

against the Polish government.[44] The Nazis maintained relations with Konovalec and his subsequent Organization of Ukrainian Nationalists (OUN) throughout the 1930's through the new intelligence organization of Admiral Canaris, the Abwehr. At first they also considered the hetmanite followers of Skoropadsky and miscellaneous Ukrainian adventurers such as Poltavets-Ostranitsa to be subordinate to the new OUN, preferring to deal with the younger and more militant Ukrainian nationalists rather than the older émigrés. The theory was that in the event of war with Poland the émigré Ukrainians might well prove useful as both a military and a political force.

Otherwise the small Ukrainian colony in Germany did not appear to be very useful. Poltavets-Ostranitsa amused himself by writing a book proving that the Ukrainians were descendants of the Iranians and tried to get money out of Amt Osten by claiming that Skoropadsky and his followers were really Freemasons. Roman Smal-Stocki, the head of the republican movement in exile, moved to Berlin from Warsaw in 1936, but the long-standing ties of the Petliura movement to Poland and France made him appear less than reliable. Skoropadsky and his Union of Hetmanites struggled along with occasional subsidies, but held little political promise. Then there was the Ukrainian Scientific Institute, a collection of scholars and students that Gerhard von Mende tried to turn into an anti-Polish propaganda institute for Amt Osten while keeping it out of the hands of Skoropadsky's supporters. Other than passing numerous books, pamphlets, and clippings on to Leibbrandt, however, the Institute could offer little in return for its subsidies. In general, the Ukrainians slipped into the background in the 1930's until the Blitzkrieg against Poland again reminded their German sponsors of their potential utility.[45]

The exception was Skoropadsky, whom the Germans subsidized

[44] Dallin, *German Rule*, pp. 114–115; J. Lipski, *Diplomat in Berlin, 1933–1939* (New York and London, 1968), pp. 135–142.

[45] *Chasovoi*, No. 114–115 (1933), p. 8; Records, T-81, roll 11, EAP 250-4-18-05/4 and roll 15, folder 9; the correspondence of Amt Osten officials with the Ukrainian Scientific Institute is contained in T-81, roll 16, flash 2 for the period 1932–1941.

as the only sufficiently pro-German Ukrainian leader. Since 1927 Skoropadsky had received an annual subsidy of 12,000 Reichsmarks from the Reichspräsident's "dispositional fund," although his request in 1935 that the Wilhelmstrasse provide him with 10,000 Reichsmarks per month was rejected. In general the Germans followed the activities of the hetman and his family closely (such as his son Daniel's visit to Canada and the U.S. in 1937) but gave him only funds sufficient for his personal needs. With the outbreak of the war even Skoropadsky was largely ignored by his eminently practical sponsors.[46]

The Georgians fared as poorly as the Ukrainians. In Warsaw there was a diverse group known as the Prometheus Society united around the Menshevik leader Zhordaniia, which was all too clearly supported by the Poles and the French and was, as the Wilhelmstrasse observed, "in no way friendly to National Socialism." Its rival in Paris, a group of Georgians and Armenians around the journal *Le Caucase,* was far more sympathetic to the Nazis. But even this circle received only verbal support from Germany. Eager to take advantage of the anti-Soviet mood of the non-Russian nationalities, the Germans again found no single group worth serious consideration.[47]

The Russian Germans, in contrast to the other non-Russian nationalities, had established themselves as a political lobby long before the Nazis came to power in Germany. In the wake of the First World War a bewildering number of different organizations had appeared: Johannes Schleuning's Union of Volga Germans (1918), Theodor Hümmel's Union of Caucasus Germans (1918), Adolf Eichler's Union of Germans from Congress Poland (1919), the Union of Colonists and other Germans from North Russia (1919), the Union of Black Sea Colonists (1920), the Union of German Volhynians, and the Union of Germans from Moscow and St. Petersburg. In the early 1920's the functions of these groups

[46] AA IV Russland, Po. 11 (Ukraine), Vol. 3 especially Kiewitz to State Secretary, January 20, 1935.

[47] August 10, 1937, report on the Prometheus Society (AA IV Russland, Po. 26 (Ukraine), Vol. 1, October 1936–December 1937); report of General Kwinitadze dated October 6, 1941 (Records, T-454, roll 16).

were mainly limited to caring for Russian German émigrés in Germany, arranging for aid to relatives inside Soviet Russia, and organizing further migration from Germany to North and South America. It was only in the 1930's that the value of the Russian Germans as embittered anti-Soviet critics became apparent.

In contrast to the Russian émigrés, the Russian Germans managed to unify themselves reasonably well in the 1920's. The first unity group established in 1919—the Committee of German Groups from Old Russia—soon broke up into factions in a manner typical of the émigrés in general.[48] But in the spring of 1921 a congress of Russian-German groups in Stuttgart under the sponsorship of the Deutsche Auslandsinstitut succeeded in forming a Central Committee of Germans from Russia to coordinate the welfare work of the various individual organizations. In the following years this Committee guided the resettlement of Russian Germans in Canada, the United States, and South America and kept alive the memories of home in such journals as *Heimkehr*, the *Wolgadeutsche Monatshefte*, and its own organ *Deutsches Leben in Russland*.[49]

The Russian Germans soon found fertile soil in Germany, thanks to the prewar publicity given them by Balts such as Schiemann, Rohrbach, and Alfred Geiser. In addition, there had been attempts to resettle Russian-German families in Prussian Poland before the war. But it was the war itself which succeeded in driving so many Russian Germans back to their ethnic homeland; thousands of them arrived as refugees in 1918–1919 with the encouragement of the Germans themselves, who had enthusiastically publicized their ties to the motherland in areas under German occupation. Those Russian Germans used by the German army for wartime propaganda, such as Georg Cleinow and Adolf Eichler, found it a simple matter to continue their agitation in the interests of *"Russlanddeutschtum"* in Germany as well. Eichler, a Polish-German journalist from Lodz, and Johannes Schleuning, a minister from Tiflis, were particularly influential in organizing relief work during the famine of 1922 through the Union for Germans Abroad and resettlement to the

---

[48] Adolf Eichler, *Deutschtum im Schatten des Ostens* (Dresden, 1942), pp. 437–440.

[49] *Der Auslanddeutsche*, X (1927), 463–464.

Americas in the mid-1920's.[50] In Germany, as in Russia, they remained firm supporters of the interests of Russian Germans.

By 1925 about half of the Russian Germans who had fled to Germany after the war had moved on. The German census of that year listed a total of about 58,000: 35,000 Volhynian Germans, 10,000 Polish Germans, 5,000 Baltic Germans, 2,000 Black Sea and Volga Germans, 5,000 Moscow and St. Petersburg Germans, and 400 Germans from the Caucasus.[51] By this time the Russian Germans thus constituted an inordinately large proportion of the "Russian" emigration still in Germany, perhaps as much as one quarter of the whole. For the Russian Germans, cultural assimilation was easy and the German government solicitous. To cultivate German public opinion further the Russian-German Committee established in 1925 its own journal, *Deutsche Post aus dem Osten,* edited by Eichler. This journal carried news of the fate of Russian Germans in Russia and the diaspora in the 1920's and 1930's, and later became a Nazi organ. Throughout these years it featured a strident German nationalism, constant attention to the plight of its Russian-German constituency, and an outspoken condemnation of the Soviet regime. Nobody more than the Russian Germans, wrote Eichler, "recognized the primary danger which an expanding Communism represented to the German people and they know best the means Moscow employed in order to lead Bolshevism to victory in the Reich." [52]

Besides Eichler, a number of other Russian Germans worked for the *Deutsche Post aus dem Osten:* Carlo von Kügelgen, the son of the former editor of the German-language *St. Petersburger Zeitung* who later continued his activity under the aegis of Anti-Comintern; [53] Georg Löbsack, a Volga German active in relief work and journalism; B. H. Unruh, a Mennonite leader; Karl Stumpp, in

[50] Carlo von Kügelgen, "Adolf Eichler und das Russlanddeutschtum," *Deutsche Post aus dem Osten,* XIV, No. 2 (February 1942), pp. 6–9.

[51] Otto Kredel, "Die Russlanddeutschen im Reich," *Der Auslanddeutsche,* X (1927), 175–176.

[52] Adolf Eichler, "Russlanddeutsche im Reich," *Der Wanderweg der Russlanddeutschen* (Stuttgart and Berlin, 1939), p. 271.

[53] *Deutsche Post aus dem Osten,* XIII, No. 11 (November 1941), pp. 1–2; XIV, No. 4 (April 1942), pp. 20–23.

charge of Russian-German matters at the Deutsche Auslands-institut; and Axel Schmidt, a Baltic German historian. This group of men, along with such well known Baltic German publicists as Paul Rohrbach and Max Boehm, continued to keep alive in Weimar Germany the consciousness of a German island in a Russian sea.

In 1929–1930 a new wave of Russian-German refugees emigrated from the Soviet Union in flight from the terrors of collectivization. If anything, they were more bitter than their predecessors and would provide a series of anti-Bolshevik witnesses for the Nazis a few years later. Faced with the grain collection campaign, new taxes, and compulsory entry into collective farms, thousands of Russian-German peasants fled toward Moscow in the autumn of 1929 seeking permission to leave the country. During the winter of 1929–1930 several thousand of them were living outside the city in wretched conditions. Faced with mounting pressure from official circles and public opinion in Germany, the Soviet government finally agreed to permit a number of them to emigrate.[54]

The leader of the German campaign to help the Russian-German colonists was Otto Auhagen, the agricultural attaché at the German embassy in Moscow and later director of the Osteuropa Institute in Breslau. Auhagen believed that as long as the Bolsheviks ruled Russia the very existence of Russia's German peasant minority was in jeopardy, a point which he made in a telegram to the Wilhelmstrasse in November 1929. In the following months Auhagen sent to Berlin a stream of reports emphasizing the desperate position of the German farmers and their families, the terror, the deportations of suspected kulaks, and the growing desire for emigration to Canada or elsewhere, a virtual *Auswanderungsfieber*. It was partly through Auhagen's campaign that the first relief measures were instituted in Germany.[55]

The great German *Hilfsaktion* that winter involved both public

[54] Otto Auhagen, *Die Schicksalwende des Russlanddeutschen Bauerntums in den Jahren 1927–1930* (Leipzig, 1942). The diplomatic correspondence relating to the Russian-German migration of 1929–1930 is in AA IV Russland, ORuss, Vol. 24.

[55] Auhagen, *Schicksalwende*, pp. 78, 139–140; on Auhagen see also the short biography in *Deutsche Post aus dem Osten*, XI, No. 10–11 (October/November 1939), p. 23.

and private circles. The Foreign Office procured the necessary passports for emigration, President Hindenburg donated some 200,000 marks from his discretionary fund, and additional material support was provided by labor, business, religious, and Red Cross organizations. The various Russian-German and *Auslandsdeutschen* groups were also naturally involved in the campaign. As a result some 5,700 refugees were brought to Germany in December 1929 in two transport ships, and another 1,000 over the next two years.[56] Here they were placed in camps in Prussia, Hamburg, and Holstein for a few months until the necessary health and passport documents could be obtained for the journey to North and South America. Most of the émigrés passed through Germany in this manner. But others, impressed by the warm welcome offered by Russian-German leaders, decided to stay.[57]

Thus German sympathies for the Russian Germans and hatred for the government that had mistreated them were well established even before the Nazis came to power. As early as 1918 men like Johannes Schleuning were speaking out in public on the plight of their countrymen and the need for German support. Some of their works, like Karl Lindemann's report of his 1919–1921 trip through the towns of South Russia, were sensible first-hand accounts of life in Russia under the Bolsheviks. But in general there was a persistent nostalgia and German nationalism in the writings of the Russian Germans which later, with Nazi encouragement, turned all too easily into a harsher anti-Bolshevism and anti-Semitism. In the summer of 1930 Botkin noted in his last report to Giers that the new wave of German colonists coming from Russia had helped effect a shift in public opinion to an increasingly hostile view of Soviet Russia.[58] For the moment the plight of the Russian Germans was dramatized by influential opinion-makers in Germany, among them Auhagen and Otto Hoetzsch of the Osteuropa Institute and Georg Cleinow. But soon the Russian Germans began to tell their own story: *Pictures from Soviet Russia* (1930) and

[56] H. J. Willms, ed., *At the Gates of Moscow* (Yarrow, B.C., Canada, 1964), pp. 102, 138.

[57] "Russlanddeutsche Bauern auf der Wanderung," *Der Auslanddeutsche,* XII (1929), 776–779, 822–823.

[58] Botkin to Giers, August 20, 1930 (BA/RD, folder 60).

My Flight (1931) by the Mennonite refugee Abraham Kroeker, and the trilogy of Volga German life by Josef Ponten appeared at the same time.[59] Such books described the trials and tribulations of Russia's German colonists over the past fifty years, of which collectivization was only the most recent example. The Mennonites were the children of God, suffering the torments of the Soviet Hell, persecuted by the Devil through his Bolshevik agents. The Russian-German colonies had been the most orderly and productive in Russia; now they had been destroyed by a new government devoted to the destruction of both private property and religion. The bitterness of the Russian Germans was understandable; so too was the Nazi discovery of a German-speaking reservoir of anti-Bolshevik émigrés willing to serve as propagandists for the Third Reich.

The Russian Germans thus filtered easily into positions of responsibility after 1933 in every area of German life related to Russia. The activity of individuals in Rosenberg's Amt Osten and Anti-Comintern as anti-Soviet propagandists is one obvious example. In addition, the Nazis continued to use Russian Germans as intermediaries in posts in Russia: the military attaché Ernst Köstring, the commercial counselor Gustav Hilger, and two Baltic German journalists, Klaus Mehnert and Arthur Just.[60] These men, however, were educated and intelligent people from the Baltic or from Moscow and Petersburg. On most issues they appeared as "Easterners," interested in preserving the tenuous ties between two societies indulging in mutual hatred and moderating the anti-Soviet campaign at home. But the Russian-German colonists were an entirely different breed, men of lower-middle-class or peasant origin, far more hostile to Bolshevism, and useful to the Nazis not as intermediaries but as propagandists. Through Ehrt and Leibbrandt, in cooperation with the Russian-German leaders, the Nazis found it a relatively easy matter after 1933 to enroll this group in its service.

[59] Abraham Kroeker, *Bilder aus Sowjetrussland* (Striegau, 1930), *Meine Flucht* (Striegau, 1931); Josef Ponten, *Wolga Wolga* (Berlin and Leipzig, 1930), *Rhein und Wolga* (Stuttgart and Berlin, 1931), *Im Wolgaland* (Stuttgart and Berlin, 1933).

[60] H. Teske, ed., *General Ernst Köstring* (Frankfort-on-the-Main, 1966); Dallin, *German Rule*, p. 6; H. von Dirksen, *Moscow, Tokyo, London* (Norman, Okla., 1952), pp. 120–123.

A number of Russian Germans simply joined the Nazis as individuals: Guida Diehl became the head of the nationalist women's group Neuland Haus and then a leader of the Nazi women's movement; Herbert Backe, a German from the Caucasus, joined the Nazis in the early 1920's and later represented them in the Prussian Landtag and as director of the Food Ministry of the Ministry of Agriculture during the war; Adrian von Renteln, a Balt, was a Reichsführer of the Hitler Youth; through Leibbrandt and Ehrt a number also found temporary service as writers or secretaries in Amt Osten and Anti-Comintern. But the Nazis also faced the problem of coordinating the activities of the many Russian-German organizations, which they did by creating a new group known as the Union of Germans from Russia (Verband für Deutschen aus Russland), or VDR.

The VDR was founded in 1935 under the nominal leadership of Adolf Frasch. In fact it was a project of Leibbrandt at Amt Osten. Its functions were twofold: first, to unite the various Russian-German groups under a single head responsible to the German government and, second, to provide a political weapon for pro-Nazi agitation among the Russian-German colonies in other lands, particularly North and South America. Subsidized variously by Amt Osten, the Foreign Office, and Anti-Comintern, the VDR was conceived by Rosenberg as a frankly "political" organization to enroll the multilingual Russian Germans in various Nazi propaganda activities at home and abroad.[61] To this end the VDR took over the *Deutsche Post aus dem Osten* and, with Nazi subsidies, made it into the chief organ of the Russian Germans under the editorship of Carlo von Kügelgen.

Many of the Russian-German journalists continued to write for *Deutsche Post*—among them Kügelgen, Georg Löbsack, Axel Schmidt, B. H. Unruh, and Hans Rempel—but with a substantially more vicious message appropriate to their new masters. The familiar themes now began to appear in its pages: Bolshevism was a "Tatar Empire," a form of "Asiatic-Muscovite Marxism under Jewish

[61] Aktennotizen of Amt Osten, December 11, 1935, and February 5, 1937, and Rosenberg memorandum of September 28, 1935 (Records, T-81, roll 11, EAP 250-4-18-05/4-5).

leadership," in contrast to the Nazis who were the defenders of European civilization against "Asian and African bastardizing." [62] Scheubner-Richter was fondly remembered as one of the first Russian Germans to join the Nazi party, and the occupation of the Sudetenland in 1938 was greeted with enthusiasm. The Russian Germans, wrote Harald Siewert, have not only found a "new homeland" in Germany, but have helped enlighten the Germans as to the dangers of Bolshevism, Judaism, and Freemasonry. In the future they would help the Germans engage in "cultural work" in a new Russia freed from the communist yoke. [63]

Another organization interested in the fate of the Russian Germans was the Deutsche Auslandsinstitut in Stuttgart. The head of its Russian-German section, Karl Stumpp, edited books and pamphlets in the 1930's on the life of the colonies in Russia and conducted research to demonstrate the "Aryan" origin of particular individuals. He also made attempts to solicit additional funds for welfare work among the Russian-German émigrés, most of whom by the late 1930's had scattered to the Americas. There was naturally a certain rivalry between Frasch and Stumpp over refugee work, part of the usual bureaucratic feuding over the control of émigré affairs in general. In July 1938 the VDR and the Auslandsinstitut signed an agreement to cooperate in Russian-German matters in an attempt to overcome the "differences of opinion" between the two groups. But they continued to pursue their political and welfare activities more or less independently. [64]

Much of the work of the Russian Germans in the 1930's was simply devoted to the well-being of the widely scattered émigrés. But no single group was more numerous in the various areas of the Nazi bureaucracy where anti-Bolshevism was being cultivated. Deeply embittered by their treatment at the hands of the Soviet government and capable of rapid assimilation into German life, the Russian Germans found it all too easy to shift their allegiances and develop their anti-Bolshevism into a marketable commodity.

[62] *Deutsche Post aus dem Osten*, IX, No. 5 (May 1937), p. 4.

[63] *Ibid.*, XI, No. 2/3 (February/March 1939), pp. 24–27; X, No. 11 (November 1938), pp. 1–2; XI, No. 6/7 (June/July 1939), pp. 25–27.

[64] DAI, folders 45, 207, 1128, and 1146. Also available on film in Records, T-81.

In the summer of 1939 the careful Nazi cultivation of the Russian emigration came to an abrupt end with the signing of the Ribbentrop Pact between Germany and the USSR. Until this time the émigrés had been useful to a certain degree as anti-Bolshevik spokesmen; now they were a definite political liability standing in the way of smooth Soviet-German relations during the occupation of Poland, the war in the West, and the Battle of Britain. Only with the German attack on the Soviet Union on June 22, 1941, did they re-emerge to play a role in wartime policy.

Immediately after the attack on Poland in September 1939 émigré activity in Germany was severely curtailed. *Novoe slovo* was closed down within a few months. A Gestapo circular of October 25 concerning the "Russian, Ukrainian, Cossack, and Caucasus Emigration in the Reich" announced that the Ribbentrop Pact now meant that émigré activity—anti-Soviet polemics, public meetings, marches, and demonstrations—must be "sharply limited." This was essentially Nazi policy until the outbreak of war with the Soviet Union in 1941. The membership in émigré clubs and organizations was limited to stateless persons and forbidden to German citizens. The émigré press was muzzled and the wearing of uniforms or carrying of flags prohibited. As late as June 1941 official policy was that the "present political situation" made any émigré political activity dangerous to the preservation of Soviet-German relations.[65]

The non-Russian émigrés found life equally difficult. *Deutsche Post aus dem Osten* was closed down for a time, and Adolf Frasch and the VDR found it increasingly difficult to procure funds for the Russian Germans, even though the Nazis allowed German colonists living in occupied Poland to "return" to Germany. The Ukrainians fared somewhat better. Skoropadsky continued to receive a subsidy from Rosenberg's Amt Osten during these months, Admiral Canaris' Abwehr still cultivated the more radical nationalist leaders of the OUN, and Leibbrandt arranged for the release of a number of Ukrainian émigré leaders from Gestapo jails in the

---

[65] Records, T-175, roll 424, 952916-9; June 20, 1941, report of the *Reichssicherheitshauptamt* (Institut für Zeitgeschichte, Munich: Document Fa 506/11, pp. 207–212).

winter of 1939–1940. But it was only when preparations for Operation Barbarossa were well under way in the spring of 1941 that the Ukrainians were able to continue their anti-Soviet activities under German guidance and with German support.[66]

It was the German attack on the Soviet Union which made the émigrés useful again. Despite an official ban by Alfred Rosenberg's Ostministerium, the main civil administrative body for areas of the Soviet Union under German occupation, émigrés from Paris, Berlin, and Warsaw continued to drift back toward their homeland to find service with the Germans as doctors, engineers, translators, and in other lesser official posts. The Russian-German coterie around Rosenberg, notably Leibbrandt, Schickedanz, and von Mende, now became the key administrators for the eastern territories. Finally, there was a series of attempts to use émigrés and war prisoners in military detachments available for service on the eastern front, first with the shadow OUN formations organized by Canaris and later with the army of Soviet prisoners under the captured General Vlasov.

Few of the older generation of Russian émigrés played any role at all in German policy during World War II. Most Russians involved in the Vlasov movement were either second-generation émigrés in organizations such as the NTS or Russian war prisoners converted to the new anti-Soviet campaign. The only group trusted by the Nazis with positions of responsibility were the Russian Germans, and only through them could other émigrés expect aid and comfort. This was true not only of the Ostministerium but of the Vlasov army as well. The most important Russian German associated with Vlasov was Wilfried Strik-Strikfeldt, a Moscow German in charge of the main camp for Soviet prisoners at Dabendorf.[67] Other Russian Germans involved were Nikolai von Grote, a Baltic German who headed the army Aktivpropaganda Ost section; Ernst

---

[66] *Deutsche Post aus dem Osten,* XI, No. 12 (December 1939), pp. 1–4; on Skoropadsky see Document NG 3055 of the Institut für Zeitgeschichte, Munich; the difficulties of the Russian Germans are described in DAI, folder 1127.

[67] George Fischer, *Soviet Opposition to Stalin: A Case Study in World War II* (Cambridge, Mass., 1952), pp. 76–77. On the Vlasov movement see also Gerald Reitlinger, *The House Built on Sand* (London, 1960) and Dallin, *German Rule.*

Köstring, appointed "General for the Caucasus" in 1942 where he organized a detachment of Georgian war prisoners; Gustav Hilger, who returned from Moscow in 1941 and became the Foreign Office liaison with the Vlasov movement; and Gerhard von Mende of the Ostministerium, who maintained the closest ties to the non-Russian émigrés, particularly those from Georgia and Turkestan.[68] Indeed it was the presence of so many Russian Germans which gave an anti-Russian, rather than anti-Soviet tone, to so many German operations during the war and produced deep rivalries with Himmler's SS over questions of policy in the East.

In the end both the Vlasov movement and the various schemes of the older generation of émigré Russians came to little. Krasnov's Central Cossack Office in Berlin, the Ukrainian National Committee of Paul Shandruk, and other similar organizations of Belorussian and Georgian émigrés and war prisoners were largely paper operations, never trusted by the Nazis as capable of any real contribution to the military effort in the East. A small group of Turkestani and Azerbaijani prisoners did actually fight as part of the 162nd Turk Infantry, and a number of Cossacks were enrolled in the XV Cavalry Corps of the SS.[69] But this was all. Vlasov, like Krasnov, saw action with his troops only at the very end of the war and was captured near Prague by the American army and turned over to the Russians for trial and execution. Like a generation of German officials before them, the Nazis permitted their émigré Russians a freedom of action sufficient to raise their hopes of an eventual non-Soviet Russia but not sufficient to contribute to German policy-making with respect to Russia. By 1945, if not by 1941, the role of the older generation of émigrés was over, and a second wave of wartime refugees from the Soviet Union had initiated a new phase in the story of Russians in Germany.

In Nazi Germany only a few of the most embittered Russian émigrés could find life palatable. The organizations and way of life of the old emigration collapsed with the *Machtergreifung*, and what remained was subsumed under German control. Most attempts by

[68] Jürgen Thorwald, *Wenn Sie verderben wollen* (Stuttgart, 1952), pp. 82–83, 89–92, 106–107, 111, 158, 344, 406.
[69] Fischer, *Opposition*, pp. 48–49.

the émigrés to use the Nazis ended in failure; most attempts by the Nazis to use the émigrés ended in confusion. Anti-Semitism and anti-Bolshevism were obviously useful to the Germans in giving a certain tone of authenticity to their propaganda. But only the Russian Germans, particularly the Balts, were trusted enough to find positions of responsibility and influence in the Third Reich. Their ability to assimilate gave them a distinct advantage over their Russian countrymen. More fateful, it enabled them to pass on to Germans the view that the Soviet Union was not only hostile but inferior. If they did not create this view in Germany, they nurtured and legitimized it.

⸺⊶⟨ IX ⟩⊷⸺

The Legacy

Historians have too long neglected the social and cultural side of the Russian Revolution in favor of its more obvious political and economic aspects. This is not surprising in view of the paucity or scattered nature of the sources, the concerns and origins of the Soviet leadership, and the traditions of Western scholarship. Seen as a seizure of power by an elite of Russian Marxists who subsequently industrialized the country, the revolution is impressive enough as a major upheaval in a century visited by mass tragedies in so many forms. But its meaning runs deeper.

What a study of the Russian emigration reveals is that the revolution also suggested a dramatic change in human values. For many contemporaries it was not simply a Marxist *coup d'état* but a fundamental break with bourgeois Europe, a break long anticipated by European intellectuals and completed by the devastation of World War I. Although the various émigré factions and parties failed to achieve their political aims, they succeeded in conveying to the West this anticipation of a new cultural age. The Russian Revolution in this sense was delimited by the novels of Dostoevsky, the music of Stravinsky, the painting of Kandinsky, the constructions of Tatlin and Gabo, the cult of the machine among the Futurists and Maiakovsky, and the cinema of Eisenstein. On the eve of the war European audiences were thrilled by the Moscow Art Theater and the Diaghilev ballet; in the 1920's they were equally impressed by the Van Diemen Gallery exhibit of 1922, the stories of Bunin, and films such as *Potemkin* and *Strike*.

364

If the émigrés consciously rejected the Bolshevik revolution as a political phenomenon, they unconsciously disseminated this more general cultural revolution which had preceded the war and which ultimately died under the heavy hand of party control in the late 1920's. The cultural revolution, of course, was not uniquely Russian, but was deeply bound up with European developments: the Russian themes of *Firebird, Petroushka,* and *Rite of Spring* were presented through a musical idiom close to Berg, Schönberg, and Webern; Kandinsky's abstractionism drew on the anthroposophy of Rudolf Steiner, as well as the aesthetic novelties of the Fauves and German expressionists; the theater of Meyerhold drew on Greek drama, the *commedia dell'arte,* and the staging of George Fuchs and Max Reinhardt; the Futurists took their clue from Marinetti, even though they found him wanting when he visited Russia in 1913. The revolution appears to have provided an arena for experiment and innovation not possible in a war-weary Europe; after 1917 anything seemed possible in the utopian mood of the new Russia. Even as they fled this revolution, the émigrés took its cultural baggage with them.

There is thus a certain irony in the relationship of the Russian emigration to the Russian Revolution. Although Russians had come to Germany before and after World War I for political reasons, their ultimate impact upon German life was cultural. Few émigré political messages found support in Germany unless those messages confirmed already accepted views on events inside Russia. Rather it was Russian literature, music, art, and even food which the émigrés conveyed to Germans, along with the sense that the revolution was acceptable as a cultural phenomenon bringing a new breath of life to a dying Europe. The expectation that Russia offered a religious solution to the alienation of modern man from life and work in industrial society was a popular one in German intellectual circles before the war. It was the Russian critique of the West, rather than the Bolshevik critique of capitalism, that gave emotional content to the *Rapallopolitik.* The reception of Russian émigrés in Germany revealed a political hostility to revolution tempered by cultural enthusiasm, an enthusiasm which sometimes destroyed the very political anti-Bolshevism the émigrés so desired.

Was the Russian emigration a movement with any unity? Certainly the differences between Grand Dukes and anarchists, monarchists and socialists, Russians and non-Russians suggest the very same political and cultural divisions which characterized the Russian Empire itself. The common heritage of these diverse exiles was a sense of survival and despair, rather than a comity of interests. The apocalypse of the revolution had destroyed everything— except their culture. The clock of historical time had stopped at 1917, and most exiles chronicled the events of their life only up to that year, or the year of their flight. Conscious political activity proved chimerical within a few years, and only the unconscious cultural heritage remained. Reality was not the defeated cities of Weimar Germany but the memory of Russian things past, made more vivid by the unacceptability of the present.

The common cement of culture was the Russian language. It not only obscured the political and social fissures of the emigration, but it provided the metaphors for communication. For an exile, language *is* politics in many instances. Books, periodicals, and arguments in German cafés replaced political activity for the vast majority of exiles. In this way the metaphors of "East" and "West" also became a kind of symbolic language for communication between Russians and Germans, symbols laden with ambiguity reflecting the confused identity of the users. By employing them each émigré circle was able to define its own "Russian Revolution" that might have been, a great historical possibility rendered impotent by Bolshevik perfidy: for the right, it was a restoration; for the liberals, a parliamentary democracy; for the socialists and anarchists, an economic or stateless Utopia; for the non-Russians, federal autonomy; for the intellectuals, a vaguer "new age."

What these metaphors enabled émigrés to communicate was a sense that their particular revolution had universal meaning, a promise for the West as well as the East, a way out of the crisis of modern man. Yet the Germans did not read these metaphors by émigré logic. Too often they blurred the line between Soviet Russia and the imagined New Russia of émigré hopes, and in so doing created an enthusiasm for Russia upon which the Bolsheviks could capitalize.

For many Germans the Russian Revolution, like Russian culture before the revolution, promised renewal and reintegration of man's spirit, not merely institutional or social change. This promise had long been articulated in Germany by exiles who were themselves often thoroughly Europeanized yet drawn to romanticize their native land along lines desired by receptive Germans. The post-1917 emigration likewise helped satisfy a European need for Russian culture—as well as a European hostility toward Russian politics—with the aid of those individuals sufficiently Europeanized to convey a Russian message to Germans. Whether Russia promised a cultural renewal or a political threat, exiles were ready interpreters. Nor were anti-Bolshevism and cultural Russophilia contradictory. Often those who had found a way out to the West politically continued to seek a way out to the East culturally.

In 1938 Walter Schubart, a Baltic German émigré, wrote that the Russian emigration was "as important an event for the relations between the West and the East, and therefore for the spiritual destiny of the Western world, as was the stream of Humanists which overflowed into Europe after the conquest of Constantinople by the Turks in 1453." Since the eighteenth century, Europeans pessimistic about the future of their own civilization had turned to non-Western cultures, particularly Russia, China, and India, in search of a better world. Now such a culture had been brought into Europe through the Russian emigration. "Three million human beings belonging to an Eastern culture, of whom the majority were members of the intellectual elite, overflowed into the European countries bringing with them a culture which up till then had been practically unknown and inaccessible to the West." As a result the West, which had "robbed the human race of its soul" by its mad dash toward material progress and a technological civilization, had rediscovered the Russians in the 1920's as a "way out to the East," a culture which could "give back to mankind its soul." [1]

Much of Schubart's argument bears the marks of a Balt attracted to the exotic nature of the Russia left behind. The Russian wants

[1] Walter Schubart, *Russia and Western Man* (New York, 1950), pp. 31–32, 36.

to suffer, has a primitive trust in God, is spontaneous, capable of great sacrifice, and childlike. The West is dying and the East offers life; the future belongs to the Slavs. What is unusual is that Schubart was conscious of the dilemma of the Baltic Germans, suspended between East and West. No single group was better prepared to mediate between the "form without life" of the West and the "life without form" of Russia. But in the end no single group did more to attack the Russians as an inferior and hostile culture on the margin of civilization.[2]

In fact, as this study has suggested, the Balts and the Russian Germans in general were perhaps even more ambivalent than Schubart claimed. As one scholar has noted, there was a certain distinction between the educated middle-class Russian Germans from St. Petersburg and Moscow and the more irredentist Balts, many of whom became German nationalists in emigration.[3] More than this, there appears to have been within the Russian Germans themselves a latent attraction toward both countries and cultures whose magnitude depended primarily on the audience they encountered as émigrés in Germany. Some came with their German nationalism already developed; Paul Rohrbach recalled later that "our consciousness of being German was so strong that we did not understand why people at first considered us 'Russians' in Germany."[4] Others, like Alfred Rosenberg, acquired their distaste for the Russians only after arriving in Germany. Conversely, cultural friends of Russia such as the St. Petersburg German Lou Andreas-Salomé learned their enthusiasm for Russia from Russian friends (the cultural historian A. L. Volinsky) and developed it as a kind of "self-Russification" because of its appeal to German friends (Rilke).[5] It was only in Germany that many Russian Germans realized how much they loved or hated their country of origin, which Andreas-Salomé dubbed "my land that I so long neglected."

Thus the process of assimilation, of "becoming German," could

[2] *Ibid.*, pp. 30, 298.

[3] George Fischer, *Soviet Opposition to Stalin: A Case Study in World War II* (Cambridge, Mass., 1952), pp. 76–77.

[4] Paul Rohrbach, *Um des Teufels Handschrift* (Hamburg, 1953), p. 9.

[5] Rudolf Binion, *Frau Lou: Nietzsche's Wayward Disciple* (Princeton, 1968), pp. 279–280.

mean either hostility or attraction toward Russia, depending on the German environment. For Germany itself, as Thomas Mann suggested, was a land in the middle, neither Eastern nor Western, torn as to its identity and its future. In this sense the Balts found in Germany no solution to their problems of identity but a mirror of their own dilemma. Yet in the end they did have a choice, as Schubart noted, because of their German culture, as to the message they would convey and the Germans they would seek out. It was this very freedom of assimilation which made them so different from and so crucial to the Russian emigration in general. The Russians might agree among themselves that Russia formed a community of people different from and superior to "the West." But whereas the Russian Germans suffered and benefited from the problems of a mixed national identity, the Russians themselves became ever more conscious that no such choice was open to them.

The properly Russian elements of the emigration never assimilated into German life, which they rejected as symptomatic of the general decline of Western culture long prophesied by Russian intellectuals and all too apparent in the wake of the First World War. Life in exile heightened the sense of cultural distinctiveness, and hence of isolation within the German environment. The Russians had to live in the West, which they rejected culturally, because they could not live in Soviet Russia, which they rejected politically. Thus many were forced to seek a "way out" by fantasizing another Russia, either in a nostalgia for the past or a forlorn hope for some future return to a better Russia, a dream country which in the end they took with them into emigration. The generally anti-Western nature of this dream, as in the writings of the Eurasians, the Scythians, Berdiaev's circle, and Smena Vekh, contributed to German intellectuals' cultural Russophilia, but also to their more positive attitude toward the Russian Revolution, viewed as some purifying anti-Western apocalypse. Thus the émigrés' cultural nationalism in the end contributed to their political isolation.

What was the effect of the emigration on German life in the 1920's and 1930's? Politically it is obvious that the existence of tens of thousands of anti-Bolshevik Russians did little or nothing to alter the warm relations between Weimar Germany and Soviet

Russia after Rapallo. More significant was the influence of specific groups—the Mensheviks, the Baltic Germans, the right-wing Russians, the intellectuals—on German public opinion concerning Russia. Here again, however, one gets a sense of resonance rather than influence. Those Russians whose political Russophobia or cultural Russophilia fitted the mood of German public opinion were listened to and well received. They provided expertise, firsthand knowledge, and direct contact with the world of Russian culture and the Russian Revolution; they rarely changed anyone's mind.

In general, the influence exerted by German and Russian émigré public opinion was mutual rather than one-way. An eager reception by a German audience often exaggerated the very message the émigrés brought with them. The effect of Spengler's metahistory on Berdiaev, the staunch anti-Bolshevism which Kautsky encouraged in his Russian and Georgian Menshevik friends, and Rosenberg's discovery of anti-Semitism in Munich all bore witness to this phenomenon. So did the virulent Russophobia which the Third Reich drew out of the Russian-German colonists. The Balts who were so troubled by their mixed Russian-German identity both before and after the First World War might exhibit the Russophobia of a Scheubner-Richter or the Russophilia of a Karl Nötzel; in either case, like Russians in general, they were greatly influenced by the mood of the Germans with whom they came in contact.

Within the Russian emigration those groups who were able to influence German public opinion had generally been "Westernized" in some sense prior to exile. They had a knowledge of the German language and German culture, or they were ethnic Germans by origin. By 1923 the political life of the Russian elements in exile had ended in despair; only the Alexander Steins, the Rosenbergs, the Scheubner-Richters, or the Fedor Stepuns were able to move easily into a new life in Germany. They assimilated, and they provided a kind of bridge between Russians and Germans. This was particularly true of the Baltic Germans and the Jews, not because of any peculiar national or ethnic characteristics but because the Russification policies of the Imperial Russian government had sent them into exile before the revolution, as well as after.

The continuity with the past is striking. Russians and Germans had always had a certain ambivalence about each other. For many Germans, Russia's "Eastern" nature was a fusion of life-giving religiosity and exotic simplicity and death-dealing barbarism and despotism. For many Russians, Germany was a land of both Kant and Krupp, philosophy and war, the highest culture and the lowest bourgeois commonplaces. As the mood in Germany changed, so did the emotions and influence of those Russians who lived there. Despite the enthusiasm for Dostoevsky, the years before 1914 were marked by a general Russophobia well cultivated and reinforced by Balts like Theodor Schiemann. Under Weimar the mood was generally Russophile, and the enthusiasm for Russia and the "East" among émigré intellectuals was welcomed and reinforced by similar sentiments among German writers such as Spengler, Mann, and Hesse. With the Third Reich came the new anti-Semitic virulence of the Nazis nurtured by the extreme right-wing Russians and Balts who had discovered Hitler in Munich in the early 1920's. In every case Germans listened to those Russians they wished to hear.

Within the Russian context the tragedy of exile has its roots in the traumatic process of modernization and revolution which characterized Russian life from the 1890's through the 1930's. Many émigrés saw their world come apart, and were seeking a new faith even before the revolution. The political extremism of the *Protocols of the Elders of Zion* and the cultural messianism of the "way out to the East" circulated widely within the emigration; their origins lay in the political violence and cultural millenarianism of the Silver Age. Relativity theory, nonobjective art, the twelve-tone row, World War I, and the Russian Revolution all testified to the "decline of the West" and the need for some new principle of order. The literature of the emigration is full of extreme answers to that need, answers for a world in crisis which are central to the Russians' culture of despair.

In the end the despair of exile produced two sets of answers to the global crisis of the twentieth century. For the Russian intellectuals the way out lay in the "East," in the preindustrial world beyond the borders of Europe whose integrated life styles offered a new meaning to Faustian European man whose soul had been sacrificed to modernization. For the political right and the Russophobic Russian Germans the way out lay in the "West," in a shoring up of the bastions of Western civilization against the subhuman forces of destruction threatening Europe from outside.

The tragedy of the Russian emigration was that it found in Russia and Germany after 1933 a choice only between two forms of totalitarianism. From the permanence of the exile experience itself there was no exit.

The Russian emigration to Germany may be thought of as a movement of the "Westernized" elite of a "non-Western" society into the West. In Russia this elite had conceived of itself as "Western"; now it found itself viewed as something exotic and "Eastern" when living as refugees in the West. The continuity of alienation from society provided the touchstone of émigré thought, with its rather desperate attempts to identify with either East or West, Russia or Germany. The home which was unavailable in the real world might yet be found in literature, in journalism, in art, in political activity. The émigré is a man who belongs nowhere:

> since the self he was continues to smolder beneath the person he is about to become, his identity is bound to be in a state of flux; and the odds are that he will never fully belong to the community to which he now in a way belongs. (Nor will its members readily think of him as one of theirs.) In fact, he has ceased to "belong." . . . just as he is free to step outside the culture which was his own, he is sufficiently uncommitted to get inside the minds of the foreign people in whose midst he is living.[6]

Looked at in this way the Russian emigration takes on an even more universal significance as an archetypal situation of twentieth-century man in general. Uprooted and alone in a world changing too fast, the émigré can live anywhere because he lives nowhere. His home is a memory; his house is a temporary residence. Only in his mind can he live comfortably amid the furnishings of old dreams and new expectations.

[6] Siegfried Kracauer, *The Last Things before the Last* (New York, 1969), pp. 83–84.

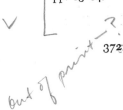

--◦◦⊰{ }⊱◦◦--

Biographical Notes
and Glossary

Abramovich (Abramowitz), Rafael (1879–1963), Jewish socialist, leader
of Bund and Menshevik factions abroad after 1920.

Alexanderheim, home for needy Russian refugees established in Berlin
in the 1890's by the Orthodox Church.

Ammende, Ewald (1893–1936), Baltic German active in famine relief
efforts, General Secretary, European Congress of Nationalities.

Amt Osten, eastern section of Nazi Foreign Policy Office.

Anderson, Paul B. (b. 1894), American YMCA worker in Berlin, founder
of the Russian correspondence school.

Andreas-Salomé, Lou (1861–1937), St. Petersburg German author and
psychologist, friend of Nietzsche, Rilke, and Freud.

Anti-Comintern, Nazi anti-Soviet propaganda organization established
in the 1930's and staffed with émigrés.

Antony, Metropolitan of Kiev (1863–1936), head of the Sremtsy Karlovtsy wing of the Russian Orthodox church in exile.

Aronson, Grigory Yakovlevich (b. 1887), member of the "right" Menshevik faction in Berlin in the 1920's.

Arshinov, Peter Andreevich (b. 1887), head of the Group of Russian
Anarchist-Communists Abroad (Berlin) in the 1920's.

Aufbau, right-wing organization of Russians and Germans in Munich in
the early 1920's headed by Scheubner-Richter.

Auhagen, Otto (1869–1945), agricultural attaché in Russia (1900–1906
and 1927–1930), director of the Osteuropa Institute, Breslau.

Avalov (Bermondt-Avalov), Paul Mikhailovich (b. 1881), Russian commander of the Baltic Northwest Army, 1919.

Akselrod, Paul Borisovich (1850–1928), leading Russian socialist living in Berlin in the 1920's.

Bauer, Max Hermann (1869–1929), artillery officer involved in the Kapp Putsch of 1920.

Belgard, (Bellegarde), Aleksei Valerianov (1861–1942), Baltic German monarchist politician, Chief of Press Administration (1905–1912).

Belyi, Andrei (Boris Nikolaevich Bugaev) (1880–1934), leading symbolist poet and writer living in Berlin, 1921–1923.

Berdiaev, Nikolai Aleksandrovich (1874–1948), Russian religious philosopher, edited *Sofiia* while living in Berlin, 1922–1923.

Berg, Ludwig (b. 1874), head of the Catholic Emigré Welfare Office in Germany in the 1920's.

Bethmann-Hollweg, Theobald von (1856–1921), German Chancellor from 1909 until 1917.

Biskupsky, Vasily Vasilievich, Russian general and monarchist politician close to Scheubner-Richter and the Nazis.

Blücher, Wipert von (b. 1883), official of the Eastern Section of the Wilhelmstrasse responsible for Russian émigré affairs.

Bobrinsky, Aleksandr Aleksandrovich (1852–1927), archaeologist and diplomat active in the émigré monarchist movement.

Bobrishchev-Pushkin, A. V., writer active in Smena Vekh, formerly an Octobrist in Denikin's army.

Boehm, Max Hildebert (b. 1891), Baltic German writer and expert on European national minorities.

Botkin, Sergei Dmitrievich, Russian ambassador to Italy, head of the Russian Delegation in Berlin, 1920–1936.

Brant, A. F., Russian colonel in charge of the Russian Military Mission in Berlin, 1919.

Broederich, Sylvio (1870–1952), Baltic German who colonized his estates with Volhynian Germans before 1914, journalist.

Bucholtz, Wilhelm Adolfovich (b. 1867), Russian-German socialist, *Vorwärts* correspondent and editor, *Russisches Bulletin,* 1910–1914.

Bülow, Bernhard von (1849–1929), German State Secretary (1897–1900) and Imperial Chancellor (1900–1909).

Bund, Jewish labor organization in Imperial Russia, overlapping in membership with Russian socialist parties.

Burtsev, Vladimir Lvovich (1862–1942), leading Social Revolutionary, editor of the Paris newspaper *Obshchee delo.*

Chakhotin, Sergei (b. 1883), writer for *Nakanune* associated with the pro-Soviet *smenovekhovstvo* movement.

Chernov, Viktor Mikhailovich (1873–1952), Social Revolutionary Minister of Agriculture (1917) and president, Constituent Assembly.

Chenkeli, Akaki (1874–1959), Georgian Menshevik, president of the Transcaucasian Federal Republic (1918).

Cleinow, Georg (1873–1936), St. Petersburg German, press chief of Poland and Governor-General, Warsaw (1914–1916), edited *Die Grenzboten*.

Council of Ambassadors, (Soveshchanie Poslov), Paris émigré organization of former Russian diplomats.

Dallin, David Yulevich (1889–1962), Menshevik writer and member of the Foreign Delegation, living in Berlin, then the U.S. (1940).

Damanskaia, Avgusta Fillipovna (b. 1885), poetess and translator employed by *Dni* in Berlin in the 1920's.

Dan, Theodor (Fedor Ilich Gurvich) (1871–1947), leader of the Menshevik Foreign Delegation in Berlin, then Paris, and finally New York.

Defensists, Russian socialists who supported their country's war efforts during World War I.

Denicke, Yury Petrovich (George Dekker) (b. 1887), Menshevik writer for *Die Gesellschaft* specializing in economics.

Denikin, Anton Ivanovich (1872–1947), one of the leading White Russian commanders during the Russian Civil War.

Deriugin, G. M., right-wing Duma politician active in the émigré monarchist movement.

Deutsche Auslandsinstitut, Stuttgart institute for Germans abroad engaged in scholarship and propaganda.

Despotuli, Vladimir, Russian émigré of Greek ancestry who edited the right-wing *Novoe slovo* in Berlin in the 1930's.

Doncov, Dmitro (b. 1883), Ukrainian nationalist, head of Union for Emancipation of the Ukraine in World War I.

Eckardt, Julius Wilhelm Albert von (1836–1908), Baltic German publicist, edited *Die Grenzboten*, cofounded Verein für Sozialpolitik.

Eckart, Dietrich (1868–1923), German poet and playwright, edited the anti-Semitic *Auf gut deutsch* in Munich, 1918–1921.

Efimovsky, E. A., moderate monarchist, formerly a Kadet, editor of *Griadushchaia Rossiia*, Berlin, 1921–1922.

Ehrenburg, Ilia Grigorievich (1891–1967), Russian-Jewish writer living in Berlin in the 1920's, co-editor of *Veshch*.

Ehrt, Adolf (b. 1902), Russian-German Nazi active in the propaganda work of Anti-Comintern.

Eichler, Adolf (b. 1877), Polish-German journalist and editor of Pan-German *Deutsche Post aus dem Osten*.

Eisenstein, Sergei Mikhailovich (1898–1948), Soviet film director whose *Potemkin* enthralled Berlin audiences in the late 1920's.

Eliasberg, Alexander (1878–1924), Russian-Jewish translator and writer, cofounded Society to Aid Russian Citizens in Berlin (1916).

Esenin, Sergei Aleksandrovich (1895–1925), Russian lyric poet of peasant origin, married for a time to the dancer Isadora Duncan.

Eurasianism, émigré movement originating in Sofia, Bulgaria, in 1920 which identified Turkic and Iranian roots of a "Eurasian" culture.

Evlogy, Metropolitan of Western Europe (1868–1946), head of the Russian church eparchy in Paris, as named by Patriarch Tikhon in 1922.

Ewald, F. F., Baltic German colonel and chairman of the Russian émigré committee in Munich.

Ewart, Major General Sir Richard (1864–1928), President of the Inter-Allied Commission for the Repatriation of Russian POW's, Berlin, 1919.

Foreign Delegation (Zagranichnaia delegatsiia), Menshevik exile organization established in Berlin in 1921.

Frank, Semion Ludvigovich (1877–1950), Russian philosopher and writer, lecturer at the Russian Scientific Institute.

Frasch, Adolf, Russian-German head of the Verband für Deutschen aus Russland.

Gabo (Pevsner), Naum (b. 1890), Russian sculptor involved with the Constructivist movement after 1917.

Gamm, A. F., Russian consul-general in Berlin, later associated with the Russian Military Mission (1919).

Garvi, Peter (Petr Abramovich Bronstein) (1881–1944), Menshevik journalist and politician living in Berlin in the 1920's.

Geiser, Alfred (b. 1868), Baltic German business manager of the Pan-German League.

Gessen, Iosif Vladimirovich (1865–1943), leading Kadet lawyer and politician, editor of prewar *Rech'* and émigré *Rul'*.

Giers, Mikhail Nikolaevich (1855–1932), Imperial Russian ambassador in Rumania, Turkey, Italy; headed the Council of Ambassadors.

Glants, R. Ya. (A. Grigorianz), socialist journalist who wrote for *Vorwärts* and *Zhizn'* in the 1920's.

Goltz, G. A. J. Rüdiger von der (1865–1946), German general in command of Free Corps troops in Finland and the Baltic, 1918–1919.

Gorky, Maxim (A. M. Peshkov) (1868–1936), Russian writer living in Germany in the 1920's, where he edited *Beseda* 1923–1925.

Goul, Roman Borisovich (b. 1896), writer associated with *Zhizn'* and *Nakanune* in Berlin, later editor of *Novyi zhurnal* (New York).

Grzhebin, Zinovy Isaakovich (1869–1929), Soviet book publisher in Berlin, friend of Gorky.

Guchkov, Alexander Ivanovich (1862–1936), Octobrist leader living in Berlin in the 1920's.

Gurko, General Vasily Iosifovich (1864–1937), Imperial Russian chief of staff, Provisional government commander-in-chief.

Harnack, Adolf von (1851–1930), Baltic German theologian and professor in Berlin, friend of William II.

Harting, A. M., head of the Berlin section of the Okhrana before World War I.

Hehn, Victor (1813–1890), Baltic German journalist, author of widely read *De Moribus Ruthenorum* (1892).

Heiseler, Henry von (1875–1928), St. Petersburg German writer in Munich (1898–1914).

Hilferding, Rudolf (1877–1941), leading socialist theoretician of the USPD, German Finance Minister in 1923 and 1928–1929.

Hilger, Gustav (b. 1886), Moscow German involved in POW exchange, later diplomat in Weimar and Nazi Germany.

Hoetzsch, Otto E. G. (1876–1946), German politician and Russian scholar, founder of the Society for the Study of Russia (1913).

Hurwicz, Elias (b. 1884), Russian-Jewish writer for *Hochland* and *Die neue Rundschau*.

Ilin, Ivan Alekseevich (b. 1883), Social Revolutionary writer who emigrated to Germany in 1922 and worked for the YMCA.

Iollos, Grigory Borisovich (1859–1907), Kadet, Berlin correspondent for *Russkie vedomosti* and editor of *Russische Korrespondenz*.

Ivanov-Razumnik, Razumnik Vasilievich (1878–1946), writer and leading theoretician of the Scythian group.

Biographical Notes and Glossary

Ivanovich, Stepan (Semion Osipovich Portugeis) (1881–1944), anti-Bolshevik socialist and editor of *Zaria* in Berlin.

Kadet party, Constitutional Democratic party, or Partiia Narodnoi Svobody, founded in 1904.

Kaminka, Avgust Isaakovich (b. 1877), Kadet leader and co-editor with Nabokov and Gessen of *Rul'*.

Kandinsky, Wassily (1866–1944), Russian abstract painter who worked in Munich 1897–1914 and later at the Bauhaus.

Kaplun-Sumsky, S. G., Menshevik journalist and director of the Epokha publishing house in Berlin.

Kapp Putsch, attempted military takeover in Berlin in March 1920 lead by an East Prussian civil servant, Wolfgang Kapp.

Karsavin, Lev Platonovich (b. 1882), Russian religious philosopher who lectured at the Russian Scientific Institute.

Kautsky, Karl (1854–1938), leading theoretician of German Social Democracy, close to some of the Berlin Mensheviks.

Kazem-Bek, Alexander Lvovich, head of the Young Russia movement (Mladorossy) living in Paris.

Kerensky, Alexander Fedorovich (1881–1970), Trudovik politician, Minister of Justice and, later, of War, Provisional government.

Keyserling, Hermann (1880–1946), Baltic German mystical philosopher who founded the Wisdom School at Darmstadt in the 1920's.

Khol'msen (Holmsen), General Ivan Alekseevich (1865–1941), head of the "military section" of Botkin's Russian Delegation.

Kirdetsov, G. L., writer associated with *Nakanune* and *smenovekhovstvo*.

Kirill, Vladimirovich, Grand Duke (1876–1938), cousin of Nicholas II and pretender to the Imperial throne in exile.

Kleinmichel, Countess Maria Eduardovna (b. 1846), Baltic German head of a Berlin "political salon" in 1919.

Kliuchnikov, Yury Veniaminovich (b. 1886), active in *smenovekhovstvo*, former "foreign minister" of Kolchak government.

Knorring, Ludvig Karlovich (1859–1930), Baltic German representative of the Council of Ambassadors in Baden-Baden, former diplomat.

Kolchak, Alexander Vasilievich (1873–1920), White commander in Siberia, 1919–1920.

Kolyshko, Iosif Iosifovich (b. 1862), émigré writer for *Novoe slovo* in the 1930's as "Baian."

Krasnov, General Peter Nikolaevich (1869–1947), White commander, author of Cossack novels, German collaborator in World War II.

Krivoshein, Alexander Vasilievich (1858–1923), monarchist politician, Minister of Agriculture in 1917.

Krüdener-Struve, Baron A. A., Baltic German Duma representative involved with the Northwest Army.

Krupensky, Anatoly Nikolaevich (1850–1923), monarchist politician, ambassador to Norway (1905–1912) and Italy (1912–1915).

Kuskova, Ekaterina Dmitrievich (b. 1869), socialist theoretician and wife of Prokopovich, follower of Eduard Bernstein.

Ladyzhnikov, Ivan Pavlovich (1874–1945), Bolshevik publisher with an outlet in Berlin in the 1920's.

Lampe, General Aleksei Aleksandrovich von, representative of General Wrangel in Berlin.

Leibbrandt, Georg (b. 1899), Russian-German Nazi, head of Amt Osten, the "eastern section" of Rosenberg's party Foreign Policy Office.

Leuchtenberg, Duke Georg Nikolaevich (b. 1872), lesser Russian royalty, liaison between Kiev and Berlin (1918), "Anastasia" host.

Lieven, Prince Anatoly Pavlovich (b. 1872), Baltic German commander of Yudenich army in the Baltic in 1919.

Lissitsky, El (Lazar Markovich) (b. 1890), Russian-Jewish artist connected with Constructivism, co-editor of *Veshch*.

Litvin, Paul, Russian-Jewish businessman, part of Brest-Litovsk negotiating team.

Lokot, Timofei Vasilievich (b. 1869), former socialist active in monarchist politics in the 1920's.

Lütz, L. B., Russian-German chairman of the Society for Russian Citizens of German Origin, Zemgor member.

Lukianov, S. S., writer for *Nakanune* and other periodicals of *smenovekhovstvo*.

Luther, Arthur (1876–1954), Russian-German translator and editor of the journal *Osteuropa*.

Luxemburg, Rosa (1870–1919), radical socialist theoretician from Poland, a major figure in the SPD, USPD, and Spartacist parties.

Lvov, Prince Georgy Evgenievich (1861–1925), first head of the Provisional government, chairman of Zemgor.

Maklakov, Vasily Alekseevich (1870–1957), Kadet party leader and Duma representative, Provisional government ambassador in Paris.

Malcolm, Major-General Neill, head of the Inter-Allied Commission for the Repatriation of Russian POW's in Berlin in 1919.

Maltsev, Aleksei Petrovich (1854–1915), Russian Orthodox priest, founder of the St. Vladimir Brotherhood in Berlin in 1890.

Maltzan, Ago von, head of the eastern section of the German Foreign Office in the early 1920's.

Markov II, Nikolai Evgenievich (b. 1866), Union of the Russian People leader, member of Supreme Monarchist Council in exile.

Martov (Tsederbaum), Yury Osipovich (1873–1923), Menshevik leader, editor of *Sotsialisticheskii vestnik*.

Maslennikov, A. M., constitutional monarchist and former Kadet, member of the Supreme Monarchist Council.

Matchabelli, Prince, Georgian émigré politician active in Germany during World War I.

Mende, Gerhard von (b. 1904), Baltic German Turkologist, head of the Ukrainian Scientific Institute, employed by Amt Osten.

Mensheviks, literally "men of the minority," democratic socialist wing of the Russian Social Democratic Workers' Party.

Merezhkovsky, Dmitry Sergeevich (1865–1941), novelist and critic popular in pre-1914 Germany, later right-wing émigré journalist.

Miliukov, Paul Nikolaevich (1859–1943), leading Kadet politician, historian, and editor of the Paris newspaper *Poslednie novosti*.

Minsky (Vilenkin), Nikolai Maksimovich (1855–1937), symbolist poet and head of the House of Arts intellectual circle.

Mirbach, Count Wilhelm von (1871–1918), German ambassador in Moscow, assassinated in 1918.

Nabokov, Vladimir Dmitrievich (1870–1922), Kadet party leader and editor of *Rul'* in Berlin.

Nabokov, Vladimir Vladimirovich (b. 1899), the leading chronicler of émigré life, living in Berlin 1922–1937.

Nansen, Fridtjof (1861–1930), polar explorer, League of Nations High Commissioner for Refugees.

Nansen passport, refugee identity card issued under the auspices of the League of Nations, little used in Germany.

Nazhivin, Ivan Fedorovich (1874–1940), writer and editor active in the monarchist movement.

Nemirovich-Danchenko, G. V., Wrangel's press chief, journalist active in the Nazi movement.

NEP, New Economic Policy of limited capitalism in Russia after 1921.

Nicolaevsky, Boris Ivanovich (1887–1967), Menshevik historian and archivist living in Berlin in the 1920's.

Nikolai Nikolavich (Romanov), Grand Duke (1856–1929), army commander-in-chief, 1914–1915, in exile pretender to the Romanov throne.

Nötzel, Karl (1870–1937), Baltic German author and translator whose interpretations of Russia were widely read in Germany.

Northwest Army, anti-Bolshevik army in the Baltic in 1919 staffed by Russian officers and POW's and German Free Corps troops.

NTS, *Narodno-trudovoi soiuz* (National Labor Alliance), right-wing émigré organization formed in the 1930's.

Oberost, administrative command for the German-occupied areas of eastern Europe during World War I.

Okhrana, Imperial Russian political police with offices in Paris and Berlin before 1917.

Olberg, Paul (1878–1960), Menshevik journalist for *Vorwärts* who emigrated to Germany in 1906.

Oldenburg, S. S., leading member of the "constitutional monarchist" movement after Reichenhall.

Orlov, Vladimir Grigorievich (b. 1882), intelligence officer for Wrangel involved in the forging of the Zinoviev Letter.

Ostjuden, German term for Jews living in the territories of Russia and Austria-Hungary before World War I, especially Poland and Galicia.

Parvus (Helphand), Alexander (1896–1924), Russian-Jewish socialist involved in the organization of anti-government Russians in World War I.

Pasternak, Boris Leonidovich (1890–1960), Russian writer, poet, and translator, student at Marburg and resident in Germany in the 1920's.

Petliura, Simon (1879–1926), Ukrainian nationalist politician who emigrated to Paris.

Pevsner, Antoine (1886–1962), Russian architect associated with Constructivism, brother of Naum Gabo.

Pianov, F. T., Russian YMCA worker active in refugee work in Berlin in the 1920's.

Poltavets-Ostranitsa, Ivan, Cossack officer under Skoropadsky, later active in the Nazi movement.

Potekhin, Yury Nikolaevich (b. 1888), émigré writer connected with the Smena Vekh movement.

Pototsky, Major-General, Volunteer Army delegate in Berlin 1918–1919, head of first Russian Delegation.

Prokopovich, Sergei Nikolaevich (1871–1955), socialist economist and follower of Bernstein, taught at the Russian Scientific Institute.

Purishkevich, Vladimir Mitrofanovich (1870–1920), anti-Semitic writer and head of the Union of the Russian People.

Randstaaten, German term for the western borderlands of Russia from the Baltic to the Black Sea, including Finland, Poland, Ukraine.

Reichenhall Congress, June 1921 gathering of Russian émigré monarchists at the town of Bad Reichenhall in Bavaria.

Reventlow, Ernst (1869–1943), German right-wing journalist and editor.

Rimsky-Korsakov, A. A., State Councillor and Senator, governor of Yaroslav province, émigré monarchist.

Rodzaevsky, Konstantin Vladimirovich (b. 1908), head of the All-Russian Fascist Party in Harbin, China, in the 1930's.

Römmer, A. K., Baltic German "civil governor" of Baltic territory occupied by the Northwest Army in 1919.

Rohrbach, Paul (b. 1869), Baltic German journalist, colonial administrator, and diplomat, head of the German-Ukrainian Society.

Rosenberg, Alfred (1893–1946), Baltic German theoretician of the Nazi party, head of the party Foreign Policy Office [Ostministerium].

Rosenberg, Paul von, Russian guards officer involved with the Northwest Army in the Baltic in 1919.

Russian Delegation, recognized by the German government as the official organ of the Russian colony, headed by S. D. Botkin, reporting to the Council of Ambassadors in Paris.

Scheubner-Richter, Max Erwin von (1884–1923), Baltic German officer in German army, Nazi, head of Aufbau Society in Munich.

Schickedanz, Arno, Baltic German schoolmate of Rosenberg and Scheubner-Richter, Nazi, anti-Semitic journalist.

Schiemann, Theodor (1847–1921), Baltic German Professor of Russian History at Berlin University, *Kreuzzeitung* writer close to William II.

Schlesinger, Moritz, German socialist and businessman active in POW repatriation and refugee work for League of Nations.

Schleuning, Johannes, Russian German minister from Tiflis who worked for Russian-German organizations in Germany.

Schmidt, Axel (1870–   ), Baltic German journalist, headed the German-Ukrainian Society.

Scythians, loosely-linked literary circle which published in Berlin in the early 1920's, headed by R. V. Ivanov-Razumnik.

Shabelsky-Bork, Peter Nikolaevich (1893–1952), right-wing Russian officer who helped kill Vladimir Nabokov in 1922, later a Nazi.

Shirinsky-Shikhmatov, Aleksei Aleksandrovich (1862–1930), Procurator of the Holy Synod, member of Supreme Monarchist Council.

Shklovsky, Viktor Borisovich (b. 1893), Russian "formalist" critic and writer, author of *Zoo* and *Sentimental Journey*.

Shlippe, Fedor Vladimirovich (b. 1873), Moscow German, chairman of the Berlin branch of Zemgor in the 1920's.

Skoropadsky, Paul Petrovich (1873–1945), German-sponsored "Hetman" of the Ukraine in 1918, Nazi collaborator in World War II.

Slovo, Russian publishing house created by the Ullstein Verlag in Berlin in the 1920's.

Smal-Stocki, Roman, Ukrainian nationalist author and politician representing Petliura in Berlin in the 1920's.

Smena Vekh, "Changing Directions," émigré movement urging support of Soviet government during NEP.

Snessarev, Nikolai (?–1928), writer for *Novoe vremia*, supporter of Grand Duke Kirill in emigration.

Social Revolutionary party (SR's), peasant socialist party centered in Paris and Prague in exile.

Spartacists, left-wing socialist party formed in Germany during World War I.

Stadtler, Eduard, German journalist, POW in Russia in World War I, professional anti-Bolshevik politician in 1920's.

Stankevich, Vladimir Benediktovich (Vladas Stanka) (b. 1884), socialist author and head of *Zhizn'* circle of intellectuals in Berlin, 1920.

Stein, Alexander (1881–1949), Jewish socialist from Riga, intermediary for the Mensheviks and the USPD in the 1920's.

Steiner, Rudolf (1861–1925), Viennese mystic and theosophist who founded his own "anthroposophy" movement in Germany.

Stepun, Fedor Avgustovich (1884–1966), Russian author and editor, helped organize pre-war Russian-German philosophical journal *Logos*.

Struve, Peter Berngardovich (1870-1944), Russian liberal politician and economic historian, editor of *Osvobozhdenie* (Stuttgart).

Stumpp, Karl, Russian German active in the Deutsche Auslandsinstitut and Russian-German émigré politics.

Taboritsky, Sergei, Russian officer involved in Nabokov's murder in 1922, and later with the Nazis.

Talberg, N. D., Skoropadsky's Minister of Internal Affairs, editor of monarchist journal *Dvuglavyi orel*

Teitel, Jacob (1850–1940), attorney, judge, and former State Councillor, head of the Union of Russian Jews in Germany.

Tikhon, Patriarch (1865–1925), head of the Orthodox church during the early years of the post-1917 emigration.

Tödtli, Boris (b. 1901), Swiss Nazi of Russian-German origin, involved in defense of the *Protocols* in 1935.

Tolstoi, Aleksei Nikolaevich (1882–1945), Russian poet, playwright, and journalist who emigrated in 1919 but returned to Russia.

Tsereteli, Irakli G. (1882–1960), leading Georgian Menshevik active in socialist exile politics.

Ukhtomsky, N. A., journalist writing for periodicals of *smenovekhovstvo*.

Union of the Russian People, right-wing anti-Semitic political organization active in Russia between 1905 and 1917.

USPD, Independent Socialist Party of Germany.

Ustrialov, Nikolai Vasilevich (b. 1890), Kadet professor, Kolchak's press chief, leader of *smenovekhovstvo* movement.

Vinberg, Colonel Fedor Viktorovich, right-wing Russian officer, editor of anti-Semitic *Luch sveta*.

Vorst, Hans, Baltic German journalist and correspondent on Russian affairs for the *Berliner Tageblatt*.

Vysheslavtsev, Boris Petrovich (1877–1954), émigré writer and philosopher associated with the Russian Scientific Institute.

Winckler, Pastor, delegate of South Russian German colonists to Berlin in 1917–1918.

Wrangel, Baron A. A., head of the Russian Red Cross in Berlin, active in welfare work for *Zemgor*.

Wrangel, General Peter Nikolaevich (1878–1928), last of the White commanders (1920), Paris head of the army in exile.

Yashchenko, Aleksandr Semenovich (?–1934), writer of the *Zhizn'* circle, then *smenovekhovstvo*, director, YMCA Correspondence School.

Yasinsky, V. I., rector of the Russian Scientific Institute in Berlin in 1922–1923.

Yudenich, Nikolai Nikolaevich (1862–1933), White commander of anti-Bolshevik forces in the Baltic, 1919.

Zemgor (Zemstvo and Town Committee), émigré welfare organization growing out of the wartime Union of Zemstvos and Towns.

Zenkovsky, Vasily Vasilievich (b. 1881), Russian religious philosopher associated with Berdiaev and the YMCA.

Zhordaniia, Noi Nikolaevich (1870–1952), Georgian Menshevik and leader in the independence movement of 1918–1920.

—⦃ ⦄—

Selected Bibliography

The following brief bibliography lists only periodicals and unpublished materials. Books and articles are given in the notes.

UNPUBLISHED MATERIALS

Columbia University Russian Archive, New York

Botkin Collection (BC). Reports from S. D. Botkin in Berlin to M. N. Giers in Paris, as well as personal materials of Botkin relating to émigré affairs in Berlin

Damanskaia, A. F. "6 otryvkov iz vospominanii Avgusty Filippovny Damanskoi." Recollections of émigré life in Berlin by a poetess employed by *Dni*.

Holmsen, Lieutenant-General I. A. "Na voennoi sluzhbe v Rossii: Vospominaniia ofitsera general'nago shtaba." New York, 1953. Memoirs of the head of the military section of Botkin's Russian Delegation.

Rosenberg, Rittmeister Paul von. "Formirovanie russkikh natsional'nykh chastei na pribaltiiskom fronte." Berlin, 1919. The war in the Baltic in 1919 from the Russian side (contained in BC).

Shlippe, F. V., Untitled memoirs. The recollections of the head of the Berlin Zemgor.

Zenkovsky, V. V. "Moe uchastie v russkom studencheskom khristianskom dvizhenii." Describes the author's work among Russians for the YMCA after 1921.

Hoover Library, Palo Alto, California

Antikomintern Collection (A). Drafts and final versions of anti-Soviet publications from the 1930's and World War II.

Botkin Archive (BA). The files of S. D. Botkin, including the archives of

386

the Russian Delegation (RD, 67 folders), materials relating to Mrs. Tchaikovsky (TA, 64 folders), and the files of pre-1914 Russian consulates and legations at Weimar, Stuttgart, Breslau, Leipzig, and Darmstadt.

Gessen, I. V. "Gody skitanii." The memoirs of émigré life by the Kadet journalist, editor of *Rul'*, and head of the "Slovo" publishing house.

Giers Archive (GA). 131 folders of reports from throughout the diaspora in the 1920's. Communications to the Council of Ambassadors, including reports of Botkin to Giers from Berlin for 1920–1926 (folders 32–35), reports from L. K. Knorring in Baden-Baden for 1921–1922 (folder 21); materials on Berlin Zemgor for 1923 (folder 49).

Konstitutsionno-demokraticheskaia partiia (K-D) (Partiia narodnoi svobody); archives, 1920–1922 (KDA). 2 volumes. Records of the Kadet party in exile; especially important is the section on the Berlin group in volume I, pp. 193–241.

Lampe Archive (LA). The papers of A. A. von Lampe, the representative of General P. N. Wrangel in Berlin, in 57 folders.

Maklakov Archive (MaA). Materials from the files of V. A. Maklakov concerning the official life of the Berlin colony in the 1920's and its relations with Paris and other émigré centers.

Markov, Anatolii. "Entsiklopediia belago dvizheniia s 1917 po 1958 g.: vozhdy, partizany, fronty, pokhody i narodnyia vozstaniia protiv sovetov v Rossii." 4 volumes. A huge, indexed collection of uneven value which contains useful biographical data.

Miller Archive (Archiv Generala Miller Predstavitelia Generala Vrangelia vo Frantsii) (MiA). Materials on the army in exile.

NSDAP Hauptarchiv (HA). The filmed Nazi party archives; includes a clipping file on the Reichenhall congress of 1921 (roll 51, folder 1197), scattered issues of Scheubner-Richter's journal *Aufbau* for 1922–1923 (roll 53, folder 1263), and material on Rosenberg (roll 53, folder 1259). See the guide by A. F. Peterson and G. Heinz, *NSDAP Hauptarchiv* (Stanford, 1964).

Ustrialov Archive (UA). Papers and correspondence of the leading figure in the Smena Vekh movement in the 1920's, N. V. Ustrialov.

Wrangel Archive (WA). Reports of Holmsen on the activity of army organizations in Germany in the 1920's.

National Archives, Washington, D.C.

Archives of the German Foreign Ministry (AGFM). This is part of the larger RG 242 "Records" collection, consisting of the "Records of the

German Foreign Office Received by the Department of State" (T-120) and the materials given by St. Antony's College, England, to the U.S. Department of State (SA, T-136), on film in the National Archives and available elsewhere. The materials are indexed in G. O. Kent, *A Catalogue of Files and Microfilms of the German Foreign Ministry Archives, 1920–1945* (3 vols.; Stanford, 1958–1966).

"Captured Records filmed at Alexandria, Virginia," part of "World War II Collection of Seized Enemy Records," RG 242, National Archives, Washington, D.C., to which AGFM also belongs. The most useful materials are indexed in the following guides to the records: *Records of the Reich Leader of the SS and Chief of German Police* (Parts I–III); *Records of the Reich Ministry for the Occupied Eastern Territories; Records of the National Socialist German Labor Party* (Parts I–III). Unfilmed materials are also available in the Bundesarchiv at Koblenz. The Institut für Zeitgeschichte in Munich has an excellent cross-indexed card file for selected filmed material.

YMCA Historical Archive, New York

Colton, E. T. "Memoirs of Ethan T. Colton, Sr.—1872–1952." Includes a report on the author's work with Russian émigrés.

Klepinin, N. "Survey of North American YMCA Service to Russians in Europe." 2 volumes. Mimeo. A good summary of YMCA work among émigrés in Berlin and Paris in the 1920's and 1930's.

"Report of the Russian Department for the Month of December 1921." Berlin, 1922. World Service Box 146-A. Describes YMCA work among Russian students and war prisoners.

"Russian Church Interpretations—YMCA Relations, 1926." World Service Box 9, folder F. A report by Paul Anderson to E. T. Colton dated Paris, November 26, 1926, on the ideological problems raised by Protestant work among Orthodox émigrés.

"Russian Correspondence School." World Service Box 9, folder E. A history of the correspondence school for émigrés in Berlin (1921–1924) and Paris (1924–1939).

"Work for Russian Students in Berlin." Berlin, 1924. World Service Box 8, folder D. Survey of religious and educational work for 1921–1924.

Wiener Library, London

Freyenwald Collection (FC). Materials collected during the Berne trial of 1935 relating to the *Protocols* and including reports from various émigrés.

Bibliography

"Querschnitt durch die Tätigkeit des Arbeitsgebietes Dr. Taubert (Antibolschewismus) des RMVP bis zum 31.12.1944." A summary of Anti-Comintern activity prepared for the Gestapo; film of the original in the YIVO Institute for Jewish Research, New York.

Tödtli Collection (TC). Materials relating to Boris Tödtli's work for the Nazis among the émigrés in the 1930's.

International Institute of Social History, Amsterdam

Kautsky Archive (KA). Correspondence of Kautsky with various Russian socialists from before and after World War I, particularly the Mensheviks.

Rocker, Rudolf. "Revolution und Rueckfall in die Barbarei." Memoirs of a leading German anarchist who befriended like-minded Russians in the 1920's.

Stein, Alexander. "Erinnerungen eines Staatenlosen, 1881–1906." Memoirs of a leading Menshevik covering his life in Riga prior to his emigration to Germany; written in 1945.

Bundesarchiv, Koblenz

Deutsches Auslandsinstitut Archiv (DAI). The files of the DAI for 1917 to 1945, containing material on the Russian Germans; also on film in Records.

Auswärtiges Amt, Bonn

Politisches Archiv (AA). Reports of the German Foreign Ministry on and by the émigrés in the 1920's and 1930's.

Bavarian State Archive, Munich

Bayerische Geheime Staatsarchiv (BGSA). Scattered reports on the émigrés; folder MA 104351 is informative on the activities of Grand Duke Kirill.

Bayerische Hauptstaatsarchiv (BHSA). Useful reports on the émigrés by the Bavarian Ministry of the Interior, the police, and Bavarian representatives in Berlin; especially MInn 71623–71626 on Russians in Bavaria from 1892 to 1936.

Private

Goldenweiser, Alexei. "Die Rechtslage der Russischen Flüchtlinge." Washington, D.C., 1938. A report for the "Refugee Survey" conducted by the Royal Institute of International Affairs.

PERIODICALS

Two useful guides to the periodical literature of the Russian emigration are: *Ukazatel' periodicheskikh izdanii emigratsii iz Rossii i SSSR za 1919–1952 g.g.* (Munich, 1953) and P. Bruhn, *Gesamtverzeichnis Russischer und Sowjetischer Periodika und Serienwerke in Bibliotheken der Bundesrepublik Deutschland und West-Berlin* (Berlin, 1962, I, A–N). An interesting early survey is V. Belov, *Belaia pechat'* (Petrograd, 1922).

Emigré periodicals published in Germany

Al'manakh mednyi vsadnik: Kniga pervaia. Berlin, 1923. Literary collection edited by Sergei Krechetov (Sergei Sokolov).

Anarkhicheskii vestnik. Berlin, 1923–1924.

Arkhiv russkoi revoliutsii. Berlin, 1921–1937. Historical journal on the revolution and civil war edited by I. V. Gessen.

Aufbau. Munich, 1921–1923. Right-wing weekly edited by Max Erwin von Scheubner-Richter.

Beloe delo. Berlin, 1926–1933. White memoirs of the revolution and civil war edited by Krasnov, Wrangel, Lampe and Duke Georg of Leuchtenberg.

Beseda. Berlin, 1923–1924. Literary-scientific journal edited by Maxim Gorky.

Biuleten' get'manskoi upravi. Berlin, 1929–1930. Ukrainian journal of Skoropadsky's followers.

Le Caucase: Organ de la Pensée Nationale Indépendante. Paris and Berlin, 1937–1939. Right-wing Georgian journal.

Contra-Komintern. Berlin, 1937–1939. Official journal of Anti-Comintern.

Daite zhizn'/lasst uns Leben. Altengrabow, 1920. Camp newspaper of the interned troops of Avalov.

Detinets: Sbornik pervyi. Berlin, 1922. Monarchist literary journal edited by Ivan Nazhivin (one issue).

Deviatyi val': Vestnik rossiiskago natsional-sotsialisticheskago dvizheniia. Berlin, 1935. ROND journal.

Dni. Berlin and Paris, 1922–1928. The "republican-democratic" daily newspaper of Alexander Kerensky.

Dvuglavyi orel'. Berlin, 1920–1922. Biweekly journal of the Supreme Monarchist Council, edited by N. E. Markov II.

Ekonomicheskii vestnik. Berlin, 1923–1924. Technical journal of economics edited by S. N. Prokopovich.

Epopeia. Berlin, 1922–1923. Literary monthly of Andrei Belyi.

Evraziiskii vremennik. Berlin, 1922. Four-volume essay collection by the Eurasians.

Golos Rossii. Berlin, 1919–1922. Daily newspaper run successively by "democrats," Kadets, and SR's.

Grani. Berlin, 1922–1923. Literary almanac, two issues.

Griadushchaia Rossiia. Berlin, 1921–1922. Daily newspaper of the constitutional monarchists, edited by E. A. Efimovsky.

Istorik i sovremennik. Berlin, 1922–1924. Historical journal edited by I. P. Petrushevsky.

Kazachii sbornik. Berlin, 1922. Cossack monthly edited by P. N. Krasnov and I. A. Rodionov, monarchist and anti-Semitic.

Luch sveta. Berlin and Novyi Sad, 1919–1926. Extreme right-wing literary-political journal edited by F. V. Vinberg.

Molodaia Rossiia. Berlin, 1922. Pro-Soviet literary almanac edited by Aleksei Tolstoi.

Moment. Altengrabow, 1919–1920. Prison camp journal of the Avalov army.

Na vidič. Berlin, 1939–1940. Ukrainian journal of Skoropadsky.

Nakanune. Berlin, 1922–1924. Daily newspaper of the Smena Vekh movement.

Nash vek. Berlin, 1933. Short-lived right-wing newspaper.

Natsiia v pokhodi. Berlin, 1939–1940. Hetmanite journal.

Novaia russkaia kniga. Berlin, 1922–1923. Pro-Soviet literary monthly edited by A. S. Yashchenko.

Novoe slovo. Berlin, 1933–1939. Main Russian journal financed by the Nazi government.

Novosti literatury. Berlin, 1923. Literary monthly edited by Mark Slonim.

Nuzhdy derevni. Berlin, 1922. SR monthly edited by G. I. Shreider.

Pravoslavie i kultura. Berlin, 1923. Collection of articles on religious philosophy edited by V. V. Zenkovsky.

Prizyv. Berlin, 1919–1920. Monarchist daily newspaper edited by S. Zolotnitsky.

Rabochii put'. Berlin, 1923. Anarcho-syndicalist monthly.

Razsvet. Berlin, 1922–1924. Jewish periodical edited by S. P. Gepstein.

Rul'. Berlin, 1920–1931. Daily newspaper of the Berlin colony, edited by I. V. Gessen, A. I. Kaminka, and V. D. Nabokov.

Rus'. Berlin, 1920. Popular literary monthly for émigrés and war prisoners.

Russische Korrespondenz. Berlin, 1905–1914. Socialist bulletin on events inside Russia, edited by G. B. Iollos.

Bibliography

Russisches Bulletin. Berlin, 1906–1914. Menshevik journal edited by Alexander Stein and Wilhelm Bucholtz.

Russkii ekonomist. Berlin, 1922–1923. Economic journal edited by A. Gan (Gutman).

Russkii emigrant. Berlin, 1920–1921. Popular literary journal of the Russian Colony cooperative society.

Russkii inzhener. Berlin, 1921–1923. Monthly scientific and technical journal edited by M. Beilenson.

Russkii kolokol. Berlin, 1927–1930. Conservative literary journal edited by I. A. Ilin.

Sofiia: Problemy dukhovnoi kul'tury i religioznoi filosofii. Berlin, 1923. Journal of religious philosophy edited by Nikolai Berdiaev (one issue).

Sotsialisticheskii vestnik. Berlin, 1921–1933. Menshevik biweekly of the Foreign Delegation; moved to Paris in 1933 and New York in 1940 and became a "non-periodical collection" in 1961.

Spolokhi. Berlin, 1922–1923. Literary monthly edited by Alexander Drozdov.

Strugi. Berlin, 1923. A literary almanac (one issue).

Svobodnaia Rossia. Berlin, 1924–1926. Liberal-democratic journal of literature and politics.

Teatr. Berlin, 1922. Journal of the theater arts.

Teatr i zhizn'. Berlin, 1921–1922. Biweekly review of the theater, art, and music edited by E. Iu. Griunberg.

Trudy russkikh uchennykh zagranitsei. Berlin, 1922–1923. Review of émigré scholarship edited by A. I. Kaminka.

Vereteno: Literaturno-khudozhestvennyi al'manakh. Berlin, 1922. Literary almanac publishing work by émigré and Soviet authors.

Veshch/Gegenstand/Objet. Berlin, 1922. Monthly journal of "constructivist" art edited by El Lissitsky and Ilia Ehrenburg.

Vestnik russkogo monarkhicheskago ob"edineniia v Bavarii. Munich, 1923. Biweekly monarchist journal supporting the Grand Duke Kirill.

Voina i mir. Berlin, 1922–1924. Military-technical journal edited by P. Kosmel.

Vysshii monarkhicheskii sovet: Ezhenedel'nik. Berlin, 1921–1923. Weekly bulletin of the Supreme Monarchist Council.

Zaria. Berlin, 1922–1925. Biweekly journal of the "right" Mensheviks who supported Stepan Ivanovich, edited by A. Khomsky.

Zhar'-ptitsa. Berlin and Paris, 1921–1924. Illustrated art journal edited by A. Kogan.

Zhidoved. Berlin, 1935. Anti-Semitic Russian-language edition of the Nazi journal *Judenkenner.*

Zhizn'. Berlin, 1920. Biweekly journal of the Peace and Labor circle edited by V. B. Stankevich (Vladas Stanka).

Znamia bor'by. Berlin, 1924–1930. Monthly journal of the Left-SR's and anarchists.

German periodicals

Antibolschewistische Korrespondenz (A. B. C.). Berlin, 1918–1920. The organ of Eduard Stadtler's Anti-Bolshevik League, edited by Heinz Fenner.

Auf gut deutsch. Munich, 1918–1921. Anti-Semitic journal of Dietrich Eckart.

Berliner Tageblatt. Daily newspaper, examined for the period 1919–1923.

Deutsche Post aus dem Osten. Berlin, 1925–1942. Journal of the Union of Germans from Russia, edited by Carlo von Kügelgen.

Freiheit. Berlin, 1918–1922. USPD newspaper edited by Rudolf Hilferding.

Die Gesellschaft. Berlin, 1924–1932. Socialist journal edited by Rudolf Hilferding.

Der Reichswart. Berlin, 1920–1922. Nationalist and anti-Semitic weekly edited by Count Ernst Reventlow.

Die rote Fahne. Daily newspaper of the KPD, examined for the period 1920–1923.

Völkischer Beobachter. Anti-Semitic Munich daily newspaper purchased by the Nazis in 1921; examined for 1920–1923.

Vorwärts. Berlin newspaper of the SPD edited by Friedrich Stampfer; examined for 1921–1923.

Other periodicals

Belaia ideia. Paris, 1939. Right-wing émigré journal.

Chasovoi. Paris, 1929–?. Journal of the ROVS.

Fashist. Putnam, Connecticut, 1933–?. Journal of the All-Russian Fascist Organization edited by A. A. Vonsiatsky.

Heimatbuch der Deutschen aus Russland. Stuttgart, 1956–. A Russian-German annual edited by Karl Stumpp.

Literaturnye zapiski. Moscow, 1921–1922. Soviet literary journal.

Mladorosskaia iskra. Paris, 1931–1935. Organ of Alexander Kazem-Bek's Young Russians.

The New Russia. London, 1919–1920. Liberal anti-Bolshevik journal edited by Paul Miliukov and V. D. Nabokov.

Bibliography

Obshchee delo. Paris, 1918–?. Anti-Bolshevik daily of the Paris SR's, edited by V. L. Burtsev.

Poslednie novosti. Paris, 1920–1940. Liberal-democratic daily edited by Paul Miliukov.

Smena vekh. Paris, 1921–1922. Weekly journal of the Smena Vekh movement, subsequently moved to Berlin as a daily newspaper, *Nakanune*.

Sovremennye zapiski. The most important literary journal of the emigration, published in Paris and briefly in Berlin (1922–1923).

Index

Index

Index

Index

Index

Russian Student Christian Movement, 250

Russian Student Union, 33

Russische Korrespondenz, 31, 192

Russisches Bulletin, 35, 192

Russkaia Koloniia, 126

Russkii emigrant, 126

Sadyker, P. A., 266, 271

Sailors' Mutual Aid Society, 120

St. Petersburger Zeitung, 18, 37, 57, 354

St. Petersburg Germans, *see* Germans, Russian

St. Vladimir Brotherhood, 20, 55, 121, 124, 284

Sakharov, K. V., 297

Savitsky, Peter, 260

Scheler, Max, 252, 304

Scheubner-Richter, Mathilde, 220

Scheubner-Richter, Max Erwin, von, 159, 164-167, 174-177, 179, 180, 188, 201-202, 204-205, 211, 214-221, 339, 349, 359, 370

Schickedanz, Arno, 164, 175, 220, 331, 334-335, 350, 361

Schiemann, Paul, 163, 165

Schiemann, Theodor, 40-41, 45-48, 52, 58, 62-64, 353, 371

Schlesinger, Moritz, 84, 107, 109-110, 130-131, 141-142, 145, 199, 284, 286

Schleuning, Johannes, 352-353, 356

Schmidt, Axel, 61, 355, 358

Schubart, Walter, 367-369

Schwarz, Solomon, 226

Scythians, 252-258, 268, 277, 369

Seeberg, Reinhold, 40

Semenov, Ataman, 177, 214

Seraphim, Bishop, 348

Shabelsky-Bork, P., 86, 176, 208-209, 211-212, 333

Shandruk, Paul, 362

Shapiro, Alexander, 239

Shcherbachev, General, 85, 95, 97

Shestov, Lev, 255

Shirinsky-Shikhmatov, A. A., 117, 176, 179

Shkliaver, S. Ya., 125

Shklovsky, Viktor, 132, 279-280

Shlippe, F. V., 119-120, 140-142, 286

Shreider, Alexander, 255, 316

Shulgin, V. V., 217

Sievers, Marie, 42

Siewert, Harald, 336, 349, 359

Simons, Walther, 109-110

Skoropadsky, Paul, 75, 97, 147-150, 165-166, 176, 332-333, 351-352, 360

Slovo publishing house, 134-136, 185, 276

Smal-Stocki, Roman, 61, 149-150, 351

Smena vekh (book), 265-266

Smena vekh (journal), 266-268

Smena Vekh movement, 130, 256, 263-275, 277-278, 369

Smilg-Benario, Michael, 126-127

Smirnov, S. A., 141-142

Snessarev, Nikolai, 213, 215-216

Socialist Party of Germany (SPD), 29, 34-36, 45-46, 50-51, 189-198, 231-232

Social Revolutionaries (SRs), 66-67, 208, 222-225, 233-238

Society for Officers of the General Staff, 120

Society for Russian Citizens of German Origin, 152

Society of Employees of the Ministry of Foreign Affairs, 118

Society of Russian Doctors, 124

Society of Russian General Staff Officers, 286

Society to Aid German Returnees, 153

Society to Aid Russian Citizens in Berlin, 56, 114, 125

Sofiia, 251-252

Sokolov-Baransky, V. P., 179

Sologub, Fedor, 244

Soloviev, Vladimir, 28, 42, 245, 254

Sonnenberg, Libermann von, 47, 50

Sorokin, Pitrim, 137

Sotsialisticheskii vestnik, 196-197, 232, 297-298

Southern Army, 77, 92

Sovremennye zapiski, 134, 138, 234, 326

Spartacists, 82

SPD, *see* Socialist Party of Germany

Spengler, Oswald, 43, 248, 252, 256, 259, 269, 279, 313-314, 316-318, 370-371

Sremtsy Karlovtsy sobor, 121-122, 347-348

SRs, *see* Social Revolutionaries

Index

CULTURE IN EXILE

Designed by R. E. Rosenbaum.
Composed by Vail-Ballou Press, Inc.,
in 10 point linotype Caledonia, 3 points leaded,
with display lines in Weiss Series III and Weiss Roman.
Printed letterpress from type by Vail-Ballou Press,
on Warren's 1854 text, 60 pound basis,
with the Cornell University Press watermark.
Bound by Vail-Ballou Press
in Interlaken ALP book cloth
and stamped in All Purpose foil.

Library of Congress Cataloging in Publication Data
(For library cataloging purposes only)

Williams, Robert Chadwell, date.
Culture in exile.

Bibliography: p.
1. Refugees, Russian. 2. Russians in Germany.
3. Russians in Berlin. 4. Russia—History—Revolution, 1917–1921. 5. Germany—Politics and government—20th century. I. Title.
DD238.W54   301.451′917′043   77-162543
ISBN 0-8014-0673-0